Anthony C. Lang
14 September 1978
Athens

❧ The Duke's Province

The Duke's Province

A Study of New York Politics and Society,

1664–1691

by Robert C. Ritchie

The University of North Carolina Press
Chapel Hill

Copyright © 1977 by
The University of North Carolina Press
All rights reserved
Manufactured in the United States of America
ISBN 0-8078-1292-7
Library of Congress Catalog Card Number 77-681

Library of Congress Cataloging in Publication Data

Ritchie, Robert C   1938–
  The Duke's Province.

  Bibliography: p.
  Includes index.
    1. New York (State)—Politics and government—Colonial period, ca. 1600–1775.
  2. New York (State)—Economic conditions. 3. New York (State)—Social conditions.
  I. Title.
  JK99.N69R57   309.1'747'02   77-681
  ISBN 0-8078-1292-7

To My Parents

◆ Contents

ᴇᴢ List of Tables

❧ Acknowledgments

Anyone laboring for many years on a project such as this acquires many debts to people and institutions. I wish to take this opportunity to express my gratitude to those who have helped me in my work.

It is a pleasure to recall the many courtesies extended to me by the librarians of the Henry E. Huntington Library, the New York Historical Society, the New York State Library, the Franklin D. Roosevelt Library, the Queens College Library, the Public Record Office, the British Museum, the Institute of Historical Research, the Bodleian Library, the Cambridge University Library, and the libraries of the University of California at Los Angeles and San Diego.

The Graduate School and the History Department of the University of California Los Angeles provided me with the resources to begin this project. I am grateful also to the committee on research of the University of California San Diego and to the Regents of the University for their support which allowed me to complete my research and writing.

I would like to thank the editors of *New York History* and the *New York Historical Society Quarterly* for permission to draw upon earlier versions of some of the material in this book published in their journals. I should also like to express my gratitude to the New York State Historical Association and its prize committee that awarded me the association's manuscript award for 1975.

My warmest thanks go to my friends and colleagues who have been so generous with their time and energy. Eugene S. Larson, Mary Beth Norton, Joyce Goodfriend, Andrew Appleby, Roger Daniels, Frances Makkreel, and Linda Mehr have patiently listened to me through the years and just as patiently offered their advice. Michael Kammen and Patricia Bonomi gave me much needed encouragement and shared their special knowledge of New York history. Arthur Joseph Slavin, Joyce Appleby, Stanley Chodorow, Harry N. Scheiber, and David

Ringrose read and critiqued the manuscript in one of its many manifestations.

I am particularly appreciative of the encouragement given me by Keith Berwick and Wesley Frank Craven who also inspired me to begin this study. Gary B. Nash offered invaluable advice during the process of its completion and without his concern this work would not be the same. Needless to say I alone am responsible for the errors and imperfections that remain.

Finally, I thank Louise Nocas Ritchie for her enthusiasm and encouragement.

❧ The Duke's Province

Introduction

This work is a political and social history of New York from 1664 to 1691. Scholars have largely ignored this period just as they have neglected it in the history of the other American colonies. But while this period lacks the drama of the Revolution or of the era of discovery and settlement, nevertheless recent work has demonstrated that it was important as an era of transition between rough-hewn settlements and established provincial life. This is the period when political institutions and practices were formulated; when entrepreneurial activity set the pattern for future commercial growth; when elite groups established their position in society and politics; when the slave system was hammered out; when the basic structure of the English empire was created; and when the colonists reshaped the social structures of the Old World to fit the imperatives of life in the new. These developments created strains that came to the fore in rebellion, riot, resistance to authority, personal anxiety, and religious doubt.

New York had all these problems and more, for its social, economic, and political history was complicated by both political and ethnic problems. Seized from the Netherlands in 1664, New York became the proprietary colony of James, duke of York, the future James II. After a brief return to Dutch rule from 1673 to 1674, New York remained a proprietary colony until York ascended the throne in 1685. Between 1685 and 1691, it became in rapid succession a royal colony, part of the Dominion of New England, the scene of a major rebellion, and once again a royal colony. Thus, on the basis of political change alone, New York compels attention. In addition, its unique bicultural population, the legacy of the original Dutch colonization, complicates the study of all of the problems afflicting the colonies. The only comprehensive study of New York's history in this period was published by John R. Brodhead in 1871. Subsequently, other historians have concentrated on places, such as Maria Van Rensselaer's work on New York City, or on individuals, as Lawrence Leder did in his study of Robert Livingston, or on events, as in Jerome Reich's *Leisler's Rebellion*. Brodhead provided a detailed narrative of events that will not be reproduced here. My purpose will be to illuminate the interaction between the government and the people and to concentrate on social, economic, and political developments.

In recounting New York's history in this period, I have focused upon four themes. The first theme is the relationship between the government and the people. During these years the colonists struggled to create systems of government consistent with their own social views that could, at the same time, gain acceptance in England, the ultimate source of legitimacy for their governments. In New York, as in the other proprietary colonies, the colonists faced the added dilemma of reconciling their wishes with the plans of the proprietor, which often did not take into account the realities of life in North America. The duke of York wanted a system of government that concentrated power in the hands of the executive. Popular government, in any of its manifestations, was anathema to him. As a result, New Yorkers struggled to gain access to the governor and, failing that, to get the government changed. This struggle should not be interpreted as the "whig" historians might have, as the fulfilment of a liberal ideology, but rather as an attempt to protect and extend the gains made by individuals and local communities. Only toward the end of this period were ideas about the nature of popular government articulated. If anything, New York politics in this period was characterized by particularism and selfishness rather than lofty ideals.

Second, New York was unique among North American colonies. After conquering New Netherland, the English found themselves in contol of Dutch colonists whose loyalties and culture differed from their own. As the number of English colonists grew and the interrelationships within and between communities became more complex, the Dutch came under increasing pressure to Anglicize. They were the first European group confronted with this problem, and their experiences prefigured those of many later immigrant groups to America.

Third, between 1664 and 1691 there emerged an elite group that was to dominate life in New York for over a century. The colonists believed the best should rule, but in the still-fluid societies of the day who were the best? Those who gained access to power during these years were able to establish their fortunes and their families.

Finally, I will analyze New York's unique place in the emerging English empire. A sign of its important position is that New York had the only garrison in North America. The decision to garrison New York stemmed not only from the fear of Dutch counterattack, but also from the colony's strategic position in the struggle between France and England. It suffered through every imperial war or threat of war. Inclusion in the empire brought other problems. The New York market was too valuable to be ignored by the London merchant community. When they finally attempted to break into this market the resulting conflict engendered far-reaching changes. Thus, imperial policymakers and individual merchants constantly affected life in New York.

The book is divided into three parts, plus a concluding chapter. The first begins with a discussion of the reasons for the English conquest of New Netherland and with a narrative of the conquest itself. The story of the conquest leads to an account of the political structure imposed by the proprietor. The concluding chapter of this section traces the evolution of local political issues—resistance to the central government, the struggle for local economic autonomy, and Anglo-Dutch tensions.

The middle section begins with the brief return of the Dutch to power during 1673–74 and the reestablishment of the proprietary government under Edmund Andros. While in power Governor Andros created a court party that would continue to dominate New York long after he left the scene. His greatest challenge came from London merchants' breaking into the New York market. They succeeded in having him recalled after a bruising confrontation. His tour of government was also marked by changes in the structure of wealth, which confirmed the political dominance of New York City, and by changing attitudes in the Dutch community. Increasingly isolated from their *Patria*, the Dutch finally confronted the multiple problems of Anglicization.

In the final section the focus is on the period 1680–91.

During this period New York experienced rapid changes. In response to a tax revolt, York allowed an assembly for the first time and sent over Thomas Dongan to oversee the change. The assembly proved short-lived, however; York did away with it when he came to the throne in 1685. Dongan then utilized the power of his office to exploit the colony for his own gain. He was replaced as governor by Andros, who returned as governor of the Dominion of New England when its jurisdiction was extended to include New York. But then the Glorious Revolution swept away the government of James II, and the colonies went through another period of flux. The pent-up tension in New York politics and society exploded as new men, led by Jacob Leisler, used the confusion caused by the revolution in England to seize power from the elite that had dominated the colony for almost thirty years. An account of Leisler's Rebellion closes the book.

Part I
The English Arrive

1 ✺ The Invasion of New Netherland

In August 1664 Peter Stuyvesant stood on the ramparts of the fort protecting New Amsterdam and cursed his fate. Across the harbor rested four weatherbeaten English ships containing an invasion force, while on the shores of Long Island militiamen, from the English towns on the island, gathered to welcome them. For years the director-general of New Netherland had received intelligence about English invasion plans. As early as September 1661 Captain Thomas Willett of Plymouth Plantation displayed letters from Boston and London making clear the pressure on the king and Parliament to invade the Dutch colony.[1] Stuyvesant reported this intelligence to the Dutch West India Company, which did nothing to aid him, and three years went by without any overt threat from England. Then in January 1664, John Scott, an English adventurer, sought to persuade Stuyvesant to grant independence to the English towns on Long Island by reporting that Charles II had already granted his brother James, duke of York, a patent for Long Island and that James was preparing a fleet to seize his colony. Similar rumors continued to circulate during the spring.[2] The grim reality behind the rumors soon appeared in the form of the four ships commanded by Colonel Richard Nicolls, a member of York's household, who had come to claim his master's property.

The ships were also symbolic of the Restoration government's new policies. The government was determined to challenge the Dutch for supremacy in international commerce and empire building, and it wanted to assert its authority over the wayward New England colonies. These were the two main reasons that brought Nicolls and his men to New Amsterdam.

The overweening economic power of the Netherlands was one of the constant problems confronting English policymakers during the seventeenth century. The Dutch mercantile empire stretched from the Baltic to the Americas, from the Levant to the coast of West Africa, and its furthest tendrils were lodged in the spice islands of Asia. The trade generated by these areas made the Netherlands Europe's leading entrepôt and processing center. As a result, wealth and envy were generated in about equal proportions. The English were the most envious. England had lagged behind the Dutch in adapting to capitalism and found it galling to confront Dutch superiority. The prime example was that of woolen cloth. The English raised the sheep and made the cloth, but the Dutch did the final processing and marketing. Accumulated resentments caused English merchants and policymakers to place the expansion of England's economy at the expense of the Dutch high on their list of priorities. In quest of this goal, Cromwell's government had gone to war in 1652.[3] The new administration of Charles II was soon treading the same path.

When Charles II assumed the throne, however, some good will existed beween the two nations and both hoped for peaceful relations. Charles had received a warm reception while traveling through the Netherlands on his way home in 1660. Once in England, Charles and his chief minister, Edward Hyde, earl of Clarendon, were inclined toward amity. Confused royal finances, economic depression, and political discontent all argued for peace. On the Dutch side, John De Witt and his republicans were concerned about the menacing power and ambition of the French and were therefore eager to conclude a peace treaty with the new English government. It was signed 4 September 1662. Ultimately the claims of war exceeded those of peace. Both sides continued to press charges of bad treatment or hostile actions and they grew more and more estranged. English public opinion became increasingly embittered until a sea captain expressed what was probably the general sentiment: "The trade of the world is too little for us two, therefore one must down."[4]

Whatever peace existed between the ratification of the treaty in 1662 and the outbreak of war in 1664 was confined to Europe. In Africa and the East Indies there were numerous violent confrontations between the merchants and seamen of the two nations. In these outbreaks the great trading companies of both nations acted imprudently. For example, in 1663 the Company of Royal Adventurers Trading to Africa, forerunner of the Royal African Company, sent out an expedition to found trading factories. Sir Robert Holmes, commander of the expedition, promptly took advantage of his local military superiority to capture almost every Dutch factory on the African coast.[5] So the hopes written into the treaty could not obscure reality: two nations intent on establishing trade supremacy in identical areas and governments unwilling or unable to control the trading companies that loomed so large in their economic systems.

Although economic conflict over New Netherland was minimal because there were no quick fortunes to be made there, the colony was important to the English Crown. Charles II faced two critical problems in North America—how to consolidate English power while New Netherland divided the English colonies and how to impose authority upon the fractious, disobedient New Englanders, especially those of Massachusetts Bay, who had welcomed the Commonwealth. These two problems became mixed.

As soon as Charles was restored to the throne, petitions and petitioners besieged him. This was true even in the case of the colonies. Some of the supplicants came as statesmen from the infant settlements. John Winthrop, Jr., and Dr. Charles Clarke came to England to obtain charters for their respective colonies, Connecticut and Rhode Island. Both men were successful, though a somewhat confused ministry left the boundaries of the two neighboring colonies undetermined.[6] Others who came represented only their own ambitions and perhaps those of their partners. Among these was John Scott of Long Island, an enigmatic adventurer who represented the Atherton Land Company, which laid claim to the Narragansett country. He also represented himself since he modestly petitioned the king for Long Island as his own proprietary.[7] This ambition was to go unfulfilled as more powerful figures entered the discussions.

Perhaps the most important man in this group of favor-seekers, as far as future policy was concerned, was Samuel Maverick, who emerged as the most persistent critic of the New England colonies. Maverick had settled as early as 1624 in what was to become Boston and had set himself up as a farmer and trader. When the great wave of Puritan immigrants arrived in the 1630s he had welcomed them and helped them through their early difficulties. For some time he kept the good will of the Puritans but ultimately ran afoul of the magistrates. He supported Robert Child's remonstrance and petition of 1646, which demanded the broadening of church membership and the franchise, and for that impertinence he was fined £75. After this he remained in the background until 1660. In that year he appeared in London as the enemy of Massachusetts Bay.[8]

Maverick and other critics of Massachusetts Bay found a ready audience in the Council for Foreign Plantations. The council appointed a special commission on 7 January 1661 to investigate conditions in Jamaica and New England.[9] This committee heard considerable testimony about New England, most of it repeating the following basic charges: the magistrates of Massachusetts Bay looked upon Massachusetts as a free state; many of the people opposed the king and wanted independence from England; freemanship was restricted to church members; the colony harbored the regicides Edward Whalley and William Goffe; men gave the oath of allegiance to the magistrates and not to the king; liberty of conscience was not allowed; writs did not run in the king's name; any who spoke against the frame of government were considered traitors.[10]

Attacks against Massachusetts Bay were accompanied by attacks on New Netherland. The basic themes of these polemics appear clearly in one of Samuel Maverick's letters to the Earl of Clarendon:

And yett the Dutch have since these Patents [the Virginia and Plymouth Companies] were granted, and many English settled on both sides, intruded into the most considerable pt of both, for trade and Comerce with ye natives gettinge yearely from them above one hundred Thousand Beaver skines, besides much other good Pelterey. The land also is exceedinge good. There are also two gallant rivers running farr up into the land And it lyeth most Commodious for commerce from and wth all pts of the West Indies, and may in tyme on that Account, prove very adventagious to ye Crowne of England if Regained, and as priudicall if not.[11]

Maverick emphasized two complaints that were to become familiar in the next few years. One was the assertion that the Dutch in New Netherland were intruders upon land that rightfully belonged to England. The other raised the specter of the persistence of the Dutch in their use of their geographic position to encroach upon English colonial trade.

These arguments were powerfully appealing to the members of the newly appointed Council for Foreign Plantations. Clearly the continued Dutch presence in New Netherland would be detrimental to England's trade and customs revenue. To the men who were at this time framing the Navigation Acts and attempting to create a new policy for the colonies, action seemed imperative. Yet it was almost three years before the cumbersome bureaucracy of the Restoration could proceed. In the interim, committees met, reports were written, and disappointments suffered.[12] Only Maverick continued to campaign for action. He urged Clarendon to send over three frigates, several hundred soldiers, and arms and ammunition in case the militia had to be called out in the New England colonies to subdue the Dutch.[13] This plan was shelved in 1662 but ultimately became the one used by the English.

Not until 10 April 1663 was some action taken. King Charles issued an order in council declaring that a commission was to be sent to New England to consider differences between the colonies and to ascertain how well they lived up to their charters.[14] Meanwhile, another committee was calling for action against New Netherland: "its humbly conceived it cals aloude upon us for remedyes that we may no longer susstains the intollerable disgrace doon to his Majestie (as far as his [Majesty] is capable of sufferinge) by the Intrusion of such monsters and the exceeding damage to his subjects by this bold usurper."[15] By the summer of 1663 it seems likely that a decision had finally been made.[16] The commission to investigate New England was to be combined with an invasion force.

The Duke of York and His Circle

The central figure in these plans was James, duke of York and Albany, lord high admiral of England, heir to the throne, and soon to be the proprietor of New York. His advice was sought on the appointees for the New England commission and evidently accepted, for by 7 April 1663 it was known that

Colonel Richard Nicolls, an officer in York's service, was a member.[17] At some point during the summer of 1663 York unofficially became the proprietor of what was to be New York. At least this is the news that John Scott carried to New England in the autumn of 1663. Further evidence of York's involvement appears in a report to the Council for Foreign Plantations on 29 January 1664.[18] It was quite simply an invasion plan written by three members of his household, Sir William Coventry, Lord John Berkeley, and Sir William Carteret. Assessing the military potential of the Dutch as inconsiderable, it advocated that three ships, two hundred men, and adequate military supplies be sent to North America to do the job. It also asked that letters be sent to the New England colonies requesting their help and that Governor Winthrop of Connecticut be appointed to lead the militia, if they were needed. Basically the plan paralleled that of Maverick and within a month it was accepted and implemented.

The duke's involvement in planning the invasion and forming the New England commission poses the question as to why he should be interested in colonial affairs, and more particularly, why he should desire a colony of his own when he stood so close to the throne. Few of his papers for this period have survived, but it is still possible to reconstruct his interests and political affinities and so gain some understanding of his motives.

As lord high admiral of England, James was the leader of a highly placed group favoring war with the Dutch. The navy, which he actively led, pressed for a larger fleet and action against the Dutch. Members of the Admiralty, among them Prince Rupert, Lord Sandwich, the duke of Buckingham, Sir George Carteret, Lord John Berkeley, and Sir Robert Holmes favored a war policy. The duke shared these anti-Dutch feelings and advocated direct action within official circles.[19]

In political circles Clarendon led a small group that favored a policy of peace, but a number of politicians, in particular Henry Bennett, the earl of Arlington, King Charles's favorite and secretary of state, worked with the naval leaders. Arlington was joined in his efforts by the duke of Albemarle, the earl of Lauderdale, and an active group of Parliamentarians that included Thomas Clifford, Sir John Shaw, Henry Coventry,

Charles Berkeley, the earl of Shaftsbury, and the ubiquitous Lord John Berkeley and Sir George Carteret. One of the most important men in this coalition was Sir George Downing, a capable man with a firm grasp of both the political and economic realities.[20] As envoy to the United Provinces, he played a crucial role in carrying out policy. But he was a man of great prejudices, not the least of them hatred for the Dutch. Moreover, in the quaint way of seventeenth-century diplomacy, he was the representative of the English East India Company, deeply involved in trying to obtain from the Dutch government the recovery of company losses incurred by Dutch seizures. This coalition dominated the councils of the king after 1662 when Arlington became secretary of state. Capitalizing on the growing war spirit in England, it was able to get that most difficult of all parliamentary prizes, a very large subsidy for the conduct of a war not yet declared.[21]

Besides taking part in policy discussions, the duke was in a position to take direct action through being lord high admiral. The Company of Royal Adventurers Trading to Africa was informally at war with its Dutch equivalent on the coast of West Africa. The duke was the governor of the company and one of its chief managers. In 1661, he lent the company three navy ships, under the command of Sir Robert Holmes, to protect its merchantmen. Holmes used his vessels against the Dutch and was able to begin a fort at the mouth of the Gambia.[22] This success was enlarged upon in 1663 when Holmes returned to the Gold Coast with more ships and men. In a quick campaign he captured or destroyed almost every Dutch factory on the coast. So successful an expedition roused the Dutch States General and De Witt, the chief minister, who could not ignore the English attacks. Their response, in sending Admiral De Ruyter to Africa to reconquer the factories, precipitated war.

The duke's interest in mercantile affairs went beyond the Royal African Company. He was the governor of the Royal Fisheries Company, another venture directly opposed to the Dutch, and he invested in the East India Company and later in the Hudson Bay Company.[24] He also associated with some of the most powerful members of the London mercantile community. Sir Richard Ford, who with his partner Sir William Ryder was a major supplier to the Navy Board, was the duke's most important advisor in mercantile affairs. Ford and Ryder were active in Parliament and both favored war with the Dutch. Ford also had strong interests in the East India Company, which he twice served as a commissioner, and in the Royal African Company, of which he was, for a time, subgovernor under York. He participated actively in the politics of London and rose to be lord mayor. As a publicist of the mercantilist cause, he was the licensee for the first printing of Thomas Mun's *England's Treasure by Foreign Trade*, perhaps the most influential work of the time on mercantilist thought. Ford dedicated the first edition to the earl of Arlington.[25] In Ford, the duke had an advisor well known to the mercantilists, an active lobbyist for their cause in many offices and commissions, and a man who favored war with the Dutch.

The duke surrounded himself with other men who were interested in trade and colonization. As has already been pointed out, three members of his staff, Coventry, Berkeley, and Carteret, submitted the final plans for the invasion of New Netherland to the Council for Foreign Plantations. Sir William Coventry was the duke's secretary and a commissioner for the navy; in fact, he virtually ran the navy. Along with the other authors of the report, he was a member of the Council for Foreign Plantations as well as of the Council for Trade. Above all, he was a member of the king's Council for Foreign Affairs, the most important policymaking group in the government. In this council, however, he actively favored peace with the Dutch—a position that finally led to his leaving the service of the duke.[26] Despite this, he did favor the expansion of the navy, for which he worked diligently. Berkeley and Carteret seemed to spend much of their time and influence working for the welfare of Berkeley and Carteret. Both were members of the duke's Commission of Revenue and so were intimately involved in running his household. They were also naval commissioners, members of Parliament (both served on the committee considering the Navigation Acts), members of the Royal African Company, proprietors of Carolina, and later proprietors of New Jersey. While serving the Crown well, they served themselves better.[27] One other member of James's household had close ties with colonial policy; Philip Frowde, secretary to Anne, the duke's wife, served as the first secretary of the Council for

Foreign Plantations.[28] Thus, the duke of York emerges as a man with a great deal of power in naval affairs and close connections with the mercantile community. He was well placed to influence decision making at the highest level through his own person and through his servants and associates.

One other factor may have played a role in York's desire for a grant in North America. He was having financial difficulties. Since his return to England in 1660 he had been given parliamentary gifts, including large estates in Ireland, monopolies of the revenue of the Post Office, and certain excise taxes and manors in England. His Commission of Revenue estimated that by March 1664 he had received from these sources a total of £211,641, which still did not satisfy his household's needs. By 1677 its wages alone, grown only slightly from 1664, required £36,991 annually. As early as May 1663 the commissioners estimated that if expenditures held steady the duke's debts would increase by £27,475 a year.[29] Thus, any additional increase in the duke's income would relieve his financial situation. In this light, the estimated £10,000 annually in customs revenue from New Netherland may have had an attraction for the duke.[30]

A final compelling reason for conquering New Netherland was that once the Dutch colony was removed, England would dominate the North American coast from Carolina to Nova Scotia. This long line of settlement would be easier to administer and defend once it was completely English, especially since the connecting link was to be held by a permanent military garrison under the command of a member of the royal family. Charles and his councilors must have thought, too, that it would aid them in their future dealing with the New England colonies. They hoped that New England would be overawed and more susceptible to royal blandishments. Thus, for reasons of state and simple venality, New Netherland was to be conquered.

York's Patent

The duke of York received his patent on 12 March 1664. This document was notable for the rapidity with which it passed through the various offices and seals and the extent of the territory granted to the duke. It was rushed through the bureaucracy in the remarkable time of four days, and it granted the duke a huge new proprietary that can only be appreciated by reciting it. He was given:

all that parte of the mayne land of New England beginning at a certain place called or knowne by the name of St. Croiz next adjoining to New Scotland in America and from thence extending along the sea coast unto a certain place called Petuaquins or Pemaquid and so up the river thereof to the farthest head of the same as it tendeth Northward and extending from thence to the river of Kenebeque and so upwards by the shortest course to the river of Canada Northward. And also all that Island or Islands commonly called by the several name or names of Mattowacks or Long Island scituate lying and being towards the West of Cape Codd and the Narrow-Higensetts abutting upon the maine land between the two rivers there called or knowne by the several names of Connecticutte and Hudsons river together also with the said river called Hudson river and all the lands from the west side of Conecticutte to the east side De la Ware Bay And also all those several islands called or knowne by the names of Martin Vineyard and Nantukes otherwise Nantufat. [31]

In modern terms the duke owned most of Maine, part of Connecticut, New York, New Jersey, and part of Pennsylvania, all for a quitrent of a mere forty beaver skins a year. In addition, the patent assumed that this land was vacant and devoid of prior title. This was far from the truth, of course, for the Dutch were inhabiting parts of the grant and had been doing so, on the Hudson River at least, since 1618. But this was of little consequence to the English. Sir George Downing told John De Witt disingenuously that he "knew of no such country but only in mapps; that, indeed, if their people were to be believed, all the world were New Netherland."[32]

The man chosen to lead the combined enterprise of conquering and investigating New England was the duke's aide Richard Nicolls. Descended from the Scottish gentry who had come south with James I, Nicolls's family settled at Ampthill, in Bedfordshire. He and his three brothers joined the Royalist army and followed Charles and James into exile in France. During this sojourn, Nicolls entered the service of York and continued his military career. He reaped his reward for loyalty at the Restoration when he was appointed a gentleman of York's bedchamber and received other signs of favor.[33] On 2 April 1664 he received a commission appointing him deputy-governor for York's proprietary colony. Nicolls was the best governor York ever appointed. Sensitive to the anxieties of the Dutch, he proved patient but firm in his dealings with them. Unable to establish a cordial relationship with the New Englanders on Long Island, Nicolls at least gained their respect if not their affection. By the time he left New York in 1668 he had created a government, faced four invasion attempts, and kept the peace between the English and Dutch planters.

The three other members of the commission were Samuel Maverick, Sir Robert Carr, and Sir George Cartwright. The selection of Maverick, a declared enemy of Massachusetts Bay, indicates that the commissioners were not chosen for their objectivity. Joseph Williamson, secretary to the earl of Arlington, attested to this when he noted that "Maverick was of all men the worst to do it; debauched idle and under great prejudices." Of the other two he wrote, "Cartwright persuaded himself to be a Jesuit by old Bellingham of the Society of Jesus. Sir R. Carr a weak man."[34]

The two sets of instructions given to the commission reveal why impartiality was not needed for their duties.[35] The public instructions enjoined the commissioners to subjugate the Dutch and then hold hearings in New England to investigate boundary disputes, Indian welfare, civil and religious liberties, enforcement of the Navigation Acts, and to soothe apprehensions about possible royal interference, particularly in Massachusetts Bay. The secret instructions were quite different. Their first goal was still to conquer the Dutch, which would presumably ingratiate them with the people of New England. They were then to try to influence the leaders of Massachusetts Bay to submit their charter for alterations "necessary for their owne benefit." Indeed, they were to try to get all of the New England charters submitted for revision. One suggested change was royal approval, if not nomination, for governors. While discussing these matters with the leaders of New England, they were ordered to interfere in the elections for the General Court of Massachusetts Bay in order to obtain a majority of royalists willing to bring the magistrates into submission. In addition to this folly they were to get Nicolls made governor of Massachusetts Bay. Altogether an impossible set of instructions that do hint at a design of creating a single administrative unit out of

New England and New York. It was a plan that would come to fruition in the Dominion of New England in 1685, but considering the limited resources of the 1664 commission, the government expected a great deal.

The Invasion and Its Aftermath

The expedition left Portsmouth on 15 May 1664. The commission plus three hundred soldiers sailed in three naval vessels and a chartered freighter. A rough passage forced them apart, and none made their intended landfall at the eastern end of Long Island. Nicolls and Cartwright anchored at Nantucket Island and made preparations for the invasion while waiting for Maverick and Carr to come from Piscataway, Maine. As part of their preparations Nicolls contacted Massachusetts asking for help if the need arose. The answer, which was to become familiar, was a polite refusal. The magistrates pleaded that poverty and harvest time made it impossible for them to send aid. The fleet reassembled by 29 July, ready to end Stuyvesant's career.[36]

While he had been forewarned of the English expedition, Stuyvesant was not forearmed. His requests for arms and ammunitions had been spurned by the West India Company. The company directors believed that the expedition was directed at New England, not New Netherland.[37] As a result, Stuyvesant faced the English with about 150 soldiers, 250 men of the burgher watch, a dilapidated fort, an indefensible city, and the only source of relief three thousand miles away. When the fleet dropped anchor on 18 August, Stuyvesant sent a letter demanding to know their intent as they raised "much admiration in us."[38] Simultaneously, he wrote to the Dutch towns on Long Island and up the Hudson River warning of the arrival of the fleet and asking for all possible aid.[39] It was to no avail.

Stuyvesant and the soldiers wanted to fight, but the burghers wished to avoid such a calamity. In an assault, the city was indefensible and a sack inevitable. The townspeople feared any soldiers, English or Dutch, but their greatest apprehension was reserved for the Long Island militia, whom they considered "our deadly enemies, who expected nothing else than pillage, plunder, and bloodshed."[40] Nor did the people have strong feelings of loyalty toward the West India Company or Stuyvesant. They had been struggling for a long time, with little effect, to gain a larger voice in government.[41] Many may have felt that, at the very least, English government could not damage them as much as an attack upon the city. In the end a concern for property overrode the calls of martial ardor.

While New Amsterdam seethed, Nicolls carefully gathered his troops and the Long Island militia and moved from Gravesend to Brooklyn. Two ships were sent up the Hudson to outflank the city.[42] As Nicolls increased the pressure, Governor John Winthrop, Jr., of Connecticut provided the last turn of the screw. Placing himself in the role of a mediator, he received assurances from Nicolls that two of the prime concerns of the Dutch, continued trade with and immigration from their homeland, would be permitted.[43] He then went into the besieged city. In a waterfront tavern he urged Stuyvesant, his council, and two burgomasters to surrender. The meeting broke up without results, but Winthrop left behind him a letter from Nicolls giving the assurances the Dutch sought. This letter proved to be the decisive blow. The two burgomasters wanted it read to the magistrates. Stuyvesant refused and, in a fit of anger, tore it up. News of the letter spread throughout the city, feeding the hopes of the inhabitants. A crowd assembled at City Hall demanding to know what Nicolls had written. Stuyvesant rushed to the scene and urged defiance of the English. His pleas fell on deaf ears, for many believed "to resist so many, was nothing less to gape before an oven."[44] Reports also circulated that the officers of the West India Company were sending their wives over to the English side.[45] Such rumors sapped morale even among the soldiers, and so, recognizing the growing hopelessness of the situation, Stuyvesant had the now-famous letter pieced together.

After its contents were revealed to the people, ninety-three of the most substantial men in the community signed a remonstrance to Stuyvesant and the council. They pointed out the impossibility of holding out for very long in either the city or the fort as supplies were low and relief so distant. Above all, they expressed their fears of "misery, sorrow, conflagration, the dishonor of women, murdered children in their cradles, and, in a word, the absolute ruin and destruction of about fifteen hundred innocent souls."[46] Finally recognizing that the people were in no mood to fight and, perhaps, accepting the validity of these arguments, Stuyvesant surrendered.

On 27 August representatives of both sides met at Stuyvesant's farm to conclude an agreement. Their discussions were brief since the English had the upper hand and were offering good terms. Nicolls's policy was based on good sense. He knew that the English militiamen would soon return to their farms, leaving him to control the area from Albany to the Delaware settlements with three hundred men. He also knew that he would soon lose the ships with their powerful guns. What he needed was a contented, docile population, and the treaty reflected these realities. The Dutch soldiers were to leave the fort with all military honors. If any soldier or inhabitant of New Netherland wanted to return home he was welcome to do so, and immigration from the Netherlands was permitted. This clause had the effect of getting rid of the truly disgruntled and the only organized force that could oppose the English. All ordinary facets of Dutch life such as religion, contracts, property, and inheritances were to remain undisturbed. The status of denizens was accorded the Dutch and trade with England or her colonies permitted. As a further concession, direct commerce with the Netherlands was permitted for six months. Even the West India Company was to continue holding and using its property. Finally, in local government, all officials were to remain in office until the next election; however, after the next election all magistrates would have to swear an oath to England.[47] This agreement was quickly ratified. On Monday, 29 August, Stuyvesant and the garrison marched out of the fort, flags flying, drums beating, and matches lit. Because the Dutch soldiers were ashamed at surrendering without firing a shot, they were not paraded before the English but quickly put aboard the *Gideon* of Amsterdam. With the soldiers out of the way, Nicolls conducted his men into the fort and opened the history of New York by renaming the fort, Fort James.[48]

The surrender agreement came to be an important document to the Dutch. They took it to be a declaration of rights that recognized many different aspects of Dutch life such as partible inheritances. As will be seen later, whenever the English attempted to change an aspect of Dutch life that the Dutch community believed was guaranteed in the surrender agreement, they were quick to demand that the English live up to its terms. Needless to say, the English government viewed it as a surrender agreement—no more, no less.

Having achieved his initial goal in capturing New Amsterdam, Nicolls moved to seize the rest of the territory in the duke's patent. Sir George Cartwright was sent up the Hudson River to take possession of the river settlements and Fort Orange. He was preceded by Johan De Decker, a member of the council and a signatory to the articles of surrender. Decker, seemingly acting alone, wanted to raise a rebellion, but the planters knew that whoever controlled the mouth of the Hudson controlled their fate. Cartwright received the surrender of Fort Orange and named it Albany after one of York's titles. Accepting their new name, the *handlaers* or fur traders got the one thing that they desired—a monopoly of the fur trade.[49]

Cartwright, at Nicolls's behest, performed another vital task. He undertook to sign a treaty with the Iroquois. Since they were essential to the fur trade, the Indians had to be convinced of the good intentions and trading terms of the English. A treaty was signed on 26 September promising the Iroquois a ready market for their fur in Albany, where they would find the traditional trade items.[50] The other important clause guaranteed aid to the Iroquois should they be attacked. Sovereignty over the Five Nations and their lands was not mentioned in the treaty. That was assumed to be English.

The other expedition sent out by Nicolls was cruelly managed. Sir Robert Carr was sent to the Delaware with instructions to offer terms to the Swedish and Dutch settlers similar to those granted to New Amsterdam.[51] Unfortunately, Carr chose to ignore the spirit of his instructions. The farmers of the river valley quickly accepted the terms offered, but Governor Alexander d'Hinoyossa and his troops at New Amstel refused to surrender. Carr assaulted their tiny fort, killing three and wounding ten of the defenders. The soldiers and sailors then plundered the place. Carr joined in the plunder, seizing the property of the city of Amsterdam and the people of New Amstel. Unsatisfied with this loot, he appropriated the estate of d'Hinoyossa for himself, that of *schout* Gerrit Van Sweringen for his son, Robert, and that of Ensign Peter Alricks for his ensign, Arthur Stocke. As a fitting conclusion to this rapacity, he reportedly sold the Dutch soldiers into servitude in Virginia and raided the rest of the river, including a colony of Mennonites.[52]

Carr's behavior outraged Nicolls. At all times the latter had pursued a policy of conciliation and attempted to keep friction between the two national groups to a minimum. Despoiling the Delaware settlements could only poison the relationship. Nicolls was also embittered at Carr's personal claim to the plunder while the soldiers of the expedition were in need.[53] In November, Nicolls visited New Amstel but failed to make Carr disgorge all of the goods and produce he had seized. After renaming New Amstel, New Castle and appointing a new commander, Nicolls returned to New York without Carr, who stayed on to enjoy his plunder.[54]

The legality of Carr's activities can be questioned in other ways. York's patent included the Delaware River, but under normal usage that would have meant the east bank only. Nearly all the settlements were on the west bank. Nicolls must have decided that establishing English sovereignty over Dutch territory superseded observing legal niceties. From this time on the settlements were part of New York—patent or no patent.

The relatively peaceful conquest of New Netherland was a propitious beginning. Had blood been spilled and New Amsterdam and Fort Orange subjected to the sack, the problems of governance would have been great. A sullen, vengeful Dutch population would have needed constant watching, straining the resources of the new government and making life miserable for the English minority. As it was, the major areas of Dutch population went unscathed and received good terms upon surrendering. This is not to say that there were no ill feelings. The rival nations had denounced one another for a long time and had propagandized their people about the manifest iniquities of each other. Nicolls, for his part, shared in the distrust of the Dutch; however, he recognized their value to England and the duke. They were seasoned planters and merchants who had established a growing economy. That alone made them much greater assets than the many Englishmen who came to North America with chimerical schemes.

2 ❧ The Structure of Government

The conquest of New Netherland brought a pleasing symmetry to English maps of North America. The gap between the Chesapeake Bay and New England colonies was removed. Richard Nicolls, however, had to assess the meaning of the conquest in more practical terms, and he discovered that New Netherland was not the source of easy wealth depicted by those who had urged the expedition. There was one thing of great value—a large number of planters and an established economy. Nicolls and his successor Francis Lovelace confronted the task of imposing a government upon these people. Their principal dilemma was how to administer a vast area with varying traditions of government while respecting the wishes of York, who wanted a highly centralized government. The resulting patchwork of administrative units was unmatched elsewhere in the colonies.

The duke of York, unlike other proprietors, did not have the problem of obtaining new planters. York never had to embark upon a campaign to encourage immigration; therefore he was able to avoid the problems and expense that afflicted the Carolina proprietors or, later, William Penn. The presence of ten thousand people in New York would have brought joy to any proprietor.[1] York and his governors were to find that the colonists also presented numerous problems, and they in turn created problems for the people. The population of New York was spread from Albany to the capes of the Delaware River, and while there were towns and villages, many people had dispersed in order to hunt and trade for furs and to farm small plots. The reliance on the fur trade derived from the policies of the West India Company, which had encouraged many men to eschew farming for the more immediate, albeit often slight, gains of the fur trade. The company's policies had also brought a polyglot population to New York. Eighteen languages were reportedly spoken, and the number of religious groups was hardly less. New York's already heterogeneous population foreshadowed that of the middle colonies in the eighteenth century.

New York City was the center of York's vast domain. The city, or perhaps more accurately the town, was clustered at the southernmost tip of Manhattan Island, and because the East River provided protection from the spring ice floes and floods, the town was oriented toward Long Island.[2] Seen from the perspective of the island, New York was a collection of docks, warehouses, and houses lying at the foot of some low hills inside the wall that protected the city on its land side. At the very southern tip of the island sat Director Stuyvesant's house and the large homes of some merchants. Above them rose Fort James, which, due to a lack of funds, was a dilapidated pile of stone and earthworks. In the fort's interior were barracks, a chapel, and housing for the officers. Unfortunately, the fort was unprotected from the vigorous hogs that ran at will all over the city. They rooted in the earthworks, undermined the palisades, and exposed the interior.

Running north from the fort was Broad Way, aptly named since it was the widest street in the city. To the west of Broad Way lay orchards, gardens, and a few homes lining the Hudson. To the east lived most of the inhabitants. Between Broad Way and the East River two streets, Prince Gracht and Smee Street, ran back from the river, turning to run parallel to Broad Way. These three thoroughfares were the main streets and, with a few small alleys, made up the city of New York. A canal ran up the middle of Prince Gracht, almost to the wall. It provided access into the city for small boats carrying wood, bulky parcels, and goods. The rest of the streets were unpaved and filled with wood piles, garbage, and the same hogs that were destroying the fort. These side streets were also deeply rutted by the wagons of the carters who, along with the porters, had a monopoly on transportation of goods. Even in the most populous section, gardens and orchards were still quite frequent.

Beyond the wall, Broad Way ran up the middle of the island toward the village of New Haarlem. On this road, a mile or so beyond the city limits, was the city's first ghetto. Directors

William Kieft and Stuyvesant had granted farm plots to free Negroes and, in 1667, Nicolls confirmed these grants.[3] However, the Negroes were not exactly free. The city fathers, worried over the conduct of servants on the Sabbath when they went beyond the city walls, warned the freedmen not to entertain "Christian or Negroe" servants in their homes for more than twenty-four hours or their freedom would be forfeit.[4]

The population of New York City was approximately 1,500 according to a tax list of 1665.[5] There were 254 individuals listed and the overwhelming majority of them were Dutch. Using surnames as a guide, one concludes that only 16 Englishmen lived in the city. This is an approximate figure, however, since the Dutch had a habit of changing English names. Charles Bridges, for instance, was always referred to as Carel Van Brugge. The number of English residents was probably very small, but the English and other Europeans gave the city a metropolitan quality.[6] The tax list also provides an approximate guide to the economic gradations in the community. There were six categories of taxation. Only 24 taxables (3 of them English) ranked in the top two categories. The three middle groups had 94 and the bottom two 136 taxables. Unsurprisingly the list indicates an already stratified society in the city. At the top were the officers of the Dutch West India Company and the leading private merchants. The rest were smaller retail merchants, brewers, tanners, shoemakers, other skilled and semi-skilled artisans down to the porters and other laborers.

New York City lived on trade. The first export commodities developed were furs and hides. Coming from the interior, particularly Albany, they were prepared and then shipped to Amsterdam. In return, manufactured goods were sent to New Amsterdam for dispersal in New Netherland or the neighboring English colonies. Maryland and Virginia were the most important trading partners because their tobacco was highly prized on the Dutch market. To this base the merchants added a trade in foodstuffs to the Dutch Caribbean colonies of Surinam and Curacao and later to the British colonies. Sugar, dye goods, and other commodities flowed into New Amsterdam for transshipment to Europe. There also developed a trade in African slaves destined for work in New Netherland or the tobacco plantations of the Chesapeake.[7] With this economic base already in place, Nicolls was optimistic about the future. He believed New York would shortly eclipse Boston as the leading port in the colonies and was already the "best of all his majesties Townes in America."[8] The most important asset the city had was the Dutch inhabitants. Nicolls wanted them encouraged because they knew economic conditions in America.

The rest of the colony consisted of disparate elements. In the immediate area of the city there were a few villages. Located at the northern end of Manhattan Island was New Haarlem, a small, predominantly Dutch farming village. Since it was on Manhattan, it came under the jurisdiction of the city government, and its constable and overseers annually traveled to New York to be confirmed and sworn in.[9] Just north of New Haarlem were a few scattered English settlements, products of expansion from New Haven and Connecticut. These villages were small and were interspersed with the landholdings of the three largest landowners, John Archer, John Pell, and John Richbell.

To the west along the banks of the Hudson lay a few Dutch hamlets. On viewing the lands to the west of the river, Nicolls decided that they were the best in New York and planned to settle the area, which he called Albania, as soon as possible.[10] Farther west and south lay the scattered Dutch, Finnish, and Swedish settlements on the Delaware. The recently renamed New Castle was the largest settlement and the center of government and trade. The farmers of the Delaware were distant from New York and went their own way, caring only for their crops, but unlike the rest of New York, they concentrated on growing tobacco as a cash crop.[11]

Across the East River from New York lay the largely Dutch villages of Long Island—Brooklyn, New Utrecht, Flatbush, Boswyck, and Amsfort. Gravesend had a mixed Dutch and English population and Flushing was predominantly English. These villages were small agricultural plantations that supplied produce for the city and for trade. The villagers also spent a great amount of time arguing among themselves about boundaries and land patents. Other villages of Long Island hugged Long Island Sound and were populated by New Englanders who had crossed the sound from Connecticut and New Haven.[12] At the eastern end of the island, clustered around Shelter Bay, lay the most distant English settlements—Southampton, East-hampton, and Southold. The southern part of the island was largely uninhabited.

For the inhabitants of the island, life was confined to hard work and the community life of small villages. They traded with New York City, Boston, and Connecticut for manufactured necessities and the few luxury goods they could afford. This trade was paid for by foodstuffs, animals, and whale oil. Trade in the latter was growing rapidly and methods for securing the oil were changing, from merely locating beached whales to organizing regular whale hunts. Indians played a prominent role in the whale hunts because of their knowledge and skill, but this cooperation between the races was rare.[13] The Indians continued to diminish in numbers. The Reverend Daniel Denton wrote naively in his *A Brief Description of New York*: "it is to be admired, how strangely they [the Indians] have decreast by the Hand of God, since the English first settling of those parts; for since my time, where there were six towns, they are now reduced to two small villages, and it hath been generally observed, that where the English came to settle, a Divine Hand makes way for them, by removing or cutting of the Indians either by Wars one with the other, or by some raging mortal Disease."[14] But the Indians were still an object of fear, as was shown by a scare about an Indian rising that ran through the towns in 1669.[15] By and large, life on Long Island was rigorous for both races and one must view with skepticism Denton's contention "that if there be any terrestrial happiness to be had by people of all ranks, especially the inferior rank, it must certainly be here."[16]

North and west of New York City stretched endless miles of untamed wilderness. Although the coastal tribes had been subjugated during the Peach War of 1655, the Indians still remained masters of the forest. The only outposts of Europe were far up the Hudson at Esopus and Albany. The Esopus River Valley was a prime farming area. It had only one village of note, Wiltwyck (renamed Kingston), which was predominantly Dutch. Albany, also, was the center of an expanding farm area, but the main reason for its remote location was the fur trade. Albany was completely isolated for many months, separated from New York and Massachusetts by the severe winters. The community, therefore, quivered to every nuance of war and peace between Iroquois and Algonquin or Iroquois and French, because not only its economic but its military security depended on the outcome. The town was small, consisting of a palisaded fort and a number of houses clustered at the bottom of a hill on the Hudson. In the summertime, troops of Indians swarmed along its streets, trading with the inhabitants, and the docks were thronged with yachts to carry out the furs. During the rest of the year Albany was isolated and the inhabitants paid a price for this. Jasper Dankaerts, a visitor to New York, wrote of the Albanyites, "these people live in the interior of the country somewhat nearer the Indians, they are more wild and untamed, reckless, unrestrained and haughty." Heavy drinking was rampant and the sight of women staggering on the streets prompted the magistrates to pass many ordinances against drunkenness.[17] Violence, profanity, and Sabbath breaking were common and of constant concern to the magistrates. Intolerance also flourished. The magistrates and townspeople harassed the members of the Lutheran church and its minister, contrary to the orders of the duke and the laws of the province.[18]

The remainder of the new colony was far from New York City. The islands of Nantucket and Martha's Vineyard lay to the east of Long Island and were settled by New Englanders. On Nantucket the Coffin family was in control, as were the Mayhews on the Vineyard. To the north and east, on the mainland between the Kennebec and the St. Croix rivers, lay the most distant lands under Nicolls's charge. Along the shores there were a few fishing villages that had a marginal existence. The interior was left to the Indians. Nicolls's estimation of this part of New York was succinct; it was "not worth a farthing."[19]

While New Netherland had extended over a wide area, it had never become a strong entity. Its population growth lagged far behind its English neighbors, a result, in part, of the policies of the Dutch West India Company. The company had stressed fur-trading stations, not farming plantations. An experiment to found large landed estates or patroonships had failed in all but the instance of Rensselaerswyck. When the company opened the fur trade to all residents, the growth of farming slowed even more as people gave up agriculture for the easy riches of the fur trade. One other factor hindering growth was the unwillingness of the Dutch to emigrate. The economy of the Netherlands was prosperous, and the discontented or ambitious could go to other, more attractive, areas within the Dutch empire.[20]

The Proprietary Government

Institutional life in New Netherland had been weakly rooted. The director of the West India Company and his council exercised the executive, legislative, and judicial functions of government. The extensive powers of the director had been challenged by local merchants, who protested to the West India Company and the States General about trade policies that acted to exclude the independent merchants. The merchants lost this struggle and continued to live under the control of the company.[21] Local government in the Dutch towns was limited and the ultimate choice of the magistrates was in the hands of the director, as the towns nominated only men for office. Since nominations were in the hands of the magistrates, local governments were controlled by oligarchies. The English towns of Long Island had negotiated for their charters with the Dutch and as a result had gained considerable independence over their own affairs.[22] The Delaware River settlements were under the jurisdiction of the City of Amsterdam and had failed to develop a strong tradition of local government because the settlements were very small and widely scattered. With the exception of New Amsterdam, Nicolls did not have to contend with vigorous Dutch institutions. Instead he faced a scattered population under the control of an unpopular trading company. An English administration which promised trading opportunities and little interference with Dutch religious and social customs may not have been entirely bad in the eyes of some.

The new administration was to be unlike that of any other English colony. The man most responsible for it was York. His charter gave him complete power to organize his government as he wished, reserving to the Crown sovereignty and the right of judicial appeal. York's instructions to Nicolls have not survived, making it impossible to know with certainty what his plans for the proprietary were, but the actions of Nicolls and later events leave little doubt about York's preferred style of government. The duke wanted a strong executive without the interference of an elected body. This meant lodging nearly all executive and legislative authority in the hands of the governor. No assembly or any other popular forum was permitted. Later, when his own governors suggested that this policy be changed, York ignored them and continued the forms of government that Nicolls had instituted.[23]

Nicolls took his time organizing the government. In the surrender agreement, the Dutch magistrates were permitted to stay in office until the next election. This provision insured continuity, but it also implied changes in the future. In his dealings with the English communities on Long Island, Nicolls also moved cautiously. He had antagonized the towns in one of his first actions as a member of the New England Commission. The commission was charged with aligning boundaries and the first task it undertook was to define the overlapping boundary lines between New York and Connecticut. New York's boundary line was the Connecticut River while Connecticut's extended to the South Sea. To complicate matters, Connecticut exercised jurisdiction over the English towns of Long Island. When Governor Winthrop was in New York at the time of the surrender, he evidently came to an understanding with Nicolls whereby the coastal islands would be in New York and the boundary between them would be drawn to the east of the Hudson River Valley. To confirm this agreement, a meeting was held in New York of the commission, magistrates from Connecticut, and two representatives from the Long Island towns. On 30 November 1664 an agreement was signed committing both sides to the boundaries agreed on previously. The Long Island representatives, John Young of Southold and John Howell of Southampton, refused to sign the agreement and returned home embittered about being separated from Connecticut. Afterward, Nicolls approached the English towns with care. He wrote to Howell and Young on 1 December confirming all magistrates and promising treatment equaling any in New England.[24] In particular there would be no new taxes or duties. To mollify them Nicolls promised to meet with town representatives after the winter abated.

In February 1665 Nicolls sent letters to the Dutch and English towns on Long Island and to the English settlements in Westchester announcing a meeting at Hempstead on 28 February to discuss the governance of the colony.[25] The freemen of the towns were to elect two men "sober able and discreet . . . without partiality or faction." No directives were sent as to how the elections were to be held, and freemen were defined only as those who were rateable.[26] Nicolls also took the opportunity to send one order to the towns in his letter. The representatives were to bring with them all the town records relating to boundaries. Boundary disputes had become a sore subject with Nicolls because of the many land cases he had to settle after his arrival.[27] At the conference, he hoped to decide the disputed boundaries, once and for all.

The Hempstead meeting was called to erect a government and establish a legal code for the colony. However, apart from the small Dutch towns of western Long Island, only the English were invited, and of the thirty-four delegates who attended, only nine were Dutch.[28] New York City, Albany, and the other Dutch settlements were excluded. Thus, the meeting was really called to inform the English of the shape of the new regime.

After receiving the announcement of the meeting, the English townsmen of Long Island formulated their position on the nature of the new government. They did not want to break their ties with Connecticut because Connecticut represented the New England tradition of local autonomy and representative government, which they treasured. Nor did they look with favor on the possibility that they would have to abandon the trade with Connecticut since traversing the Long Island Sound was much easier than going through Hell's Gate to the East River and Manhattan. They faced the future with apprehension but hoped the Hempstead meeting would give them the opportunity to preserve their way of life. Before the meeting, townsmen met together to formulate instructions for their delegates. The Southold proposals were representative: title to the town lands in free and common socage; election of town officials by the freemen; election of militia officers by the militia; three court sessions each year, held by elected officials, to try all actions and causes under £5; no taxes for fortifications built outside the town; no militia training outside the town boundaries; no yearly maintenance for provincial officials; no rate, tax, or levy raised without the consent of a "General Court"; and the expenses of their deputies to the court to be met by the government.[29] In summary, the Southold townsmen wanted to continue the same arrangements that they had had with Connecticut, preserving as much autonomy as possible in their own affairs.

When Nicolls arrived at Hempstead, he brought with him a frame of government and a civil and criminal code. This code came to be known as the Duke's Laws and remained the basic law of New York for some time.[30] Nicolls probably supervised the compiling of the Duke's Laws, while the provincial secretary Mathias Nicolls, a barrister, played an important role in actually writing them.[31] The code borrowed much from the laws of other colonies, particularly those in New England. Copies of the laws of Massachusetts Bay and New Haven were sent to New York, but not those of Connecticut. The laws of Maryland and, probably, Virginia were also consulted. In addition, the ordinances promulgated in New Netherland were available. The accumulated experience of the English colonies was mined for the new code.[32]

In writing to Lord Clarendon, Nicolls stated, accurately, "Our new Lawes are not contrived soe Democratically as the rest."[33] There was no provision for an elected assembly. Apart from ideology, practical reasons may have mitigated against an assembly. Any elected body representing the whole colony would have had a Dutch majority. Such a majority would be unacceptable in England and to the English colonists.

The governor and his council, sitting together, were the supreme governing body in New York.[34] The governor was responsible for day-to-day administration and his hand-picked council helped him make policy. They also met annually with the high-sheriff and the justices of the peace as the court of assize. This court was the supreme court, but not the court of last appeal, as York's patent provided for appeals to the king. Because it was the only body that brought together leaders from the whole colony, the assize's function was not strictly limited to justice. It was a clearinghouse for orders and information gathering. Frequently, laws were promulgated and taxes announced at the end of its sessions. Whether the assize discussed and voted on these acts or was merely a convenient forum in which the governor could promulgate them is difficult to tell. The evidence indicates that the governor listened to his hand-picked officials and then decided what action was called for.

The only unit of local government created by the Duke's Laws was the county of Yorkshire. It contained the areas of English occupation—Long Island, Westchester, and Staten Island—and like its namesake, it was divided into three ridings. The east riding comprised the towns at the east end of Long Island (now Suffolk County); the west riding, the middle section of Long Island (parts of Suffolk, Nassau, and Queens counties) and Staten Island; and the north riding, the west end of Long Island (Queens and Kings counties) and Westchester. The focus of administration in the ridings was the court of session. The officers of the court were justices of the peace and under-sheriffs who were chosen by the governor. Their duties were to hear appeals from the town courts, supervise the collection of taxes, and entertain petitions from aggrieved individuals or towns. The high-sheriff of the county supervised the work of the courts of session. In theory, he was chosen from nominations made by the sessions in a three-year cycle. In practice, the governor chose his own man and kept him in office as long as he liked. As the chief liaison with the towns the sheriff had to be someone who had the confidence of the governor.

The towns were the lowest level of administration, and the only level on which there was any popular participation. Each town was governed by a constable and eight overseers elected by the freemen. Each year four overseers were elected and of the four whose terms were up, one had to be elected constable. This was done to insure that an experienced individual held this important office. The constable was the town's chief official presiding over the town court, assessing and accounting for the rates and carrying out the orders of the governor. As a sign of his importance he was confirmed by the court of session where, after taking an oath, he was given his stave of office. While this type of town government resembles that of New England there was one significant difference. In New York, no provision was made for town meetings. Nicolls thus deleted the heart of town democracy so beloved in New England.[35]

Compared to government in other colonies, this was a highly centralized system. The governor and the council were left to carry out provincial affairs relatively unhindered by local opinion. The governor appointed the sheriffs and justices and they, in turn, controlled the constables. In practice, however, the governor did not have total control since all of his appointees were local men who lived and worked among their relatives and neighbors. If their community strongly objected to a policy, they would in all likelihood not carry out orders. Time and local resistance could nullify a policy unless the governor felt strongly enough about the matter to descend in person. His stay could never be for long, and the community would be left on its own. So the governor's authority was limited in practice, if not in law, as the people of Long Island were often to demonstrate. Tension between the local authorities and the provincial government became the normal state of affairs in New York.

Discord first reared its head at the Hempstead meeting. The delegates came to the meeting expecting to share in the formulation of the government and, above all, to arrange for the assembly that Nicolls had promised them by inference in a letter shortly after the surrender of New Amsterdam. Instead, they discovered their role was merely to observe and accept a prepared body of law. Nicolls wrote to John Winthrop, Jr., that after he submitted his code he "mett with great tryalls and exercises of Patience and some very disobliging persons whom I sought to satisfy both with reasons and Civility, but they were throwne upon very undeserving persons namely Captain Young and Mr. Howell for whose sake onely I had made divers condesensions and alterations in the Lawes in open Court."[36] Young and Howell could not be dissuaded from following their instructions, even by bribery. As Nicolls put it, "I had acquainted them that I would give them the most honorable share in Government but I found they struck at all or none and sullenly refused any office at all which you know passeth not unpunished in other Colonies, but I am too well natured to deal harshly with the worst of men."[37] Nicolls must have found this stubbornness very strange after watching the fight for offices in England. He even had to pressure Thomas Topping to write an address to the duke thanking him for the colony's dependence on him. Part of the message, which read "And wee doe publikely and unanimously declare our cheerful submission to all such Lawes, Statutes and ordinances which are or shall be made by virtue of Authority from your R.H.," was extremely displeasing to many, and John Baker, John Young, and John Howell refused to sign the statement.[38] Baker was finally won over, but not even Nicolls's warning that those who did not sign should not expect to enjoy the "fruit and benefit" with the others could bring the other two to sign it.[39] To emphasize this point, Topping was made a member of Nicolls's council, and William Wells, Young's fellow delegate from Southold, was appointed high-sheriff of Yorkshire.

This was not an auspicious beginning for the relationship between the townsmen and the provincial government, especially those of the eastern end of Long Island, who remained unreconciled. Nicolls did, however, wring a tax of £200 from them for the costs of government. This was a small amount, but, as he reported to Lord Clarendon, "I durst not endeavor to stretch their purses farther in the infancy of this change least their affections should be perverted."[40] But their "affections" were "perverted" and the payment of rates without representative government was to become the focus of dissent.

The Hempstead convention was a bitter disappointment for the townsmen. A comparison of the instructions of the Southold delegates with the Duke's Laws reveals the disparity between the townspeople's hopes and the reality of the Duke's Laws. Their desire for representative government had been dashed. Along with the lack of an assembly went the loss of control over taxes and the payment of salaries to provincial officials. They were able to elect their own town magistrates, but their governments were under the scrutiny of the court of sessions, made up of the governor's appointees. Nor did they get satisfaction in local control of the militia. The militia companies were only allowed to nominate three men to be officers; the governor chose the man he favored. If no man on the list was to his liking, he could send it back to the constable with a demand for additional nominees. The townspeoples' request for legal title to their lands was not considered, and Nicolls avoided this issue until he was more secure. Thus, the townsmen were disappointed in the three main areas of concern—a representative body in the government, control over town affairs, and the militia.

Unmentioned in the Southold instructions, but of great importance to the townsmen, was the religious freedom of the inhabitants. ·Here was an area where the duke's preferences matched those of the colonists. York gave religious liberty to all Christians; Jews were not allowed public worship. However, individuals did not have a guarantee of total religious freedom. Each town was given the right to tax for the support of a minister acceptable to the majority. Where towns had inhabitants of different religious preferences, the minority had to support the religion of the majority. If the minority happened to be Quakers, as in a number of Long Island towns, their Calvinist neighbors made sure that they were taxed in full.[41]

The Duke's Laws provided government only for Long Island and a small part of Westchester. The system of sheriffs, justices, constables, and overseers was only gradually extended throughout the colony. Nicolls made exceptions creating other forms of government where needed. For instance, he granted manorial rights to Fisher's Island, Shelter Island, and Pelham in Westchester. His successor, Francis Lovelace, created Fordham in Westchester and Fox Hall in the Esopus region. These grants resulted from both the desire to reward friends and the need to create English government in distant or isolated places. Fisher's Island, the plantation of John Winthrop, Jr., lay close to the Connecticut shore. Shelter Island was the property of Giles Sylvester, who had testified against New England after the Restoration.[42] Pelham, Fordham, and Fox Hall rewarded prominent English landowners for loyalty and provided a form of English government for scattered English settlers, particularly those of Westchester who petitioned Nicolls for protection against the Dutch.[43] Because they lacked the provisions for courts leet and baron these grants were not, accurately speaking, manors. The charters all used the term "manors or township," which makes it more likely that the grants were essentially means of providing local government. This was, however, government in which the manor lord exercised private jurisdiction.[44]

Beyond creating manors, Nicolls did little for the outlying

areas of the colony. This work was largely left for his successors. Prior to leaving New York, Nicolls did issue directions for settling an administration on the Delaware River. Captain John Carr, the garrison commander, was to act as the chief magistrate in conjunction with two elected officials. The New York government normally neglected the Delaware towns, however. In 1671, Captain Carr wrote Governor Lovelace requesting aid and an answer to the planters' question—by what right did they hold their lands? Only after a particularly brutal Indian raid in March 1672 did Lovelace visit New Castle. Unable to do much about the Indian problem, he made two of his protégés, William Wharton and Edmund Cantwell, justice of the peace and sheriff, respectively, and made New Castle a bailiwick (the only one in New York) governed by a bailiff and six assistants.[45] Even with these changes, it was not until the administration of Edmund Andros (1674–80) that a copy of the Duke's Laws was sent to New Castle.

The patchwork nature of administration is also seen in the offshore islands. Staten Island was brought under New York's jurisdiction after a struggle with New Jersey in 1668–69. To consolidate his hold, Lovelace bought the island from the Indians in April 1670, but it was left without a civil administration, with the exception of a ranger—an English officer who watched the royal parks.[46] Martha's Vineyard and Nantucket were left in the control of the dominant family on each island. In 1671, Lovelace made Thomas Mayhew governor and customs collector of Martha's Vineyard for life, with three elected assistants to aid him. In return, Mayhew agreed to an annual quitrent of six barrels of fish. Tristram Coffin, patriarch of the Coffin family on Nantucket, was made chief magistrate of that island. He too was aided by elected assistants, and he paid a quitrent of four barrels of fish. The portion of present-day Maine included in York's patent was without a settled government until July 1677, when Governor Andros sent a garrison whose commander exercised civil jurisdiction.[47] These areas were remote from New York and were essentially autonomous. Communication was rare, and the provincial government could only approve or disapprove of actions already taken. In all but the form of their governments, they remained part of New England.

In creating the county of Yorkshire and extending varied

forms of government throughout New York, Nicolls and Lovelace revealed a pragmatic turn of mind. They used whatever institutions seemed best suited for an area. This attitude was especially necessary when it came to creating local government for the Dutch settlements in the Hudson River Valley. Unlike the Dutch communities of western Long Island, these were treated separately and given different forms of government. The only exceptions were the towns of the Esopus River Valley, where Lovelace encouraged the settlement of English soldiers in two towns near Kingston—Hurley and Marbletown. After all three towns had elected constables and overseers, the governor ordered the officials to meet together in October 1671 as a court of sessions. Thomas Chambers, manor lord of Fox Hall, was made justice of the peace to preside over the court.[48] This arrangement kept leadership in the hands of the English.

New York City and Albany had to be treated differently from the small communities. In both places, the articles of surrender had continued the magistrates in office. The elections for new officers were held in New York City at the usual time in February 1665, and Nicolls confirmed the new officeholders. Then, on 13 June Nicolls appeared before the magistrates, dissolved the Dutch form of government, and proceeded to incorporate all of Manhattan Island under an English form of municipal government with a mayor, aldermen, and a sheriff.[49] Seven new officials were appointed and commissioned by Nicolls. When he appeared before the burgomasters' court to install the new government and its officers, Nicolls met with resistance. The deposed burgomaster, Oloff van Cortlandt, objected to the change in government as a violation of Article 16 of the surrender agreement, which guaranteed that all magistrates were to remain in office until the next elections. Nicolls maintained that the article had been fulfilled by holding elections in February. After lengthy debate, Nicolls announced that he was making the change by order of the duke of York. He also said he had "qualified some English for the office on purpose, that parties may be better aided on both sides, as well as English and Dutch, who go to law and be better to strengthen the peace and quiet of the inhabitants."[50] The new mayor's court did have an ethnic mix different from that of the old burgomasters' court. The only Englishman in the former administration was *schout* Allard Anthony, a long-term resident of the city. The new municipal government had four Englishmen and three Dutchmen. The two most important offices—mayor and sheriff—were in the hands of Englishmen. Thomas Willett, from Plymouth Plantation, was mayor and Allard Anthony went from the analogous office of *schout* to that of sheriff. In order to record the proceedings of the administration in English as well as Dutch, Nicholas Bayard, who was bilingual, was appointed cosecretary with Johannes Nevius.[51] Nicolls had made the city government more amenable to English rule.

In actual structure and distribution of power, the city government had not changed very much. Instead of a burgomaster with four *schepens* and a *schout*, there was now a mayor with five aldermen and a sheriff. The old burgomasters' court had been chosen by the director general from double nominations for each office presented to him by the outgoing court. Nicolls appointed the first set of new officers and he probably continued to do so without reference to the magistrates. In 1669, when Lovelace presented the mayor's court with a seal and a set of crimson robes (a gift from the duke), he reverted to the system of nominations. On occasion, however, he overlooked some of the nominees to appoint his own choices to the court.[52] The mayor's court, in its legal capacities, acted as a court of probate, a surrogates court, and a court of sessions. As a sign of the change to an English system, a jury was impaneled ten days after the new government came into being. Nicolls also abolished the office of treasurer and brought the financial administration under the city collector. The old taxes, except the burgher tax, were continued in order to support city government.[53]

Albany presented problems different from those of New York City. As the center of the colony's government and trade, New York City needed a government shared between the Dutch and the English, along with the legal powers of the jury system and the court of session. It was not as critical to have the same arrangement in Albany. What was important was to have a proper defense for the isolated town. The English garrison commander participated with the magistrates in making Indian policy and in some town affairs relating to the garrison. The town was administered by five *commissaries* (magistrates) plus a *schout*. Two of the *commissaries* represented Albany, two Rensselaerswyck, and one Schenectady. The patroon of Rensselaerswyck was allowed to nominate his own men subject to the governor's approval. The others were selected by the governor from double nominations made to him by the outgoing magistrates. Lovelace changed this pattern of representation since distance made it difficult for the Rensselaerswyck representatives to appear. The Albanyites, also, were never very happy about having representatives of the patroonship on the town council. To remedy this, Lovelace increased the representation of Albany and Schenectady to five, thereby guaranteeing a quorum.[54] One other reform was pushed through by Lovelace. In 1670, when Sylvester Salisbury was garrison commander, Lovelace sought to enhance his power by having him elected *schout*. After the *commisaries* reluctantly acquiesced, Salisbury assumed an office that gave him increased civil authority.[55] It also meant that Lovelace had a key man of his own in Albany's government.

One political unit on the upper Hudson retained a special autonomy. Surrounding much of Albany was the patroonship of the Rensselaer family, the only remaining survivor of the West India Company's experiment in feudalism. The patroonships represented the company's attempt to attract settlers and pacify the appetite for land among certain stockholders. All the others failed except Rensselaerswyck. The family retained both its land and its political control over the inhabitants. Nicolls himself negotiated with Jeremias Van Rensselaer, the resident director, and agreed to let him exercise his usual powers, provided a new patent was obtained from England. In return, Nicolls sought an annual rent of 200 beavers a year, but settled for 50 beavers and 600 boards. This rent was an important source of revenue to Nicolls since it could be collected in wheat, which was always needed to feed the garrison. It was a less favorable agreement for the Rensselaers, who had difficulty obtaining a new patent.[56]

Who Rules?

In the government of the colony as a whole, there were really only two important institutions—the council and the corporation of New York City. The council advised and consented with the governor and sat on the court of assize. The mayor and aldermen represented the largest center of population and the economic hub of the colony. The governor controlled both groups by appointing their members, either directly or indirectly. Only on the city council was there any sort of election, and that was merely the nomination of new members by the old members at the end of their year's tenure. This meant that New York City was governed by a self-perpetuating oligarchy. Both bodies were closely tied together through interlocking membership. During the years 1665 to 1673 Nicolls and Lovelace appointed only ten men to the council. From these ten were chosen the mayors of New York City during this period. Of the thirty-nine aldermanic offices available during those eight years, twenty-two were held by eight of the ten councilors.[57] The membership of both bodies was closely intertwined, making for a close liaison that favored the city over the other regions of New York.

The only two members of the council during this period who did not reside in the city were Thomas Topping and Thomas Willett. Topping lived on Long Island and was on the council for only one year.[58] Willett came to America on the *Mayflower* and had become a trusted leader in Plymouth Plantation and a trader who went as far afield as New Amsterdam and Fort Orange.[59] Because he was a friend of Stuyvesant and familiar with the Dutch, Nicolls talked him into leaving retirement and becoming the first mayor of New York City in the hope that he would ease the transition. Willett's trade activities and distant residence in Plymouth kept him from regularly attending the council. The other eight councilors were identified with New York City. Three of them, Robert Needham, Ralph Whitefield, and Thomas Lovelace, served on the council for short periods. Needham and Whitefield were officers in the garrison. Thomas Lovelace was the governor's brother and held a number of posts in New York besides being a merchant.[60] Two of the five remaining councilors, Cornelius Van Ruyven and John Lawrence, were longtime residents of the city. Van Ruyven had served the Dutch West India Company and, as a result, knew the mercantile community as well as any man.[61] Lawrence was an Englishman who had emigrated to New England and had found his way to Long Island. His original interest was land, which led him to become a patentee for Hempstead in 1644 and for Flushing a year later, but after a time his trading activities became more important, and he moved to New Amsterdam in 1658, where he gained the confidence of Stuyvesant. His attempt to remain neutral in 1664 aroused Nicolls's suspicion to the point where Lawrence had to take the oath of allegiance with the Dutch.[62]

The three most important men on the council were Mathias Nicolls (no relation to the governor), Thomas Delaval, and Cornelius Steenwick. Governor Lovelace particularly valued the advice of Delaval and Steenwick. After dispatching them to take care of problems in Albany and Kingston, he ordered them to return quickly as "you well knowing how much I am destitute in your absence of any helps."[63] Nicolls was important because he was the provincial secretary and the only barrister in New York. As noted earlier, he helped prepare the Duke's Laws and as the informal chief legal officer he attended many meetings of the courts of session to supervise their proceedings.[64] Delaval, the receiver general, was on the council because of his office. In England he had been a surveyor for the Farmers of the Customs and prior to that a customs collector in Dunkirk. Besides being receiver general, he was also the original commissary for the garrison, a position of importance since some of the support for the garrison normally fell upon the government of New York.[65] Cornelius Steenwick was one of the wealthiest men in New York. About 1652 he came to New Amsterdam and one year later his wealth was commented upon. Most of his fortune derived from an active trade in tobacco in Maryland and Virginia.[66] In 1658, his nomination as a *schepen* was approved and he continued to hold office thereafter. Thus, of the ten councilors, eight were merchants or officeholder-merchants whose base was in New York City. Their concern for its prosperity was a constant in New York politics.

The ethnic composition of the council and the mayor's court was also important. Of the ten councilors, only two were

Dutch. Nicolls completely excluded the Dutch from the council. Only after Lovelace took over in 1668 was Steenwick appointed and a year later Van Ruyven. At the same time Lovelace went back to the Dutch system of double nomination for offices in the city. Both of these actions probably stemmed from a recognition that the Dutch had remained quiet during Nicolls's tenure and so should be brought into the government. Lovelace's actions certainly made him popular with the Dutch. The reality of the situation was that the English controlled matters. The office of mayor was in English hands except for the two-year tenure of Steenwick. The only two sheriffs were likewise English, and thus the two most important city offices were held almost exclusively by Englishmen. The aldermanic offices were more evenly divided. Of the forty-seven positions in eight years, seventeen were in English hands and twenty-two in Dutch. The ratio of English representation was far greater than that of their numbers in the population, however, and the Dutch had to tolerate this disparity as one of the burdens of conquest. However, the fact was that the members of the council and the mayor's court were united in their economic interests.

The structure of government created by Nicolls and elaborated by Lovelace was a mosaic of governmental units. At its center were the governor and his hand-picked council. This was the pattern of governance favored by the duke of York and the sweeping powers granted to him in his charter allowed him to fulfill his plan. The preeminence of the executive was the chief weakness in the system. Much of the vitality of the government depended upon the governor. When he was a vigorous and moderate man like Nicolls, the government could operate reasonably well. Should the governor, however, be authoritarian, or greedy, or both, tremendous tensions could be created between the government and the people. Another danger resulted from this centralized system. Because the central administration relied so heavily on the governor, a crisis could easily occur if he were ill or removed from office or indecisive. At such times a vacuum ensued that invited dissidence.

The special relationship between the central government and New York City was also a problem. It was natural that each governor relied upon the merchants of the city for support.

They were his social peers and companions; furthermore, they could help him finance the expensive garrison. Should he also want to engage in trade they were willing to help. In return, they expected access to power and favorable treatment for the city. The result was a "city" versus "country" split that runs through New York politics.

The "country" in New York comprised the various regions —Long Island, Albany, Esopus, and Delaware. These areas had differing demographic patterns, economic interests, and governmental structure. Nowhere else in the English colonies at this time was such diversity brought within one system. Separated by great distances they remained autonomous units, and without an assembly in which to voice their discontents, the regions were prey to the policies of the central government. As a result, time after time, in the crucial areas of economic monopolies and taxation, the city merchants had their way.

The geographic isolation of the settlements had one beneficial effect. Local government, no matter what sort, was in close touch with the people. Magistrates were easy to influence and any misbehavior could be punished. Within this narrow sphere families could attempt to fulfill their hopes and dreams of prosperity and well-being. On the one hand, this local particularism bred distrust of outsiders, and in New York, it increased tension between the two national groups. On the other hand, it created a tradition of local self-reliance and trust in local government. Unfortunately the central authorities could and did impinge upon them, for the people needed the legitimacy provided by the government to sanction their governments and their land dealings. This contact with the local source of ultimate authority in the metropolitan community was crucial for people at the edge of the wilderness. Yet in New York this meant dealing with a government that was frequently insensitive to their needs. The result was a system in which the regions struggled to minimize the impact of the central government. This conflict began during the first decade when the issues dividing the "city" and the "country" were created. The pattern of the conflict was to remain the same for a very long time.[67]

3 &amp；ᑌ The Emergence of Political Issues, 1664–1673

After the exciting events of 1664 the people of New York slowly adapted to the new government. In turn, the members of the government reacted to the initiatives of the people. This interaction was contained within the narrow framework of the new structure of government. The people had to discover these parameters, just as the government had to recognize the limits of its authority. This process is revealed in three major problems that emerged during the first period of English administration from 1664 to 1673. First, there was the continuing struggle of the New English towns on Long Island to preserve local autonomy and extend representative government. Second, competition developed between the various regions to exploit their own economic potential. This struggle was complicated by the desire of the government to collect duties to defray the costs of the proprietary. Third, the tension between the Dutch and the English became a major problem as the Dutch were forced to begin the long process of Anglicization. During this period, the pressures on the Dutch varied considerably. They also could retain the hope of returning to Dutch rule, a hope that was realized in 1673 when a Dutch fleet sailed into New York harbor. These three problems were not discrete. Economic rivalries enhanced ethnic tension, and vice versa. Struggles for local autonomy were sharpened by economic rivalries. An understanding of the growth of these three issues and the conflicts they engendered illuminates the working of the new government.

The Struggle for Local Autonomy

At the Hempstead meeting, Nicolls confronted the prickly local pride of the New Englanders on Long Island and managed to overcome their objections to the new government. Their grudging acquiescence rather than joyful loyalty had to be tolerated until he established the government. The vigor of local autonomy did not wilt in the presence of the new government and shortly after the Hempstead meetings the townspeople left no doubts about how they felt.

The principal issue was taxation. The normal costs of government were no greater in New York than in other colonies, but imperial politics and good sense demanded that after the conquest the soldiers remain in the colony to watch the Dutch. Later, when the rivalry with France came to dominate imperial policymaking, the strategic position of New York required that a trained force be stationed there. The garrison thus became the oldest established British military force on the continent.[1] It also placed a financial burden upon the proprietary government.

The soldiers needed wages, clothing, shelter, munitions, and fortifications. The state of the records does not permit a complete accounting of expenditures for the garrison, but those records that have survived reveal the extent of the financial burden it created. For 1674, when 100 new soldiers joined the garrison, the annual cost of salaries for the men and their officers was £2,062.[2] Who paid these salaries was no small matter to the governors. The soldiers of the 1664 expedition were members of York's own companies and were paid by the Treasury. Not until 1674, however, did the Treasury agree to pay for munitions and other supplies, besides salaries. It is impossible to estimate how much of this money found its way to New York. But when York became king in 1685 a statement of his accounts revealed the Treasury owed £6,750 of the £1,000 per year extra compensation it had agreed to pay in 1674. From 1674 to 1685, only £905 in military supplies was forwarded to New York.[3] Thus, one must conclude that York was paid irregularly and that he in turn did not remit all that was due to the garrison. The governors were left with the responsibility of financing the garrison. During this period they were aided by Thomas Delaval, the commissary, who may have prospered from his position, as any funds sent by York or the Treasury would be in hard money. In an economy short on specie, cash or bills sent from England were highly valued.[4] Whatever he received was simply not enough and the governors used local taxes to house the garrison and keep up the fortifications.[5] Nicolls found this system inadequate and he recommended reductions in the size of the garrison, while pleading for help from the duke and the Crown. When they did not respond, he, like many other colonial governors, spent his own funds and pledged his credit to get supplies in New York and Boston.[6] Embittered by his experience, he wrote ruefully, "My ignorance made mee bold to undertake so great a charge, which will become a much wiser man and of a more plentifull fortune."[7] By the time he returned to England, Nicolls was at least £8,098 in debt.[8] The figure takes into account only expenses from 1 April 1666 to 1 May 1668 which were accepted by York. On a yearly basis, therefore, it cost Nicolls £3,890, personally, to finance the proprietary. The duke promised to repay Nicolls, but the latter's will requested that his executors obtain payment from York for his debts.[9] Lovelace was obviously in the same situation but the tangled estates of Lovelace, Delaval, and Isaac Bedloo, Lovelace's factor, make any accurate assessment of expenditures impossible.[10]

York did nothing to help the situation. In fact he acted contrary to his own interests. One obvious means of gaining a broader tax base was to expand the number of planters throughout New York's extensive territory. Nicolls immediately seized this opportunity by granting patents for the new towns of Elizabeth and Monmouth west of the Hudson River.[11] Unknown to him, however, York had already begun the dismemberment of New York by granting the area between the Hudson and Delaware rivers to his faithful friends Lord John Berkeley of Stratton and Sir George Carteret.[12] Governor Nicolls vehemently opposed York's munificence. His letters argued that the best farmland had been stripped from New York, customs would be diminished because ships could berth on the Jersey side of the Hudson, and the Delaware settlements would be more difficult to administer. In addition, if New Jersey had trouble with the Indians and the garrison was called out, who would pay? Nicolls advised the duke to divest himself of his proprietary unless the gift to Berkeley and Carteret was rescinded.[13] York disagreed and his governors had to do without the quitrents and customs of the Jerseys. They were left to finance the government from their own pockets and a restricted tax base.

No principle animated the English planters more than that taxes ought to be levied by an elected body; thus it was in New England and Old England; thus it should be in New York. On 26 February 1666 Nicolls issued warrants to assess a rate of one penny on the pound of assessed valuation in the county of Yorkshire. The local overseers were to assess the estates of all men over sixteen and the constables had to collect the tax under threat of heavy penalties.[14] To those who thought the rate announced at Hempstead was the last of its kind, this second rate promulgated by the governor was an alarming event. Oyster Bay protested immediately but Nicolls rebuffed the town, stating that the costs of government had been underestimated, and he needed to collect £200. Taxpayers, he continued, could assure themselves that nothing was improper because the government's accounts were presented to the court of assize for review. To justify further his action Nicolls asserted that his power to tax derived from the duke's patent. This was his last line of defense, although on another occasion he had claimed the right to tax had been granted by the deputies at Hempstead.[15]

The issue of the new rates soon became intermixed with another one. The burden of tax collection fell on local magistrates, who had to assess and collect the new rates. Town magistrates were already unpopular because they administered laws for an unpopular government, and the new tax raised their unpopularity to greater heights. The constables of Hempstead and Brookhaven were assaulted while trying to collect the rates. In Brookhaven, discontent escalated into a riot. Nicolls responded by sending a commission to investigate the "mutinous" conduct in the town.[16] A far more serious problem was created by the refusal of Southold, Southampton, and Easthampton to elect magistrates in compliance with the Duke's Laws. An exasperated Nicolls wrote to Sheriff Topping, "I am not a little moved agst. close and seditious practices of some who secretly distill into ye hearts of his [Majesty's] good subjects, such refractory and mutinous humours as tend to ye disturbance and breach of the Lawes Establish't." Through the sheriff, he ordered the towns to elect new officials or be declared "mutinous contemmers of ye Lawes Establish't and disturbances of the peace of this Government."[17]

Through the months of April and May 1666 the English towns remained in turmoil. As discontent flourished, the deputies who had attended the Hempstead Convention and agreed to the Duke's Laws became objects of revulsion. Stung by the feelings of their neighbors they wrote a "Narrative and Remonstrance" in defense of their actions.[18] In it, they asserted that they had not just accepted the laws: amendments they proposed were accepted by Nicolls, but when a committee went to him about electing all of the government officers, he refused to consider their proposal because his instructions gave him the power to choose magistrates. So heated was the attack on the deputies that the next court of assize made it a crime to criticize them and, by implication, the laws themselves.[19]

To Governor Nicolls, the continuing disturbances were threats to the government. He wrote to John Underhill, the collector and high constable of Long Island:

I have received yours of the 29th of April, wherein you represent the distempers of some people, against the p'sent form of Government by which (you say) they are inslav'd under an Arbitrary Power, and that I do exercize mor than the King himselfe can do, which is so high an imputation, that I can not suffer my selfe to be reputed or Blasted in the hearts, or by the Tongues of such false and malicious men, therefore instead of writing to mee under the notion of some people say thus and thus, be think yourself or some particular Persons who do thus slander mee with a charge of no less weight than High Treason.[20]

Chastened by this blast, Underhill made an example of the Reverend Samuel Doughty by removing him from his pulpit for preaching against the government.[21]

As a royalist and an army man, Nicolls found the intransigence of the towns extremely obnoxious. The only comparable experience he could draw on was the Revolution in England and in it found a lesson: "The Late Rebellion in England, with all ye ill consequences thereof, began with the selfe same steps and pr'tences." He could not understand "men too fractious as to hazard both life and Estate in a mutiny or Rebellion."[22] To Nicolls, order was more important than rights. The men who refused to pay public rates and who made demands for the election of magistrates were republicans and a threat to the stability of society. When he wrote of his troubles to Lord Clarendon, he complained, "Democracy hath taken so deepe a Roote in these parts, that the very name of a Justice of the Peace is an Abomination, whereof I have upon due Consideration of his [majesties] interest layd the foundations of Kingly Government in these parts so farre as is possible which truely is grievous to some Republicans."[23] These sentiments show the division between Nicolls and the townsmen. To him, their actions verged on rebellion. From the townsmen's point of view, he was the chief magistrate in a government that taxed them illegally.

For all his fulmination against "Republicans," Nicolls ultimately could not force the townsmen to obey the laws. He discovered the limits of his powers. Had he been a petty tyrant he could have ordered the garrison to march into the towns in a show of force. But was it worth it? The Dutch population would have been left unguarded with who knows what consequences. Sooner or later the troops would have to return to the city, the most strategic point in the colony, leaving behind them embittered townspeople with even more reason to hate the duke's government. These were the very real limits on the governor's powers. Without popular consent to the government's policies, the governors would have to conciliate local opposition just enough to defang its worst opponents.

At the end of May 1666, when tension was still high, Nicolls wrote, "Their designs [are] to give [me] a just provocation, thinking to overcome my patient Temper. . . . But they will be mistaken in their Measures, for I will take my owne time and not theirs."[24] Nicolls marked time until the autumn. Unwilling to cancel the rates altogether, thereby capitulating to the towns and disobeying his instructions, he sought a compromise. He turned over payment for some public bills to the towns. Town services provided by individuals, whether for labor or supplies, were no longer reimbursible by the provincial government. These services were now left to the communities to pay from their own rates. This cut the burden of the central government while enhancing local control over local expenditures. Next, Nicolls abolished the salaries of the justices of the peace. He had waited six months after the Hempstead meeting before announcing the salaries and fees of the provincial office-holders. Undoubtedly, he wanted the wounds caused by the meeting to heal before the townspeople discovered what the new government was going to cost. The justices were the chief beneficiaries, as their pay was £20 a year plus fees.[25]

Easthampton, Southold, and Southampton instantly disapproved and called a meeting of all the towns to object to the salaries.[26] No record of a meeting survives, but protests over the salaries helped fuel the protests over taxation in the spring of 1666. When the assize met in October 1666, the justices were stripped of their salaries and the privilege of not paying rates in their towns of residence. There remained only the fees they collected for services performed at the assize and sessions. To complete the economy move, the high-constables and under-sheriffs of the ridings were dismissed and their offices discontinued. In the future the high-sheriff and town constables were to collect the rates, a job most of the high-constables and under-sheriffs had refused to do anyway. To make sure that orders were obeyed hereafter, fines were set for noncompliance.[27]

Local autonomy had been strengthened at the same time central administration had been tightened—a nice compromise. A balance had been sought by Nicolls and, according to his lights, achieved. The Duke's Laws were modified but not fundamentally changed, since his new arrangement was well within the mandated system. If only the townspeople had seen it this way. In their opinion their fundamental objections to the unrepresentative nature of the government had not been met, and they maintained a watchful attitude. Soon they were engaged in another dispute with Nicolls.

Land and Politics

At the assize meeting in 1665, Nicolls moved to rationalize the land system because of constant controversies between the towns. Arguments over boundaries and contradictory land claims had bedeviled him from the start. The confusion endemic in land grants in all the colonies had been magnified in New York by the English conquest, when, according to Cornelius Van Ruyven, "many old matters [were] ripped up and misinterpreted."[28] The resulting litigation forced Nicolls to regulate new land sales so that future problems would be avoided. During the assize session Nicolls revealed plans to review and reissue all the old patents. He announced that patents held from the States General of the Netherlands or the West India Company were made by foreigners and thus were contrary to English law and the duke's orders. All landowners were commanded to bring in their patents for renewal.[29]

The order was virtually ignored. Only Jamaica bothered to comply. Faced with this recalcitrance, the 1666 assize reissued the order of 1665 and added some teeth to it. Patents unconfirmed by 1 April 1667 would not be pleadable in law.[30] With this threat hanging over their heads, the towns reconsidered and started to capitulate. One reason they did was that Nicolls had acted to remove their chief complaint about repatenting. The English towns believed they were being discriminated against because the Dutch were allowed to remain unmolested in their grants. To satisfy them Nicolls extended the new law to cover all patents. Orders went to Albany and New York City to bring all "Ground Briefes" in for inspection and reissuing.[31] This proved to be a sore point with the Dutch, who, like the islanders, did not like interference in matters of land ownership. One man wrote to the local constable, "I will see you tomorrow to comply with ye orders of ye new government. . . but not without very strongly protesting against the injustice which has long been heaped upon us. . . ."[32]

With the Dutch conforming to the law, the English followed suit. By the 1 April deadline, Brookhaven, Easthampton, Flushing, Newton, Huntington, Smithtown, Westchester, and Eastchester had submitted their patents for confirmation. This left a number of towns without new patents, but as the assize session of October 1667 approached, Gravesend, Flatlands, Flatbush, Brooklyn, and Bushwyck submitted. Hempstead, Oyster Bay, Southold, and Southampton continued to ignore the order. These four towns had provided much of the resistance to the Duke's Laws, the rates, and now the new patents. Nicolls kept the pressure on them until Hempstead obtained a new patent in March 1668.[33] The remaining three continued to resist, even in the face of threats. The people of Oyster Bay argued that they had recorded their patent at Hempstead and that a new patent would "bind us and our posterity forever to ye subject of all unknown Laws without exception . . . which may be imposed upon us many years after ye Kings and Dukes Decease."[34] In other words, to give up the patent was to forfeit what remained of their rights. They believed that they should obey a higher law than the duke's—God's law—and it was not until the imperious Sir Edmund Andros became governor that they capitulated.

A collateral issue to repatenting was that of quitrents. While there are no fiscal records for this period, other evidence indicates that Nicolls decided not to press the issue of quitrents in 1666 but instead to leave this issue for later. He did this by issuing the new patents with a clause stating that "duties and acknowledgements" might be demanded in the future. In a few instances, however, quitrents were charged on especially large holdings. The Lloyd family, for example, had an annual rent of four bushels of wheat on their holdings at Lloyds Neck.[35] But with few exceptions Nicolls left the inhabitants alone, thereby keeping the argument on taxes from becoming even more raucous. Future quitrents were not wholly unde-fined, however. The Duke's Laws set a rent of two shillings, sixpence for every newly purchased 100 acres.[36] In practice this provision was ignored as succeeding governors decided to let sleeping dogs lie and forego collection.

The opportunity to benefit from the repatenting was not wholly overlooked. Fees were charged as always, for the privi-lege of obtaining a new grant. In New York City, for instance, the charge was one beaver, although the magistrates could waive the fee for poor homeowners.[37] Those individuals who had extensive grants paid special, and large, fees. Nathaniel Sylvester paid £150 for the manor of Shelter Island.[38] Quit-rents might be deferred, but a one-time windfall was not over-looked.

From the very beginning of New York's history the English towns on Long Island showed their desire for autonomy. Had there been an assembly in which they participated in policy-making and above all voted for taxes, they might have been integrated into, or at least reconciled to, the new government. Without an assembly they remained deeply suspicious of the government. They had won some concessions from Nicolls, but they continued to watch for any future advances by the central government. They discovered very quickly that they not only had to fight over the system of government, but also had to suffer attacks on their economic well-being.

The Provincial Economy

New York had four regional economies. The Delaware River region was the most important tobacco-growing area in New York. Frequent voyages between New Castle and New York City and land acquisition there by New York merchants testify to its importance as an alternative to Virginia and Maryland. Long Island's towns specialized in grains and livestock with an expanding whale-oil business that became a lucrative export trade. Albany was famous as a fur-trading center, but the region around it was also gaining recognition as a grain-exporting region. The same was true of the settlements along the Esopus River. Hundreds of miles separated these regions, yet they all had the same focal point—New York City. The strategic position at the center of this web made the city an entrepôt. European imports flowed in while colonial exports flowed out, sometimes after processing by local artisans. At first glance this was a natural trading system, yet it was one that engendered bitter battles. The English towns of Long Island preferred to take their business to the nearer ports of Connecticut or Rhode Island or even to Boston. These voyages were easier than the long haul down the sound or around the island. Albany, on the other hand, preferred to be the master of its own destiny and trade directly with Europe. Delaware, the stepchild of this system, was too weak to go it alone. Regional battles for autonomy were built into New York in 1664, and, in the years following, they would unfold to create dissension and distrust.

During the years 1664 to 1673, New York's economy responded directly to events in Europe. The second Anglo-Dutch war was a fight between two maritime powers that disrupted trade in northern Europe. The onslaught of war in 1664 impaired New York's trade immediately. Only after the war ground to an end in 1668 did the economy, both of the warring states and of the colonies, recover. The exceptional year of 1671 did not follow this trend because bad weather in North America curtailed crops and forced delays in trade.[39] Then while they were recovering from this setback the colonies began to suffer again as England and the Netherlands began to drift into war for the third and last time. Against this general background New York's economy continued to grow and develop.

Caught up simultaneously in a war and a trade slump, Nicolls was left to his own devices. As a result his policy was one of encouraging trade from England while placating the local Dutch merchants. In one of his first letters to Lord Arlington, the secretary of state, Nicolls insisted that supplies be sent to New York by April or May 1665.[40] He emphasized that the Dutch provided European goods, not only for themselves, but also for the planters from Long Island to Maryland. Should there be no ships from England this trade would continue and the tobacco trade would go directly to Holland in Dutch ships. His pleas were apparently in vain, however, since during Nicolls's four years in office there is record of only one ship that sailed from London to New York.[41]

The Dutch merchants of New York could not wait for English enterprise. Nor could Nicolls for that matter. Commerce was the lifeblood of the city and unless Nicolls wanted a discontented citizenry, he had to improve trade. So while waiting and hoping for a response from England, he supported the Dutch merchants by making them denizens, a status that permitted them to trade within the English empire.[42] He also made it possible for them to continue to trade as they had in the past. The articles of surrender suspended the Navigation Acts and allowed trade with Holland for six months. This measure was probably designed to allow the Dutch to settle accounts in Holland, but Nicolls continued to grant exceptions after the six-month grace period elapsed.[43] He even allowed Cornelius Steenwyck, the wealthiest and most important merchant in New York, to continue trading with the Netherlands for one year because trade was "the only means of supporting the Government, and the welfare of the inhabitants."[44] The independent merchants got more good news in November 1664, when Nicolls abrogated the privileges of the Dutch West

India Company. The articles of surrender had granted the company the right to collect duties on cargoes going to the Netherlands. This policy was quickly reversed and the company lost the right to trade, and its assets were first frozen and then seized.[45] Encouraged by this action, the magistrates of the city wrote to York expressing their thankfulness at being under his protection. If he would only grant them exemptions from duties, they promised York he would "learn with hearty delight the advancement of the Province even to a place from which your Highness shall come to derive great revenues."[46]

As the months went by and ships failed to arrive from England, Nicolls went to greater lengths to aid the Dutch mercantile community. He wrote to England requesting that four to six ships be allowed to make the round trip from New York to Holland each year.[47] If granted this privilege, he asserted, the Dutch community would be won over to England. It may have appeared in England that Nicolls had instead been won over by the Dutch. His request was not realized until 1667, when Peter Stuyvesant, on behalf of his countrymen, petitioned the king and York for special treatment.[48] Stuyvesant argued in favor of allowing the Dutch to continue trading with the Netherlands on the grounds that all their commercial contacts were in their mother country. If the Crown forced them to break the old ties, they would be ruined, and the fur trade, which was based on the Dutch trade, would be lost to the ever-ready French, depriving New York of this trade. He concluded by pointing out that ships had not come from England and that if the settlers went unsupplied they would have to move. As a minimum concession, he argued, two ships should be allowed to go to the Netherlands immediately.

Stuyvesant's petition was referred to the Council for Trade. There it received a sympathetic reading from the many friends of the duke. After due consideration the council recommended that, in light of England's inability to supply New York, three ships be allowed to go between New York and the Netherlands annually for seven years, and on 22 October 1667 an order in council was issued to this effect.[49] Considering the policy of the Crown and Parliament as reflected in the Navigation Acts, this decision was an unusual one, but in this instance, as in other Restoration affairs, expediency outweighed policy. The needs of York's new proprietary were just too important to overlook.

Only a year later, however, the order permitting trade with the Netherlands was canceled. The end of the second Anglo-Dutch war, the revival of trade, and the jealousy of English merchants had brought about a reconsideration. The Council for Trade advised the king that English merchants were withdrawing from trade with North America because Dutch ships were supplying not only New York, but also Virginia and New England. Such arguments brought about the end of legal trade with the Netherlands after November 1668.[50]

This was a heavy blow to the New York merchants who had rushed to Amsterdam. Such leading merchants as Oloff Van Cortlandt, Jacques Cousseau, Nicholas De Meyer, and Margareta Philipse (wife of Frederick) were stranded along with thirteen other merchants who had gone to settle accounts and arrange trade. Cornelius Steenwyck and Stuyvesant were particularly hard hit. The order of 1667 required that those who wished to trade with Holland obtain permits from the proprietor. Stuyvesant and Steenwyck had quickly obtained these permits and sold their rights to a group of Dutch merchants. Now their permits were invalidated along with the hopes of the other merchants. They petitioned for, and received, permission for a return voyage in the *King Charles*. Further efforts were made to get dispensations for New York but without the vigor of those made in 1667. These too ended in failure, putting a finish to hopes for creating a special trade relationship for the new proprietary.[51]

Internal Trade Rivalry

Frustrated in their hopes for a legal export trade to the Netherlands outside the Navigation Act system, the New York City merchants were very successful in controlling the economy of the proprietary. Their ability to do so was enhanced by the nature of the government. Overrepresented on the council, the merchants were its dominant voice, and their control over the city's government was never in doubt. What enhanced their influence were the men appointed to the governorship. All four of York's appointees were military men to whom the governorship was a means of advancing their fortunes. As a future assembly would ruefully remark about the governors, "they know the Time of their Continuance in the Governments to be uncertain, all Methods are used, and all Engines set to work to raise Estates to themselves."[52] Of the first two governors, Nicolls seems to have had little interest in advancing his fortune through trade. Lovelace, however, took full advantage of his position. He came to New York with his brother Thomas, who was a merchant, and together they acquired land spread from Esopus to Delaware, with an especially large estate on Staten Island. They also financed the building of a ship, the *Good Fame*, in New York, and after selling shares in the *Good Fame*, they bought shares in at least two other vessels, the *Duke of York* and the *Hopewell*. Trade with Amsterdam was an important aspect of Lovelace's entrepreneurial activities. His interests in the Netherlands were maintained by such New York merchants as Eagidius Luyck, François Hooghlandt, Nicolas Gouverneur, and Isaac Bedloo. The latter also acted as commissary for the garrison and was Lovelace's private factor. As commissary, Bedloo had access to the public treasury, which Lovelace appears to have used as a means of financing his own ventures. So intermingled were Bedloo's and Lovelace's accounts with those of the government that they were extremely difficult to disentangle when his administration was brought to a close in 1673. With a governor so heavily involved in mercantile activity, it was no wonder the merchants had an easy time extending their influence.[53]

One further factor aided the merchants—the heavy burden imposed by the garrison on the governors. Because funding from England was irregular, the governors had to rely on the merchants to supply provisions. In return they gained further political leverage. Often it took the form of favoritism such as a special dispensation from the rules, special passes to trade in New Castle and Albany, or the right to take whales in a certain area. Ultimately their influence gave New York City a leading position in the provincial economy.

The merchants first capitalized on their influence immediately after Lovelace arrived in the colony. During the summer of 1668, a group of merchants led by Frederick Philipse argued in a petition that Albany's trade should not be restricted to its residents.[54] Of course, this was a trade the city merchants desired for themselves. The issue was left unresolved until June 1670, when Lovelace issued an order restricting trade on the river. All goods going upriver had to be unloaded in New York City to pay duties. Once customs were paid, the goods could continue only on a vessel owned by a freeman of the city; all other ships were banned. The next year the order was renewed and made binding forever.[55] In the autumn of 1670 the monopoly was made complete. That summer, traders had arrived overland from New England with horses, cattle, and trading goods. This was an important venture on behalf of New England fur merchants, who needed Albany's peltries. Such competition was not condoned, as it meant the loss of valued trade and customs revenue. The result was an order prohibiting all overland trade.[56] Goods needed for the Indian trade now had to come through New York City and to be shipped upriver in city vessels.

The growing foodstuffs trade soon attracted the attention of the merchants. Wheat, flour, and bread for ships' stores were increasingly important in trade up and down the coast and to the West Indies. Control over this trade was, therefore, highly desirable. Supplies of wheat were usually sufficient until 1670–71, when a severe winter was followed by devastating spring floods that heavily damaged crops along the Esopus and Hudson river valleys.[57] Faced with tight supplies and difficulty in fulfilling contracts for flour and bread, the merchants moved to control the situation. On 7 March 1671 the bakers of the city were called before the mayor and aldermen. Asked if it were feasible to export grain from the city, they replied that if exports were allowed, there would be no bread in the city by summer, and they requested a ban on the export of grain, although not of flour or bread. Such a ban was not unprecedented. When wheat was scarce in 1666 and 1667, the export of wheat and its products had been banned. However, the embargo requested by the bakers in 1671 was unusual because it exempted flour and bread. As they explained it, the coopers and other "mechanics" in the city would still be able to gain a livelihood if these exports were allowed. The magistrates followed the bakers' advice and requested that the governor place a ban on the export of grain. Their proposal was considered by the council on 8 March, and on the following day an order to this effect was issued.[58]

The principal beneficiaries were the merchants, mill owners, and bakers. Those outside this circle protested immediately, forcing the council to reconsider the matter on 18 May. At this meeting, the council noted that the mayor and aldermen agreed with them that a ban on wheat was necessary.[59] Without retracting the order the council decided to consult other people. Their actions to this point could only have pointed out to other groups in the colony the influence of the merchants. What followed could only confirm their worst fears. The justices of the peace were ordered to discuss wheat supplies at the sessions and then report their findings at the assize in October. Predictably, the justices reported widespread discontent over the ban and many requests that it cease. Because of a good summer crop, predictions of severe shortages could no longer justify the prohibition. The assize, dominated by the governor and council, refused to retract the order, however, and, in fact, extended the ban to cover meal straight from the mill. Their reason was that New York City's trade had increased in flour and bread, which were selling at good prices.[60] The continuation of the embargo revealed the ascendancy of the city, since such prices benefited only the wealthy city merchants.

Policing the ban was another matter, especially on Long Island. Too many small harbors and unseeing people vitiated the effectiveness of any law. Lovelace sent Sheriff Manning to the sessions with orders to check on the transportation of wheat and the ship traffic and to find anyone who would be willing to act as customs officer in every port suitable for landing cargo.[61] A standoff was inevitable, but such unenforced orders only added to the tensions on Long Island, particularly when the council made exceptions to the embargo to reward the favored few. Such was the case in 1672 when the wheat crop was so abundant that some merchants were allowed to send wheat to Connecticut for grinding. At this point, the assize buckled under pressure and lifted the ban on grain, although with special conditions on its sale. When prices were four shillings, sixpence per bushel for winter wheat and four shillings for summer wheat, it could be sold. If the buyer was a nonresident, and in New York City, the prices were six pence less.[62] This was a very nice bargaining point for the merchants and further proof of their influence.

These new rules lasted for a short time. In April 1673, after another severe winter, exports of wheat were halted again except by special license from the governor.[63] Two months later, the government issued new regulations on the inspection of all grains to insure the quality of exports. The number of inspectors and packers was also increased, and no bread or meal could leave New York without their stamp. Thus, the city continued to benefit from special legislation. Nor did Governor Lovelace help his image when he issued himself a special license to ship wheat to Boston.[64]

Control over Albany's fur trade was relatively easy to achieve. Its geographic position made it susceptible to control and, besides, the *handlaers* were still left with the valuable fur trade. Long Island was a different story. The economy on the island was diverse, and economic disputes inevitably became intertwined with political issues. During Lovelace's administration, the interplay between control of economic policy and local autonomy brought about frequent clashes.

As his first move, Lovelace appointed customs collectors for the easternmost towns of the island. The produce and whale oil of these three towns regularly flowed to Boston and Connecticut, depriving the duke of customs revenue. The appointment of new customs collectors created little reaction among the townsmen, but Lovelace soon enraged them with a second move. In an attempt to regulate the value of produce received for payment of the rates, Lovelace set prices on the most common items.[65] The set prices, however, were lower than those prevailing for grains, beef, and pork. Such pricing gave the government a tidy windfall profit, and the towns responded accordingly. The chief fear of the farmers was that ultimately the set prices would become the standard ones, thereby lowering their profits. Huntington held a town meeting in January 1669 to draw up a petition of grievance. Other towns quickly joined in and a general meeting was held at Jamaica to "agitate." Giving vigor to this meeting was a bumper grain crop in 1669, which reduced prices and brought about a scarcity of money among the farmers.[66] After the towns met, Richard Gildersleeve, the representative for Hempstead, carried a petition of protest to the governor. Lovelace was taken aback by the action of the townspeople.[67] He maintained that the set prices were good only for public, not private, debts and that prior transactions where payment was in produce would remain unaffected. Those transactions made in the future would be influenced only in that the new set prices would be guidelines. No answer from the towns has survived, but the fixed prices remained one of their foremost grievances.

The assize of November 1669 brought about a confrontation that revealed the economic grievances of the towns. The catalyst was the announcement of another new rate of one penny on the pound of assessed valuation.[68] Petitions were immediately formulated in Hempstead, Oyster Bay, Flushing, Jamaica, Westchester, Eastchester, Newton, and Gravesend. For once, the towns on the west end of the island and in Westchester took the lead. They agreed to make the Hempstead petition their official protest.[69] Six of its eleven complaints dealt with economic matters. The main one requested price controls on the goods of New York City merchants and on what they offered for the produce of the island. Specifically, the farmers wanted grain prices to return to those set by Nicolls, not just for trade, but also for taxes, as the towns were still displeased with Lovelace's prices. Their other demands were a miscellany: they wanted wampum to pass at six pieces per penny or not be used at all; a ban on the export of deerskins; free trade in all harbors; standardized English weights and measures for the colony; and all land patents legalized without delay. Never missing an opportunity to register their displeasure about the form of the proprietary government, the townsmen also demanded an assembly. The petition claimed Nicolls had promised them one, so that their representatives could make laws for the good of the "Commonwealth."

Lovelace gave little comfort to the townsmen. He dismissed most of their requests and defended the city and the merchants.[70] While keeping the set prices, he ordered the justices of the peace to discuss prices at the next sessions and report at the 1670 assize. On two points the townsmen obtained satisfaction. A one-year ban was placed on the export of deerskins, and English weights and measures were made standard for the colony. The governor followed this response to the farmers with a further order, revealing once again the influence of the merchants; wills proved at the courts of session must be reported in New York City so that creditors would know the details. The townsmen got very little solace from the assize of 1669.[71]

Tensions rose to new heights after the assize meeting of 1670. Few of the justices from the three ridings attended the meeting and thus it was dominated by officials of the provincial government. The result was a stream of orders regulating the economy.[72] The much-hated grain prices remained the same, the prohibition on the export of deerskins was ended, no dead hogs could be brought to New York for export, and strict laws were placed upon the breeding of horses to upgrade the stocks for export. All these regulations benefited the city and affected the towns. For instance, bringing live hogs to New York meant that the butchering was done by a licensed butcher, a butchering tax was collected, and the city coopers packed the pork. The worst blow came in the form of an order levying a special tax to replace the decaying palisades around Fort James. A single sop was thrown to the towns. Reports received by the assize indicated that poor people were buying small lots in the towns and then expecting to vote with the freeholders. The assize responded with an order stopping this practice, as it would "in time prove ye Destruction of ye Place, In that it [a town] will come to be Governed by the worst and least concerned of ye Inhabitants."[73] If a town felt victimized by poor inhabitants the local sessions court could remedy the situation.

As the news of the assize meeting filtered throughout Long Island, it created dismay. No matter that townsmen's own internal control had been strengthened; the orders issued by the court were a catalog of horrors, and protest meetings quickly followed. Typical was that of Jamaica, where the constables and overseers called a town meeting to inform the townspeople about the assize. The tax levied for repairs on the fort became the symbolic issue. Here was something real and quite fearsome. The fort was too far away to provide them with protection; it could only defend the despised merchants. Besides, the garrison and the fort represented a potential threat to their liberties. The Jamaica meeting issued a statement opposing taxes for Fort James, declaring that the town had obeyed the Duke's Laws, even though they were contrary to English law, but it had done so only to keep the peace and in the hopes that the future might bring them their "just liberties."[74] As the dissidence grew a highly unusual meeting was called for the west riding sessions court. The justices of the peace from the west and north ridings met with members of the council to respond to the towns. They read the petitions of Huntington, Hempstead, and Flushing and declared them "false, scandalous, illegal and seditious tending to disaffect peaceable Subjects."[75] The assembled justices and councilors requested that the governor suppress such proceedings. On 29 December 1671, Lovelace ordered the petitions burned in front of the city hall in New York.[76] He glossed over the fort tax issue by stating that all he had done was ask the justices to consult the towns on the best way of repairing the palisade and that before this could be done, illegal meetings had been held and seditious papers issued.

The orders of the court of assize outraged the three eastern towns of Easthampton, Southampton, and Southold. Their ire was roused not only by the economic and tax legislation, but also by the fact that their patents had been invalidated and their title to the town lands threatened. In early February, Southampton sent a letter to the governor protesting the court's action. At the same time the townsmen protested against the fort tax, raising the issue of taxation without consultation. As with the other letters and petitions, this, too, was publicly burned.[77] After discussing the matter in council on 8 March, Lovelace sent a letter to Southampton announcing a commission to discuss their mutual concerns. After the commission debated with them, he promised to report the town's position to the duke. In closing, he said that he was unwilling to use harsh methods and hoped they would agree with his actions. The language in the instructions to the commissioners, Thomas Delaval, Mathias Nicolls, and Isaac Bedloo, indicated, however, that Lovelace felt that "ill-minded" people had infused "ill principles" into the people.[78] The commission was empowered to talk to the towns at the east end of the island, but if it met resistance, it was authorized to call out the train bands.

No records have survived of the discussions between the commission and the townspeople, but whatever happened was displeasing to the towns. On 4 May a town meeting at Easthampton voted to send two representatives to meet with deputies from Southampton and Southold. On 6 May Southold followed suit, sending five deputies. Southampton must have done the same. The Southold delegates were instructed to discuss writing to England to obtain a separate charter for the three towns.[79] This was no idle talk, for on 29 June 1672 the king referred a petition from the three towns to the Council for Foreign Plantations. As well as any document, this petition expresses the feelings of the islanders.

The only version of the petition that survives is the order in council referring it to the Council for Foreign Plantations; thus, the language of the original is distorted. The petition stated that the inhabitants of the three towns had:

spent much time and pains and the greatest part of their Estates in settling the trade of whale fishing in the adjacent seas, having endeavoured it above these twenty yeares, but could not bring it to any perfection til within these 2 or 3 years, last past, and it now being a hopeful trade at New York in America the Governor and the Dutch there do require ye Petitioners to come under their patent, and lay very heavy taxes upon them beyond any of his [majesty's] subjects in New England, and will not permit the petitioners to have any deputys in Court, but being chiefe, do impose what Laws they please upon them, and insulting very much over the Petitioners threaten to cut down their timber, which is but little they have to make casks for oyle.[80]

Asserting that Connecticut was closer to them than New York, the petitioners asked that the towns be returned to Connecticut's jurisdiction or else be granted their own charter. The petition was assigned to a council on which the duke of York sat—nothing was heard of it again.

This petition reflects the tenuous relationship between the townsmen, especially those of the east, and the government. Embittered by the lack of an assembly and believing that New York City was trying to take over their trade and land, they wanted to return to Connecticut. It is indicative of the centripetal forces in the proprietary. Unable to separate from New York or totally to free themselves from the economic control of the city, Albany and the Long Island towns could only watch

ruefully as the merchants pressed their control of the hinterlands. A barrier of distrust was erected between the "city" and
the "country." So, while the merchants built "great houses" of
stone, the jealousy of the outlying areas was also building.[81]
The resulting tensions remained close to the surface and would
emerge at any time if given a chance.

Anglo-Dutch Tensions

The third problem affecting New York in this first decade
was that of Anglo-Dutch tensions, which easily became intertwined with other problems. For instance, the 1672 petition of
the eastern Long Island towns specifically mentions the Dutch
of New York City as their oppressors. The Dutch merchants
were accused of subverting the English townsmen's trade and
imposing arbitrary laws on the province.

Anglo-Dutch relations in New York were inevitably
strained. The long rivalry between the two nations had created
intense feeling on both sides and these feelings increased
steadily until the second Anglo-Dutch war erupted. Nicolls
distrusted the Dutch, kept them out of government, and wrote
to Governor Benedict Arnold of Rhode Island that "the Dutch
pay no more than a forc't Obedience to his [Majesty] and their
practices have been always treacherous to the English Nation."[82] An old Dutch soldier probably expressed the thoughts
of many of his countrymen when he wrote, "If God has designed . . . That ye Dutch people should become victims to ye
treachery and rapacity of ye English, then all they can do is
submit."[83] However, Nicolls was a practical man and knew
that the Dutch in New York could not be permanently alienated
from the government. In giving instructions to subordinates at
Esopus and Albany, he cautioned them to treat the Dutch well.
He admonished Captain John Baker at Albany to "Lett not
your eares bee abuzed with private storyes of the Dutch being
disaffected to the English, for generally, wee cannot expect
they love us."[84] On another occasion he ordered Captain Daniel
Brodhead to mete out equal justice to soldiers and Dutch alike
and not to become the leader of a party or become prejudiced
against the Dutch, for, "though I am not apt to believe they

have a natural affection for the English, yet without ill usuage, I do not find them so malicious as some will seek to persuade you they are."[85] In order to encourage understanding between the two ethnic groups, Nicolls held a weekly meeting for selected individuals in New York City.[86] Lovelace went much further than Nicolls in encouraging the Dutch by admitting them to high office and tying his own prosperity to Dutch merchants. In the background, however, a number of incidents revealed the existing tensions.

Nicolls faced an immediate crisis with the Dutch over the oath of allegiance. He had invited the leading inhabitants of the city to a special meeting of the city magistrates on 14 October 1664. When he arrived and discovered the domines of the Dutch church and the officers of the West India Company were not present, he had them summoned. On their arrival, he presented to the gathering a simple oath of loyalty to the king and the duke of York, and of obedience to the officers sent by the duke to administer the colony.[87] After the oath was read a heated discussion took place. The Dutch, believing that it negated the articles of surrender that had guaranteed their rights, refused to swear to it unless a clause was entered stating that the oath did not abrogate the articles. Nicolls refused, and the argument continued until he became so enraged he walked out. Four days later Nicolls, Cartwright, and Thomas Willett again confronted the city magistrates about the oath. Nicolls accused them of stirring up the people by casting false aspersions on the oath and, in particular, by stating that it made the articles of surrender null and void. The magistrates denied this and declared that they were willing to take the oath if it contained clauses stating that it did not nullify the surrender agreement. Nicolls was adamant and handed the magistrates a prepared statement that said: "I do think fitt to declare that the Articles of Surrender are not in the least broken or intended to be broken by any words or expressions in the said oath than is herein declared I shall account him or them disturbers of the peace of his Majesty's Subjects and proceed accordingly. I do further appoint and order that this Declaration be forthwith read to all the Inhabitants and also that Every Denizen under my Government do take the said Oath who intend to remaine heere under his Majesty."[88] Two days later, the magistrates and leading citizens met to review the controversy and decided that Nicolls's guarantee was sufficient. During the next few days, the oath was administered to, and signed by, over 250 male inhabitants of New York City. A few refused to sign and left New York as soon as they had settled their estates.[89]

A much more serious problem arose as winter sealed off New York from most of the outside world. The presence of approximately 150 soldiers in the relatively small community of New York City proved disruptive. The invasion over, the soldiers lapsed into garrison life. Their idleness gave them time to drink, carouse, and generally disrupt the life of the town.[90] To top it off the soldiers hated and distrusted their officers. And pay and supplies were short. In November 1664, when Nicolls was in New Castle, the soldiers mutinied when they found out they might have to pay for their passage to New York. In a petition submitted to Nicolls on his return, the soldiers aired their grievances and complained that the Dutch belittled them and lied about their misdeeds.[91] Nicolls resolved some of the problems, but the soldiers were still resentful and bitter about their treatment by the Dutch and continued to fight with and steal from them. In turn the Dutch were vexed because Nicolls kept jurisdiction over the soldiers in courts-martial, where he occasionally punished offenders but not with the vigor the Dutch hoped for.[92]

The situation remained unsettled until March 1665, when Nicolls resolved to carry out the wishes of the soldiers and put them in private homes. Perhaps he hoped family life would curb the soldiers' bad habits. The benefits to the Dutch were that they would get paid for room and board and be able to put the soldiers to work. The Dutch response to the quartering proposal was chilly. They were not convinced that the trouble-makers would change while living in households. The magistrates felt compelled, however, to compile a list of forty-eight people (none of their own names were on it) whom they asked to quarter the soldiers. Forty refused or excused themselves.[93] Having made an effort, the magistrates allowed the matter to lapse until Nicolls forced the issue by calling a special meeting of the magistrates and leading citizens for 7 April 1665. At the meeting, Nicolls confronted those in attendance, asking them to accept the soldiers. They all refused to do so but stated they would contribute to the costs. The governor then requested a list of all the homes capable of lodging soldiers. The magistrates responded by stating that "the Commonality dread receiving the soldiers witnessing the insolence they at present commit."[94] The impasse continued until 19 August, when Nicolls presented his demands again, raising, at the same time, allowance to the homeowner from one guilder to three, plus rations. Still, no one came forward until the magistrates agreed to raise the allowance to five guilders a week. With this high weekly allowance, quarters were soon found for one hundred soldiers, and the city fathers then had to seek the funds for the program. A special tax was assessed according to a now-unknown property formula. It yielded two hundred guilders per week and was supposed to last only six weeks. However, since Nicolls was short of funds, he put the tax into effect before the soldiers were transferred to their new quarters and then continued it long after it was supposed to terminate.[95] Incidents between the soldiers and townsmen continued, and the latter were now paying an added tax for this dubious arrangement.

The same ethnic tensions that bedeviled New York City existed in Albany and Esopus. During the first winter after the English conquest, there was a painful readjustment to new conditions in the upper Hudson River communities. Small garrisons were posted in Albany and Kingston, and, cooped up by the winter weather, the soldiers and the inhabitants engaged in fights and verbal abuse. In Kingston one Dutchman threatened, "I don't care a snap for you, we shall kill all of you next Spring."[96] Emotions ran high, particularly among the Dutch, because they had to pay for the upkeep of the garrisons. To have their enemy as a visitor was difficult; to pay for the visit intolerable. Tension rose to such heights that Nicolls had to leave New York City in August 1665, at a time when a Dutch invasion was threatened, and sail up the Hudson. He relieved Captain John Manning and appointed Captain John Baker to command the garrison at Albany. Baker's instructions dwelt on the problems between the town and the garrison. He was to observe the soldiers' relations with their landlords and with the commissaries, and while Nicolls granted amnesty for past actions, Baker was ordered to watch the "raisinge up of those Godes of distrust and jealousy amongst us, which above all things ought principally to be avoided." But the irritant of paying for the soldiers remained, for the *schout* had to remit one-half of his fees to Baker, who was also receiving two hundred guilders wampum from the town's revenues.[97]

After leaving Albany, Nicolls went to Kingston, where he placed Captain Daniel Brodhead in command of the garrison, with orders similar to those of Baker.[98] In the end, it was in Kingston, not Albany, that Nicolls's fears of an outbreak between the Dutch and English were realized. The soldiers once again were the troublemakers. Their thefts and assaults had become commonplace. Brodhead not only failed to deter the activities of his men, but even became himself one of the chief offenders. He and his men were so distrusted that when Brodhead was ordered to take some of the militia to attack the French who were destroying the Mohawk villages, he met with resistance. One Dutchman was heard to say, "Shall wee go and fight against our friends and leave our enemies at home."[99] The insults and assaults grew and the divisions deepened. Brodhead provided the catalyst for a full-scale riot. For reasons unknown, Brodhead argued and fought with Cornelius Barentsen Sleght, the brewer in Kingston. As Sleght's wife and children ran screaming through the streets, Sergeant Berrisford and four soldiers rushed into Sleght's house and found him with his gun on Brodhead. Before he could shoot he was disarmed and then imprisoned. The Dutch, inflamed by this, rushed to arms and about sixty men paraded in front of Sleght's home. Brodhead then appeared with his fifteen soldiers to confront the militia. The Dutch hurled death threats at the English, who replied by threatening to burn the town to the ground. Thomas Chambers, a longtime English resident trusted by the Dutch, was summoned. Even he could not calm the militia and not until late at night did they disperse. The local magistrates met and tried to defuse the situation by asking that Sleght be turned over to them for trial. Brodhead refused, causing another wave of hatred to sweep through the Dutch. Albert Heymans was reported to have said that if he had command of the militia, "he would not have left an English souldier alive in Esopus." Finally, the inevitable happened when William Fisher, a soldier, killed Hendrick Cornelissen, the town ropemaker.[100]

On getting the first reports of these events, Nicolls dispatched a special commission composed of Captain Robert Needham, Thomas Delaval, and Cornelius Van Ruyven to investigate. The commissioners held hearings from 25 through 27 April 1667 under the guidance of Nicolls's strict instructions.[101] They were empowered to hear all the evidence and dispense justice; Nicolls, however, prejudged some of the issues for them. William Fisher was to be tried first, but he was to be found guilty of manslaughter "if it appeare that the Dutchman rann upon the sword to assault Fisher." He appears to have been acquitted. Sleght's imprisonment was judged proper by Nicolls because no burgher could strike an officer of the crown. The militia's actions were judged to be an armed rising. The commission was to hear the evidence on the most notorious incendiaries, then choose six or less and convict them of treasonable riot. Two men, Antonio d'Elba and Albert Heymans, who had been involved in other disturbances, were named by Nicolls for special scrutiny if they were found to be actors in the disturbance. D'Elba, Heymans, and two others were convicted and banished from the province for life. The commissioners were also instructed to relieve Brodhead of his office because he had refused to turn Sleght over to the magistrates. Finally, the commission was instructed to reprimand both the soldiers and the people. Needham was assigned to admonish the soldiers, Delaval and Van Ruyven the burghers. But Needham was warned to "discourage not the soldiers too muche in publiche least the Boores insult over them."

A sense of proportion was maintained in the Esopus investigation. Only the chief participants suffered for their actions. Admittedly, the Dutch had to suffer more than the English. Brodhead and Fisher were sacrificed for four troublemakers from the community. Nicolls later reduced the sentences for the Dutch after receiving petitions on their behalf.[102] He could not afford to alienate the Dutch majority by exacting harsh punishments upon harassed townspeople.

Lovelace, in his turn, acted in a very different way when confronted by the only serious outbreak of ethnic tensions during his administration. This disturbance did not occur among the Dutch, who were the constant concern of the English government, but among the Finns and Swedes of the Delaware region. In late July 1669, Marcus Jacobsen, a Swede, and his confederates, Henry Coleman and Laurentius Lokenius, spread the rumor that a Swedish fleet was on the way and that Delaware would be taken from the English.[103] For a short time, a number of people joined them in a rebellion that was to prepare the way for the fleet. The magistrates and the garrison of New Castle quickly brought the situation under control, however, and the ringleaders were apprehended. The government had been given a scare, for it had feared that the dissidents would join with the Indians to create havoc, and thus it was in no mood to treat the insurgents kindly. Captain John Carr wanted to try Jacobsen—or the Long Finn as he was called—and his associates immediately, but Lovelace insisted that he, or a member of the council, be present. In fact, Lovelace had already decided on the punishment for the Long Finn. He was not to be put to death, but whipped, branded on the face with the letter R, and shipped as a servant to Barbados. Meanwhile, proceedings were begun against his followers. Approximately seventy persons were fined, some for as much as two thousand guilders. These were harsh fines and must have fallen heavily on the farmers. Finally, in November, Mathias Nicolls arrived and conducted the trial of the Long Finn, with its predetermined results.[104]

Dutch-Anglo tensions during this period centered on the relationship between the English government and the Dutch planters. The established Dutch and English communities were separated physically and were accustomed to coexisting. The only new element in their relationship was the feeling on the part of the English on Long Island that the Dutch merchants of New York City were attempting to control their trade. The government, however, presented a threat to the Dutch. The loyalty oath controversy revealed their sensitivity to any threat to the community and its customs. Such touchiness needed delicate handling. Unfortunately the soldiers, the most visible Englishmen in the larger Dutch communities, made poor diplomats. They disrupted community life and physically threatened the people. At a very tense period of transition the soldiers represented England and Englishmen to the harassed Dutch. Their behavior only increased the distrust and bitterness of the Dutch community. Lovelace attempted to blunt these feelings by admitting Dutchmen to office on the council. This undoubtedly pleased those who were granted office and comforted others. Yet those admitted to office and the other members of the merchant community were made aware that their trading activities were being pushed into an English mold. Like it or not, they served an English government in an environment increasingly English.

Imperial Wars and Local Tensions

Enhancing the tension between the English and Dutch colonists were the imperial struggles between England and the Netherlands, on the one hand, and between England and France, on the other. The Dutch continued to covet the furs and tobacco of North America. France desired control over strategic fur-trade routes and access to an ice-free port, such as New York City, for New France. Both powers moved actively to fulfill their desires, causing periodic panics in New York as warnings of invasion swept the colony.[105]

The Iroquois, who controlled a large part of the ground between New France and New York, were simultaneously a buffer and a decisive element in the balance of power. The number of warriors they could put into the field was sufficient to influence the outcome of any conflict, and their military importance was enhanced by their growing control over the fur trade.[106] France and England, therefore, had to choose between destroying or befriending the Five Nations. The French were to remain basically hostile to them, while the English maintained friendly relations. What made this policy somewhat difficult for the English was the overwhelmingly Dutch character of the population in the upper Hudson River area. The Dutch, however, were not eager to endanger their own prosperity and remained neutral when fighting occurred between the French and the Indians.[107] Peace was uppermost in their minds, for war disrupted the web of interactions necessary to the success of the fur trade. Still, the English worried when France and the Netherlands were allies. On these occasions, one factor was in their favor: even though the Netherlands and France might be united by treaties there remained a fundamental and profound difference between the Dutch and the French. The members of the Dutch Reformed church were unremittingly hostile to the Catholic church. Their fears of the papacy exploded into hysteria on occasion, as in the case of Leisler's Rebellion, and in normal times it made them suspicious of governors appointed by a Catholic proprietor or king.

The French made two early incursions into New York. The first was made during the severe winter of 1665–66 when the French hoped to take advantage of the weather for a surprise attack against the Iroquois. By the time they reached the vicinity of Albany, however, the men were exhausted, and they discovered to their dismay there was an English garrison. They returned home, bedeviled by Indians most of the way.[108] A second expedition in 1666 succeeded in destroying Indian towns and supplies north of Albany, and before turning homeward the French performed a ceremony claiming the whole territory for King Louis. This was the basis for their later claims to this region.[109]

These expeditions caused Nicolls many anxious moments. The second expedition had 1,400 soldiers and volunteers, far outnumbering any force New York could muster around Albany. He could only hope the French would concentrate on the Indians and leave the upper Hudson Valley unmolested. To maintain some form of defense he urged peace between the Dutch and the English. To this end he asked that "English and Dutch . . . live as brothers [and] keep a strict hand upon the authors or reporters of strange newes which commonly tends to the dividing of mens hearts."[110] It was not so much the French threats, however, as those that came from Dutch sea power that helped sharpen Anglo-Dutch tensions.

While Nicolls was busy establishing the English regime in New York, England had once again gone to war with the Netherlands.[111] The attacks and counterattacks on the periphery of the empires finally brought war to Europe. The diplomats retired while the battle fleets readied for combat. The immediate causes of the war were the seizure of New Netherland and the success of Admiral De Ruyter's fleet in dismantling the work of Sir Robert Holmes on the Gold Coast. In addition, De Ruyter had orders to retake New York after finishing his work in Africa. A letter was sent on 8 January 1665 warning Nicolls of the danger and ordering him to prepare a defense for New York and New England.[112] Nicolls received this warning on 22 June, but he had already been warned. On 5 June Cartwright had written from Boston informing Nicolls that De Ruyter had descended on Barbados with fourteen sail and had been repulsed. Ten days later Nicolls announced the state of war and confiscated the property of the Dutch West India Company.[113]

Fort James, which Nicolls had captured less than a year before, was still of little value in defending the city. Forty pieces of ordnance had been placed on the walls, but the fort still needed extensive repairs. Like Stuyvesant before him, Nicolls had to go to the inhabitants of the city for help in reconstructing the fort and fortifying the city. But Nicolls's position was worse than Stuyvesant's because he had armed the English inhabitants and disarmed the Dutch.[114] Such was the condition of the city, however, that he had to appeal to the disgruntled Dutch. On behalf of Nicolls, Thomas Willett spoke to the city council about the open and unfortified state of the city and, in response, the magistrates ordered the people to assemble to consider the problem. At a public meeting on 28 June Willett repeated his message to the people. As an encouragement, he informed them that Nicolls promised two thousand wooden palisades and one thousand guilders in wampum for the work. Somewhat disingenuously, Willett added that the intent was not to get anyone to fight against his own nation, but to protect them against any enemy. Since the Dutch had long hoped for and expected Admiral De Ruyter, Willett's plea persuaded very few to work for the English, and many noted that by taking their arms away, Nicolls had done little to strengthen the defense of the city. As a result, they refused to work on the defenses until their arms were restored.[115]

What Nicolls did not know was that the danger had already passed. De Ruyter had arrived on the Gold Coast on 22 October and had been continuously at sea or in battle for ten months when he arrived in the West Indies. The setback at Barbados, after he had been so long at sea, effectively put an end to any serious plans to assault the English colonies. Fearing that he would face resistance in New York, De Ruyter sailed to Newfoundland where he appeared in early June 1665, and after destroying some fishing stages he set sail for home.[116]

Another Dutch threat came in 1667 when Captain Abraham Krynessen, with three ships, sailed into the Chesapeake and destroyed all of the English vessels there, including a man-of-war. With a Dutch fleet on the loose, New York was again endangered from the sea. Once again defenses were prepared and, once again, they went unused as Krynessen, satisfied with his haul of tobacco, sailed home.[117]

The hopes of the Dutch planters were dashed in 1667 by the treaty of Breda, which brought the second Anglo-Dutch war to an end. The Netherlands ceded New Netherland to England. Jeremias Van Rensselaer spoke for many of his countrymen when he wrote: "For we did not have the least idea here that the country would remain English, since the Lord God blessed the arms of their High Mightenesses the States General so during the war. . . . Now it seems that it has pleased the Lord [to ordain] that we must learn English . . . as yet I [have] learned so little. The reason is that one has no liking for it."[118] The prayers of the Dutch went unanswered until 1673 when a Dutch fleet sailed into New York harbor, temporarily disrupting English rule.

English Efforts to Counterbalance the Dutch

The problem of Anglo-Dutch relations required a solution, especially at a time when the Netherlands and France were making designs on the colony. Nicolls sought to effect a solution by increasing the number of English settlers. The means of attracting colonists were readily at hand, for there were ample lands within the duke's patent to provide for a liberal land policy. Assessing the lands under his control, Nicolls concluded that Maine, Martha's Vineyard, and the smaller islands were useless; the upper Hudson Valley was too cold; and Long Island was barren of soil and "meanly inhabited by a poore sort of people who are forct to labour hard for bread and cloathing."[119] This left the lands west of the Hudson River, which, unfortunately, the duke gave away. Later, he was to change his mind about the upper Hudson and decide that the Esopus area was excellent farming country. If English farmers could be lured there, they could counterbalance the fractious Dutch.

When he was in Boston in the spring of 1665, Nicolls took action to attract more settlers. He had Samuel Green of Cambridge print a promotional broadside.[120] This venture into advertising reveals clearly the conditions offered to new colonists. As in New England, Nicolls was making land available only for the settlement of communities and not for individual speculation. The purchasers had first to obtain title from the Indians and then record the transaction before the governor. Nicolls had laid down this rule early in his administration because of the many disputed land titles.[121] Each town would elect its own civil and military officers by vote of the freemen (defined as men who owned a lot and took the oath of allegiance to the king). Within the towns, the magistrates would have the power to settle minor civil or criminal suits. On the very important topic of religious liberty, the broadside was specific—liberty of conscience was guaranteed for all Protestants. In essence, therefore, the broadside promised a township pattern similar to that of New England. Undoubtedly, Nicolls realized that these were the minimum conditions he must promise to attract new inhabitants.

Nicolls's hopes of large-scale immigration were not realized, however. Many new settlers did come, but they settled in the colony of New Jersey, doing nothing to balance the ethnic composition of New York's population. Esopus, designated in the broadside as an alternate area for settlement, turned out not to be attractive to Englishmen. An established Dutch community existed there, and it was a great distance from the coast. In addition, not many New Englanders were attracted to New York, with its prerogative government, when they could go to New Jersey, whose proprietors offered more liberal concessions, including an assembly.

York was aware of the need to counterbalance the Dutch in his proprietary and attempted to send out Scot settlers. In 1669, he requested permission to allow Scottish subjects to emigrate.[122] He also requested consent for the ships to engage in trade at New York or the West Indies. Scenting another attempt to subvert the Navigation Acts, the customs officers moved quickly to block the petition because of the loss of revenue. A counterproposal was submitted downgrading the objections of the customs officials, arguing that it was more important to send the king's subjects to New York in order to outnumber the Dutch. The government temporized by granting permission for two ships to make a return voyage.[123] When this news was received in New York plans were made to settle two hundred Scots families at Esopus. Only one ship even attempted the trip, however, and it went aground on the sands of Cairnburg. It may have been for the best, for the Scottish Privy Council had sent out warrants to officials stating that "strong and idle beggars, vagabonds, egyptians, common and notorious whores, theeves, and other dissolute and louse persons" be recruited for the voyage.[124] How long such people would have lasted at Esopus is questionable.

A somewhat more promising group of immigrants was that from the West Indies and Bermuda. Economic and political changes brought on by the rise of the planter class in the islands made the mainland colonies more attractive, and Samuel Maverick and Governor Lovelace encouraged any inquiry about New York. Maverick urged the Reverend Samuel Bend and his flock to leave Bermuda. His correspondence with Bend stressed New York's religious liberty, the rights of freeholders, the growing trade with Spain, Tangier, and the Caribbean, and the province's need for "shipping and stirring merchants" and "honest diligent people."[125] Lovelace hoped to settle the new colonists on Staten Island. The island was claimed by York, and the need to settle it before people from New Jersey did so was urgent. Lovelace bought the island from the local Indians and promised ample house lots and farms, if Lovelace's own newly acquired estate were cleared first.[126] The Reverend Mr. Bend and his flock do not appear in New York's record, and it is probable that the Carolinas were far more attractive to them. The only notable immigrants were the Quakers, Richard and Lewis Morris, the founders of the Morris family. What appears to have discouraged new immigrants from the islands was the gloom, prevalent in the proprietary, about New York's economic prospects. Reports circulated that as many as six hundred people were ready to leave New York, and substance was given to these rumors when Lovelace imposed a passport system because ships were luring planters to other colonies. Many who went left behind unpaid bills.[127]

The way Lovelace finally developed the Esopus region

reveals the difficulties in recruiting colonists. On 6 April 1668 Nicolls had issued a promise to provide farmland for the thirty men of the Esopus garrison and for any other soldier who wanted to settle in that area. There was a variety of reasons for eliminating the Esopus garrison other than an attempt to get new settlers. After the treaty of Breda the threat of invasion had diminished, providing an opportunity for cutting the expenses of the garrison. Moreover, if the soldiers became farmers, they would strengthen the militia and perhaps become better neighbors to the Dutch farmers. Within a week after Nicolls left New York in August 1668, Lovelace acted on Nicolls's promise. All soldiers who wanted to settle at Esopus, and any colonists who thought they had land claims there, were promised land. On 23 September Lovelace arrived in Kingston to survey the sites near the Esopus River. However, after strengthening the defenses and admonishing the soldiers and farmers to live in peace, Lovelace left with little or nothing accomplished.[128]

It was not until two years later, in 1670, when the Scottish and West Indian ventures had failed, that two new towns were started with soldiers. Hurley and Marbleton, as they were named, were settled by fifty-four men. Hurley had a sprinkling of Dutch and French settlers and one black; Marbleton was composed entirely of English soldiers. Each man was given a ten-acre house lot and twenty acres of land. But the soldiers thwarted the plan because they proved to be unwilling farmers. Five months after the men received their lands, Lovelace had to issue orders prohibiting the soldiers from selling their lands for three years and voiding all sales made prior to his orders.[129] His experiment had failed and English immigration continued to be very slow, no matter what the inducement. Only after many years had passed did the English surpass the Dutch in numbers.

By 1673 the proprietary government and the colonists had tested the parameters of the government's power. The colonists accepted the legitimacy of the government, for it, in turn, gave their land grants and other transactions legitimacy. The government and the people had also initiated a dialogue of sorts that defined the nature of the relationship between them. At the center of the discussion was the desire of the colonists to maintain autonomy in local affairs. The townspeople of Long Island argued that their rights as Englishmen were violated by a government that taxed them without their consent. The Dutch waged a struggle for their rights as embodied within the articles of surrender. The controversy over the loyalty oath was just the first battle and in the future any threat to their rights as defined by the articles would evoke a similar outburst. Both national groups had specified their rights and demanded that the government observe them. Admittedly these "rights" centered on simply being left alone but they did begin a tradition of anti-proprietary rhetoric.

Another important development was that of Dutch attitudes toward the English. These ethnic tensions brought a dimension to New York society not found elsewhere in the English colonies at this time. As the Scotch-Irish, Germans, and other peoples were to experience in the eighteenth century, the pressures to conform to English governmental, cultural, and societal patterns were constant. While non-English groups enriched English traditions, these groups would all have to conform to them. The Dutch experienced this process first and the effects were unsettling for many individuals. While there seemed some hope of a return to their *Patria* the Dutch could treat the English as invaders and perhaps just an aberration. After 1674 when the Netherlands renounced their claim to New York the Dutch would develop different patterns of behavior in dealing with the English.

A by-product of all three developments was the creation of a strong sense of regionalism. The Dutch on the upper Hudson were isolated geographically and concerned about their control over the fur trade. Ethnicity combined with geography to create what would remain the most lasting Dutch community in New York. Their feelings about New York City would certainly be shared by future generations right down to the present day. The New Englanders on Long Island also had their own regional identity. They resented the city and worked up a thorough dislike of the merchants, and since many of the merchants were Dutch their perception of the city's influence was doubly tainted. The city, with its polyglot population, already prefigured its future. Thus by 1673 regionalism had already become an element in New York's politics and would only gain strength in the future.

Part II
The Divisions Appear

4 ❧ Once Again Dutch, Once Again English

While brief, the third Anglo-Dutch war was not without effect on New York. A Dutch fleet, intent on sailing home after raiding Virginia, stopped at Sandy Hook. Dutch farmers quickly boarded the vessels, appealing to the commanders to lift the English yoke from their shoulders, and a brief, bloodless attack made New York New Netherland once again. Unfortunately for the Dutch colonists, they were a piece on the international chessboard. England and the Netherlands sought a quick end to the war and when the treaty of Westminster was signed in 1674, New Netherland was a pawn the Netherlands quickly surrendered. York was restored to his proprietary and he now embarked upon a policy of more vigorous administration. This policy was personified in the dominating figure of the new governor, Edmund Andros, whose actions had a lasting effect on New York's political and social structure.

Once Again Dutch

The Treaty of Breda proved to be more of a truce than a permanent peace. After the second Anglo-Dutch war a rapprochement occurred between the Netherlands and England. Under the guiding hand of Sir William Temple, this culminated in 1668 in the formation of the Triple Alliance between these two Protestant nations and Sweden. King Charles, however, soon slipped back into his normal allegiances and secretly signed the Treaty of Dover with France on 1 June 1670. In return for funding from King Louis, he turned England away from Dutch toward French interests; thereafter relations between England and the Netherlands deteriorated quickly until a new war was declared. As in 1665, it was Sir Robert Holmes who provided the catalyst for war by attacking the Dutch Smyrna fleet in the Channel. On 13 April 1672 messages and proclamations alerted the colonies to the renewed hostilities and ordered them to organize and maintain a convoy system to insure trade.[1]

As the likelihood of war grew, Lovelace saw to his defenses. In doing so he increased the tension between the English and Dutch and placed further strain on his relationship with Long Island. New York's defense rested on the fort and garrison that guarded the city, but the fort was still quite dilapidated because of the lack of support by the duke. The soldiers' faith in it can be seen in the increased desertions that plagued Lovelace.[2] To get the fort back into shape Lovelace was forced to appeal to the people for contributions. All areas of the colony, even Long Island, responded favorably to this appeal. Typically, Lovelace was very circumspect in raising the issue with the townspeople. In his letters he wrote, "You will know I have been very tender to press this Point to you; It being now the first time I have desired of you in that kind."[3] It was also typical that some of the towns tried to use their contributions to exact privileges, and Lovelace had to rebuff them.[4]

The war forced Lovelace to make very unpalatable personal decisions. On 24 May 1672 he received a message announcing a state of war between England and the Netherlands. This was doleful news in New York. Mathias Nicolls reported to Richard Nicolls that "the news thereof was very unwelcome to most especially those of the Dutch nation."[5] Lovelace was ordered to proclaim the war and seize all the property belonging to the United Provinces or its subjects; yet he hesitated. On 26 June, in a tortured letter to John Winthrop, Jr., Lovelace wrote that he had not declared war because he doubted that he had the legal right to do so. His immediate concern was the seizure of his ship, *Good Fame*, in Holland. Not only his ship, but Thomas Delaval's *Margaret*, Cornelius Steenwyck's *James*, and Frederick Philipse's *Frederick* had been confiscated.[6] While Lovelace was trying to negotiate the release of his vessel, events forced him to relinquish his neutrality. On 6 July he temporized by proclaiming a state of war without confiscating any enemy property. Three months later he finally expropriated property belonging to the United Provinces.[7] Undoubtedly he had given up hope of ever recovering the *Good Fame*. He may also have been prompted by the knowledge that a Dutch fleet was on its way to America.[8] This fleet ended his career as governor.

Two separate squadrons left the United Provinces in 1672. One was prepared by the Province of Zeeland and was under the command of Cornelius Evertsen, the younger. The other one, from Amsterdam, was led by Jacob Binkes. Rendezvousing at Martinique in May 1673, the combined fleet of eight ships captured St. Eustatius. After this success they sailed to Virginia in July, arriving just as the annual tobacco convoy was assembling. After a short fight, the Dutch overcame the English escort vessels and seized the tobacco ships. With no opposition they were free to raid and plunder up and down the Chesapeake.[9] The fleet left the James River seeking an anchorage further north in order to get fresh water for the voyage home. After an unsuccessful try at getting past the sand bars at the mouth of the Delaware, the squadron sailed for Sandy Hook. Almost as soon as they anchored there on 30 July, Dutch farmers from Long Island came on board to complain of the harsh treatment they suffered from the English and to plead with the commanders to reconquer New York. They told Evertsen and Binkes that Lovelace was not present and that Fort James was poorly garrisoned and in bad repair. The two commanders called a council of war and, after assessing the evidence, they decided to attack the next day.[10]

The Dutch could not have arrived at a more propitious time for an invasion. Lovelace was on his way to Connecticut to meet with Governor Winthrop, probably to discuss a new mail post between New York and Boston. He had left the fort in the hands of Captain John Manning, recently injured in a bad fall.[11] With the governor gone and the commander hampered by injury, the small garrison of about sixty men was hard pressed to defend the dilapidated fort. Manning tried to muster the Long Island militia without success. In the city all but ten or twelve of the inhabitants remained neutral and refused to enter active service in the fort.[12]

The Dutch forced a showdown on 30 July. It began with an exchange of messages, in which Manning demanded to know by what rights they were there; the Dutch replied that their rights were in the mouths of their cannons. Evertsen then landed six hundred men behind a screening attack on the fort. After a period of confused negotiations Manning accepted the logic of Dutch superiority and surrendered. That same evening the garrison left the fort without putting down its arms and was placed on ships in the East River. Lovelace, meanwhile, had received a letter from Manning and went immediately to Long Island hoping to raise the militia and keep the island out of Dutch hands. He failed completely. The islanders felt no great sympathy for New York City or the governor and undoubtedly did not want to risk their lives and property if they could help it. Lovelace's nerve failed, and on 31 July he wrote to the victorious Dutch asking for a pass. On Saturday, 2 August, he and secretary Mathias Nicolls surrendered. So ended the reconquest of New York. The ease with which it was accomplished surprised the Dutch as much as it scandalized the English.[13]

Lovelace did not remain long in New York. He, Manning, and the garrison were shipped off to Europe in August. Behind him lay a confiscated estate and ahead, a very uncertain future. During the journey he had time to contemplate the way in which both the Dutch and English inhabitants of New York had deserted the government. The Dutch had encouraged Binkes and Evertsen to attack New York by providing information about the weakened condition of the fort and garrison. They had then welcomed the return to Dutch rule. The English had stood aside, unwilling to get involved in a losing enterprise. Any oath they or the Dutch had taken to obey the duke's officials was quickly forgotten when danger threatened. Who can blame them when those same officials had neglected the garrison and the fort and pocketed their taxes and contributions?[14] When Lovelace arrived in England King Charles appointed a commission, under the leadership of the duke of Monmouth, to investigate his actions and accounts. He was imprisoned in the tower until April 1675. He died shortly after his release.[15]

Meanwhile, in New York, Evertsen and Binkes faced the problem of governing a colony for which they had neither orders nor the ability to defend permanently. They could not remain in New York because they were under orders to return to Europe with their much-needed ships. Before leaving they did what they could. All of the areas inhabited by the Dutch were easily brought under their control. Albany, the towns of western Long Island, and the Delaware River settlements rapidly came over to them and the whole of New Jersey was added.[16] Once again sheriffs were *schouts* and overseers, *schepens*, as the old institutions of government were restored. The government of the colony was placed in the hands of Captain Anthony Colve, who suddenly found himself promoted from the infantry to a governor-generalship. To help him administer the colony, a council was formed, and the first man appointed to it was Cornelius Steenwyck, one of Lovelace's most trusted councilors.[17]

Having supplanted the old government, Evertsen and Binkes proceeded to dispossess it. A proclamation announced the seizure of the property of all subjects of King Charles. This policy was never wholly carried out because the proclamation was aimed primarily at the duke and his officers, all of whose property was seized.[18] To confiscate the property of all Englishmen would endanger trade with the English colonies; therefore the merchants probably counseled against this.

The Dutch inhabitants of New Netherland were appalled when Evertsen and Binkes announced that the fleet would leave. The burgomasters and *schepens* of New Orange, as New York City had been renamed, petitioned the two commanders to stay. Rejoicing to be under their *Patria* again, they feared the English and French would not allow them to remain unmolested in the middle of the English colonies. Without protection they would inevitably be attacked and made "slaves."[19] In response, the *Zeehond*, a forty-gun frigate, was left behind along with a small garrison. Even with this defensive force, the Dutch colonists could only look grimly into the future and watch their English neighbors.

Initially impressed by the power of the Dutch fleet, the English towns at the east end of Long Island submitted. Southampton, Southold, Easthampton, Brookhaven, and Huntington petitioned together for privileges in trade and government, most of which were met.[20] After this they submitted their magistrates to Colve for approval and settled down to coexist with the new government.

A new complexion was placed upon matters when Connecticut and the United Colonies of New England began to organize against the Dutch. Immediately after the fall of New York, Connecticut sent two emissaries to New Orange to declare that it would defend its interests—which included the eastern end of Long Island. This was mostly bravado, since the vulnerability of the Connecticut coast line, in the face of the Dutch men-of-war, was manifest. Indeed, this danger forced the assembly to create a committee that had the power to impress everything it needed for defense.[21] It also meant that Connecticut's two envoys in New Orange were given powers to negotiate some form of truce. Arguing that their religions were similar and that they had maintained good relations in time of peace and war, the envoys hoped good relations would continue. When the Dutch asked for these sentiments in writing, the envoys demurred.[22] Since it might be difficult to explain a local truce to the home government at a later time, their reticence was understandable. The Dutch reply to Connecticut was brusque; this was wartime and they would do what they must. Governor Winthrop quickly searched for allies and, by the end of August, the United Colonies of New England agreed upon a common defense.[23]

After the Dutch fleet left in the middle of September, there was less to fear. In early October, when commissioners from New Orange came to administer the oath of allegiance to the people of Southampton, Southold, Easthampton, Brookhaven, and Huntington, they were met with refusal.[24] This rebuff was followed by a sharp note from Connecticut expressing disbelief at the Dutch browbeating the farmers to take the oath and promising retaliation against the Dutch if the provocations continued.[25] As a symbol of support, Connecticut sent Samuel Willys and Fitz-John Winthrop to give aid to the towns and urge them to continue their resistance. Although Colve threatened Winthrop, he was unwilling to open hostilities. Indeed, he hesitated to use force at first since the English colonies, with their greater manpower resources, might use any attack as an excuse to invade New Netherland. After Colve received assurances from Lewis Morris and Nathaniel Sylvester (both Quakers) that submission of the towns was probable, he sent another expedition. Again, the townsmen refused to take the oath.[26] Peaceful measures failed because the townspeople were not convinced that the new government had power enough to humble them and their ally and protector, Connecticut.

Colve's last attempt to coerce the towns was made in February 1674. The towns had returned to their old relationship with Connecticut, providing the Hartford Grand Committee with the excuse to send over Fitz-John Winthrop with the impressive title of "Sarjt Major over the military forces of his [Majesty's] subjects." In February 1674 Winthrop embarked a company of Connecticut militia to aid the islanders. Shortly after he arrived a fleet of four ships appeared. They were Colve's answer to Connecticut's presumptuous conduct. Nathaniel Sylvester, now a friend of the Dutch after they had restored his rights to Shelter Island, asked for the surrender of Southold. Winthrop refused, and a battle ensued between the ships and the militia. After expending quantities of powder without inflicting injuries, the engagement ended with a Dutch withdrawal. So went the only "battle" of the campaign. Afterward, each side returned to its favorite weapon, the bristling letter.[27]

Colve's relations with Connecticut influenced his government of New Netherland. After the fleet returned home and he realized his exposed condition, he spent his time and energy in building defenses. He reorganized the militia and increased its training, rebuilt the deteriorating fort in New Orange, and, in general, put the colony in a state of preparedness. With the frigate *Zeehond* he harried the New England coast, seizing vessels in order to keep his enemies impressed.[28] All of this activity took its toll. His privateering discouraged trade, as did his seizure of English property; as a result the effects of the slump were compounded by the expense of fortifying his command. Taxes were raised and, when they proved insufficient, he had to mortgage public property as security.[29] Along with these measures went a heightened sense of insecurity. All strangers were ordered to depart and all correspondence with New England interdicted. Colve even interfered with the city government of New Orange as he forced one of his officers upon them as president of the court in order to monitor its activities. The protest of the magistrates was rewarded with a rebuke.[30] So, while liberated, New Netherland was unhappy. Surrounded by the English and overlooked by the *Patria*, which was fighting a more serious war in Europe, the Dutch viewed the future with apprehension.

The English Plan Their Return

While the New Netherlanders fretted, the English fumed. Whatever reasons were offered for the capture of New York, they were not sufficient. While Lovelace suffered humiliation, others plunged forward to make their careers on his misfortune. As always, it seems, there was a New Englander in London full of information, proposals, and hope of preferment. This time it was William Dyre. Dyre had followed a career at sea and served as a captain in the expedition against Nevis in 1667. He may also have been the William Dyre who testified in a maritime case in New York in May 1672.[31]

Dyre appeared before the Council for Trade and Plantations with the first proposal for retaking New York. His plan contained the elements of others presented later.[32] It recommended that an expedition be sent to New York and Virginia to undo the work of the Dutch fleet. All the reasons used in 1664 to advocate an English attack on New Netherland were brought forth again. The assertion that New Netherland would subvert the trade of the English colonies and could be used as a base to harry English shipping headed the litany. And, once again, the same conclusions were drawn—there would be damage to English trade and a reduction in the king's customs. Dyre's plan also repeated the familiar old chestnut that great riches awaited the English in New York. This time, however, a new element was added as Dyre advocated the complete removal of the Dutch residents from the colony or isolating them in Albany. Most of these suggestions found their way into the report the council made to the king on 15 November 1673.[33] This report was superfluous, however, since the government was already involved in negotiations that were to return New York to the English peacefully.

The third Anglo-Dutch war proved a bitter trial for the Netherlands. Pitched against the English at sea and the French on land, the Dutch were sorely beset. William of Orange and the States General sought peace with England in order to concentrate on the greater enemy—France. On 15 October 1673 King Charles received a letter requesting negotiations. Faced with an obstreperous Parliament and an embarrassing shortage of funds, the king treated this request seriously. In their next letter the States General again urged negotiation and, as a sign of esteem, offered to return New Netherland. The Treaty of Westminster, signed on 9 February 1674, was the end product of the negotiations. Its sixth article returned New Netherland to England.[34] With this formal cession the States General gave up all rights in the area and England secured uncontested control. Another invasion had been avoided.

York's New Administration

York quickly regained his patent and moved to assert control over his proprietary. Prior to 1674 little correspondence passed between the duke and his governors, leaving the impression of slack administration. After 1674 frequent correspondence and a tightened administration characterized the new relationship. In England York used his commissioners of revenue to watch over affairs in his proprietary. In New York the new governor, Edmund Andros, proved a vigorous administrator.

York's commission of revenue was created in 1667 to oversee his household finances and rescue him from "great debt."[35] Its primary duty was to manage York's financial and legal affairs. After 1674 it took over the management of New York, operating as a miniature Lords of Trade. Finances, economic policy, relationships with other proprietors and the Crown were part of its regular duties. Its members were York's friends, relatives, and household officers. The latter were the most important, especially Sir John Werden and Sir Allan Apsley. Werden was the duke's secretary and was responsible for correspondence, issuing orders, and for appearances before official bodies on York's behalf. Apsley, the treasurer of the household, was responsible for the accounts.[36] Both men were proven friends of York and came from families with long records of service to the Stuarts.

The duke continued to recruit the same type of governor.

When Edmund Andros was appointed governor in 1674 he was beginning a long career in colonial administration that included terms as chief executive in Virginia and the Dominion of New England.[37] Following in his father's footsteps, he had become a soldier at nineteen in the service of Prince Henry of Nassau. After the Restoration he returned from service in Holland and France to a position of favor with King Charles. After getting a commission in the household regiments, he was transferred and made a captain in Sir Tobias Bridge's Barbadian Regiment during the Anglo-Dutch war. Until 1674 he remained attached to this regiment and saw duty twice in the West Indies—1667 to 1669 and 1672 to 1674. These tours of duty in the colonies gave him a reputation for colonial service. He was further identified with the colonies by marriage to Mary, daughter of the earl of Craven, a proprietor of Carolina. Through this connection he became a landgrave in Carolina and was granted four baronies. On his return to England in 1674, when the duke was casting around for a governor, Andros was probably an early choice. Not only did he have extensive colonial service, but he had also served in the Netherlands, which gave him invaluable experience with the Dutch. In short, the duke had in his service a soldier seasoned in the colonies and well connected at court.

In office Andros displayed an autocratic personality. He relished his powers and few curbs were placed upon a temperament that thrived on dominating those around him. He was most offensive when defending the duke's rights. When Connecticut was engaged in a desperate struggle during King Philip's War, Andros sailed into Saybrook and proclaimed York's rights to western Connecticut. Badly needed militia were detailed to shadow his movements while the General Court suffered collective apoplexy. Later he disputed Governor Philip Carteret's right to govern New Jersey. Andros went to New Jersey and confronted Carteret in a document-waving contest that succeeded only in gathering large crowds. After this failure to stop Carteret, Andros brought him to trial in New York where he bullied the jury in an unconscionable manner, all to no avail as the jury stuck by its verdict in favor of Carteret.[38] Andros did not inspire affection, but he did command respect and, often as not, fear.

Soon after getting his patent and selecting Andros, York settled his government for New York. He issued a commission as lieutenant-governor and instructions to Andros on 1 July 1674, along with a commission as captain of a company of foot for New York.[39] Because Andros's instructions were the informal constitution of New York, they are worth examination. He was ordered to receive the colony from Colve and assure the colonists that their possessions would not be disturbed (except, of course, those of any Englishman who had helped Evertsen "in any way"). The Dutch, or other foreigners active in Colve's government, were to be persuaded to go elsewhere. To aid him in administering the colony, Andros was to choose a council of no more than ten men whom he was to consult on "extraordinary" occasions. The Duke's Laws were to be reinstituted and applied without variance, except in emergency conditions, and only with the advice of the council. Any new laws remained in effect for only one year until the duke could approve them. A later warrant empowered Andros to put laws into effect and amend them with just the advice of the council.[40] The old courts were to be reestablished and justice impartially administered to the English and Dutch alike. While the rights of the inhabitants were held inviolable, the only right specified was freedom of religion. As chief executive Andros exercised great powers with only the curb of his hand-picked council. For a man with his disposition, it was a heady brew.

Andros arrived in New York on 18 November 1674. He brought with him one hundred soldiers for the garrison, a warrant to seize Lovelace's property, and a cargo of goods belonging to York for which he was the factor.[41] On arriving in the colony he was immediately confronted with the problem of the emotional state of the Dutch colonists at being abandoned to the English. After rejoicing at being restored to their *Patria* they were disillusioned by the Treaty of Westminster. Forsaken, many no doubt echoed the sentiments of Jeremias Van Rensselaer who wrote home to his brother, "I notice with great sorrow that their High Mightinesses [the States General] again offer and give away this country to his Majesty of England. It is true that we prayed for him to Almighty God, but mostly on the regular days of prayer and not in secret and that we did not count on such a blow God knows."[42] He also looked with some apprehension on the return of the English to power because at "my farewell to the English last year, when they had to leave, I showed them nothing but friendship, but they were uncivilly treated by some."[43] Apprehensive eyes watched for the sails bringing the English back.

As soon as he arrived, Andros sent Governor Philip Carteret, the newly appointed governor of New Jersey, and Ensign Caesar Knapton to demand the surrender of the fort and the city.[44] Although he had received orders to surrender New Netherland to Andros, Colve demurred until he received promises of good treatment for the Dutch. Andros gave assurances that they would have the same treatment as the English and sent Mathias Nicolls, who had joined him from his exile in Connecticut, to convince Colve of his intentions. This still did not placate the fearful inhabitants. Cornelius Steenwyck and Johannes Van Brugh were sent out to Andros's ship *Diamond* to negotiate. They returned unsatisfied and not until Colve drew up a set of proposals, to which Andros mostly agreed, did the city relax. These proposals were basically concerned with the economic consequences of the exchange of governments. Andros granted Colve permission to collect his debts after he left the colony, guaranteed everyone in the possession of their goods and lands, accepted all of the sentences and judgments of the courts, and agreed that the Dutch could keep their religion and inheritance customs and would not be forced to fight against their own countrymen. He refused to approve articles restricting the imposition and use of taxes.[45] In all, these articles were quite similar to the surrender terms of 1664. Clearly, the Dutch continued to view the terms of the 1664 agreement as a statement of their fundamental liberties. When Andros arrived with the sanctions of a treaty to accept the return of New York, they were willing to lose his good will in order to gain his acceptance of their rights.

On 31 October Colve appeared before the assembled magistrates of the city. In an emotional ceremony he discharged them from their oath to the States General and the prince of Orange and then turned the colony over to Andros. Soon afterward Andros settled any remaining doubts by issuing a proclamation confirming all prior grants, concessions, and legal proceedings and established the Duke's Laws once again.[46]

Andros quickly made the acquaintance of the New Englanders on Long Island who were equally concerned with their rights. For a brief interlude the towns had returned to the authority of Connecticut, a relationship they preferred to the one they had with New York. Andros disenthralled them. On 2 November he ordered the restoration of all of the magistrates who were in office at the time of the surrender. Gradually most of them were sworn in and, by the end of November, the justices of the peace for both the west and north ridings of Yorkshire had come forward.[47] There were others on Long Island, however, who looked upon the restoration as a time to restore their local rights. On 1 December a petition came from Jamaica welcoming Andros and expressing the townspeople's gratitude at his desire to help them in any way. But, because Andros probably did not know what they wanted, the petition asked that he call the people together so that they could tell him what was best for the public interest. The Jamaicans recalled that Nicolls had promised them an assembly that had not been granted, and that they had no representatives sitting on the council.[48] Three days after getting this message, Andros had to turn his attention further east to Southampton, Easthampton, and Southold. While Jamaica asked for an assembly, the three eastern towns opted for independence. They declared that they had been left to fight the Dutch and had succeeded in doing so only through the aid of Connecticut; as a result they had returned to Connecticut's jurisdiction. At the same time they appealed their case to the king. Governor John Winthrop, Jr., approved this plan and hoped Andros would acquiesce to it.[49] He did not know Andros.

Andros ordered John Mulford, John Howell, and John Youngs, the town leaders, to appear before the council or be declared rebels. The towns were ordered to submit or suffer the same fate. At the same time a courteous but direct letter was sent to Winthrop warning him not to help the towns or obstruct the royal prerogatives. Winthrop was quick to reply that Connecticut had helped the brave people of Long Island only until the king's will was known.[50] Andros, having admonished Winthrop, ordered Captain Sylvester Salisbury, the newly appointed high-sheriff, to visit the three towns, receive their surrender, and assure them of Andros's desire to aid them and guarantee all their rights. On reconsidering, Andros decided that his own presence would be more impressive and so descended upon the towns in person. While there he met Fitz-John Winthrop and John Wyllis, the Connecticut envoys who were still on the island, and learned more from them about the "battle" of Long Island.[51] In the course of exchanging pleasantries, Andros brought the three towns back within the fold. For the last time they had tried to escape from New York, but even within the fold they were not docile sheep.

When Andros turned to organizing his government, he all but excluded the Dutch from office, as Nicolls had a decade before. This policy was not permanent, as Andros gradually gathered around him a group of men, of English and Dutch extraction, with whom he administered the colony. But in the beginning the Dutch were treated harshly.

On first arriving he restored for six months all magistrates who were in office prior to the arrival of Evertsen and Binkes. The only exception was Peter Alricks, bailiff of New Castle, who had too readily offered his services to the Dutch. Later, Andros carefully appointed new sheriffs and other officers such as clerks, secretaries, and revenue collectors for Albany, Esopus, and Delaware. All were English, either new men to whom he extended his patronage or old officials. When the towns of the Esopus area protested against his appointees, they were warned that they were expected to obey and not to form parties opposing the government.[52]

The English also dominated the two main agencies of government—the council and the city aldermanic board. Andros appointed four men to his council in 1674. One of them was the well-seasoned John Lawrence and the other Mathias Nicolls, who was also reappointed to his post as provincial secretary. The other two were Andros's second in command, Captain Anthony Brockholls, and the receiver general, William Dyre. After these initial appointments, Frederick Philipse, William Darvall, and Stephanus Van Cortlandt were added in 1675, 1676, and 1680, respectively. Continuing past patterns, merchants dominated the council. Nicolls and Lawrence, besides being old officeholders, were merchants and landowners.

Philipse and Van Cortlandt were in the first rank of New York merchants. Darvall was a newcomer without their prominence, and his appointment may have come from being the son-in-law of Thomas Delaval, who was in England seeking to have his property restored by the Dutch.[53] The council still interlocked with the city government. Andros appointed a new group of city magistrates in 1674. Mathias Nicolls was mayor and Lawrence, Darvall, Gabriel Minvielle, Samuel Winder, and Frederick Philipse were the aldermen.[54] After 1674 Andros reinstated the old system of double nominations. The result was a steady turnover in office. During the seven years that Andros was governor there were forty-five positions available. These were held by twenty-three individuals; one man served for four years and only four for three years.[55] The city's government still remained in the hands of the merchants and officeholders who made up the city's oligarchy. The men chosen for the board of aldermen were also unrepresentative of the ethnic balance in the community. Twelve of the twenty-three magistrates were English in a city that had a population approximately three-quarters Dutch. Most of the Dutch chosen for the board were admitted to office after 1677 when Andros, casting aside his old distrust, decided to allow more Dutchmen into the government.

The council remained an unrepresentative body. The most obvious bias was geographic. All of the members lived in New York City. Albany, Delaware, and Long Island were kept from positions of power. The practical problem of having members of a body that met frequently living at great distances may have influenced Andros. Yet this did not prevent the eastern towns from complaining about their exclusion in their 1672 petition to the king. Frequently the mayor of the city sat with the council, and if the agenda included trade items, the aldermen were invited. When military officers such as Sylvester Salisbury or Caesar Knapton visited New York City, they joined in the meetings. Finally, distinguished members of the community who did not hold office, such as Thomas Delaval or Lewis Morris, were called frequently to offer their counsel. But the outlying regions went unrepresented, for merchants and officeholders were Andros's only advisors.

Of the seven members of the council, five were English.

From this one would presume that the Dutch would resent the ethnic composition of the council; however, it was actually the other way around. As Andros gained control over the colony and became firmly established, he turned to two men as his chief advisors. Frederick Philipse and Stephanus Van Cortlandt attended upon Andros constantly and, as will be seen later, the three of them were suspected of being trade partners. To the farmers of Long Island and the English merchants attempting to obtain a foothold in New York these two men represented an overweening Dutch influence in a supposedly English government.[56] From Andros's point of view, his alliance brought him the friendship of two of the leading merchants in the colony. As will be shown later, Philipse and Van Cortlandt, in turn, developed their English contacts, unlike their rivals in wealth, such as Jacob Leisler and Cornelius Steenwyck, who remained identified with purely Dutch interests. The families of Philipse and Van Cortlandt also intermarried and were related to the Schuylers, Van Rensselaers, Darvalls, and Delavals by marriage. Through these families the interconnections led to nearly every important family in New York. Thus, Andros not only gained an alliance that was potentially profitable but also fashioned a powerful political interest group. This group strengthened the position of the "court" faction. The "country" faction, on the other hand, still had no institutional means of opposition in the restricted world of New York politics. They could only protest, petition, and seek solutions in England.

The Revenue Problem

York sent Andros to his new position with one major goal—to insure a sufficient revenue. A great concern of all proprietors was realizing a profit on their grants or, at the very least, meeting expenses. York, however, was no ordinary proprietor and New York no ordinary proprietary colony. The problem he confronted in making New York profitable was still the garrison. Andros's instructions ordered him to "take ye best advise you can and transmit an Account to me ye most easy and speediest means to lessen ye chardge of ye government without weakening it or hazarding it; that soe by degrees

I may reape from thence some advantages, in return for ye great expence and trouble I have been at in protecting that Colony."[57] Andros was never allowed to forget this order; almost every letter from Sir John Werden or York contains some comment on finances. Werden was particularly pointed about repaying the duke for the £2,000 it cost him to regain New York in 1674.[58]

York sent a new receiver general to New York with Andros to try to make New York pay. William Dyre got the office as a reward for his testimony before the Council of Trade and Plantations. His commission ordered him to collect all forms of revenue but stressed the importance of the customs. York collected his own customs, not royal customs, in his proprietary and this was the major source of revenue.[59] Dyre's zeal in carrying out his instructions would ultimately put him under a charge of treason and help undermine Andros.

Andros entered his administration without a clear picture of what the revenues were. Shortly after he took power the courts were full of suits and countersuits revolving around the question of blame for the seizure of New York in 1673.[60] Wrapped up within this question was the problem of who had lost or benefited from the various confiscations carried out by Colve and Andros. The estates of Lovelace, collector Delaval, Bedloo (Lovelace's factor), and Colve were entangled in litigation.[61] Andros and Dyre, therefore, had very confused evidence on which to make tax estimates.

When he turned away from this legal morass, Andros discovered that many considered the creation of an assembly as the best way to fulfill York's desires for a profit.[62] When Andros wrote to York about this advice, the duke commended him for discouraging any requests for an assembly and stated that redress could be obtained in the court of assize "where the same persons [as justices] are usually present, who in all probability would be their Representatives if another constitution were allowed." Andros had the tact not to point out that the governor chose the justices, not the people. In another letter York was even more negative: "I cannot but suspect they would be of dangerous consequence, nothing being more knowne then the aptness of such bodyes to assume to themselves many priviledges wch prove destructive to, or very oft disturbe, the peace of ye governmt wherein they are allowed."[63] Killing the proposals for an assembly meant that Andros and Receiver General Dyre were forced back upon the same methods employed by Nicolls and Lovelace to acquire money. The failure of Nicolls and Lovelace did not augur well for Andros and Dyre. If they were to succeed, every possible tax source would have to be squeezed dry. Such a policy meant difficulties with the people of New York.

Andros and Dyre were limited in what they could do to satisfy the demands of York and Werden. The sources of revenue available to them were limited, and there was always the problem of collection. Taxes can be divided into two categories, local and provincial. Local taxes were assessed, collected, and disbursed by the magistrates. These were the taxes begun by Nicolls and authorized in the Duke's Laws. The money was collected by a rate made on assessment of land, animals, and, sometimes, polls. The funds collected were disbursed for local expenses such as the salary of the minister, services rendered by individuals to the community (for instance, delegates going to New York City), allotment to cowherders and the poor, and for extraordinary expenditures such as Indian gifts. In other words, the towns had to pay their own way. Andros reviewed their proceedings to ascertain that they were meeting their obligations and not collecting taxes without his approval.[64]

New York City and Albany had special problems and privileges in taxation. The critical position of Albany, close to the Indian nations and the French, meant that the town had to conduct diplomacy for the colony. Because of the debts accrued in doing so, Andros allowed the magistrates to assess and collect a special tax of every three-hundredth penny in the pound of assessed valuation. After granting this special tax Andros stopped the excise on butchering since it was a burden on the poor. Later, the magistrates were permitted to charge a special tax of every hundredth penny.[65] Besides these special taxes ordered by the governor, the magistrates also collected an excise on liquor, gunpowder, and lead, in addition to regular town rates; and, when King Philip's War threatened to spill into the Hudson, they were allowed an additional special tax for support of the militia. To collect all of these taxes and keep the books, the court finally appointed the town clerk, Robert Livingston, as treasurer.[66]

New York City chronically needed money. Besides paying its officials and providing for local needs, the city had an additional burden to bear as the center of the colony. Proper facilities for ships and the fort had to be maintained. While the fort was supposed to be a bulwark for the whole colony, the special "contributions" collected by Colve and Lovelace to pay for repairs fell heavily on the city. In early 1677 a check of the city's finances revealed debts of 24,505 guilders (wampum). The treasurer, Peter Stoutingburgh, was ordered to repay all creditors.[67] With the limited tax resources, this was an almost impossible task. There were a number of incidental fees such as those for the burgher or freeman right, legal fees in the mayor's court, and use of the dock. The main source of revenue for many years was the "Small Pacht," or excise, or retail sales of liquor. Andros stopped this tax throughout the colony and instituted a fee on licensed alehouses. Thereafter, the city fathers relied on a tax based on property assessment. They also made sure that any new project was paid for by a special tax and not from regular city revenues. Thus, when Andros ordered the building of a larger dock, a special tax was levied.[68] Andros had the Long Island towns contribute building materials for the dock since he felt that they too would benefit from better facilities. The towns, however, were never happy about paying taxes for projects benefiting the city. Thus, when Andros placed another special levy for the fort on them in January 1676, the townsmen's animosity came to the fore again. Andros sent them a detailed list of contributions he expected in January, and by September he had to threaten them with action in the court of assize.[69] In a further attempt to help the city, Andros allowed a special hearth tax and ordered all vacant land in the city to be built on or forfeited for sale.[70] Such special treatment helped, but the city remained in debt.

The larger field of provincial taxes was the area of greatest concern. The provincial revenues came mainly from customs. The duties were set at 2 percent ad valorem on all imports from England and English colonies and 10 percent on foreign goods. Trade goods continuing up the Delaware or the Hudson had to pay an additional 3 percent. The only goods taxed on leaving the colony were furs and tobacco. All of these rates remained in effect for three years, beginning in 1674, unless the duke decided to change them.[71] Andros and Dyre were responsible for putting the duke's regulations into effect, and in the process a number of them were changed. For instance, salt and tobacco were made customs free—salt because a tax on it was detrimental to the general welfare, and tobacco because it made up too important a part of New York's trade.[72]

The most difficult problem confronting Andros was that of collection. Innumerable places of entry studded the coastline from the Delaware River to Southampton. New York City was the natural center for collection, but in order to accommodate the islanders, Southold and Southampton were made ports of entry. However, because of tax collection irregularities, the eastern towns lost this privilege after a short time, leaving New York City as the only legal point of entry.[73] Poor, distant, sparsely inhabited Delaware received special treatment for a short time also. New Castle and Whorekill charged the same customs as New York until 1678, when New York City also became the collection center for Delaware.[74] Thus all customs collection came under the sharp eye of Dyre in the colony's capital.

The next important source for funds was the taxes on polls, animals, and lands in the three ridings of Yorkshire specified in the Duke's Laws. They were used to meet the operating costs of government on the island and other expenses such as the garrison. Andros ordered a rate made on 5 August 1675, and in succeeding years other rates were consistently collected, as is evident from the surviving assessment lists for 1675, 1676, 1678, 1680, and 1683.[75] Most of the funds were disbursed locally. The accounts of Sheriff John Youngs for 1680 indicate that the total revenue from the rates was £563. Most of this money was used for expenses such as entertainment, salaries, and hue and cries charged against the court of sessions in each riding. Youngs, himself, had a yearly salary of £20 plus expenses of £38 for incidentals and £21 for entertaining the court. An even more intriguing figure is a total of £207 paid out to six individuals. Four of these six were later found as judges or lawyers in New York, so at this time they probably went on the sessions circuit as lawyers. If so, it was highly lucrative for some. In 1680 George Merritt made £79.13. In contrast, Anthony Brockholls, who was acting governor at the time, received only £36. Whatever share the governor received after expenses were met was mostly in produce, not in cash, and was used to feed the garrison.[76]

The rates remained a source of contention. The Duke's Laws, as amended by the court of assize, specified the assessed value of each item of property assessed. Polls, horses, oxen, cows, hogs, sheep, and land were all enumerated. Problems arose, however, when values changed rapidly. For example, horses had declined drastically in price by the 1670s, but were still assessed at the high rate of £12 for a four-year-old. When Southampton unilaterally lowered the assessment to £4 on four-year-olds (and the others proportionally), Andros ignored the townsmen and recalculated their total assessment, adding £1,156. The next assize confirmed Andros's valuation of horses.[77] Another continuing point of discord was the price of goods used when paying the rates in kind. Since these prices never fluctuated exactly with the market, the government continued to get produce at the cheap set price and then sold it at the higher market price. The towns hated this practice and now and then delayed payment, which always brought a warning to be prompt.[78]

Quitrents made up a very small part of the revenue. There is no evidence that they were collected on Long Island or in the vicinity of New York City. Nicolls had charged a quitrent on a few private patents and merely left the possibility of doing so on the rest. Few, if any, were collected. The tension with the towns over the rates and the lack of an assembly kept Nicolls and his successors from extracting the quitrents. Perhaps they also downplayed quitrents in an attempt to attract more planters from New England. When Andros finally forced Southampton, Southold, and Oyster Bay to accept patents under pain of forfeit, he placed nominal quitrents in the patents.[79] The remaining records indicate that only Rensselaerswyck, the Delaware settlements, and Esopus paid quitrents. The quitrents substituted for the rates charged on Long Island, although on one occasion the Delaware settlements got a three-year reprieve.[80] No such relief was granted Esopus, where the farmers paid infrequently until the collector, Lieutenant George Hall, received permission to seize the property of those who refused to pay.[81] The amounts collected in quitrents are hard to calculate, but it probably added up to little more than the costs of local government.[82]

The three other regular sources of revenue were the weigh-house at New York City, the monopoly over liquor licensing, and the excise on liquor of all kinds. The government farmed all of them to the highest bidder in an auction by candle. The farm of the excise, or the "Great Pacht," yielded 10,300 guilders in 1675.[83] After his successful bid, the farmer of the excise charged set fees on all liquor sold wholesale in New York. Since most of the wines, brandies, rums, and other favored drinks came in through New York City, the farmer had a near mono-poly. The farmer of the weigh-house also had a monopoly since goods going in or out of the city, from silks to iron, beaver to tea, and sarsaparilla to pork, all needed weighing. The success-ful bids for the weigh-house have survived from 1675 to 1680, indicating an average yearly income of 6,700 guilders.[84] The remaining farm of the "tappers" license gave the successful bidder a monopoly of granting licenses to all those retailing alcohol in the city. In 1677 it yielded £180, but this is the only year for which accurate information survives.[85]

The only other sources of revenue were incidentals. When the colony was captured, Nicolls seized the property of the West India Company and that of the City of Amsterdam on the Delaware. Drift whales and shipwrecks, from time to time, benefited the public coffers. Admiralty courts presided over by the governors also added occasional amounts.

In the end, all of the sources, whether local, provincial, or incidental, failed to meet the desires of the proprietor. Andros tried to extract the maximum revenue by collecting every tax he felt he could and authorizing special taxes when he felt they were called for. But only once did Werden strike an optimistic note in his correspondence with Andros about revenue. In May 1677 he wrote that the commission was pleased by Dyre's last report to Apsley, which showed a credit of £126.[86] Within a year this was shown to be false optimism. Andros obtained permission to return home in 1678 to attend to private business and accept his knighthood. Before he arrived, Apsley reviewed all of his accounts and estimated the deficit from June 1674 to November 1677 as £1,100. To balance the books and signal approval of Andros's stewardship, the duke paid him this amount.[87] Compared to the much larger debts Nicolls brought back, Andros had achieved a great deal. But a profitable colony still eluded York.

The early years of Andros's stewardship yielded mixed results. York's central concern of profiting, or even breaking even, remained a faint hope. The taxable resources of a still-developing plantation proved insufficient to meet the heavy costs of the government and the garrison. Not even Andros's domineering style of politics could guarantee a sufficient revenue. The tax burdens only heightened the tension between the people and Andros, further alienating them from the proprietary government that seemed more and more in the hands of a clique.

The most important long-term result of this period was Andros's success in creating a "court" faction of merchant-landowners. This clique, centering on Stephanus Van Cortlandt and Frederick Philipse, was not dislodged from power until 1689, and then only temporarily. The court faction generated almost as much hatred and jealousy in the towns and villages as the domineering Andros. Those groups outside Andros's circle can hardly be called the "country" *faction*; New York's regionalism isolated the malcontents and kept them from forming a faction. A further hindrance was the lack of a political institution, such as an assembly, where an opposition could gain coherence and establish alternatives. Without such a base the centripetal forces present in regionalism would overcome the tug of common animosity toward the "court." The "country" was left to bluster, petition, and attempt to avoid the law. The more defined group of officeholders and merchants around Andros remained undisturbed until events outside the colony intruded upon their happy situation.

5 &ℯ Trade and Politics: The Recall of Edmund Andros

Between 1674 and 1680 the central figure in New York was Governor Edmund Andros. During these years he ruled with an autocratic manner. His recall to England in 1680, surrounded by charges of malfeasance, corruption, and favoritism, was the central drama of this period. His downfall illuminates many aspects of his administration. In particular it reveals the intrusion of powerful external agents of change. The entry of London merchants into the closed market created by the New York merchants was an economic and political event. Until the new merchants arrived the only external figure of major political importance was the duke. With the entry of this new group the colonists were made aware of powerful forces at work within the empire. In addition the Stuart government was now intent on exerting more control over the colonies. Colonial charters were challenged and investigators sent to the colonies to examine economic and political trends. An era of intense reexamination was underway that would reach a climax with the creation of the Dominion of New England in 1685.

A Changing Economy

After 1675 New York's economy underwent dramatic changes. The familiar patterns of New York trade were explained by Andros in a report he submitted to the Lords of Trade and Plantations in 1678.[1] He described New York City as the center of all trade with ten to fifteen ships of about one hundred tons entering the harbor annually; Albany and Southampton were the only other places of consequence. The chief exports were wheat, peas, beef, pork, fish, whale oil, tobacco, beaver pelts, wood products, and horses. Most of these items were local products with the exception of tobacco, which came from the Delaware settlements and Chesapeake Bay colonies. The foodstuffs were sold mainly in neighboring colonies, Newfoundland, and the increasingly important West Indian market. Boston was an important factor in the economy. The Bostonians carried much of the English trade of New York and the Long Island whale oil. Andros ruefully admitted that Boston was of greater importance in colonial trade than New York. The import-export trade with Europe was glossed over by Andros in his report. He mentioned that the chief imports were English manufactured goods and Indian trade goods. He failed to mention the extremely important trade that continued with the Netherlands.

Although by 1668 they had given up trying to get some form of legal trade with the Netherlands, the Dutch and English merchants of New York continued their familiar trade patterns.[2] Tobacco, logwood, whale fins, sassafras, cotton, sugar, and the skins of the beaver, otter, fox, mink, and raccoon filled the holds of ships bound for Amsterdam. To make the trade legal, most of them stopped in at Dover on the way to and from Holland.[3] A significant exception was Frederick Philipse, who sent his vessels in and out of Falmouth, an out-of-the-way place where Philipse dealt with more compliant customs agents.[4] On their return trip from Holland to New York the ships passed out of the English channel loaded with all sorts and types of cloth and clothing, nails, millstones, pipes, fishing hooks, window glass, tools, guns, combs, dyes, buttons, starch, dishes, and all the other necessary and extravagant things needed in North America. Not even the ballast was wasted on the return voyage, as many ships had loads of as many as seventy thousand bricks.[5] During the 1670s this was a regular voyage for as many as six ships per year.[6] In contrast, the number of English vessels was limited until 1675. From 1664 to 1674 only five vessels are recorded as making a direct voyage from England to New York.[7] English goods could come from Boston but the bulk of New York's export trade was still basically Dutch.

The trend in New York's economy at the end of the 1670s was primarily downward. By 1679 a number of vital exports were bringing all-time low prices: winter wheat, normally priced at about 4½ to 5 shillings per bushel, dropped to 4 shillings;

summer wheat declined from 4½ to 5 shillings per bushel to 3 shillings per bushel; rye went from 4 to 2½ shillings per bushel; a barrel of beef went from £3.5 to £2 and pork, from £3.10 to £3.[8] Price cuts in these important staples hurt farmers and merchants alike. This slump was followed by a series of bad harvests. By the end of 1681 grain was scarce and Anthony Brockholls, temporarily in charge of the garrison, was desperate for foodstuffs. Shortages of grain continued until 1683, slowing economic growth.[9]

Regional economic rivalry was still a feature of the provincial economy. New York City, Albany, Delaware, and Long Island remained four distinct centers. However, significant changes were occurring.

Long Island continued to be divided in its orientation. The towns of the west end looked to New York City, those at the east end to Boston and Connecticut ports. Southampton was emerging as the most important of the eastern towns. Boston merchants traded there regularly for the growing quantities of whale oil that supplemented the island's foodstuffs.[10]

Albany's wealth still came from the rivers and streams of the Great Lakes region. The fur trade was jealously guarded, although the growth of Schenectady called for vigilance on the part of the sheriff. The swelling number of merchants coming up from New York City during the high season of August and September also bore close watching.[11] Internally the magistrates had trouble policing their own people. For the protection of the town, bartering with the Indians was supposed to occur outside the gates. Temptation was so great, however, that the sheriff had to arrest children who attempted to lure Indians into houses where their parents used liquor to acquire the furs from the Indians.[12] Protecting the fur trade was a constant task for the magistrates and large fur wholesalers. Supplementing the fur trade and growing in importance were the grain crops of Albany and the Esopus River settlements, which sent increasing amounts of grain down the river.[13]

Delaware experienced a population boom after 1674. Prior to York's renewing his grant to Berkeley and Carteret in 1674, Berkeley sold his rights in New Jersey to two Quakers, John Fenwick and Edward Byllynge, for £1,000. Carteret claimed the eastern half while the two new proprietors took over the more sparsely settled western half. Although aspects of his title were clouded, Fenwick arrived in America in 1675 ready to organize his colony. Andros denied him the rights to administer the area because York had not granted the old proprietors the right to govern. This was only the beginning of a running battle with the Jersey proprietors that climaxed in Governor Carteret's trial.[14] Unmindful of the legal maneuvering, Quaker colonists began arriving in 1677. An initial group of two hundred was shortly followed by two more shiploads from Hull and Liverpool.[15] While distrusting Fenwick in particular and Quakers in general, Andros was happy to get new colonists. The merchants of New Castle were also pleased because the new colonists needed supplies. To insure their control over trade on the Delaware they asked for and acquired control over imports and exports.[16]

New York City remained the center of economic activity. Dominance over the hinterlands and the export-import trade were the city's lifeblood. As it expanded, the city followed a familiar pattern of controlling the internal economy so as to assure local monopolies and control of quality. Newcomers had to register with the magistrates and purchase the status of freeman before entering commerce or practicing a craft. Having entered the economic life of the city, the newcomers faced a variety of controls. Viewers and searchers were appointed to inspect pipe staves, hides, grain for distilling, flour for export, casks, and horses.[17] Labor, even that of skilled craftsmen, was closely controlled. One example occurred in December 1679, when the city's coopers set their own prices. When complaints of their price fixing reached the council the twenty-one coopers were summoned to a hearing. The coopers argued that their agreement did not raise prices, but the council fined them all and fired two who worked for customs.[18] In typical seventeenth-century style, the government watched the economy very closely and was quick to punish those who violated the many regulations.

York and Andros shared economic policymaking; however, York and his commissioners were distant, infrequent meddlers in the proprietary's economic life. York at one time ordered a ban on ships from Boston going up the Hudson and on the importation of European goods from Boston unless they had an English clearance. Massachusetts remained an object of distrust for the duke and one report passed among his advisors advocated an attack on the Bay colony.[19] In another action York denied a petition requesting him to grant a currency for New York, which struggled with many different kinds of coins and wampum. Since he would be providing the coinage, York refused, noting that unless the money was cheaper than that obtainable in surrounding colonies, it would quickly leave New York.[20] Beyond these actions Andros was left by York to exercise wide discretionary powers over the economy.[21] Andros used them to the benefit of New York City. Like his predecessors he was surrounded by merchants in government and in his social life. The merchants continued to reap the benefits of their monopoly of the governor's ear.

Andros did more than his predecessors to expand New York City's control over vital sectors of the economy. As in the past the merchants wanted to control the Hudson River trade that had lapsed during Colve's tenure. Andros first banned all river trade except by vessels owned by inhabitants of the colony who had his permission. This was followed by another order directing the inhabitants of the Hudson River towns to bring their European goods through New York City.[22] The Albany magistrates immediately responded with a "Remonstrance," which asserted that Albany's right to trade overseas was an old one and that they would suffer terribly if it were not continued. They argued that "they will have to sell their beavers at such low prices as those of New York will be pleased to give and consequently pay for all their merchandise, both Indian and Christian trading goods, as much as those in New York may be pleased to demand."[23] They even conjured up the French specter by arguing that if they were unable to attract the Indians through the lack of goods, the tribes would go to Canada. This was not an idle threat, and even though Andros had officially claimed the Iroquois lands for England, the boundary and the allegiance of the Iroquois were still in dispute. The "Remonstrance" was unsuccessful. Andries Teller and Dirck Wessells, who delivered it to Andros, were sent home with orders that Stoffel Abeel, Hendrick Cuyler, and David Schuyler, who had signed the petition on behalf of the inhabitants, were to present themselves before the council. Accompanying the summons went a message to the magistrates demanding to know if they wanted general trade privileges or a monopoly of the Indian trade.[24] Knowing where their wealth came from, the *commissaries* acquiesced and agreed to "do therein as his honor [Andros] in his wisdom and sound judgment shall see fit, which no doubt will tend to the preservation and benefit of the place."[25] To confirm the fur monopoly, two New York merchants were fined for fur trading. One appealed his conviction to the council, which approved the fine and charged him more for protesting.[26] At the same time Timothy Cooper, John Pynchon's factor, was forced to leave Albany. This meant that Pynchon, the leading fur trader in the Connecticut River Valley, was cut off from the richer fur trade in the west.[27] To complete the pattern of enforcement, Sheriff Pretty of Albany went to investigate trade at Schenectady. He was physically barred from doing so and quickly lodged a complaint. As a result Andros confirmed Albany's monopoly and reminded Schenectady that it was a farming community and nothing more. So, while they had the pleasure of enforcing their monopoly of the fur trade, the *handlaers* had to acquiesce to New York's control of their foreign trade and could only watch apprehensively when further orders were issued on 11 April 1679 controlling the movement of cargo to and from Albany.[28]

While wresting control of the river traffic from its competitors, the city's merchants regained the important wheat monopoly that now challenged furs as the colony's premier export. According to Andros's report of 1678, sixty thousand bushels were shipped annually from New York.[29] When surpluses made it possible to ship grain in 1676, directives were issued to insure the quality of the wheat. First, two viewers were appointed to examine all grain used for distilling in New York City to insure that it was unfit for grinding. Later, two cure masters were given power to examine all flour in barrels to make sure that summer wheat and winter wheat were not mixed.[30] This action was followed with an order granting the seaport towns sole authority to inspect wheat for export because the seaports needed to guarantee the quality of the wheat to protect their reputations in the trade.[31] Since this meant that final packaging of upriver wheat was done in New York, the Albany magistrates complained of this in their "Remonstrance" but to no effect.[32]

These preliminary moves were followed by decisive orders granting the city a wheat monopoly. After three council meetings in January 1680, orders were issued prohibiting the packing of wheat for export and the bolting of flour outside the city, and restricting all retailing of wheat and ownership of bolting mills to freemen of the city.[33] The merchants now had a monopoly of packaging and exporting wheat and flour, which benefited not only them, but also the coopers, millers, bakers, and other workmen in the city. Joined with control of packaging beef and pork for export, the wheat monopoly gave the city control over the major exports of the province. The city received another important monopoly when it was designated the only port where cargoes could be loaded for export.[34] This undoubtedly aided Dyre in collecting customs and was thus desirable for revenue collection, but the result was to strip away privileges won by New Castle and the towns of eastern Long Island. The outlying regions could only look on with dismay as the council decreed law after law cutting away their autonomy and further benefiting the city's merchants. They had to turn to smuggling or await new political developments. Their wait was not for long; a new group entering the life of the colony acted as a catalyst for change.

London Merchants and the New York Market

After 1674 London merchants entered the New York market. As has already been noted few English ships ventured directly to New York prior to 1673. Opening up a new market in the seventeenth century meant sending out relatives or trusted factors. The dominance of the Dutch no doubt deterred

Englishmen from trying to compete, and the few English merchants in New York had ties to Boston or Holland. This changed in 1674 when London merchants decided to open up the New York market. Cargoes and factors went in the same ships that took Andros to his new post. The years that followed witnessed continued interest.

In 1675 four ships left London for New York, only one in 1676, none in 1677, five in 1678, four in 1679 and 1680, and then none in 1681.[35] Significantly, 1681 was the year Andros was tried for malfeasance in office. The merchants entering this new market were men who traded regularly with Boston and other colonial ports prior to 1674. Approximately fifty men shipped cargoes to New York; however, there was a core group that made substantial investments. The most active were William Antelby, Mathew Chitty, Thomas Crundall, Gerrard Dankheythusen, William De Peyster, Edward Griffith, Thomas Hart, John Harwood, Benjamin Hewling, John Lewin, Edward Mann, Samuel Swinock, Gerrard Vanheythusen, and Robert Woolley.

The means by which they entered the new market were diverse but typical of business practice in the seventeenth century. William De Peyster of London traded with his cousin Abraham in New York to knit together the De Peyster family's widespread influence.[36] Samuel Swinock appears to have met Thomas Delaval when the latter was in England in 1673 trying to regain his estate after the Dutch had confiscated it. It appears that Swinock sent him goods on account, for when Delaval died he owed Swinock £1,657 sterling.[37] Mathew Chitty joined with Nicholas Cullen of Dover to send cargoes over on New York vessels leaving Dover. The latter may have shared religious ties with some of the New York merchants, for in his will he made Abraham De Peyster and Jacob Leisler executors for gifts to the Dutch churches in New York City and Albany.[38] Some merchants settled for venturing cargoes with captains and factors. One of the factors was Samuel Winder, whose accounts went into litigation after his death. Among his creditors were John Lewin, Mathew Chitty, Robert Woolley, Alderman Francis Warner of London, and Sir Henry Tufs.[39] One prominent New York personality who built his trade on factoring was Robert Livingston. He made his way to Albany as a factor for Boston merchants. Once established in Albany he sought English suppliers. Later he sorely abused Jacob Harwood's credit.[40]

The number of new traders entering New York can be seen in a special order issued by the aldermen on 31 October 1676 warning twenty-five individuals to pay their taxes prior to leaving the city.[41] Twenty-three of the twenty-five were English and nine of them are readily identifiable as London merchants. The remainder could very well be factors or captains whose names would not be listed in customs accounts. Some men of substance are notable. Five men—John Robinson, George Heathcote, Edward Griffeth, James Lloyd, and John Robson—had estates valued at £2,000 and those of Thomas Thatcher, Robert Sandford, and Abraham Whearly were over £500. These were sizable valuations indicating significant taxable estates.

A clash between the new merchants and Andros was not inevitable. However, the English invasion threatened the city merchants just as the economy began to slump. Andros naturally defended his constituency in the city and, as a result, a number of the new men were roughly treated.

The first merchant to be the object of Andros's wrath was George Heathcote, a familiar face in New York. A member of one of London's most distinguished merchant families, he first appeared in New Amsterdam in 1661. Gradually, he acquired property in Albany, on the Delaware River, in Southampton, Long Island, and New York City. A Quaker, he revealed a disposition to defy authority. In an incident in Massachusetts he refused to take off his hat to Governor Bellingham and was placed in jail for his impertinence. Unfortunately he exercised this trait before Andros in a public place.[42] During the summer of 1676 he was charged with trading illegally at Albany after trade was restricted to freemen of the town. Since he owned property in Albany and thought himself a resident, Heathcote protested the charge. Confronting Andros in the customshouse to plead his case, he made the mistake of complaining about the quantity of cheap and illegal Dutch goods in Albany. The situation was so bad that he could not sell his goods and thus was denied "ye Priviledges of an English man." Sheriff Thomas Ashton of New York City complained to Andros that Heathcote had defamed the city's good name and as a result the latter found himself a guest of the magistrates in the city jail. Before a specially convened court of assize Heathcote was found guilty of "scurrilous" speech and fined £20 plus costs. The fine was large, but the court costs were an incredible £61.5.6. After many petitions the fine was suspended, but the court costs remained.[43]

The next victim was John Robinson. He foolishly testified during Heathcote's trial that Albany was indeed flooded with illegal Dutch goods. Perhaps as a warning, Dyre, the customs collector, took him to court for payment of £97 in duties for which he had been given credit.[44] He remained untroubled after Heathcote's trial until he made the mistake, about one year later, of telling Andros that there were still illegal Dutch goods in Albany. Tried in the mayor's court instead of the assize, he managed to escape Heathcote's fate. Andros exacted his own revenge by denying Robinson permission to trade at Albany.[45] Others such as Robert Story, Richard Mann, and James Graham shared the fate of Heathcote and Robinson in trials for illegal trade and contempt of court.[46]

Andros committed a serious error when he had Edward Griffeth tried on similar charges as those brought against Heathcote and Robinson. Griffeth had complained about preferential treatment for the Dutch, an inability to trade at Albany, and, in general, being denied the rights of an Englishman. For acting in "derogation and contempt of the Kings Authority," he was fined £20.[47] Outraged by his treatment, he sought revenge. Unwilling, or perhaps unable, to attack Andros in New York, Griffeth had his family begin a court case against Andros when he returned to England during the winter of 1677–78 to receive his knighthood and attend to family business. Two weeks prior to Andros's sailing for New York, a group of merchants petitioned York to detain him until witnesses and evidence arrived from New York, but the duke denied their request.[48] Andros escaped this time but would finally be brought to bay by the merchants.

The Recall of Governor Andros

The merchants' petition reveals the many sources of friction between Andros and them. Andros, they charged, had violated the Navigation Acts by allowing direct commerce with the Netherlands that avoided the royal customs; he had granted special privileges to Philipse and others; he had obstructed trade with Albany in order to favor a few; he helped his friends avoid customs; and he carried on a private trade of his own. There were other complaints not relating to trade. Andros was accused of manipulating trials against the defendants and, in one instance, of throwing one of the new merchants, John Robson, in jail without a hearing.[49] Taxes collected for the garrison were diverted by Andros for his private advantage. Andros also used his tax power to dissuade English merchants from trading in New York. Finally, he interfered with the practice of religion and subjected the English to humiliation by installing a Dutch whipping post. The effects of his tyrannical administration were to hinder further English immigration and cause such outrage among the people that they would not defend the colony. York's response was to allow Andros to return to New York. Two years later, after a rising chorus of complaints from New York and further pressure from the merchants, he recalled Andros to England.

York and Werden wrote separate letters to Andros on 24 May 1680.[50] In his letter recalling Andros, York explained that his chief reason was to ascertain the true revenues of New York. In order to do so he was sending over an unbiased person to investigate and impartially assess all facets of the colony's finances. He also pressed Andros to return immediately in order to defend himself against those attempting to blemish his record. Their accusations were left to Werden to explain. He wrote: "As to ye rest wt relates to your behavior in your government, whether ariseing from complaints of some private men, or anger of ye Quakers, or Captn Billop or from some suggestions of yor favoring Dutchmen before English in trade, or makeing by Laws hurtful to ye English in general, or delaying ships unduly for private reasons, or admitting Dutch ships immediately to trade with you, or trading yourself in ye names of others."[51] This catalog of mismanagement and inequitable government reveals the confluence between the external and internal sources of discontent, and that Andros's critics were vigorously pressing their case in England.

It is difficult to tell what specific incidents lie behind the charges against Andros, but the accusations reflect many different aspects of the inhabitants' ire at the proprietary regime. The charges break down into two broad categories—economic and political. The latter are fewer in number. The anger of the Quakers is easy to explain. Andros's hounding of Fenwick had aroused them. Further, from the beginning, he had treated the Quakers, especially those of Long Island, differently because they refused to take a loyalty oath.[52] The Quakers promised to be faithful subjects, but during King Philip's War, when the militia system was strengthened, they refused to participate in the militia and were fined. The Quakers also disturbed other religious meetings, turning local congregations against them. Their own meetings were banned, but this did not prevent them from continuing to meet, even after special warnings. Individual Quakers were heavily fined for not paying the ministers' rates and for refusing to accept office.[53] They were even fined for marrying in ceremonies not prescribed by law, and when they protested against the government's actions, they were fined again.[54] Life was difficult for Quakers in New York; however, they had an important friend in William Penn, a friend of York. Penn had become a trustee for West New Jersey in the wake of Byllynge and Fenwick's business reverses. He was in a position to report on Andros's conduct toward the new settlements.

The family of Captain Christopher Billop, an officer in the garrison, made a different type of complaint against Andros. Shortly after his arrival, Billop obtained 1,300 acres on Staten Island. He asked to leave his command and develop his estate, but the duke refused him permission to do so. In 1677, he was sent to the Delaware settlements to control the Quakers arriving there and to watch Fenwick. Billop, however, fell in with Fenwick, denounced the governor, and acted against the older planters. For this he was removed from his office in Delaware and ordered back to New York. After Billop defended himself by making "extravagant" speeches, Andros dismissed him from his position. Billop had family and friends in England to defend him and protest his dismissal. Insubordination was intolerable to Andros, no matter how influential Billop's patrons, and the duke acquiesced in his dismissal by appointing another to his command.[55]

The charge that Andros made laws harmful to the English originates in his relationship with Long Island and the new English mercantile community. The chill in the relationship between the English towns and the government was an old one that deepened as the townspeople saw the continual enhancement of New York City's economic power. As the number of the city's monopolies grew, their disgruntlement flourished apace, because they perceived the Dutch merchants of the city as profiting from the actions of Andros.[56] Without representative government and taxed by a distant autocrat, many of the townspeople believed that they had "put ourselves and our successours into a state of Servitude, which, if soe, who will pitty or helpe us."[57] When they did protest or undertake a policy that angered Andros, he was quick to arrest the local constable and overseers until they were properly chastened. In 1676 he did this to the magistrates of Huntington and Hempstead. He also moved swiftly against those who imported goods elsewhere than to the city.[58] Sharpening the protests of Long Island was the growing inability of the townsmen to provide land for the young men in the villages. An uncertain future was combined with an unpopular government.[59]

Most of the other charges in Werden's letter deal with Andros's own trading activities or his favoritism to those in his circle, especially Philipse and Van Cortlandt. These charges are given substance by the journal of Jasper Dankaerts and other evidence. Dankaerts was a Labadist sent to North America to find a suitable site for a religious colony. In 1679–80 he traveled through the inhabited parts of New York, the Jerseys, the Delaware area, and Massachusetts. Although a critical, indeed dyspeptic, observer, Dankaerts relates a good deal of criticism of Andros that reflected local opinion. He charged Andros with personal trading activities, giving special privileges to Philipse, stopping the distilling of grain (thereby causing a large increase in the importation of rum, which produced customs and profitable return cargoes from the West Indies), ending flour shipments, forcing usage of land by threatening seizure if not tilled, extorting sums from merchants, and forcing the use of English leather (thereby destroying the local tanners and shoemakers).[60] This extensive bill against Andros included more charges than there were in Werden's letter. Some evidence exists for most of them.

A basic charge in Dankaerts's journal was that Andros carried on a trade with Philipse and Van Cortlandt and extended them profitable favors. Andros was not the first or last governor to enter commerce. For that matter, York himself traded. He sent a cargo of clothing, weapons, and metalware worth £1,300 to New York with Andros. When the return cargo of lumber failed to provide an adequate profit, Werden wrote a critical letter to Andros.[61] Since Andros is accused of trading as a silent partner of others, direct evidence of his activities is difficult to obtain. Dankaerts did report that Andros owned a retail shop in New York City. Beyond this, the only other references are to the governor's sloop, which carried on a coastal trade.[62] As to his partnership with Philipse or Van Cortlandt, there is simply no evidence, although there is evidence for a pattern of favoritism. Andros once wrote to the duke to get permission for Margareta Philipse, a very active merchant in her own right, to buy a Dutch ship and avoid the penalties of the Navigation Acts. When Dankaerts sailed for New York he traveled on Margareta Philipse's ship. As they sailed into the harbor a flag went up indicating their arrival, but no customs men came to inspect the cargo.[63] Considering Collector Dyre's fervor in seizing vessels, this seems unusual. Further evidence of favoritism is found in a court case pressed in 1681 after Andros returned to England. The widow of Peter DeNÿs, a one-time weighmaster, charged Philipse with not paying any fees on his cargoes from 1679 to 1681.[64] By not having to pay these fees Philipse, at least, could trade on favorable terms. It is no wonder that Griffeth, Heathcote, and Robinson complained about cheap Dutch goods in abundance. It also appears that bribery found its way into the inner circle. Maria Van Rensselaer complained of having to pay "the schout, the secretary, the governor, the councilors."[65] Favoritism and extortion carried on by a favored inner circle, apparently dominated by the Dutch, nourished hatred among the English.

Some of Dankaerts's other charges can be substantiated. No flour shipments were allowed except from New York City after the bolting monopoly was granted. Related to this was the accusation that the distillation of grain was stopped. Andros had done so in 1676. As Dankaerts pointed out, this brought in a profitable commodity—rum—that raised customs and increased the amount of grain for export. Andros had set a special tax on all unoccupied land on Manhattan. This forced the use of empty lots inside the city and curtailed haphazard expansion. Those who refused to build were subject to having their land seized. Leather tanning was curtailed and then halted in New York City, working hardships on the tanners and shoemakers. The final charge, that he licensed all merchants and received payments according to the size of their trade, is unprovable.[66]

The outpouring of frustration and hate for the regime represented in these charges is a considerable indictment. The narrow prerogative system laid down in the Duke's Laws had led to policies that alienated most of the colony beyond the charmed circle Andros had created. It was natural that a system that gave almost unlimited powers to the governor would create such a situation, particularly when the governors were all military men in charge of an expensive garrison that they had to support through difficult-to-collect taxes or special fees or loans.[67] The men who aided them were the chief advisors of the government and benefited from their special relationship. They were not working in a vacuum, however, and other groups and interests in the colony could still appeal to England for help. There is no doubt the London merchants were crucial in this regard.

John Lewin's Investigation

When York recalled Andros he informed him that he was sending over an investigator to gather information about taxes and trade in the proprietary. The duke reported that someone had offered to farm the revenues of New York and that the total revenue figures given by sources in England were greater than those sent by Andros.[68] York's information probably came from the merchants who witnessed favoritism at the customshouse. Evidence for this is seen in the choice of John Lewin as the investigator. John Lewin was no stranger to New York. He had traded to New England and New York, where he was in partnership with Robert Woolley, one of the most active of the new merchants. Since Woolley's complaints against Andros were well known to Werden, his partner Lewin was not an unbiased investigator. In fact his appointment was a victory for the merchants.[69]

Lewin's commission empowered him to investigate all aspects of revenue collection and trade. An accompanying set of instructions gave him sweeping investigatory powers.[70] There was one important exception. York specifically denied him the right to administer oaths. Only after local magistrates had administered an oath could he take testimony. It was a critical omission that proved useful to Andros's friends.

Lewin arrived on 16 October 1680 to find that Andros was in Boston. When the latter returned Lewin was able to publish his commission and set about his year-long investigation.[71] He collected evidence and testimony primarily in New York City and Albany, paying scant attention to the rest of the colony. He was unwelcome in some quarters and in one case he met with open resistance. When he went to Albany, the council ordered the *commissaries* to collect information about landholdings and quitrents prior to his arrival. Words of warning preceded him. Stephanus Van Cortlandt wrote to his sister Maria:

Capt. Lewen does not go up [the river] to deprive anyone of his rights, or to abridge the same, but to inquire into the Duke's revenues and the situation of the trade and commerce in his highness' territories, and also to inquire whether any one has any complaints against Governor Andros, whether in general or particular, against which I hope you will guard yourself, even if you should have reason thereto. Be pleased also to admonish Mr. Marten Gerritsz [Von Bergen] when he is in discourse with Capt. Lewin and mention is made of the governor, not to say anything to the detriment of Sir Edmund, but to say that all he did was for the best interest of the entire province, for they intend. . . .[72]

It is unfortunate that several lines are obliterated after "for they intend," as it would be interesting to know who "they" were and what they "intended." Albany was a special target because of the way the English merchants had been treated there. Maria Van Rensselaer conferred with Lewin a number of times about the status of Rensselaerswyck and reported to her brother-in-law, Richard, that Lewin was very interested in complaints against Andros. She went on to write that "there are many complaints" and that she hoped he would not return as governor.[73]

In New York City the obstructions placed in Lewin's way were more obvious. Frederick Philipse complained to the mayor's court that Lewin was collecting depositions illegally. Lewin had administered oaths in violation of his instructions and the law, since only the magistrates had that power. After hearing evidence, the mayor and aldermen complained to the acting governor, Captain Anthony Brockholls, that, while they were willing to help Lewin, he had acted contrary to law and had caused great "confusion" and "disorders" with his irregular proceedings.[74] With this sort of politicking going on, it is no wonder that Lewin's report is as much a political document as an economic one.

In December 1681, John Churchill, the duke's solicitor general, presided at a hearing called in London to consider the report. Present at the meeting were Lewin, Andros, Dyre, Mathias Nicolls, Edward Antill, and a Mr. Robinson.[75] Lewin's report attacked Andros and Dyre. He accused them of withholding records, of making up others especially for him, and of collecting taxes without keeping records of disbursement. Quitrents he found impossible to investigate because the records were so confused. Because of these factors he could not accurately estimate the total tax revenues except that the testimony of Edward Griffeth and other merchants indicated that the customs ought to be £5,600 a year.[76] Lewin found New York's trade a tangled web of favoritism and dissimulation. He charged that illegal trade was common, as was the practice of not charging full duties on imports. These practices were blamed on Andros and two others—Frederick Philipse and Stephanus Van Cortlandt. Disregarding the English in Andros's circle, such as Delaval, Nicolls, and Laurence, Lewin centered his attack on the two Dutchmen. He charged that as friends of Andros and his trustees·in trade matters they were allowed to trade illegally with the Netherlands and given special treatment at the customshouse. Others, outside the governor's circle, were forced to pay the full amount of taxation and had goods held in the customshouse to hinder their trade.[77] As a result of this policy English merchants suffered and English immigration was hindered. Lewin probably overlooked the English friends of Andros to give his report more effect. He obviously represented the interests of the new English merchants who were the most upset by the presence of cheap Dutch goods. In summary, Lewin accused Andros of cronyism, cheating, lying, arbitrary procedures, and private gain (before the duke's profits).

Andros denied everything and stressed his accomplishments.[78] He had rebuilt the fort, constructed a new mole, and greatly improved trade. The last meant an increase in shipping, more goods, and more money for the colony. This produced an increase in revenue that he had assiduously collected and accounted for. In answering some of Lewin's specific accusations, such as those relating to Long Island rates or the customs, Andros placed the responsibility on the sheriffs and the collectors. In turn, he attacked Lewin for refusing to cooperate with the government and for not revealing his instructions after he landed. As for the charge of favoritism, he curtly dismissed it. The result of the hearing was that both Andros and Dyre were exonerated but not returned to their offices.

The Lewin report and other contemporary accounts reveal the sources of discontent in New York. Van Cortlandt's warnings and Philipse's attempts to cast doubt on Lewin's evidence could not stop Lewin from gathering damaging testimony against Andros. The latter's arbitrary conduct outraged many people who would have agreed with one dissident who wanted to know if the "Governor was under the law," or with another who felt "a Justice of the peace may do as he pleases and noe man dare say anything to him, for if he did he was sure to be ruined."[79] Lewin acted as a lightning rod to attract and absorb the accumulated discontents and resentments.

The Impact of Andros's Recall

The recall of Andros was an important event for three reasons. First, it revealed all of the simmering discontents engendered by Andros's administration. Charges of favoritism toward the "court" faction, the establishment of monopolies, and general malfeasance all received a public airing in New York and England. Very few individuals regretted Andros's leaving, while many rejoiced at the possibility of forcing York to reconsider the course of the proprietary. After all, it was York who had brought Andros home to England and sent out an investigator. Andros's misfortune caused a flutter of hope among the colonists, who saw the possibility that some of their desires —especially an assembly—might now become a reality.

Second, the recall revealed the political influence of the London merchants. The government of Charles II favored the great trading companies and the passage of the Navigation Acts. As a result, the merchant community gained access to power in court and Parliament. Their single-minded policy was to bring wealth to England, and themselves, by exploiting markets the world over. Whenever they ran into opposition from local interest groups in a colony, they shrewdly used their influence to gain the upper hand.[80] This is the process that occurred in New York when the London merchants decided to invade the market. Andros's zeal in persecuting them to protect local merchants probably came as a surprise. However, their vengeance was quick and total. Combining their complaints with those of Englishmen outside the city clique, they painted a very bad picture of conditions in New York. The upshot was Andros's recall—a stunning example of their political clout.

Third, after having Andros recalled, London merchants exploited their victory. In 1682, the year after the hearing, five ships sailed for New York. As the merchants increased trade they also added a new group to the city's population. Men such as John Robinson, James Graham, and Charles Lodwick entered political life.[81] Under Andros's successor, Governor Thomas Dongan, they all found their way into office, broadening the elite group during his administration. They did not eclipse those Dutchmen, such as Philipse and Van Cortlandt, who were well established, but their entry closed opportunities to other Dutchmen.

A subtler effect of the growth of English trade was the effect on the Dutch psyche. The Dutch retained a strong position after 1664, because of trade with the Netherlands and a majority position in the population. The entry of more and more English goods and merchants, backed up by political power in England, diminished the Dutch position. As will be seen in the next chapter, other changes in the Dutch community created fears for the future in the face of Anglicization.

6 ✑ The Consequences of Social Change

The London merchants represented external pressure upon New York's political and economic system. After 1674 two major internal developments also influenced the proprietary: the changing social structure, particularly the distribution of wealth, reveals the growing economic power of New York City, while the Dutch community felt increasing pressures from the continuing process of Anglicization. The effects of both of these trends were not as dramatic as the intrusion of the London merchants. However, as problems mounted in New York during the 1680s their impact would help shatter the colony.

The Development of New York Society

A coherent view of New York society becomes possible for the years after 1674 because of a rising number of tax and census records generated by local government in response to demands of the central government. It is, however, a snapshot that captures only a few aspects of life. Mobility patterns are difficult to ascertain, as are the colors and textures of daily life. One thing immediately obvious, even under these conditions, is the variety of community life in New York. Perhaps the most illustrative extremes are Southampton and Albany. Founded by New England Puritans, Southampton conformed to many of the stereotypes of New England communities: a few streets of weathered clapboard houses sheltering a stern congregation playing out the dynamics of puritanism in America. In other regards it did not conform, for Southampton's whalers and Indians pursued the great whales for their oil and attracted merchants from New York City and Boston eager to exchange manufactured goods for the boiled-down residue of their catches.

The products of the sea and the land made Southampton the wealthiest town on Long Island. As the sea was the source of much of Southampton's wealth, Albany derived its income from the endless rivers and lakes to the west. The Hudson was the most important waterway. In the winter it was a wild and lonely expanse of ice; spring brought wracking floods, but in the summer it was a highway to the Indians, traders, merchants, and ordinary folk who plied its waters. Summer also brought the active trading season in furs and the expanding grain trade. Indians surrounded its palisaded defensive perimeter to barter, drink, and exchange news. At the foot of the hill on which clustered a fort, a few stone houses in the Dutch style, and many wooden structures, sloops tied up to take away the furs and grain. Autumn slowed the pace of commerce as winter's threats dispersed the traders. Another winter of heavy drinking inevitably followed.

In each and every community a small shard of European society played out its destiny in the New World. The daily interplay of social, political, and religious heritages confined within these small communities is largely beyond recovery; only a few statistics are left to describe the life of thousands. Their physical characteristics were obliterated by the detritus of industrial society.

Four growing centers of population existed within the proprietary: New York City, the Albany area, the Esopus towns, and Long Island.[1] The few tax and census records that survive provide information on the size of the communities and, somewhat less accurately, the distribution of wealth. Other characteristics of the society are difficult to reconstruct. One exception, however, was the continuing tension between the English and the Dutch.

Information on Albany's social structure is sparse. A surviving census for the city and county taken in 1687 and an assessment list for the city made in 1679 are all that remain. The census gives the total population for the county as being 2,144, but it lacks a breakdown for Albany and the three outlying settlements—Kinderhook, Claverack, and Schenectady.[2] The population was divided between 1,059 white males and 928 females, with 157 "negroes" (107 male and 50 female) completing the total. A census taken in 1698 refers to a census of 1689,

Table 1. Palisade Assessment in Albany, 1679

Rods of Fencing	Number and Percentage of Inhabitants
6	1 (0.7%)
5–5½	8 (5.4%)
4	8 (5.4%)
3–3½	31 (20.9%)
2–2½	49 (33.1%)
1–1½	51 (34.4%)
	148

stating that on the latter date there were 662 men, 340 women, and 1,014 children for a total population of 2,016 in the city and county.[3] This second estimate shows a 2-to-1 ratio of men to women, which is to be expected in a frontier community. Albany's single extant tax list, compiled to assess wooden palisades for rebuilding the fortification of the town in 1679, gives only an intimation of the town's social structure.[4] It assesses 148 individuals, considerably short of the total number of taxables in the community. For example, three of the five approved cartmen, one of the three schoolmasters, and the watchman are omitted. In addition, some of the men on the list cannot be considered members of the community. Two of the new English merchants (George Heathcote and Samuel Wilson) and city merchants such as Frederick Philipse, Cornelius Steenwyck, and Thomas Delaval owned homes in Albany only to qualify for participation in the fur trade.[5] The part of the population enumerated appears in table 1. The manner in which the list is couched makes it difficult to analyze the distribution of wealth. It would appear that the individuals on the list were those of some status in the community and that laborers and some farmers were excluded.

Few records susceptible of analysis survive for the Esopus River Valley towns (Kingston, Hurley, and Marbletown). A militia roll for the region taken in 1686 has 204 names. Another compilation made in 1689, when an oath was required of all males, lists 189 individuals to whom the oath was administered and 34 who were absent or refused to take the oath, for a total of 223.[6] These lists indicate a population of 1,020 to 1,115 for the towns by 1689. Kingston was the largest of the three towns, acting as the transshipment point for the region's wheat and other foodstuffs. It attracted such merchants as Thomas Delaval, Nicholas De Meyer, John Ward, and Cornelius Steenwyck from the city.[7] As agricultural communities, Hurley and Marbleton lacked the men of substance or the occupational diversity of Kingston. Without tax records, a profile of wealth for these communities is impossible.

Better records exist for analyzing the social structure of the Long Island towns. Tax lists compiled in 1675 survive for eleven towns, for five towns in 1676, and for seventeen towns in 1683.[8] These lists exist in various states of completion; some give nothing more than the town's total assessment, others have individual assessments, and the most valuable break down individual assessments into land, polls, and animals. It appears that all concerned ignored the Duke's Laws that stated that polls (all males over sixteen) plus all real and personal property on land and sea were subject to assessment.[9] A comprehensive law, it exempts only the aged, yearling cattle, harvested crops, and common meadowland. Since the law was not fully applied, men engaged in nonagricultural practices were underassessed. Few men in the Long Island towns, however, made their living completely from nonagricultural occupations. Still, some men went underassessed, particularly those with holdings outside their towns of residence. For example, William Lawrence of Flushing, assessed at approximately £220 in 1698, left an estate valued at £4,432 five years later. Even with this gross underassessment, it should be noted that he was fifth in assessed valuation in the town.[10] Thus, the tax lists are a poor guide to a man's total valuation but probably reflect his status in the community. Taxes were the responsibility of the whole community and the elected assessors and magistrates could not safely disregard the welfare of the town to satisfy a few individuals. The tax lists, therefore, are a valuable source of information about the number and economic status of the members of the towns.

In 1683 the population of Long Island was approximately 5,640. The towns ranged in size from the recently founded Smithtown, with 35 people (all named Smith), to Southampton, with 715. Southampton, the third largest center in the province, was exceeded in size only by Albany and New York City. The average Long Island town had 332 inhabitants. A sizable difference existed between the five Dutch and twelve English towns. The Dutch towns were much smaller, averaging 210 citizens to the 383 in the English towns. Little intermingling occurred between the two nationalities. Few English towns contained Dutch inhabitants, while only three of the Dutch towns have English surnames on their tax list: New Utrecht (2), Flatbush (2), and Brooklyn (1). Geographic isolation partly explains the lack of intermingling. Slightly over one hundred miles separated the Dutch towns from those at the eastern end of the island. However, of the four towns sharing common boundaries with the Dutch communities, Dutch families resided only in Gravesend and Newton. Jamaica and Hempstead remained aloof from their neighbors.

The Dutch towns, while smaller, had a much higher average acreage per taxable than did the English. They averaged 50 acres per taxable, while the seven English towns for which records for 1683 survive averaged only 24 acres. These averages are much lower than those in similar towns in New England.[11] The suspicion is that the law was not fully obeyed in reporting land ownership and that the towns kept all meadowland in common, out of range of the assessors. For example, when Jamaica's townspeople divided their land in 1656 each man got a 6-acre house lot, 10 acres for farming, and 20 acres of meadow. Later divisions expanded these holdings, but in 1683 the average farm contained only 18 acres of taxable land. Only five men had farms over 50 acres and none had over 70 acres.[12] Such relatively small farms in new communities leave the suspicion that townspeople held land off the tax rolls.

A sizable number of individuals did not own land. Besides the servants and working male children listed as polls, 15 percent of the taxables were landless in the English towns. In the Dutch towns this figure was 19 percent and, if Flatbush is removed, the remaining four towns averaged 24 percent. This statistic might explain the low populations in the Dutch towns. With such a high proportion of landless men, many young men may have sought employment in New York City rather than remain at home in these older communities. It was from the western area of Long Island that Governor Andros received petitions from young men pleading for land.[13]

There is one other interesting point to note about land ownership. Land in cultivation varied greatly from village to village. The acreages ranged from 3,094 acres in Flatbush to 701 acres in Easthampton. Considering that Easthampton had the fourth highest assessment on Long Island, such a small acreage for 71 taxables is intriguing. The answer lies in the large herds of cattle, oxen, horses, sheep, and swine kept by the townsmen. The town relied heavily on its common meadowland for grazing purposes and tax evasion.[14] The towns that did not attempt to obfuscate their land holdings so blatantly averaged 1,368 acres in working fields.

As a reflection of their greater size, the English towns had the highest assessments on the island. In 1676 the total evaluations of the four highest towns were: Southampton, £13,667; Hempstead, £11,532; Southold, £10,935; and Easthampton, £6,842. By 1683 Southampton, Southold, and Easthampton increased their assessments to £16,328, £10,819, and £9,075, respectively. The assessment list for Hempstead in 1683 is incomplete. Assessed valuations for Long Island towns in 1683 are given in table 2. The most obvious point in this set of figures is that three of the four highest assessments were those of the eastern towns. Among them the three towns contained 27.3 percent of the population of the seventeen towns and had 28.3 percent of the total assessed valuations for fourteen towns reporting in 1683. Population, wealth, and old loyalties spurred their search for independence. Their common interests lay in protecting the prosperity that they had wrested from land and sea.

Quite similar social structures characterized the island towns, as can be seen by comparing five tax lists selected from the nine towns that give an adequate breakdown for 1683 (see table 3). Three of the five towns—Southampton, Jamaica, and Brooklyn—represent the three ridings of Long Island. Southampton was also the largest and most developed town. The others, Flatbush and Oyster Bay, represent the highest and lowest average assessed valuations respectively.

Southampton's social structure reflected its size and wealth; the lowest one-third of the taxables had only 7.9 percent of the

Table 2. Assessed Valuations of Long Island Towns, 1683

Town	Total Valuation in £	Average Individual Assessed Valuation in £
Brookhaven	5,036	95.01
Brooklyn	5,793	91.95
Bushwyck	2,931	101.06
Easthampton	9,075	127.81
Flatbush	7,757	161.60
Flatlands	4,656	122.52
Flushing	6,430	110.86
Gravesend	3,291	109.00*
Hemptstead	11,532	n.a.**
Huntington	6,710	95.85
Jamaica	6,620	79.75
Newton	6,320	77.00*
New Utrecht	5,240	169.00
Oyster Bay	4,836	61.21
Smithtown	1,340	191.42
Southampton	16,328	114.18
Southold	10,819	110.39

*Taken from a 1675 tax list as no 1683 list has survived.
**1676 total assessment without individual breakdown.

Table 3. Vertical Distribution of Assessed Taxable Wealth in Selected Long Island Townships, 1683 (Number of Taxpayers and Percentage of Total Assessed Wealth

	Lowest 30%	Lower-middle 30%	Upper-middle 30%	Upper 10%
Southampton	43 (7.9%)	43 (19.1%)	43 (44.4%)	14 (28.5%)
Jamaica	25 (11.90%)	25 (25.9%)	25 (42.0%)	8 (21.2%)
Brooklyn	18 (10.0%)	18 (26.4%)	18 (40.0%)	6 (22.6%)
Oyster Bay	24 (15.8%)	24 (23.4%)	23 (41.8%)	8 (18.8%)
Flatbush	15 (18.2%)	15 (25.4%)	15 (37.6%)	8 (19.0%)
Totals	125 (12.8%)	125 (24.0%)	124 (41.2%)	44 (22.0%)

total assessed valuation as compared to an average of 14.3 percent in the other four towns. At the other end of the scale, the top 10 percent controlled 28.5 percent of Southampton's wealth, while in the other towns the same group averaged only 17.9 percent. In the other two categories the towns are quite similar. The broad middle section represented by these categories controlled over 60 percent of the assessed wealth in each town. Few individuals with sizable assessments lived on Long Island. Only 178, or 16.1 percent of all taxables, had assessments over £150 (see table 4). Southampton led the way with 40, Flatbush followed with 24, and then only Easthampton (23), Southold (19), and Flatlands (12) had over 10. Southampton was further distinguished by having four of five assessments over £400. This pattern of distribution of wealth is comparable to that of other colonial towns of this era.[15]

Comparing these figures with New York City tax lists puts them in an entirely different light. A number of assessment rolls survive for the city. The 1664 tax for quartering the soldiers has already been mentioned. In 1672 Lovelace collected "contributions" for the rebuilding of the fort and Colve did the same in 1674. In 1676 Andros charged a general rate for construction of a new mole. One year later the city charged a tax on real estate to help defray a growing debt.[16] The 1665 list noted 254 names and the lists of 1672, 1674, and 1676 recorded 139, 62, and 313 respectively. The census of houses in 1677 listed 369 homes. This list and that of 1676 are valuable for estimating population. On the basis of the figure of 313 taxables (and multiplying by the conversion factor of 6), the probable population was 1,876.[17] This is a conservative estimate since, as will be explained shortly, not everyone was on the list. The 1677 tax on houses is probably a better gauge of population since it is difficult to imagine many persons not living in taxable dwellings. A total of 369 houses were taxed; once again using a conversion factor of six, a population of 2,214 is indicated.

Of the five lists, only two will be used here to estimate the distribution of wealth. The 1664 list contains no assessments, but some idea of the stratification of wealth can be gained by examining the distribution of the taxpayers among seven top categories (see table 5). Thus, in 1664 the lowest 30 percent of the taxpayers paid 6.6 percent of the tax, the lower-middle 23.1

Table 4. Distribution of Taxables over £150 in Long Island Towns, 1683

Assessments	Number of Individuals
£150–199	76
£200–249	50
£250–299	27
£300–349	14
£350–450	11

Table 5. Distribution of Taxables in New York City, 1664

Tax Rate in Guilders	Number and Percentage of Individuals	Tax Collected in Guilders
0	53 (20.8%)	0
1	83 (32.6%)	83.0
1.10	13 (5.1%)	14.3
2	72 (28.3%)	144.0
2.10	9 (3.5%)	18.9
3	10 (3.9%)	30.0
4	14 (5.5%)	56.0
	254	346.2

percent, the upper-middle 44.2 percent, and the top 10 percent paid 26 percent.

The tax list of 1676 reveals much more because it contains assessments of wealth. A few cautionary notes should be observed. Not everyone was assessed; the members of the city council exempted themselves and provincial officials such as Mathias Nicolls and William Dyre. This exclusion of approximately twelve men from the upper stratum distorts the curve of wealth distribution in the direction of greater equality than actually existed. The poor and lower class provided a further source of distortion. The lowest assessment was £50, far more than many laborers and small artisans could acquire. An indication that these men were exempted from the tax can be gained by cross-checking the tax list with two lists of carters in 1677 and 1678.[18] These men monopolized the hauling of goods in the city and required a cart and horse to do their work. Of the fifteen men known as carters, four were assessed £50 and two £100, while nine were unlisted. It appears the taxation list excluded most day laborers and small artisans.

The total assessed wealth of New York City in 1676 was £95,861.[19] The distribution of this wealth differed from that of Long Island towns (see table 6). Instead of the middle 60 percent of the taxables holding over 60 percent of the total assessed value, their share in New York City was a significantly lower 41.9 percent. The wealth of the upper 10 percent shows an even more dramatic difference. On Long Island the top 10 percent controlled 21.3 percent of the assessed wealth. In New York City the figure is 51.0 percent. Another contrast is in the lowest 30 percent bracket. In the city this group had 5.9 percent of the assessed wealth, but on Long Island the figure is over twice as much at 12.3 percent. If provincial officials, laborers, sailors, and others excluded from the assessment were included, the distribution of wealth would be even less equitable.

Interesting contrasts can be made with Boston and Philadelphia. A very complete tax list for 1687 describes the property holdings of 1,036 taxables in Boston.[20] Though it is a much more complete enumeration than that for New York and was compiled a decade later, it shows a pattern of wealth distribution slightly less stratified than that of New York (see table 7). Philadelphia, on the other hand, had a far more even distribution of wealth in the tax list of 1693. Only 3.5 percent of the taxables in Philadelphia were assessed over £500 as compared to 16.6 percent in New York. At the other end of the scale, 44.3 percent were taxed less than £100 in Philadelphia as compared to 55.5 percent in New York.[21] New York City, therefore, had a more highly stratified distribution of wealth than its competitors.

Table 8 clearly shows the rising wealth of the merchant community of New York City. A comparison of the city's taxable wealth in 1664 with that of the Long Island towns in 1683 shows a similar distribution of wealth. However, by 1676 the advantages granted to the city by the governors had enriched the merchant community enormously. The top 10 percent groups are no longer comparable as the city's elite now held 51 percent of the taxable wealth.

Table 6. Vertical Distribution of Wealth in New York City, 1676

	Number of Taxpayers	Total Assessed Valuation by Group	% of Total Assessment
Lowest 30%	94	£ 5,639	5.9
Lower-middle 30%	94	£10,100	10.4
Upper-middle 30%	94	£31,200	31.5
Upper 10 %	31	£48,922	51.0
	313	£95,861	

Table 7. Highest Assessed Valuations of Boston and New York

	% of Taxables	% of Taxable Wealth
Boston (1687)	top 15	52
New York (1676)	top 15	65
Boston	top 5	27
New York	top 5	39

Table 8. Vertical Distribution of Assessed Taxable Wealth Comparing Long Island Towns and New York City

Percentage of Taxpayers	New York City, 1664	Long Island Towns, 1683	New York City, 1676
Lowest 30%	6.6	12.8	5.9
Lower-middle 30%	23.1	24.0	10.4
Upper-middle 30%	44.2	41.2	31.5
Upper 10%	26.0	22.0	51.0

The merchants' wealth was built upon control over New York City's commerce and increasingly in penetrating regional markets. For some time they had extended their control of prices and the flow of goods to local traders. Evidence of this can be seen in the records of the assize and sessions courts, which are filled with suits against local traders.[22] The merchants were also buying land in towns in order to gain economic privileges, putting even greater pressure on local traders.[23] The great stone houses erected in the city symbolized the rising fortunes of the merchants and aroused jealousy in the towns.[24] Friction between the regions and the city would become more pronounced as the economy faltered during the 1680s.

Patterns of Mobility

The limited materials extant resist analysis of mobility patterns. It can be ascertained that one group, bilingual men, had an advantage. There are two outstanding examples—Nicholas Bayard and Robert Livingston. Both were bilingual and used their talents to enter government, and they used their positions in government as a means of advancement.

Livingston arrived in Albany from Scotland via New England as factor for Boston merchants.[25] His knowledge of Dutch, acquired during a prolonged stay in Rotterdam, gained him the position of Albany city clerk. The gradual Anglicizing of New York required someone who could keep records and translate in both languages. He later added the office of city tax collector. With his profits, salaries, and fees he gradually built a modest estate. He augmented his fortune when he married Alida Van Rensselaer, widow of Nicholas Van Rensselaer. After his marriage Livingston's career as a merchant and landowner progressed rapidly.

As Peter Stuyvesant's nephew, Nicholas Bayard enjoyed immediate status when he arrived in New Amsterdam. His first reward was the office of English secretary. After 1664 he continued as the secretary to the mayor's court and added the offices of surveyor of customs, treasurer, and vendu-master. The profits of office were considerable as his earnings as vendu-master could reach four hundred guilders in one day. He, too, entered trade, on occasion as the partner of Cornelius Steen-wyck.[26] Parlaying a knowledge of language into officeholding, both men entered careers that led to positions of great influence in their later lives.

The Problem of Anglicization

The ethnic balance of New York slowly changed after 1674. The Dutch were still the great majority in those areas they had settled. Above all, they dominated the Hudson River Valley from New York to Albany. Nevertheless, there were changes in New York City. The tax list of 1676 reveals a dramatic increase in the number of English residents. Of the 313 taxables in 1676, 115 were English. From a mere handful in 1664, the English had become more than one-third of the taxable population. It is probable that their numbers were diluted in the total population because the bulk of the untaxed members were Dutch, but already they were a significant group. Andros regarded a merchant with an estate over £500 as a "substantial" man.[27] Of the forty-eight men with such estates in 1676, twenty-two were English. Most were the newly arrived English merchants whose impact was not just political.

Elsewhere it is difficult to judge if significant numbers of English people entered the colony. Staten Island experienced an influx in the 1670s when the island was developed to keep it from falling under the control of New Jersey. Englishmen acquired most of the land grants.[28] Whether these men were new immigrants coming over on the more numerous English ships or just young men looking for farmland of their own is difficult to ascertain. However, it would seem that a system of headrights, instituted by Andros in 1675 and sent to England to attract a large number of immigrants, failed in its purpose. Governor Thomas Dongan reported that only twenty English, Scotch, or Irish families immigrated to New York between 1680 and 1687.[29] Dutch immigration is similarly difficult to judge. One piece of evidence indicates that very few new immigrants arrived from the Netherlands. A list of those taking a loyalty oath in the five Dutch towns in Kings County includes information about the individual's status as native born or immigrant. There are 280 names, of which 138 are natives and 142 immigrants. Of the immigrants, only six had arrived within the past decade. The overwhelming majority arrived before 1664.[30] The only major influx of new planters that left solid evidence was that of the French Huguenots, who arrived in the 1680s. After 1685 more and more French men and women were given permission to enter the commercial life of the colony. Then, in 1687 a petition by the French sent to Governor Dongan requested the status of denizen for the new immigrants. Dongan fulfilled their desires and the steady flow of French immigration continued enriching New York's ethnic mix.[31]

Ethnic tension between the English and Dutch remained undiminished. Open brawling between the two groups abated, but new dimensions of conflict opened up.[32] To Long Island it still appeared that the city was Dutch, that the government was heavily influenced by the Dutch, and that the economic monopolies the city enjoyed benefited the Dutch. Such economic jealousy fired the discontent of the English on Long Island. Of far greater significance were the pressures exerted on the Dutch community. After the Treaty of Westminster any hope of their returning to the control of the Netherlands had to be discarded. On arriving in New York Andros did nothing to relieve their anxieties. He not only excluded the Dutch from the government but also banished Dutch as a legal language in the courts. The long and agonizing process of Anglicization was accelerating. English institutions penetrated into more areas of Dutch life, forcing either conformity or resistance to intrusion. The struggle was painfully apparent in two areas—political rights and control over the Dutch Reformed church.

On 13 March 1675 Andros issued a proclamation announcing that an oath of fidelity and allegiance must be taken by all residents.[33] Nicolls had imposed such an oath in 1664 and Andros found himself confronted with the same problems as those that afflicted Nicolls. The articles of surrender of 1664 were still taken by the Dutch community as an affirmation of their rights and privileges. Unlike their English neighbors on Long Island they never protested to the government on the abstract basis of the rights of Englishmen, but upon the specific written guarantees in the articles. This was their protection against arbitrary interference with their freedom.

On 15 March an imposing group of Dutch leaders appeared before Mathias Nicolls, who was wearing his hat as mayor of New York City.[34] Cornelius Steenwyck, Johannes Van Brugh, Johannes De Peyster, Nicholas Bayard, Jacob Kip, Eagidius Luyck, William Beekman, and Anthony De Milt were all leading political figures, having held office in Dutch and English governments. Speaking for themselves and "diverse others," they desired a confirmation of the privileges granted by Governor Richard Nicolls. Four were specifically enumerated—liberty for their church, freedom from being impressed, retention of their own inheritance customs, and the right not to take up arms against their own nation. When confronted by the same demands Governor Nicolls had solved the problem by guaranteeing that nothing in the oath abrogated the articles.

Andros was a different man. He met with the eight Dutch leaders later on the same day they appeared before Mathias Nicolls. They pressed for an affirmation of the articles or for permission to take the same oath the English took from Colve in 1674. After mulling over their proposition, Andros called them back and insisted upon his loyalty oath. The eight left without subscribing to it. The next day they petitioned Andros, pleading their cause once again and stating that they were not mutinous—a charge Andros probably threw at them. By this time one of the protesters let it be known he would leave New York if their demands were not met. Called before the council on 18 March and put to the question again, the eight remained unwilling to compromise and were sent to jail. Cautious men now came forward to take the oath. Since Andros could not afford to punish the eight for fear of alienating the Dutch completely, he formed a special committee of council members to consider the matter. They recommended, and Andros approved, a £200 bail and an appearance before the next court of assize. Johannes De Peyster reconsidered his position and capitulated, leaving seven to appear at the assize.[35]

The court of assize met on 6 October. A group more inimical to Dutch interests can hardly be imagined. Members of the council and Andros's hand-picked government for the city were joined with the justices from the three ridings of Yorkshire and those of Albany, Esopus, Delaware, and Schenectady. Of the twenty-five men in attendance, only the three from Albany and Schenectady and one from the west riding were Dutch. All twelve men of the jury were English, mostly from Long Island. One can only think that they must have relished the opportunity to try a group of New York City Dutch merchants. The results of the trial were inevitable. All of the recalcitrant Dutch were found guilty of promoting rebellion. Adding salt to their wounds, the jury convicted them of trading illegally because they were aliens who had not taken the oath. The punishment meted out was the seizure of all goods and chattels.[36]

This turn of events stunned the seven protesters and created an angry mood among the Dutch. They undoubtedly questioned the trial and its verdict because the men were refused permission to sell their estates and leave prior to the trial.[37] The comments of the convicted caused the council to summon them to a meeting on 29 October. At that meeting Nicholas Bayard's remarks were considered so intemperate that he was placed in the "Hole" and not released until 1 November. When the remaining six were questioned about their satisfaction with the judgment, they demanded an appeal, which the council granted, but only to the assize.[38] Steenwyck and his companions were undoubtedly thinking of an appeal to England. Their chances of success there, however, were about the same. In the spring they had sent a petition to the States General asking intercession with the English government on their behalf. Ambassador Van Beuningen protested at the English court, but he was rebuffed.[39] Afterward Sir John Werden wrote to Andros stating that the duke "would have you endeavor upon all occasions to keepe ye people in due obedience and subjection, and all inclinations towards mutiny severely supprest."[40] Thus ended any hope for the duke's clemency. With no hope of intercession or a pardon, the full threat of the assize sentence loomed before them. Faced with the loss of everything, they submitted and asked to take the oath. Their submission was accepted and the punishment reduced to the confiscation of one-third of their estates.[41]

This bitter trial left scars on some of New York's leading merchants. The economic and political careers of the seven representatives of the Dutch community were curtailed. Steenwyck, the most prominent man in the group, did not regain political office until 1683, when he became mayor of New York.

Nicolas Bayard suffered a similar fate, for it was 1685 before he returned to office. Luyck and de Milt seemingly left politics, while the others came back to office slowly.[42]

The effects of this controversy on the Dutch community are more difficult to judge. Domine Wilhelmus Van Nieuwenhuysen wrote to the classis of Amsterdam, "The church here does not now increase on account of the unprecedented proceedings against the inhabitants in connection with the change of government. This had excited the hatred and contempt of the rulers against the subjects. I should not be surprised if a large portion of the Dutch citizens should be led to break up here and remove."[43] There is no evidence of a mass exodus and even men like Nicholas Bayard, who threatened to leave, continued to live in New York. The Dutch did retreat from English institutions, particularly the courts. The mayor's court of New York City functioned as the primary court for suits large and small originating in its jurisdiction. Prior to 1674 the records of the city are filled with litigation, the bulk of it between Dutch litigants. After 1674 this pattern changes. Cases involving two Dutch litigants are rare except among the leading merchants.[44] More often than not, when Dutch names appear, the case involves Englishmen. In the courts English control now meant more and more juries and less reliance on arbitrators or referees, procedures favored in Dutch courts. The Dutch disliked juries because the English dominated them. For instance, from November 1681 to November 1682, 71.56 percent of all the jurors were English, 16.17 percent Dutch, and 12.25 percent French.[45] Faced with a legal system filled with English magistrates and English juries, the Dutch withdrew. The residents of the Dutch towns in Kings County similarly avoided the sessions court.[46] The question then becomes, how did they solve their legal problems? It would seem that the consistory of the Reformed church, made up of the deacons and the elders, became the source of justice for the Dutch. The consistory could appoint arbitrators in the old manner and render justice, except in criminal cases where the government was involved. As will be seen later, this is just what the Dutch did in an extremely important dispute within the Dutch community. Avoiding English courts when possible helped maintain the integrity of the Dutch community and contained the effects of Anglicization.

Problems in the Dutch Reformed Church

The Dutch Reformed church lay at the heart of Dutch life. Whenever the Dutch community was threatened, the central demand of the community was the independence of the church. While gaining respect for their church, the Dutch could not protect it from change. The changes forced upon it caused disputes within the Dutch community and between it and the government.

The decade of the 1670s was one of transition for the church. The articles of surrender brought certain guarantees to the church in 1664; nonetheless, changes crept in. The new government did not pay ministerial salaries as the old one had done. Like their English counterparts, the ministers had to rely upon their parishioners, a situation the domines considered demeaning.[47] A more deadly peril came with the passage of time. Johannes Megapolensis was sixty-five in 1669, the same age as his colleague Samuel Drisius of Albany. A church based upon two such aged men was in trouble, as was fully revealed in 1670 when Megapolensis died and Drisius became incapable of holding services.[48] The classis dispatched new ministers to fill the gaps; however, just as they endeavored to establish themselves, a controversy rocked the church. This dispute involved not only liturgical differences, but also the influence of the Catholic proprietor in church affairs.

An important cast of characters opposed one another in a struggle for the leadership of the church in Albany. On one side was Nicholas Van Rensselaer and on the other were Jacob Leisler and his future son-in-law, Jacob Milborne. Van Rensselaer came to New York with Andros with the special blessings of the duke. As a young preacher in Brussels he was said to have prophesied the restoration of Charles Stuart while Charles sat in the congregation. Having endeared himself to Charles by this act, he wisely accompanied the first Dutch ambassador to England after the Restoration. When in England he was ordained in the Church of England and licensed to preach to the Dutch congregation at Westminster. He remained in England during the second Anglo-Dutch war, but after 1671 he planned on going to New York, only to be stopped by war once again. In 1674, when the opportunity arose, he seized it and received a recommendation from York, who ordered Andros to have him called by a Dutch church as a mark of respect. In accordance with the duke's desires, Van Rensselaer was chosen as a pastor to assist Domine Gideon Schaets at Albany. About the same time, after the death of his brother, Jeremias, he became director of the patroonship. He now personified both an economic threat and a religious problem to Albany.[49]

Within a month of taking up his new office Van Rensselaer was challenged by Domine Wilhelmus Van Nieuwenhuysen of New York. Van Nieuwenhuysen questioned his position in the church because he was not ordained by the Classis of Amsterdam, which had jurisdiction over the Dutch Reformed church in New York. Called before the council to defend himself against charges made by Van Rensselaer, Van Nieuwenhuysen denied the competency of his opponent and refused to allow him even to baptize children. In his own defense, Van Rensselaer produced documents relating to his career in England, but it was not until he promised that he would conform his teaching to that of the Reformed church that Van Nieuwenhuysen withdrew his objections.[50] In Albany, however, Domine Gideon Schaets continued to disapprove of Van Rensselaer, and the outcome was a bitter struggle that climaxed in September 1676.[51] By that time Jacob Leisler and Jacob Milborne had become the chief disputants.

Jacob Leisler, born in Frankfort, Germany, was the son of a clergyman. His career is obscure until 1660, when as a twenty-year-old he arrived in New Amsterdam as a soldier in the service of the Dutch West India Company. He managed to enter trade on a small scale but greatly enhanced his prospects when he married Elsje Tymans, a wealthy widow. To secure his wife's estate Leisler entered into litigation with his wife's relatives, including the Bayards and Van Cortlandts, later his opponents in the political arena. He prospered as a merchant, building a far-flung trading network extending from New York to Surinam, Amsterdam, and London. His fortune became considerable and like many of his fellow merchants he took his turn serving as a deacon of the Dutch church or as a juror or adjudicator in the mayor's court. He cooperated with the government of Anthony Colve but did not join with those who clashed with Andros over the rights of the Dutch community.

Up to this point Leisler's career was remarkable for its lack of political activity or notoriety.[52]

Milborne came to America as an indentured servant to a New England merchant, who took him to Barbados and left him with another merchant. He later returned to New England and served out his time for his original master. On leaving service he went to New York where he served from 1668 to 1672 as a bookkeeper for Thomas Delaval. His brother William was an Anabaptist preacher in New England, an indication that the whole family had radical Protestant tendencies.[53]

Van Rensselaer accused Leisler and Milborne in September 1676 of false glosses, improper testimony, defamation, and blasphemy. They, in turn, charged Van Rensselaer with being heterodox and a poor preacher. The dispute disturbed the members of the Albany congregation so much that they called in arbitrators to reconcile the parties. To test both sides, the *commissaries* laid heavy bonds on the parties.[54] Van Rensselaer demanded an appeal to the council, which was denied, and as a result of his vociferous conduct the magistrates confined him to his house. When his situation became known to the council Andros ordered the magistrates to release him and settle the whole affair with a minimum of disruption. However, things had gone too far, as Domine Schaets had entered the quarrel on the side of Leisler. He, in turn, was sued by ten members of the congregation. As tempers flared the *commissaries* tried to follow Andros's order, but the parties remained unreconcilable.[55]

The council now moved quickly against Leisler and Milborne. They ordered Milborne to give £1,000 in security for his conduct, and when he proved unable to get guarantors they took him into custody. A warrant for Leisler's arrest followed when he also failed to post bond.[56] The council took up their case on 23 September with only Leisler present because Milborne remained in jail. Stephanus Van Cortlandt, whose sister Maria was the widow of Jeremias Van Rensselaer, represented Van Rensselaer. The council asked the parties to reconcile themselves and leave the matter of court charges to the governor and council. They refused and the matter was referred again to Albany for a decision. This time the *commissaries* forced the parties to settle their differences. Milborne was now released from custody. If he and Leisler thought the matter finished, they were mistaken. On 23 October the council reconsidered the affair and ordered Leisler and Milborne to pay all the court costs because they were adjudged responsible.[57]

Repercussions from this case continued for some time. Van Rensselaer never found acceptance in Albany and was resented so deeply as the "English" domine that at one point the congregation excluded him from his pew in church.[58] Milborne left New York in November 1677 after a parting blast at the governor and council. Leisler sailed soon after on a trading venture that ended in disaster when Algerian pirates seized his ship. Leisler paid his own ransom of 2,050 pieces of eight and returned home to collect the ransom for his sons, whom he had left behind.[59] The affair with Van Rensselaer thus drove both men out of the colony toward uncertain fates.

There are other aspects to this controversy. One wonders if the objections to Van Rensselaer were not based, in part, on his position as director of Rensselaerswyck. The Van Rensselaer family was unpopular in Albany because it claimed the city was on its lands. What is more important, Van Rensselaer was pushed into a pulpit by Andros and the duke, the latter a Catholic. The sight of a preacher who was in the patronage of the duke and who held a license in the Anglican church must have caused the faithful in the Reformed church to wince. Being English subjects was one thing, but suffering crypto-Catholics in their churches was another.[60]

The Dutch communities of Long Island had their own altercation. Domine Caspar Van Zuuren engaged in a dispute with the local Dutch schoolmaster. After the schoolmaster slandered him, the local church consistory and magistrates decided to fine the schoolmaster. The case soon became a public issue, causing Van Zuuren to fear the interference of the English. To keep the case out of the sessions court, the consistory of New York City took the case under advisement because they too did not want the interference of the English in church affairs. The consistory placed the schoolmaster under bond, but Van Zuuren was affronted by the interference of the New York City consistory in the affairs of his church. Unfortunately, the schoolmaster broke his bond and was brought before Andros, who sent him to jail. When the case came to trial, the judges were of "no religion" in Van Zuuren's eyes and their involvement in the case, which he regarded as a simple matter of ministerial censure, imperiled the freedom of the church. In a letter to the Amsterdam classis he asked, if this sort of thing continued, would the "liberty of the church remain?" Disturbed by these events Van Zuuren believed, "Our church will never be free from English politics." He blamed its problems on the "English Party [literally, the Anglicized people] who destroy our New Netherland."[61] On considering the implications of the case, Van Zuuren returned to the Netherlands.

The "Anglicized people," undoubtedly men such as Van Cortlandt and Philipse, strengthened their grip on the church after Van Zuuren departed. The growing influence of the English was inescapable. When Esopus requested a new minister from the classis, one of the terms set by the council and Andros was that the candidates speak English and Dutch.[62] Under this sort of pressure the clergy gradually changed. The new clergy who emigrated during the 1680s accepted English domination. Henricus Selyns, Rudolphus Varick, and Godfridius Dellius cooperated with the English rather than fight them. Selyns, who replaced Van Nieuwenhuysen in New York City, made friends at the highest levels of leadership. Selyns praised Andros and his successor Thomas Dongan, exchanged visits with them, corresponded with ministers in New England, and wrote of Andros as a friend of the Dutch church.[63] Van Nieuwenhuysen and Van Zuuren would have blanched at such praise for a man they considered an enemy of the church. Van Zuuren denounced the complacency among the new clergy, but their desire to accommodate was too powerful.[64] The new clergy would suffer for not providing proper leadership, for during Leisler's Rebellion their coreligionists drove them into exile or threw them in jail for their support of the English.

Finally, the Dutch were put on the defensive during King Philip's War, an event that influenced English attitudes toward the Dutch. The initial onslaught of the Indians during King Philip's War took a heavy toll of the New England colonists before they regrouped and counterattacked. Connecticut faced the additional strain of Andros's hectoring in Saybrook over the boundary lines. This affair embittered Connecticut's leaders, for in their eyes Andros appeared to be like an ally of King Philip. While not the soul of discretion, Andros did know his duty. Throughout the conflict he fought to keep the allegiance of the Iroquois and other New York tribes.[65] His efforts went totally unappreciated in New England. When rumors reached Connecticut that King Philip was in the vicinity of Albany, the General Court demanded that the Mohawks be sent to capture him. In the same letter they asked Andros to stop trade with the Indians, especially among "the Dutch people, who you [Andros] know are soe much bent upon their profit."[66] In reply, Andros was bitter and sarcastic. They presumed to give him orders, but above all "I cannot omitt yor great reflection on the Dutch. . . . There being none in this Government but his [Majesty's] subjects."[67] The General Court was equally biting, assuring Andros that the Albany traders had indeed supplied their enemies.[68]

In December 1675, the accusation that the Dutch were supplying King Philip was printed in Boston.[69] The New Englanders had developed a conspiracy theory to explain the continuation of the uprising. By supplying the Indians, the Dutch allowed the Indians to continue their depredations, thereby stabbing New England in the back. The truth of the matter can never be known. New York certainly tried to halt this trade, but keeping individuals, particularly the farmers, from making a trade in the forest was impossible. Andros, for his part, demanded the names of any illegal traders, and when William Loveridge, an English resident in Albany, accused the Dutch of trading, the sheriff arrested him on Andros's order. Bound over to the assize to make good his charges, Loveridge failed to do so and as a result suffered heavy fines.[70]

The war forced Andros into the position of defending the Dutch and his government against the deeply suspicious New Englanders. They heaped abuse on him for aiding the uprising. Returning to England for a short visit in 1678, Andros found that the charges made in New England preceded him. The abuse he received forced him to petition the king for relief. As a result the Privy Council defended Andros and called upon the Massachusetts agent to explain the charges. Shortly thereafter the matter was dropped and Andros vindicated.[71] The Dutch, however, remained damned in the eyes of New England as wretched profit-seekers intent on aiding and abetting King Philip.

The Anglo-Dutch Families

Despite the pressures on the Dutch community, some individuals and families among the Dutch had extensive relationships with the English. Stephanus Van Cortlandt and Frederick Philipse are outstanding examples. Neither joined the oath controversy with Andros and, in fact, both shortly became Andros's and later Dongan's chief councilors.

Van Cortlandt was born and raised in New York.[72] His father, Oloff, arrived in New Netherland as a soldier, but shortly thereafter became a carpenter and a trader. After Oloff married a wealthy widow his fortune grew considerably, allowing Stephanus to enter politics and become one of the most important men in New York. During his career he was a *schepen*, officer of militia, alderman three times, first native-born mayor of New York City, director of Rensselaerswyck, and a councilor.

Philipse, one of the wealthiest men in New York, first entered the colony as a butcher and carpenter.[73] He was a contractor for some time before hiring a West India Company sloop to trade in Virginia. He, too, increased his fortune by marrying a widow, Margaret De Vries. She was a merchant in her own right and a factor on her own vessel, the *Margaret*, on at least two trips to Holland. Vigorous and shrewd, she made a fitting wife and partner for Philipse. He developed into a multifaceted entrepreneur, acting as a pawnbroker, land speculator, wampum manufacturer, shipowner, mill owner, fur trader, and merchant in the colonies, Europe, and England. From the time Andros made him a councilor until he left the council in 1698, Philipse was a major figure in New York life.

There is nothing in the life of either man to mark him as especially susceptible to the English. Jacob Leisler's career, for instance, was remarkably similar to that of Philipse. One assumes that some men saw the future belonging to the English and accepted the situation. Others, perhaps more attached to a Dutch way of life and susceptible to atavistic impulses, refused to accommodate.

These two men and their families carried on relationships with the English at a variety of levels other than politics. Jacobus Van Cortlandt, brother of Stephanus, went to Boston to learn English and to trade. Later, he was sent to the West Indies as the family factor, until illness forced his return.[74] Maria Van Cortlandt, widow of Jeremias Van Rensselaer, sent her son, Killiean, to Boston as an apprentice. He disliked the living conditions in Boston, for it was reported that "Killiean is not used to living so plainly as they do there." While he was in Boston two prominent merchants, John Usher and Richard Pattischal, cared for him. Usher later served with Stephanus Van Cortlandt on the council of the Dominion of New England. Some of Maria Van Cortlandt's other children went to live with her sister, Catrina, wife of John Darvall.[75] Darvall and his brother William, both of whom entered trade in New York from Boston, became partners with Thomas Delaval, father-in-law of William.[76] After John Darvall died, Catrina married Frederick Philipse, uniting the Van Cortlandt and Philipse families. Two Philipse children married into the English community, which was an unusual phenomenon.[77] Among similarly prominent families such as the Schuylers, Van Cortlandts, Loockermans, Cuylers, Tellers, and Van Brughs, only two English marriages are recorded out of the first thirty-eight marriages in the second generation.[78] Philipse allied with Englishmen in other ways. In 1672 he purchased the Van Der Donck estate in Westchester in partnership with Thomas Delaval and Thomas Lewis. He gradually bought out his partners and had the land declared a manor. He and Lewis also owned a mill together. When Philipse needed an attorney in Albany, he used Robert Livingston, as did Mathias Nicolls, Anthony Brockholls, and Caesar Knapton, a nephew of Andros.[79] Livingston, in turn, married Alida Schuyler, widow of Nicholas Van Rensselaer. Two of her sisters and one of her brothers married Van Cortlandts. Built up in all these relationships is a developing clan, centered on Stephanus Van Cortlandt and Frederick Philipse. Sending children to Boston and marrying or joining English merchants in business was uncommon among their fellow countrymen. It indicates, however, that both men realized the English were in New York to stay and that they had decided to make the best of it. Their decision brought them wealth, political power, and the leadership of the "English" party in New York politics.[80]

One exception should be noted in discussing intermarriage with the English as a route to power. Jacob Leisler, future leader of the "Dutch" party, married three daughters to Englishmen.[81] While his family pattern resembled that of Van Cortlandt and Philipse and his wealth was as great, he never accommodated to the English political structure.

The four regional centers of New York were developing different patterns of trade and styles of life. Each contained a different economic pattern, ethnic mix, and structure of communal life. While unlike one another, they bore similarities to other communities in the colonies. The towns of Long Island, for instance, mirrored the New England towns from which they sprang. New York City was not unlike Boston in its distribution of wealth, although it had a far more diverse population.

Within and among these developing patterns of community life, sources of serious tension existed. Every community suffered inconsistencies in status, but the situation that elicited the most controversy was the wealth of the city merchants. These individuals, who engrossed more and more of the economic life of the colony, antagonized the people of Long Island and the Hudson River Valley. The hatred of the countryfolk generated an urban-rural tension that created yet another division within the colony. The distrust of the city became a permanent political fact of life. The wealth of the merchants also affected Anglo-Dutch tension. In the eyes of the English of Long Island the wealth and power of the city were in the hands of the Dutch merchants. This only added to their distrust of the central government and the Dutch community.

The Dutch viewed things differently. The constant pressure of English leadership and institutions inexorably squeezed the Dutch community. As the years passed its ability to reverse the process of Anglicization became less effective, particularly in the city. Albany, much more isolated geographically and with a more homogeneous population, would prove more resistant. One result of the pressure was strong atavistic impulses among the Dutch, which would contribute to the events of 1689.

Part III
Change and Crisis

7 ✍ The Experiment with Representative Government

While Andros defended himself in England a power vacuum was created in New York. Anthony Brockholls, a young, inexperienced officer of the garrison, became acting governor. Challenges to his authority started soon after Andros's departure and he quickly crumbled under the pressure. The central government faltered and then lapsed into impotency. Shortly thereafter, the system of taxes and monopolies, so carefully nurtured by the governors, was ignored. Regionalism flourished and protesters clamored for reform, above all an assemby. Fortunately for New York, the duke was in exile under considerable duress. In doubt as to his future, and increasingly doubtful of his legal position, York acquiesced to an assembly. Thus began a brief experiment with representative government.

The Challenge to Authority

Andros did not return to New York after his acquittal although he held his office until 1683, when he was replaced by Thomas Dongan. Until that time he remained under a cloud fighting numerous court battles and defending himself against Lewin.[1] His surrogate fared no better in New York. Captain Anthony Brockholls commanded the Albany garrison. His prior service left him ill equipped for the position of acting governor. He lacked experience and, as one contemporary stated, he also lacked friends.[2] Suddenly he bore the responsibilities of a governor without the necessary authority, in a system that focused on the governorship. Rapid changes in personnel on the council eroded his position evn more. At he beginning of 1681 five men (Mathias Nicolls, William Dyre, William Darvall, Frederick

Philipse, and Stephanus Van Cortlandt) were councilors. By the autumn of the same year only Philipse and Van Cortlandt remained. Nicolls went to England and John West, his replacement as secretary, did not get an appointment to the council. Dyre returned to England to defend himself against a charge of treason. Darvall was removed from office, perhaps for defending his brother-in-law, John Delaval, who contested the collection of taxes in Albany.[3] Thus, by the end of 1681 the only remaining councilors were Andros's closest cronies. Brockholls, therefore, was hampered by his own lack of power and the unpopularity of the two men aiding him in administering the colony.

The centralized nature of the government also created problems for Brockholls. Under normal circumstances the government in the colony was not highly visible. There was no assembly, therefore, no elections to involve the people in the central government. The sessions courts were operated by local men. The annual assize meeting lasted a few days and was a convocation of the governor, the council, justices of the peace, and magistrates from Albany and New York City. The governor appointed all of the members by one means or another and so they were extensions of his authority. At best, the assize was a forum of opinion, but only the opinion of appointed leaders. The most visible symbol of government, therefore, was the governor. Andros's vigor and personality had made him familiar, if unpopular, yet Andros did have the authority to carry out his will. Brockholls, a mere captain of infantry, could not manage the crisis precipitated by Andros's absence. Perhaps a respected council could have helped him, but his rump council was too unpopular. In these circumstances the duke's government all but ceased to exist. Brockholls reported in September 1681 that New York was "a government wholly overthrown and in the greatest confusion and disord'r possible."[4] The government's structural weaknesses were suddenly manifest.

Against the background of a slumping economy, which worsened with poor harvests in 1680 and 1681, Brockholls confronted an unhappy people who challenged the government on the issue of taxes. Andros caused this challenge when he committed the critical mistake of neglecting to renew the customs before he left New York. His instructions empowered him to renew these levies every three years, which he had done in 1677.[5] They lapsed on 1 November 1680 and, in leaving without renewing them, Andros created the perfect opportunity for his enemies, and the enemies of prerogative government, to attack through an assault on Collector Dyre. As the tax collector and close associate of Andros, Dyre was vulnerable. He vigorously pursued those who avoided obeying the Navigation Acts and paying customs. His exertions brought him such notoriety that he was the object of a poetic attack:

> Yr Brother Dyer hath the Divell played,
> Make the New Yorkers at the first affraide,
> He vapoured, swagger'd, hectored (whoe but hee?)
> But soon destroyed himself by Villaine.[6]

His enemies struck while he suffered from a fever and Brockholls was in Albany getting married.[7]

On 26 April 1681 Samuel Winder, acting as attorney for Edmund Gibbons of London, filed suit against Dyre in the mayor's court of New York City on a charge of illegally detaining his cargo for customs. On 9 May another London vessel landed its cargo without paying customs. The merchants, acting in concert, refused to pay customs on any goods that were unloaded thereafter because the government lacked the authority to impose them. Brockholls met with the council and, for unknown reasons, they decided that they were powerless until the duke sent over specific orders. Considering that the busiest time for trade was just beginning, this decision crippled the provincial revenue and left Brockholls the problem of paying the costs of government. He dutifully reported the problem to Werden and stated he could do nothing until he received new orders. In reply to his and the council's evasiveness and lack of decision, York wrote that the council could make temporary orders to restore the customs.[8]

Dyre, in the meantime, was defending himself in court. The trial came to a climax on 31 May when Winder, after winning his case, stood in court and charged Dyre with high treason. The basis of the charge was that Dyre had acted without legal authority in trying to collect customs. The aldermen of the mayor's court (Dyre was mayor) asked Brockholls for advice. He tried to temporize, but the case was brought to the council for a hearing. Unwilling to settle the matter on their own, the councilors committed Dyre to a trial before the court of assize.[9] Dyre, reluctant to wait until its regular meeting in October, requested an immediate special session.

The court of assize must have met with an air of expectancy and excitement.[10] For the first time an official representative of the proprietor was on trial. All of the justices were present, as were all of the aldermen. The court was dominated by local leaders of importance such as Thomas Delaval of Esopus, Major Thomas Willett, John Pell, and Captain John Youngs of Long Island, and James Graham of the city. Of the twenty-five members of the court, only six were Dutch. Before Dyre could be brought to trial, a grand jury was called to hear the evidence of Winder. Only one Dutchman, Cornelius Steenwyck, was on the jury. Englishmen dominated the court and the jury, and the whole session became their affair.

After the grand jury was sworn, Winder's bill against Dyre was read, accusing him of being a "false Traytor" who had "Tratorously Maliciously and Advisedly used and Exercised Regall Power" by imposing illegal customs. After hearing twenty-one witnesses, the grand jury found for the bill and Dyre was taken into custody. Unfortunately, the names of the witnesses are not recorded and an opportunity to identify those who opposed the government is lost. The action of the court did not scare Dyre, as he immediately challenged its right to try him because he held a royal patent equal to the authority of the court. The members of the court debated this point and decided to avoid an embarrassing situation by referring the case to England. Dyre sailed immediately on the ship of the previously victimized George Heathcote. After waiting months in London for the trial to be renewed, he finally appealed to the Crown to put an end to the affair. Samuel Winder, under £5,000 bond to press the case in England, was sought for and when he failed to appear, the charges against Dyre were dropped and he went free.[11]

At the same session of the court that tried Dyre an attack was also made on the mayor's court and, by implication, on the Dutch. The man responsible was John Tuder, who came to New York after 1674 and set up as a tavern keeper.[12] He first ran afoul of the law for allowing gambling in his inn. In November 1679 he was involved in another case before the mayor's court, where the case was decided without a jury trial. Tuder complained about the lack of a jury to Andros, who dismissed his complaint. One of Lewin's accusations against Andros was that he had denied Tuder a fair trial. Tuder took the occasion of the special assize session to get his revenge. He brought an indictment against Francis Rombouts, the mayor at the time of his trial, and aldermen William Beekman, Johannes Van Brugh, Guleyn Verplanck, Peter Jacobs Marius, and unnamed "Associates." The "Associates" were Thomas Lewis and Samuel Wilson, the only Englishmen on the court. Rombouts and the others were accused of being traitors because they did "Trayterously, Maliciously and Advisedly Plott Contrive and Practice Innovacons in Governmt the Subversion and Change of the Knowne ancient and fundamentall Laws of the Realme of England. . . ." The grand jury returned a true bill against Rombouts and the aldermen, but their trial was delayed until the regular session of the assize, at which time they were acquitted.[13]

The grand jury, now with the bit in its teeth, took advantage of the situation to present the special session of the assize with a petition protesting conditions in the colony and requesting an elected assembly. If this were accomplished, the petition asserted, New York would blossom instead of withering. The court decided to endorse the petition and send it to York. In appealing for an assembly and in attacking the proprietary form of government, the petition begged:

. . . in all submissive manner to prostrate ourselves at your royal highness' feet, and represent the miserable and deplorable condition of the inhabitants of this your royal highness' colony, who for many years past have groaned under inexpressable burdens by having an arbitrary and absolute power used and exercised over us, by which a yearly revenue is extracted from us against our wills, and trade grievously burdened with undue and unusual customs. . . our liberty and freedom inthralled, and the inhabitants wholly shut out or deprived of any share, vote, or interest in the government . . . contrary to the laws, rights, liberties, and privileges, of the subject; so that we are esteemed as nothing, and have become a reproach to the neighbours in other of his majesty's colonies, who flourish, under the fruition and protection of his majesty's unparalleled form and method of government . . . the undoubted birthright of all his subjects.[14]

This petition, along with the attack on Dyre and the mayor's court, was an indictment of the proprietary form of government and the administration of Andros. The witnesses against Dyre and the author of the petition are unknown, but there can be little doubt that they were English. The arguments used in the two court cases and in the petition were those of embattled Englishmen fighting for their ancient rights as subjects of the king. It appears that the townsmen of Long Island had joined with the disgruntled new merchants in attacking the government and its Dutch personnel. The government had failed to serve them and to their eyes it functioned primarily for the benefit of the Dutch. Looking at the council and the mayor's court, they saw Dutchmen predominating. No matter that Andros had a circle that included Englishmen; by 1681 only Philipse and Van Cortlandt were left along with Brockholls, who had married a Dutch woman. Excluded from power and kept from trading, the English wanted changes in the form of government. The thirty-nine Englishmen out of the total of forty-six men who served on the assize and on the grand jury represented widespread discontent with Andros and York.

The assize ended on 2 July, having sacrificed Dyre to popular discontent. However, the problem of taxes would not go away. On 5 July Samuel Wilson, an alderman in New York City, refused to pay excise on rum he had brought into Albany. The *commissaries*, refusing to listen to Wilson's argument that there was no law allowing the collection of such an excise, ordered payment.[15] More than a month later, on 29 August, a more serious challenge came before the *commissaries*. Robert Livingston, the excise collector, sued John Delaval, son of the ex-collector Thomas Delaval, for landing and selling 510 gallons of rum without paying the excise taxes. Livingston's case was simple. He had a commission from Andros to collect the excise that Delaval refused to pay. In rebuttal Delaval presented a six-point argument. He asked how Livingston gained this right for himself and, if not for himself, for whom was he collecting revenues? They were all free subjects of the king and "When did the King, lords and commons empower, or invest with such power, a governor of New York to levy taxes on his Majesty's subjects, since such rights belongs to all three of them jointly, and not to one of them alone." He denied owing any taxes and asked the court, "Whether a person who demands a tax or excise which is not warranted by law, should not be deemed a disturber of his Majesty's peace and . . . be proceeded against."[16] The jury unanimously found for Delaval, stating they could find no provision in the laws for the excise tax and thus the law in this case was the order of the governor. The court acquiesced to the decision and referred the case to "supreme authorities" at New York.[17]

The Livingston-Delaval trial did not end tax problems in Albany. Stephanus Van Cortlandt, brother of Maria Van Rensselaer, was acting director of Rensselaerswyck at a time when the colony within a colony suffered from poor crops and a lack of tenants. However, it still was taxed three hundred *schepels* (bushels) of wheat annually plus ordinary taxes. In December 1681 Maria Van Rensselaer informed the *commissaries* that no more taxes would be paid by Rensselaerswyck or its tenants. The magistrates refused to accede to this and ordered the taxes collected, whereupon Van Cortlandt wrote bitterly that they were punctual in observing their own interests but not those of the duke. The *commissaries* delayed collection until Van Cortlandt appeared in Albany in May 1682, when he challenged them to tax the colony. Reversing his previous role as defender of the establishment, Van Cortlandt threatened them with an appeal to the king. Stymied by Van Cortlandt, the *commissaries* did nothing and their financial difficulties grew so great that in June 1682 they had to stop all salaries.[18]

In Esopus, protest meetings were also held and petitions signed. Brockholls sent Thomas Delaval to contain the situation and collect eight hundred guilders in taxes. Lewis De Bois, an old troublemaker and now a justice, led a group of dissidents who quarreled with Delaval over a now unknown problem. De Bois was removed from office, but he remained the center of trouble. The reasons for these protests did not vanish, for Brockholls was still writing letters in April 1683, complaining about the turmoil in Esopus and restoring officers who had been dismissed.[19]

In this steadily worsening situation, it was not long before Long Island joined in the protests. As early as April 1681, Southold had sent a petition to the duke, and Easthampton had appointed two men to meet with representatives of other towns to seek redress of their grievances.[20] These initiatives apparently were not followed by the other towns at the time, as their records indicate no action was taken. By September, just prior to the regular meeting of the court of assize, a meeting was called in Huntington to discuss their "just liberties" promised by Nicolls but never attained.[21]

In response to the call for a meeting, town after town began electing deputies. Hearing of this activity, Brockholls ordered all officials on the island to prevent the "riotous Assembly."[22] Like most warnings from Brockholls, it was ignored, and when the assize met a petition was presented by Captain Josiah Hobart and four other representatives from the "assembly." The court rejected their petition and ordered the representatives home.[23] By this time the assize had had enough of protests. Most of all, it recognized that its own members and other officials were being dragged into court too often. Dyre and Livingston had already been to trial and at its October session in 1681 the assize heard the case of Peter Delanoy, the deputy collector for the province, on appeal from the mayor's court of New York City. In these circumstances the court of assize acted to protect officials in the future. It passed a law requiring two justices to approve suits against officials prior to court action. The court adjourned after threatening those who "Question or Endeavor Innovacon or Alteration or make any other Disturbance in the Government."[24]

Brockholls still would not take vigorous action against his antagonists. He dutifully reported his problems to Werden and Andros, pleading for new orders because the merchants were taking advantage of courts who "Being Scared Refuse to Justifie and maintain my Ord'rs."[25] In reply to his and the council's lack of decision, York wrote that the council could and should make temporary orders on taxes. After rebuking Brockholls, he added, "I wonder you should thus long have left so material a point undetermined."[26]

As these letters were exchanged, further problems emerged. In New York City shortages of bread and grain were reported and the magistrates ran out of money. They also squabbled with Brockholls over a letter he had written John Lewin accusing the board of being "traitors" and of illegally interfering in Lewin's investigation. Until Brockholls apologized they refused to conduct business. Such a weakened government invited further attacks. Suits to revenge old grievances were brought against Andros, Dyre, and Philipse. As a final blow New York City lost its monopolies due to the unwillingness of the regions to obey the old rules.[27]

It was clear that if the situation were to be corrected, it would have to be from the initiative of someone other than the thoroughly cowed Brockholls or his rump council. Their weaknesses, and those of the government, were now thoroughly revealed. If there was a strong governor, such as Andros, the system worked. When there was not, the colony fell into its constituent parts, each trusting its own local government and going its own way. Without a central, elective institution to bind the colony together chaos resulted whenever a strong executive was lacking.

The tax crisis of 1680 did reveal a growing political maturity among the people of New York. Heretofore, only the eastern and central towns of Long Island had protested against the form of government and its arbitrary proceedings. The demand for freedom from "Arbitrary and Absolute power" and "a yearly revenue . . . exacted from us against our wills" was now widespread. The demand also appears to have been mainly English, for they were the chief participants in all the trials. The Dutch remained passive in these affairs, watching from the sidelines while the English colonists carried out their protests. The Dutch happily avoided taxes and outside the city they ignored the monopoly system. Their unwillingness to undertake direct action may be explained on two counts. The Dutch relied upon the surrender agreement of 1664 to confirm their rights. It was over this document that they had confronted Andros. They may not have wanted to switch from this actual document to a more generalized and unfamiliar assertion of rights. Second, the English colonists went no further than challenging the government and then ignoring it. They did not attempt to overthrow the weakened remnants of proprietary government but contented themselves with sending a protest to England that requested an assembly. They knew that matters would ultimately be settled by the duke in England. Recognizing this, the Dutch were undoubtedly reluctant to get involved in the unfamiliar English political scene.

York, meanwhile, moved slowly. He apprised Brockholls that he had "severall things in my thoughts wch I hope may conduce much of ye good and satisfactaccon of all ye inhabitants and tradrs with that government."[28] It took some time for his "thoughts" to appear as policy. The first action he undertook was the hearing that cleared Andros. After his exoneration Andros was eligible for a return to his office. His stay in England and the return of his wife to join him signaled the duke's reconsideration of the affairs of his colony. York, however, delayed in coming to a decision, for he was in exile battling to retain his position as heir and deeply concerned for his own future.

Since Charles II had no legitimate sons, his brother James was heir to the throne. York, however, was anathema to many Englishmen because of his Catholicism. The issue boiled over in 1678. The revelations made by Titus Oates about a Catholic plot against the king cast suspicion on York. While he was exempted from the anti-Catholic Test Act passed in the same year, the pressure on him grew so great he had to withdraw from his offices. Ultimately, the situation became so intolerable that King Charles ordered him to leave England until the anti-Catholic fever diminished. So, in March 1679 James left for Brussels. In August of the same year, when King Charles was dangerously ill, York returned, but when the king recovered he ordered his brother out of England again. This time York went to Scotland. He lived in Edinburgh until March of 1682, when he was finally able to return to England. The duke, therefore, was a troubled man from 1679 to 1682. His political enemies were in the ascendance and his position as heir apparent in doubt. The results were an inattention to affairs in the proprietary and a vulnerability to claims against its territory and privileges. Events in the Jerseys and the founding of Pennsylvania exemplify this.

Brought together initially because of the influence of Admiral Sir William Penn, York and the younger Penn became good friends. At opposite ends of the political spectrum, they were united by their common experience of public harassment because of unpopular religious beliefs. Thus, when Penn petitioned the Crown for a grant verging on New York, the Lords of Trade referred the petition to York, who was disposed to give Penn what he wanted. Apparently against the advice of some of his advisors, York had his secretary, Sir John Werden, make a favorable reply to the lords. The only stipulation he made was that the Delaware settlements remain under his control.[29] In working out a compromise with Penn over the new boundaries, Werden revealed perhaps another cause behind York's willingness to acquiesce to Penn. Werden constantly stressed the lack of knowledge about the area, at one time suggesting to Andros that the duke's title to the Delaware region was invalid and that a new and separate patent might be necessary to insure control.[30] Penn's patent ultimately secured control over the whole region, cutting away more lands from York's original grant.

The problem of the Jerseys emerged again in August 1681, when Werden, in Edinburgh with York, wrote to York's treasurer Sir Allan Apsley hinting at new proposals for New York.[31] Werden requested that Apsley, the duke's lawyer, and the commission of revenue consider the draft of a letter York intended to send to Brockholls. This letter rebuked the latter for not collecting the customs and ordered him to issue a temporary order restoring them. Werden wanted them to ascertain if the duke had the power to order Brockholls to restore the customs. Werden stated that he was unsure if he did; was it, he wrote, "in ye Dukes power lawfully to impose Customs for the future (wch in complyance to Sir Wm Jones his opinion, I begin to doubt)." Apsley and the others were asked to consider the matter and reply quickly. Werden feared that if the customs were enacted and enforced merely on an order from the duke, many colonists would cross "ye river to New Jersey where they may trade freely without being lyable to any such publique paymts." He concluded that if the customs were to amount to anything in 1682, new orders must go to New York very quickly in the new year.

This letter reveals some of York's concerns. It shows that collecting a revenue was still a primary goal. However, the willingness and ability of the inhabitants of New York to challenge and overthrow the tax-collecting machinery caused him to reflect on his powers. He feared that the customs were illegal and that new tax-collecting officials sent from England on the basis of York's patent would be subject to the same problems as Dyre. And, if the colonists still refused to cooperate, they could go elsewhere, leaving the proprietor even greater problems. The presence of assemblies in surrounding colonies was now exerting pressure upon York, as Werden admitted when he expressed fears of an exodus to the politically more salubrious climates of the Jerseys or Connecticut.

Werden's main concern was putting the customs on sounder legal ground. Recent legal opinions in England, which were known in New York, cast doubts on York's powers to tax, especially in the tangled web that characterized the relationship between York, the Jerseys, and New York. In granting the land between the Hudson and the Delaware to Berkeley and Carteret, York never gave them clear rights to govern. Until Andros arrived in New York, the governors sent over by the proprietors governed in peace. Andros, however, attacked Governor Philip Carteret and brought him to trial in New York City.[32] After thrusting Carteret aside Andros organized East New Jersey and harassed Fenwick in West New Jersey.[33] His reason for these actions was the threatened loss of customs revenue from the ports on the Delaware and the Hudson.

When Sir George Carteret died in 1680 it seemed like a good time to challenge the situation. However, because York was in exile and politically weakened he could not ride rough-shod over Carteret's heirs or the trustees of West Jersey. After holding hearings on the question, York, for reasons that are not clear, requested Sir William Jones, a former attorney general who had become a leader of the whig opposition and was no friend of York's, to render an opinion on the customs contro-versy. Jones decided that the customs were illegal because the duke failed to reserve them in his original lease to Berkeley and Carteret. Accordingly, a deed of release to the trustees of West New Jersey was executed, granting away York's remaining rights. Exactly one month later he did the same thing for East Jersey.[34] With these two documents, James relinquished the Jerseys.

Jones figures in another influential battle over colonial rights prior to 1681. In 1677 the Lords of Trade decided to severely restrict the Jamaica assembly.[35] The lords maintained that the privileges of the assembly were derived from clauses written into the governor's commission. To carry out their plan they decided to write Poynings Law into a new governor's commission. This law gave the English government control over the Irish parliament. In Ireland, and hereafter in Jamaica, the assembly would be reduced to approving laws sent from England with no original powers of its own. The Jamaicans objected vigorously to this plan, particularly as it related to revenue bills. If the Crown had its way, taxes would be levied in England and paid in Jamaica. The resistance of the Jamaicans ultimately forced the lords to ask the attorney general and the solicitor general for a legal opinion. Jones, then the attorney general, gave the opinion that the people of Jamaica could be governed only by laws made there under the king's authority. Unhappy with this opinion the Crown consulted Chief Justice North and other judges. Their decision has not survived, but the way in which the lords dropped the plan indicates that the judges decided in favor of Jamaica. So Jones figured prominently in two decisions that limited the prerogative in the colonies. William Penn recorded that Jones believed power followed property and from this it may be assumed that he thought local property owners should decide on their own taxes.[36] His legal opinions weighed upon York and may very well have been the decisive factor in his decision to grant New York an assembly.

Thus York considered the future of the proprietary at a time when his political position was weakened in England, when legal opinions supported the independence of local assemblies, and when New York was in an uproar. The result was a dramatic change in policy.

The Assembly

The first news of a change in policy was announced to Brockholls in a letter of February 1682.[37] In it Werden hinted that he believed York might "condescend" to the desires of the colony for an assembly. He would do so, however, only on the condition that money would be raised to pay off the public debts and provide enough revenue to support the garrison and the government in the future. Brockholls was to sound out the "principall" inhabitants about this proposal, especially as to how to raise money, and get them to certify their opinions by signing them. A month after this letter was sent, long before any reply could come from America, York wrote to Brockholls confirming Werden's hint. The only reason he gave was that "I seeke ye common good . . . and ye increase of their trade, before my advantages to myself."[38] New York was finally to have an assembly.

To carry out the new policy, Colonel Thomas Dongan replaced Andros as governor.[39] He was a member of a family that had acquired lands and titles in Ireland for its loyalty to the Stuarts. As a minor son Dongan embarked upon a career in the army, where he gained preference through the earl of Tyrconnell, a friend of York's. He served for some time as a colonel in the Irish Regiment in France until he was recalled in 1667. A pension was granted to him for his services and then, in 1668, he was appointed lieutenant governor of Tangier. He was unhappy in the African enclave, but in his case, as with many others who served in Tangier, it proved a stepping-stone to higher things.[40] Two years after he returned to England, in 1680, he was made governor of New York. There was one distinction between Dongan and his predecessors—he was a Catholic. This made him a figure of suspicion in New York. Long before he arrived, rumors circulated about his religion and his plans for the construction of a "papist" church. The Dutch, in particular, worried about continuing to practice their religion in peace. None of these fears were to be realized, but they made Dongan an object of suspicion and nurtured the bitter anti-Catholicism in New York.

As governor, Dongan was on the one hand an astute politician and on the other, a profiteer. His correspondence shrewdly analyzed the growing Anglo-French conflict and prescribed a future policy for England. In governing New York, however, he used every possible means to profit from his office. His rapacity gained him few friends.

Dongan's instructions contained very specific orders about the calling of the assembly.[41] The writs of election were to be sent to the sheriffs (not many areas had them), who had to arrange elections within thirty days. The assembly was composed of eighteen representatives from the settled areas of the colony. The powers of the new representatives were less specific. York granted them the right to consider all matters of importance, but the laws they passed were subject to his approval. The governor controlled the assembly sessions, as it was his right to call elections and determine the length of the sessions. In return for the grant of representative government, Dongan's instructions reiterated the duke's strong desire for taxes. The first task of the assembly was to raise money to support the government and the garrison and pay the arrears. In order to do this the assembly had to tighten up the customs service and provide for an assessment of every man's estate prior to a new general tax.

On 13 September 1683 Dongan put his instructions into effect by sending writs to every part of the colony. Pemaquid, Martha's Vineyard and Nantucket, Staten Island, and Schenectady each received one delegate. The towns of the Esopus region were given two, as was Albany (including Rensselaerswyck). Long Island elected six members. To choose these six representatives each town had to pick four delegates to meet with those of the other towns in the same riding. This meeting elected two men to represent the riding. With four seats New York City had the next largest block. The suffrage went undefined in Dongan's order, but later the council stated that only freeholders could vote. They probably retained the definition in the Duke's Laws, allowing only male householders to vote.[42]

As the writs went out and the various elections were held, Dongan received a foretaste of the future. On 3 October the court of assize met in regular session and the officials who attended introduced Dongan to the concerns and desires of each area. At this meeting Dongan's behavior was characterized as filled with "discretion, patience, and moderation, showing in him that principle of honour not wilfully to injure any, and had a regard to equity in his judgements."[43] Easthampton tested his "patience and moderation" when it decided to send an address with the town delegation.[44] The address expressed the hope of the town meeting that Dongan was an instrument of God designed to restore their "freedom and privileges." They instructed their representatives to stand up in the assembly for the maintenance "of our priveledges and English liberties." So positive were they about their own freedoms that they wanted all writs to run in the king's name and not the duke's. As a final statement of independence they asserted that they participated in the elections, not in answer to the writ of the sheriff, but because they refused to miss any opportunity to assert their liberties. The spirit that had animated the townsmen in 1664 had never died; now, on the eve of the assembly meeting, Dongan was introduced to the prickly independence of eastern Long Island. This spirit would animate the proceedings of the assembly.

The day-to-day proceedings and membership of the first assembly are uncertain due to a lack of records. The identity of a few members is known. Mathias Nicolls, so long at the center of affairs, was the speaker. He may have represented New York City. We know that John Lawrence did represent the city, because he was compensated by the city council for his services as an assemblyman.[45] Cornelius Van Dyck and Dirk Wessels ten Broeck were elected in Albany, Hendrick Beekman and William Ashford in Esopus, and Ryer Jacobse Schermerhorn in Schenectady to represent the upriver communities.[46] Giles Goddard of Pemaquid was one of the representatives from the English settlements. The other members are unknown. The only contemporary comment on the membership comes from John West, who characterized it as predominantly Dutch.[47] It is difficult, however, to accept this characterization. The known membership was divided equally—four English and four Dutch. There were six certain English seats from the east riding (2), north riding (2), Martha's Vineyard (1), and the west riding (1). Probable Dutch members come from New York City (2), the west riding (1), and Staten Island (1). If these indeed were the results of the elections, there were ten English representatives and eight Dutch.[48]

The assembly met for three weeks, beginning on 17 October 1683, in the church at Fort James. Dongan attended to read a letter announcing his appointment as governor and to communicate the desire of the proprietor that the members consider all matters of public concern. Nothing is known of what went on afterward except as shown in the end product—fifteen laws, including the landmark "Charter of Libertyes and Priviledges."[49]

This document is not so much a law as a statement of rights and a plan of organization. It was the final elaboration of all the opinions expressed, first on Long Island and then throughout the colony, about representative government. The charter attempted to draw the duke into a contractual arrangement with the colonists. Until this time whatever government the duke had granted to the colony was written into the instructions of the governor and the Duke's Laws, which Governor Nicolls created, none of it derived from the people. It seems likely that Mathias Nicolls and his son William, both of them lawyers and recent returnees from England, knew the position of the Lords of Trade in their struggle with Jamaica. The lords' position was that the Jamaicans received all of their rights from the king and that only those present in the governor's commission were in effect.[50] The charter, seen in this light, was an attempt to gain fundamental guarantees from the proprietor about the institutions of governance and the rights of the individual.

Other influences were the struggles going on in Pennsylvania and New Jersey. William Penn arrived in his proprietary in 1682 and met immediate opposition to his proposed "Frame" of government. During March and April of 1683 he struggled with the assembly, which wanted to diminish his power and enhance that of the people. The resulting document, the Charter of Liberties, was a compromise between the factions but still a victory for those in favor of representative government. The assembly in New Jersey met three times during 1683 to restructure the government and define the rights of the individual. Seen in light of these events, the actions of the New York assembly are another instance of the people's trying to delineate their relationship with proprietary government.[51]

The first part of the charter deals with political organization.[52] Legislative authority, under the king and the duke, was to be exercised "forever" by a "Governor councill and the people, mett in a General assembly." The governor, deemed the chief administrator, governed with the "advice and consent" of the council (with a quorum of four necessary) in accordance with the laws. If for some reason (death or absence) the governor was incapacitated, and if no one else was present with a commission from the duke to take his place, then the council was to exercise the powers of the governor. Providing for the loss of a governor probably resulted from Brockholls's maladministration, another indication of the effects of that episode.

Having established the executive, the authors of the charter then turned to the assembly. Once again they asserted that "supreme and only legislative power" lay in the people's representatives, the governor, and the council. A majority vote of the freeholders elected the assemblymen. A freeholder was defined only by stating that the definition as understood in the laws of England applied in New York. Counties were established as the election districts. By this step the old administrative divisions were overthrown completely. The charter created twelve counties: New York City; Suffolk; Kings and Queens on Long Island; Richmond on Staten Island; Westchester between the Hudson and Connecticut rivers; Ulster around Esopus; Albany including Rensselaerswyck and Schenectady, although the latter was given one representative of its own; Dukes, for all the offshore islands; and Cornwall, for distant Pemaquid. Orange County, which ran from New Jersey to the southern boundary of Ulster, and Dutchess, from Westchester to Albany, went unrepresented due to a lack of population. In one stroke New York had added a new layer of government, creating a host of positions for Dongan to fill. The number of representatives remained at eighteen and only the duke could create more.

In turning to the organization of the assembly, the charter gave that body powers on a par with Parliament.[53] Meeting at least once every three years the assembly controlled the time of its meetings and adjournments. Control over the qualifications for membership was vested in the assembly and no member (or up to three of his servants) could be sued or imprisoned while journeying to and from the sessions or during them. Any laws passed by the assembly which received the approval of the governor and council remained in effect until the duke approved or they expired. The way in which the governor and council are delineated separately in this clause indicates a bicameral system. In fact, the first assembly submitted all legislation, including the charter, to Dongan and the council for approval.[54] The powers given to the assembly indicate how strongly the New Yorkers felt about an independent assembly, beyond the power of the duke to interfere. In one fell swoop they acquired powers that Parliament had only recently gained after many years of struggle.

The members of the first assembly were no less forward in claiming rights for the individual. They turned for inspiration to the Magna Charta and the 1628 Petition of Right. From the Magna Charta, II, 39 and 40, they took the right of liberty of persons, "no freeman shall bee taken and imprisoned, or bee disseized of his ffrehold on liberty, or free customes, or bee outlawed or exiled, or any other wayes destroyed, nor shall be passed upon, adjudged or condemned, butt by the lawfull judgement of his peers." The section on the rights of the individual not to be taxed without the consent of the governor, council, and assembly was taken from the Petition of Right. The charter also guaranteed trial by a jury of twelve peers from the locality, protection from quartering of seamen and soldiers in times of peace, and protection from martial law not imposed by the government. Coupled with these guarantees of political rights were a number of clauses guaranteeing ownership and control of property by the individual. It even included the right of a widow to remain in her house for forty days after the death of her spouse.[55]

The final third of the charter discussed religious liberty. All Christians were guaranteed freedom of worship. Undoubtedly, the inclusion of all Christians was a matter of compromise. The Dutch and English Calvinists probably would not have included Catholics if a Catholic proprietor and governor had not overseen their proceedings. The guarantee of freedom of worship for the individual was not absolute. It reaffirmed the old system, begun under Nicolls, of making the towns the religious units, not the churches. Here the influence of the Long Islanders was paramount. They wanted to continue the system of town ministers, elected and paid for by the community. In this way, the towns protected themselves from malcontents, especially Quakers, who did not pay the rates for the minister.[56]

The charter brought a major advance in the political life of New York. It was audacious in that it attempted to elicit a basic agreement with the proprietor about the powers of the assembly. After years of arbitrary government the representatives refused to allow the opportunity to slip by. Yet they needed York's approval for their proceedings. He and his governor could veto any offensive legislation. The governor was allowed far more power than his peers. Designated the chief administrator, he also shared legislative powers with the assembly. In Connecticut the governor was subject to annual election and had no legislative authority. The authority of Pennsylvania's executive was always under attack.[57]

The assembly had secured control over its own members and proceedings, a common power in the colonies, but its triennial sessions lagged behind the common pattern of annual elections and annual sessions. On the whole, the charter is like the early eighteenth-century royal colony form of government. In not emulating their neighbors, the representatives may have been influenced by Dongan and their speaker, Mathias Nicolls, both of whom had recently arrived from England and may well have informed the assembly how far it could go with York. It seems probable, anyway, that Nicolls, who was steeped in the government and had legal training, was the man who drafted the charter. Even so, it still met the principal objections of the colonists to the old form of government and offered them hope for the future.

During the first session of the assembly interest groups emerged to seek special legislation. During any change in government the Dutch always sought a ratification of their place in the colony's economic life. Two pieces of legislation reveal their interests in gaining security in the new system. In the area of land grants an act confirmed all titles to land in the province, assuring the farmers and speculators. Another act naturalized all non-English inhabitants of the colony, allowing them to continue their mercantile activities. Nor did the Long Island representatives miss an opportunity to get rid of an old thorn in their side. The provisions in the Duke's Laws relating to the rates never received the approval of their representatives and they disliked paying them; the assembly repealed the old rates and passed a new act to meet the costs of government and support the poor.[58] Replacing an old, disliked system with something exactly like it makes it appear that the assembly was being petty. It was, however, asserting its position that there should be no taxation without popular consent.

On the matter of taxes, the duke demanded his due. In

order to oblige him, the representatives took up taxation right after the charter and passed legislation imposing duties on a wide range of items, especially liquors and Indian goods.[59] This law replaced the duties Andros had allowed to lapse. Now, however, the regulations were permanent and the possibility of another situation such as the one that had faced Brockholls was impossible.

Besides legislating for these private and public interests, the assembly enacted new statutes to reorganize the government. The charter had established the county as the common form of local government and the unit of representation in the assembly. The assembly passed legislation delineating the boundaries of the twelve new units of government.[60] The bill creating the counties dealt only with bounds and left the governments of each to Dongan. In only one area did the assembly create wholly new institutions of local government, and that was in law courts. Dongan's instructions contained a clause ordering him to consult with the council and settle what courts they felt necessary for the proper administration of justice.[61] For unknown reasons, the assembly undertook this task. Because this did not endanger the duke's prerogatives and since he could veto any improprieties, Dongan allowed the representatives to go ahead. Four levels of jurisdiction were created.[62] The town courts had the most limited position. They could hold monthly meetings and settle minor local disputes. Above them were courts of sessions, which met less frequently and had original and appellate jurisdiction. The next step in the legal ladder was the court of oyer and terminer and general goal delivery. It replaced the court of assize, which met only once each year and was too remote from many areas of the province.[63] The courts of oyer and terminer held sessions annually in each county and consisted of one of the two judges of the court and three justices of the peace from the county. The "supreme" court was the court of chancery, consisting of the governor and the council. If anyone thought this system did not provide justice, appeals to the Crown were still allowed in the duke's patent.

One of the last, and certainly not the least, of the bills passed by the assembly provided for a "Free and Voluntary" gift to Dongan. This "gift" gained Dongan's approval of the charter and no doubt helped persuade him to approve the new legislation. Because York would be the final arbiter of the legislation, Dongan had nothing to lose. As his reward he got one penny for every pound of assessed valuation. No other act was as tightly drawn as this one in terms of a time schedule and penalties. After glancing at these provisions the people might have wondered about the "free and voluntary" title. Many did not "volunteer" to pay, so that when the assembly met one year later it had to pass an act for the "more speedy and better collecting" of the voluntary gift.[64] Having finished its work the assembly adjourned to leave its accomplishments to English review.

The Assembly's Work Reversed

The next step in the legislative process was to obtain York's approval. To this end the fifteen acts of the first session were sent to England in early December 1683. The first mention of the receipt of the documents occurred at the 28 February 1684 meeting of the commission of revenue.[65] The only reaction expressed by the commissioners was a very strong one against the way the customs rate was ascertained. They believed that estimating customs on the cost of goods in the loading port, as proposed in the laws, was fallacious. The invoices would be tampered with and the duke cheated. No matter how epochal a document the Charter of Libertyes was, the commissioners tended to business first.

The commission reviewed the charter only after reading Dongan's letters.[66] While agreeing to it in principle, the commissioners desired certain changes related mainly to the assembly's control over its membership. They wanted to grant the governor power to set the qualifications for membership and deprive the assembly of the liberty of purging its own members. Finally, representatives could not sit until taking an oath of allegiance and fidelity to the duke. The other major discussion revolved around customs. The commissioners still wanted customs charged on the value of goods at New York, not at the point of loading. They then considered in turn each act of the assembly. The commissioners objected to the bills dealing with the payment of public charges and the tenure of judges. In the act to meet the costs of government there was a passage denying entry to indigents. The commission ordered this clause struck out because the result would be to hinder new planters. Their last amendment set the tenure of judges at good behavior.

The final process was to engross the revised acts and send them back to New York. This never happened. On 22 August 1684 the commission gave final approval to the assembly's work, but not until 7 November did they put it in the hands of one of the members for engrossing. Meanwhile they asked Werden to get York's signature on the Charter of Libertyes, after which they planned to place it in a box for delivery to New York.[67] However, at this point imperial politics intruded. The duke never gave final assent to the charter because the Crown was reassessing its policy toward the colonies.

The End of Representative Government

During the last few years of his reign King Charles and his advisors took their revenge after years of retreat. The enemies of prerogative government used the Oates revelations, which unleashed an anti-Catholic search in high places, to hinder the policies of Charles and put him on the defensive. After the disastrous Oxford Parliament of 1681 Charles went on the offensive. His efforts culminated in the attack on the city charters —above all, that of London—and on his whig opponents. The Rye House plot was used to force Shaftsbury into exile and to execute Lord Russell and Algernon Sidney.[68] The reaction spilled over into colonial affairs. The Lords of Trade remained unconvinced that the colonies had the "rights" they claimed for their governments. Although the attack on Jamaica failed, the lords did rescind the charter of the Bermuda Company. Their main target was the North American colonies, especially Massachusetts. Quo warranto proceedings against Massachusetts began in 1681 but went unfulfilled until 1684 because King Charles moved slowly in pursuing the colonies. It was during this hiatus that York granted the assembly, but the Charter of Libertyes and Priviledges was not considered until the critical year of 1684. York's commission of revenue approved the acts of the assembly on 22 August 1684. The crucial revocation of the Massachusetts charter was entered in the Chancery Rolls on 13 October 1684, signifying the beginning of a wholesale assault on other colonial charters.[69] The New York legislation is not mentioned in the commission minutes until after 7 November, when it was sent for engrossment. Undoubtedly influenced by the action against Massachusetts, York turned against the assembly. Before taking further action, he became king on the death of Charles in February 1685. New York was dissolved as a proprietary and became a royal colony.

As soon as York became king, the records of New York were sent to the Lords of Trade. The lords considered the charter and prepared a set of "Observations" about it which were read on 3 March 1685.[70] Almost all of the "Observations" were hostile. The words "The People" in the clause relating to legislative powers drew the most criticism, the lords maintaining that they appeared in no other "American Constitution" of the day. Other clauses came under criticism for abridging the power of Parliament to legislate for the colonies, for restraining the governor's powers, and for establishing triennial assembly meetings. After this attack, the lords disallowed the charter and let the legislation passed by the assembly lapse.[71] Dongan was notified of these actions and of future plans to include New York in the Dominion of New England.

The dominion was the culmination of the policies of the Lords of Trade. Little doubt exists that King James favored it as a means of administering the colonies.[72] He refused to grant New York an assembly until forced to do so because of his own political circumstances and the failure to collect taxes. The government of the Duke's Laws and the opinions expressed in 1675 to Andros reflected the true feelings of York. Nothing in his experience as a proprietor caused him to change.

In fact, the advice of Andros and Dongan probably only reinforced his opinions. Andros had written after King Philip's War that the colonies were incapable of organizing defenses and that the situation would continue for "so long as each petty colony hath or assumes absolute power of peace and warr, which cannot be managed by such popular Governments as was evident by the late Indian wars in New England."[73]

Significantly, the recipient of this letter was William Blathwayt, the secretary of the Lords of Trade and a leading proponent of the dominion.[74] Dongan went even further. He was acutely aware of the growing tension with the French and the probability that New York would be subject to French attacks. Since New York could not support a sufficient garrison, he proposed increasing the tax base by returning the Jerseys to New York and then adding Rhode Island and Connecticut. Without this large tax base, Dongan believed New York exposed and endangered. An additional benefit would be derived from the expanded number of English colonists who would "balance the Interests of the French and Dutch Inhabitants of this Government."[75] With this sort of advice flowing in from his governors, it is no wonder that James made New York part of the dominion. As New York had begun life as a proprietary in the new policies of the 1660s, it ceased to be a proprietary for the new policy of the 1680s.

8 ❧ The Reassertion of Central Authority: The Dongan Administration

The establishment of the assembly and the passage of the Charter of Libertyes fueled hopes for the future of representative government. Sessions in 1684 and 1685 wrote legislation on issues such as public morals and legal technicalities, building experience and reputation for the representatives.[1] The activities of the assembly promised to broaden the political base in New York, creating the potential for an expansion of the political elite beyond the small group of government officials and New York merchants clustered around the governor. Yet, these hopes for progress were diminished after 1683 with the reversal of the assembly's work in England and the increasing dominance of Thomas Dongan.

Restructuring the Government

Dongan's administration preserved aspects of the old regime while carrying out important changes. The continuity was most noticeable in the composition of the council. York ordered him to continue Philipse and Van Cortlandt and choose eight new members and allow the council "freedom of debates and vote in all affaires of publique concerne."[2] The addition of Lewis Morris, Nicholas Bayard, and John Palmer strengthened the merchant faction. Career officials such as John Spragge (the secretary), Lucas Santen (the collector), James Graham (the attorney general), and two officers from the garrison, Anthony Brockholls and Captain Jervais Baxter, created a solid bloc for the government. Palmer, who held a number of legal offices, was also a member of this group. The single exception to the pattern of New York City merchants and officeholders was John Youngs. A merchant of Southampton and occasional local official, Youngs infrequently attended the council sessions and was relieved from office in 1687 for incompetence. Santen, the collector, was the only other member removed from the council, but in his case it was for malfeasance.[3] The council continued on in the old familiar pattern. It was predominantly English, and the three Dutchmen who served on it were associated with the English regime. As usual New York City merchants were well represented. To an old resident, the council had only three established figures—Philipse, Van Cortlandt, and Bayard. The remainder were new men who had no following in the community and were part of the ruling elite merely through their proximity to the chief executive.

The council gained considerable power after 1685. The assembly was first dissolved on 13 August 1685, then called into session in September 1686, only to be prorogued until an order for its final dissolution was issued in January 1687.[4] The council then adopted the function of the assembly. It did not settle for issuing proclamations but went through the legislative motions by ordering the attorney general to draw up legislation and then read it twice before granting final approval.[5] To those who fought for an assembly and passed the Charter of Libertyes, this must have been a farcical procedure. The fact that most of the new legislation strengthened tax collection made it galling.

Dongan oversaw the most extensive reorganization of the central and local government since 1665. At the provincial level the major reforms occurred in the court system. The new courts of oyer and terminer, chancery, and exchequer gave Dongan more flexibility in sending his own officials into a troubled locality in order to settle problems or impose his authority. The staffing of these courts also brought lucrative positions for his clique. James Graham, besides being attorney general, was a clerk of chancery. Secretary John Spragge added to his offices those of master of the rolls and register for chancery. For judges of oyer and terminer, Dongan tapped Mathias Nicolls and John Palmer. Through these men Dongan kept the administration of justice under his control.[6]

At the local level Dongan chose the officials in the new

county governments. Commissions for sheriffs, justices of the peace, tax officials, and militia officers issued from his office to trustworthy men in the country.[7] This procedure did not go unremarked. The Esopus towns objected to his choice of Thomas Garton and Hendrick Beekman as justices and William Ashford as sheriff. More than sixty residents, guided by trusted leaders such as Thomas Chambers, Henry Pawling, Nicholas Anthony, and William De Meyer, petitioned Dongan for the "liberty" to elect all officials. In light of the assembly and its work this might not have seemed like an extravagant request. Dongan saw it differently. The court of oyer and terminer descended on the towns and levied fines of £4 to £54 on over sixty persons for sedition and disturbing the peace.[8] Dongan's actions reminded those who believed a new day had dawned with the assembly that he had great powers and was willing to use them.

Dongan assumed a different position when dealing with New York City. On 9 November 1683, shortly after the first session of the assembly, the mayor and aldermen asked Dongan for a charter.[9] The first part of their petition requested the political and economic privileges gained from prior administrations. The second part was a nine-point request for changes in the city government. It proposed that the city be divided into six wards, each having a popularly elected alderman, common councilman, constable, assessors, and other minor officials. The aldermen and councilmen, along with the mayor and a recorder, would legislate for the new corporation. The mayor was not to be popularly elected but chosen by the governor from among the aldermen. Dongan later altered this practice and appointed the mayor without consulting the aldermen.[10] The recorder, a judicial official giving legal advice to the corporation and sitting as a judge when the magistrates assumed their role as a court, was also appointed by the governor, as were the sheriff, coroner, and town clerk. The corporation did get to appoint the city treasurer. The reform spirit present in the assembly still retained some vitality in the city.

While Dongan considered the city's petition, the annual elections were held and Cornelius Steenwyck, who emerged as a leader of the reform movement, was appointed mayor.[11] Steenwyck had been excluded from political life by Andros after pressing the demands of the Dutch community in 1675. Removed from public life, he used the time to increase his considerable fortune. The new mayor and aldermen pushed Dongan into accepting the proposed charter. He had tentatively decided to approve it when suddenly the new magistrates presented him with another petition. They asked that the charter be put into effect until the duke's approval was received, that the city clerk be one of their appointees, and that the fees received from the docks, ferry, and the market be turned over to them. While Dongan was taken aback by another petition, he agreed to the requests except for the power of appointing the clerk, which he referred to York. He could feel secure in agreeing to the petition because a clause in his instructions ordered him to consider special privileges for the city. He formally approved the charter on 10 December 1683, and it was hardly a coincidence that on the same day the magistrates issued a warrant to carry out the "Act for a free and voluntary gift to the Governor."[12]

Even before Dongan gave his approval, Steenwyck and the aldermen (Nicholas Bayard, Guleyn Verplanck, John Inians, William Pinhorne, John Robinson, and William Cox) instituted the reforms. The boundaries of the wards were defined and an alderman assigned to each one. The aldermen then met with the freemen of their wards and elected a common councilor, two assessors, and a constable.[13] The creation of so many elective offices (six councilors, six constables, and twelve assessors) opened a fresh era in city politics. Ambitious sons of established families or new men had a new stage on which to operate. Abraham De Peyster, one of the new men entering office at this time, went on to become mayor from 1691 to 1693 and served intermittently on the council from 1698 to 1722.[14] Of greater significance was the fact that the government was now somewhat more responsive to the desires of the electorate. The merchants, however, did not relinquish their control over the highest offices in the city.

The new city government launched a wide-ranging program of reform and renewal in the spring of 1684. On 14 February, when the common council was sworn into office, it issued a spate of orders. Three committees were formed to investigate the revenues back to 1674, the state of the public works and the cost of repairing them, and to make a collection of public regulations. One week later all three committees reported back. The committee on ordinances was ordered to draw up its findings for future publication. The committee on public works reported that £150 would be needed to repair the City Hall, wharf, market house, and other facilities. The finance group handed in a lengthy report naming names and amounts due to the city. As a result of their work, another committee was sent to wait on the governor and ask him for additional sources of revenue.[15]

This rush of activity is indicative of the spirit of renewal in New York City at this time. The work of rebuilding and repairing the public works went on all year, as did the assiduous collecting of every penny owed the city or that could be gained from Dongan. He granted the magistrates permission to tax certain trade items as they were landed in the town. When revenues continued to fall short, the magistrates merely decided to tax the inhabitants to raise £200. This levy received a stormy reaction and the city council removed one recalcitrant official to show that it meant business.[16] The magistrates acted harshly on another occasion to exert their authority. After the new city ordinances were posted on 15 March 1684, the cartmen of the city went on strike in protest against the rules relating to their monopoly. The magistrates suspended fifteen of them, and they were not allowed to return until they repented and paid a six-shilling fine.[17] With this sort of vigorous government it is no wonder that when Dongan was approached about issuing writs for a new election in October, he saw no reason to do so.[18] No city government had ever acted so vigorously on such a wide number of municipal concerns.

Albany emulated her larger and more powerful rival. On 10 April 1684, the Albany *commissaries* requested a municipal reorganization similar to that of New York City. Without waiting for a new patent the magistrates forged ahead in May and divided the city into six wards. Then in June new elections were held to complete the transition.[19] As in New York City there were now more opportunities for officeholding and political careers. Yet the *handlaers*, who dominated the city's economy, would not and did not relinquish control over the government.

Dongan forced an unwelcome change upon the smaller

towns. He compelled the repatenting of all the settlements in the province. These patents significantly changed town government. The patents appointed trustees and made them the leaders of town government and the owners of the undivided land. Town meetings could be called only by the trustees, and then only after they received a warrant from a justice of the peace. Ambitious trustees thus found themselves in a position to create oligarchies and control town government. This happened almost immediately in Flushing; for instance, the trustees could not resist the temptation to carve up the undivided lands.[20] Dongan had effected a considerable revolution in the democratically inclined towns.[21]

Dongan's reorganization expanded the presence of the central government throughout the colony and caused much unhappiness. In the first place the new county officials were appointed, not elected, a policy inconsistent with the goals of the Charter of Libertyes, which were persistently overlooked by Dongan. This meant the further suppression of long-sought ideals, particularly among the English. In the second place, the changes were potentially irritating to the Dutch for different reasons. The reorganization of the city government and the creation of county government made New York's political institutions more solidly English in form. Prior to Dongan's time English forms of government were subsumed into, or easily mixed with, Dutch forms. After Dongan's reforms there was no doubt that the government was English, heightening the sense of anxiety among the Dutch as English institutions engulfed them.

Dongan did continue some of the practices of his predecessors. He gave his favorites power and opportunities for wealth. The profits of office, opportunities to trade, and land grants came their way. Symbolic of this tendency was a lavish manorial grant that went to Robert Livingston, a favorite of Dongan.[22] Inevitably the success of the favored few bred jealousy and hatred among others in the still-fluid society of New York. Those who prospered without preferential ties and saw other men vault over them to become manor lords or gain financial stability through the profits of office were alienated by Dongan's regime.

The Continuing Problem of Taxation

A major problem confronting Dongan was financing the government and the garrison. York hoped the assembly would finally crack this old nut. Dongan discovered that the assembly did very little to aid him in his efforts, and what aid there was vanished after 1685. Dongan did not dodge the problem of taxation. He dared not in this period of close imperial scrutiny of revenues because of the rising costs for defense. What he developed in response was an enlarged tax-collection machinery and a system of extortion.

Like his predecessors Dongan had difficulty in determining what revenues were available. After conducting an audit he reported in 1685 that the debts of the government totaled £3,533.15.8.[23] Shortly thereafter he engaged in a quarrel with the collector, Lucas Santen, over the validity of his accounts. After a long struggle Santen was relieved of his office and sent home to England for defrauding the king.[24] This dispute only confused the accounts further and kept Dongan from a true understanding of the financial status of his government. He did realize that the key to his situation lay in the revenue from customs. As a result, the list of duties on goods and trade was extended to as many items as feasible.[25] The goods that moved through New York City were easily scrutinized and fees exacted. The problem of controlling Long Island's trade remained, particularly that in whale oil. Denouncing the manner in which this valuable commodity was sent off to Boston, Dongan sent customs officers to prevent the trade. The number of legally sanctioned ports at the east end of the island was limited to two and no exemptions to the trade regulations were permitted. Even Andros was refused an exemption. Ships exporting whale oil suffered further regulation for they had to go to New York City before leaving the colony. Investigating committees roamed the port towns and customs vessels watched shipping in the sound. The results must have gratified Dongan, if the protests of the islanders against his policies were any guide.[26]

Dongan's decision to collect quitrents gave the towns-people even more to complain about. Quitrents remained a sensitive issue because they were tied to the ownership of land and any innovation in land titles was vitally important to the colonists. To enhance the authority of the central government in tax disputes Dongan created a court of exchequer, modeled on its ancient namesake in England, to adjudicate disputes over taxes. Dongan justified the new court on the grounds that "Country Jurors . . . are generally ignorant enough and for the most part linked together by affinity [and] are too much swayed by their particular humors and interests."[27] Special quitrent collectors were then appointed.[28] The final step in this campaign was the most difficult—writing quitrents into land patents.

New York quitrents differed from those in other colonies. In Virginia, for instance, the tax was set at so much per acre.[29] In New York quitrents were written into patents for towns and large aggregates of land in a haphazard manner. Most of the quitrents were small and infrequently collected. To rectify this the council issued orders on 31 March 1684 to planters on Staten Island and fourteen towns on Long Island to produce their patents and any Indian deeds that related to the ownership of town land. The towns were given until 25 April to reply. When the deadline arrived, only Boswyck, Flatbush, New Haarlem, Flatlands, and New Utrecht had complied.[30] A protracted battle then broke out between the remaining towns and the governor. On one side there was foot-dragging and every possible delay, on the other, unrelenting pressure and threats. Dongan took the initiative and forwarded a representative Dutch patent to England for inspection. What specific charges he made against it went unrecorded, but the duke's commissioners of revenue could not detect any flaws in the patent. In the end they left the matter in Dongan's hands by stating that if he found a defect, he should use it to gain additional revenue. The commissioners did give him one weapon. They ordered him to call to account all holders of large tracts who were not utilizing their land. If the owners were unable or unwilling to improve their holdings, they were to be dispossessed.[31] Dongan turned this order against the towns. Before doing so, he exploited other means of coercion. On 11 November 1684 a warrant was issued to a committee, headed by Councilor Nicholas Bayard, to investigate the accounts of the Long Island sheriffs back to 1674. This commission evidently accomplished very little for a special two-man team was later appointed to inquire into tax evasion on the island. He also bypassed the towns and ordered the sheriffs to investigate all titles in their jurisdiction. Similar orders were sent to the sheriffs of Albany and New York City as the campaign broadened.[32] Still, the towns continued to resist.

Dongan then used his ultimate weapons—the court of exchequer and the power to use unimproved land. The court was a last resort and, according to Dongen, a suit there always produced the desired ends.[33] The town of Huntington, for example, ignored a letter threatening court action. On reconsidering the consequences the townspeople recanted and accepted a new patent.[34] One by one the towns succumbed to the pressure and agreed to new patents that included an annual quitrent of one pound. Oyster Bay and Southold even paid back quitrents to 1678 and 1676, respectively.[35] While others might go along, Easthampton retained its reputation for insubordination. The townspeople voted to oppose a new patent and took their case to the assembly in 1685. Unable to gain support, the town leaders continued a vain struggle against Dongan. In reply he gave thirty acres of land to nonmembers of the town. Springing to the defense of their community, the townspeople protested vehemently. For their efforts ten leading citizens were arrested. The town's minister, Thomas James, was especially singled out for preaching a seditious sermon. Ultimately, the recalcitrants were pardoned, but the town paid heavily. A special town rate of £200 was ordered to pay for the patent and legal fees.[36]

One further aspect of the repatenting episode needs consideration, as it exposed Dongan's venality. Town and other records reveal that Dongan and other officials used their powers to extort money or favors in return for patents. Before Huntington received its patent the town meeting voted £20 to Dongan to keep its case out of court and made Judge John Palmer a patentee. Hempstead granted 200 acres to Dongan and 150 acres to Secretary John Spragge. This grant abutted 400 acres given Dongan by Flushing. Brookhaven gave him twenty sheep to graze on his lands. Albany and New York City gave him £300 each for the new patents they received.[37] If a town did not pay up, Dongan simply granted land to himself or his favorites.[38] The profits of office combined with his trading and land acquisition increased Dongan's fortune; thus one tends to doubt his protestations that he had "been forc't to engage my credit soe far as t'would goe and that not sparing to pawn my Plate for money to carry on the King's affairs."[39]

The success of Dongan's efforts to increase revenues and make the colony solvent are difficult to judge. For instance, the records are silent on the costs of the expanded central government. Only fragmentary evidence exists until 1688 when Stephanus Van Cortlandt compiled a report after his appointment as deputy surveyor and auditor general.[40] His accounts indicate a total revenue of £5,288 for the fiscal year from March 1687 to March 1688. Most of this amount (£3,172) was derived from duties on imports into New York City. Another £1,707 was collected from excises charged at the local level. More than any other province New York relied on these indirect taxes.[41] However, the direct taxes were also high. In 1688 direct taxes totaling £2,556 were levied.[42] Connecticut, in comparison, had much lower taxes. In 1677, the final year of three years of heavy taxation needed to meet the considerable costs of King Philip's War, provincial taxes were an abnormally high £4,824. After the costs of the war were repaid, taxes reverted to a levy of one penny in the pound on assessed valuation. In a normal year, such as 1683, this direct form of taxation produced £941.[43] In Rhode Island the provincial tax was £160 in 1687.[44] New Jersey was almost tax-free territory compared to New York. There were no customs duties, quitrents were negligible and infrequently collected, and provincial taxes, when charged, were for sums like £50 per county in 1682.[45] New York's taxation system was thus much harsher than that of surrounding colonies. Unfortunately, worse was yet to come.

Anglo-French hostilities boiled over after 1685. In New France the old rivalry with the Iroquois and the lure of the fur trade proved stronger than the desire for peace. A major expedition was sent into the Iroquois cantons in 1687, causing a major scare in New York. Dongan could not ignore such a threat. He had emphasized to the French that the Iroquois were subjects of the English and that an attack upon them would have serious consequences. Planning for just such an outbreak, Dongan had upgraded and drilled the militia. To meet the French invasion he sailed up the Hudson in the autumn of 1687 with militiamen and a contingent from the garrison. The costs of maintaining this force in Albany for the winter were staggering. Dongan claimed that his costs were £6,482.7.11, and Robert Livingston, who helped supply some of the soldiers, submitted an account for £2,067.[46] New York's strategic position was now more than ever a heavy burden upon its people. To meet the costs of defense a special rate of one-half penny on the pound of assessed valuation was passed by the council on 14 June 1687. It was followed by another tax with discriminatory features. This second special rate took one penny on the pound of assessed valuation from Albany, New York City, and Ulster County and one and one-half pennies from Long Island. Still, the money did not flow in quickly enough and on 3 May 1688 a new levy for £2,556 was ordered, only to be canceled two months later when Andros officially subsumed New York into the Dominion of New England. This was only a temporary respite because Andros later ordered a new rate of one penny on the pound.[47]

Dongan was not unaware of the dangers of the increasing tax burden. In letters to Secretary of State Sunderland he wrote of his fears that the people would begin leaving New York for the less burdensome tax loads in surrounding colonies.[48] Such a depopulation was doubly horrible to contemplate, first, because a reduction in the number of inhabitants meant a corresponding reduction in the tax base, and second, because Dongan feared that it would be the English inhabitants who would move. He viewed this with alarm as the Dutch were not fit for "service" in the militia. To strengthen the defenses he wanted English, or even Irish, immigrants as planters.[49] Both problems had a quick solution, which was quite old by this time—the annexation of neighboring colonies. Dongan, Santen, Spragge, and other government officials requested the annexation of Connecticut, East New Jersey, and Pennsylvania at various times. Connecticut and New Jersey were thought particularly attractive because of their large population and low taxes.[50]

A Stagnant Economy

In 1685 Dongan wrote an optimistic report about New York's economy.[51] It was his last display of optimism before new conditions damaged New York's commerce. The renewal of hostilities with France in the late 1680s meant a rise in piracy and privateering, which damaged colonial commerce. As the war intensified, the slump would deepen. A second condition damaging to New York was the rapid development of Pennsylvania in general and Philadelphia in particular. By 1690 the population of Philadelphia was 4,000 while that of New York City was 3,900.[52] Since Philadelphia's boundaries were only surveyed in 1682 its growth was as dramatic as its impact on New York City's trade. Governor Benjamin Fletcher reported in 1696 that "Philadelphia in fourteen years time is become equal to the City of New York in trade and riches."[53] The first trade lost by New York was that of the Delaware region as its tobacco and grains went to Philadelphian merchants.[54] The rapid growth of population in Pennsylvania quickly produced an increase in the amount of grains for export to the West Indies, bringing vigorous competition for New York in this important market. Of equal significance was Penn's desire to control the Susquehanna River Valley. Rich in furs and potential farmlands, this region was a great prize. It had further significance because if Pennsylvania controlled the fur trade the Iroquois might be influenced by the Quakers. Dongan feared such a development at a time when England and France were drifting toward war. Alerted by Dongan to the threat of losing a potentially rich area and the imperial consequences of Quaker control of the Susquehanna, York ordered him to forestall Penn's acquisition.[55] As Pennsylvania boomed, merchants abandoned New York for the greener pastures along the Schuykill River. The end product in New York of all these changes was a slump in trade, a rise in the price of goods, and a widespread commercial recession by 1687.[56]

As commerce withered prices of farm goods dropped, hurting the farmers. Winter wheat, which sold for five shillings per bushel in 1685, dropped to three shillings in 1688 and was still at that level in 1690. A barrel of beef cost £12.0, pork £3.0 in 1685; by 1690 they slumped to £1.5 and £2.0, respectively.[57] Smuggling via East New Jersey increased as ships carried goods into Perth-Amboy without having to pay customs and then brought them surreptitiously into New York City.[58] The final blow came from the French. The very attacks that forced Dongan into expensive defensive measures badly damaged the Indian trade. Estimates were that the number of peltries passing through Albany had dropped by two-thirds to three-quarters. As profits declined land became a preferred investment no matter how distant it was.[59] The only new development in the economy was a few tentative voyages to West Africa and Madagascar, which led to the lucrative piracy and slave trade of the 1690s.[60] Inevitably, as the economy contracted the old battles over monopolies revived as the city merchants pressed their political advantage.

During Brockholls's tenure New York City had lost its monopolies. The outlying regions simply disregarded economic legislation. As soon as Dongan restored the authority of the central government the city merchants reasserted their control. In the spring of 1683, when the ice-plugged Hudson broke free from its winter lassitude, wheat went down the river in small sloops from Kingston and Albany. On arriving in New York City it was seized. Mathias Nicolls appeared before the city council on 15 March on behalf of the governor to request the release of the flour. The city council, in turn, sent a committee of Nicholas Bayard, William Pinhorne, and John Robinson to explain its actions. The committee failed, for two days later the wheat of Gabriel Thompson, a prominent Albany merchant, was released. An anxious petition from the city council to Dongan followed, requesting a reimposition of the old regulations. Dongan and the council asked for further information before granting the petition.[61]

The magistrates submitted to the council their "Reasons" for continuing the monopoly. They argued that the inhabitants of the city had, through their diligence, gained a reputation abroad that brought foreign commerce to New York and supplied jobs to the inhabitants. Flour and bread were the basis of this reputation. The "Reasons" ended with a familiar plea: "All other parts of the Province have Some Particular Advantage and way of Liveing As Long Island by Husbandry and Whaleing Esopus being fatt of the Land by Tillage Albany by Indians Trade and husbandry this City noe other Advantage or Way of Liveing but by Traffique and Dependence are on Another Chiefly upheld by the Manufacture of flour and Bread."[62]

However it may have appeared in New York, the view from Albany was very different. The Albanyites were aroused when the city magistrates seized further shipments of flour in May 1683.[63] One resident was quoted as saying, "Those of New York build large houses and try to pay for them with our goods."[64] There was despair also, for "there is no one who speaks for the good brothers of Albany."[65] The man chosen to represent Albany before the governor was Cornelius Van Dyck, one of the assemblymen. The *commissaries'* orders to Van Dyck were defiant and certainly shrewd: "You must mostly bear in mind that the granting of privileges must be done by the Assembly and you must request his honor that everything be continued until the Assembly is in session, without our being molested by those of New York about our meal or other privileges, as has taken place recently, and that the bolting, shipping across the sea and the trade may be as in the year 1677, without contradiction."[66] Their ploy was to rally the other regions in the assembly in order to end the dominance of the city. This seemed a likely approach because the assembly had jurisdiction over economic affairs. However, it enacted little economic legislation.[67] Since the city had only four votes against fourteen from the remainder of the province, it is strange that the long-awaited opportunity to escape the dominance of the merchants was not sought. The failure of the assembly in this regard sets New York apart. All of the other proprietary colonies had rambunctious assemblies that seized the initiative and forced changes on the proprietors and their deputies. For example, William Penn's economic plans were quickly laid to rest by the merchants who came to Philadelphia.[68] One reason for the assembly's reluctance may have been Dutch concern about their position. They may not have wanted to debate economic issues that would displease the duke. It was also well known that York favored the city, because as the single trade center it made the collection of customs easier. Finally, the assembly probably hesitated to attack the economic power of the city as long as the charter was under consideration in England. Dongan and Mathias Nicolls undoubtedly counseled a cautious course to those who wished to strip away the monopolies of the metropolis. All of the hopes that lay with the charter rested on York's good will and nothing was certain until positive action was taken in England. The result was inaction by the assembly.

When economic affairs were left to Dongan there was very

little doubt as to what he would do. In the end, he came down on the side of New York City. His decision was precipitated by a letter from Deputy Governor Kingsland of Barbados, complaining about the declining quality of flour shipped to his colony.[69] A week after the receipt of his letter, the council prohibited the milling and packing of flour and the making of bread for export outside of Manhattan. The reason given for the order was the complaint received from Barbados, but there is little doubt that Dongan was under heavy pressure from the merchants to restore the old monopolies. As a sop to the disgruntled, the order was to remain in effect only until the duke's pleasure was known. Since the duke's pleasure favored the collection of customs and the prosperity of New York City, the merchants retained their profitable monopolies.[70]

Having secured their old position in the economy, the merchants also cast their eyes on the increasingly important whale-oil trade. They proposed to stop the trade in oil from the island by allowing its export only through New York City. The towns of Suffolk County protested through Jacob Leisler, a prominent whale-oil shipper, only to be rebuffed. To show their further displeasure the local magistrates farmed the local excise taxes at a ridiculously low rate.[71] Undeterred, the council sent ships into the sound to enforce the new regulations. Their effectiveness was demonstrated by a petition from the soap-boilers of Connecticut asking for oil in order to remain in business.[72] Yet these increasingly harsh measures could not save the city from the depression slowly gripping New York. By 1685 the assessed valuation of real and personal property in the city was £75,694, descending to £52,192 in 1695. Personal fortunes followed the spiral. Fewer men were able to retain their positions in the top ranks of the social structure. Forty-six individuals were assessed on £500 or over in 1676. By 1695 their numbers had dwindled to six.[73] One group profited in these bad times; Dongan and his clique proved more avaricious than any similar group in the past. Money and land were their chief concerns, and their practices may be epitomized in the deal in which Dongan granted Judge Palmer the manor of Castletown on Staten Island, which Palmer deeded back to Dongan within three months.[74] Dongan thereby gained the status of manor lord—a station denied him in England. Venality combined with harsh taxation and a slumping economy was a formula for trouble.

Further Causes of Discontent

There were other sources of irritation. In 1687 Dongan, concerned about French activity on the frontier, demanded a loyalty oath from all males in the province.[75] Once again the Quakers refused and were harassed, and once again they protested their treatment.[76] The Dutch were also forced to swear their loyalty to an English king yet another time. In the face of French probes, the oath was not a vote of confidence in the people. The militia Dongan took to Albany suffered further privation. After straggling home they went uncompensated for their services. Each county had been ordered to send men; they had complied and now the men were unpaid.[77] The question around the fires and in the taverns must have been, What are all those taxes going for? Finally, New York was absorbed into the Dominion of New England. After York ascended the throne in 1685, New York became a royal colony. This proved to be a temporary arrangement as King James favored the growth of his experiment—the Dominion of New England. Dongan and others had argued for an expansion of New York to create a larger tax base and provide for a more efficient defense. Their advice was taken, but instead of a greater New York the boundaries of the dominion were extended to the Delaware. Andros, returned to power and favor in 1685 as governor of the dominion, found himself in charge of New York once again in September 1688. In the eyes of many New Yorkers, Andros was hardly a welcome replacement to Dongan. They also had more parochial fears. For most of the colonists the government was far enough away in New York City, but in Boston it was very distant. The problem of distance was compounded by having their old commercial rival as a capital. Who would control trade and in which city's favor? Yet the event that aroused the most comment was Andros's removal of the public records from New York to join the archives of the dominion in Boston.[78] This struck a note of fear among the people. Future land disputes would entail incredibly expensive litigation in Boston. The wells of distrust produced even greater fears over how the records might be used. Could any man's land be safe with the records moved beyond the people's observation?

By the end of Dongan's administration New York was a deeply troubled province. Denied the bright fruits of their struggle in 1680, the people were left with the familiar bitter dregs of arbitrary government. The assembly and the charter remained only as memories, and the future promised a continuation of prerogative rule. The accession of York to the throne, given his well-known aversion to popular government, meant the permanent imposition of Stuart tyranny. This was doubly onerous because of King James's Catholicism. Those given to conspiratorial theories could dwell on a peculiar constellation of Catholics: King James, Governor Dongan, Collector Matthew Plowman, and two garrison commanders—Jervais Baxter of Albany and Anthony Brockholls of New York City. With the French plotting on the northern frontier the conspiratorially minded had much to brood about. How could popular government make a comeback under these conditions? Compounding their problems was the slumping economy. Everyone was affected by the difficulties, even the very wealthy. In a still-fluid society how could a man be assured of his wealth and position? Indeed, what was certain in these times of trouble?

With problems mounting on all sides, in no small part because of Dongan's policies, one is struck by the lack of political activity in New York. There were petitions and occasional "riotts" but no cohesive opposition confronted Dongan. Compared to the rapid creation of an antiproprietary party in Pennsylvania, New York was positively backward. The paucity of central political institutions may be to blame. The short term of the first assembly failed to generate a coherent opposition to the "court" group. Even on the issue of monopolies, Albany and Easthampton could not rally support in the assembly. The curtailment and final termination of the assembly made the task of creating an opposition highly problematic. The old pattern of regionalism emerged again. It is also true that New York City occupied a crucial position because it could have sustained an opposition on its own. There were two reasons for this failure. First, the city benefited greatly from Dongan's economic policies. Realization of this blunted any desire to cause trouble. Second, the overwhelmingly Dutch population of the city desired not to do anything that might jeopardize their rights and antagonize English authorities in New York and England. They may have feared a complete severance of their trade with the Netherlands and the end of their contacts with the *Patria*. The result was political inertia. Without an opposition having an established institutional base the central administration continued to dominate affairs. During a period of serious economic and political disequilibrium that administration had to be extremely adroit to meet the challenges.

9 ❧ Leisler's Rebellion

During August 1688 Sir Edmund Andros journeyed to New York and New Jersey to proclaim his commission extending the government of the Dominion of New England over New York and New Jersey. His arrival coincided with gay celebrations for the birth of the heir to King James. Bonfires lit the nights; free food and beer encouraged the people to join in the thanksgiving.[1] Andros had no intention of staying; accordingly, he appointed Francis Nicholson, a member of the Boston garrison, lieutenant governor in charge of the southern area of the dominion. Andros's old friends had additional reasons for thankfulness. John West, James Graham, and John Palmer acquired offices in the new government while Philipse and Van Cortlandt, among others, were raised to the dominion council.[2] The dominion had reached its greatest extent with the incorporation of New York and New Jersey. The imperial experiment was in its heyday with only one pressing problem, French intentions in the north. Andros was unaware that his greatest danger actually lay to the east where William, prince of Orange, displaced his father-in-law as king of England.

The Crisis

William and Mary landed in England in November 1688, at the invitation of Englishmen displeased with King James's administration and frightened by the continuation of a Catholic ruling family. News of the turmoil gradually filtered to the colonies and by 1 March 1689 secret dispatches were received in New York alerting Lieutenant-Governor Francis Nicholson to events in England.[3] He and the council kept the news a secret in New York while sending word to Andros. However, the Williamite invasion opened the floodgates of frustration in Massachusetts, inspiring a movement that put Andros and other officials in the common gaol. News that the leaders of the dominion had been imprisoned in Boston's jail arrived in New York on 26 April.[4] The next day Nicholson called a meeting of the council and invited the mayor and aldermen of the city, the local justices of the peace, and militia officers to meet and discuss events. By this time the news from England was no longer a secret and this meeting had to cope with rumors of invasion and other wild tales that were sweeping the colony. To quiet the people and take some positive action, the council decided to fortify the city and have the four militia companies aid the twenty-two soldiers in the fort. After issuing these orders the council wrote to Andros giving him the comforting news that they were sure the "rabble" of Boston had imprisoned him, as no one of "quality" would have done so, and assuring him, and perhaps themselves, that the people of New York were inclined to peace.[5] It would be the last time they could give such assurances.

The emergency struck New York at a particularly awkward moment for the ruling elite. Some of their number were already in jail in Boston, and Dongan had retired to his Long Island estate, leaving only a few of them in positions of power. Lieutenant Governor Nicholson was a thirty-three-year-old military officer with no connections or influence in New York.[6] To aid him there were only three council members: Stephanus Van Cortlandt, Frederick Philipse, and Nicholas Bayard. When called upon to aid this rump government, Colonel Andrew Hamilton of New Jersey and Colonel William (Tangier) Smith of Long Island begged off for fear of personal retribution.[7]

The situation now closely resembled that of 1680—an inexperienced young man at the head of a council composed of Andros's cronies. This had been the recipe for disorder and proved so again in 1689. A narrowly based government concerned mainly with its own aggrandizement had failed during the proprietary and would do so again in the dominion; it was a legacy from York's distrust of representative government. If an assembly had been granted in 1665, it seems likely that years of confronting problems in a body that diffused political power throughout the colony and extended the numbers of politically active citizens might have made New York's governing institutions somewhat more stable. As it was, whenever there was a crisis the people had no common trusted institutions to rely on, and the result was fragmentation of the province into its constituent parts. It had happened in 1680 and did so again in 1689. The problem was an even more difficult one in 1689. Nicholson led a de facto, not a de jure, government after King James fled England. In 1680 Brockholls was the de jure authority and everyone knew that York was the final arbiter of events in his proprietary. The problems confronting Nicholson were, therefore, much greater. He and all other officials in New York held their commissions from King James, who was now at war with William and Mary. Confusion mixed with anxiety created great insecurity.[8]

The climax came during the month of May. Rumor piled upon rumor until hysteria gripped New York. The central element in the stories spreading through the colony was a Catholic threat to take New York. The chief officials of the government were charged with being papists. Nicholson was not immune to these charges and even those councilors who were members of the Dutch Reformed church were accused of papist leanings. Catholics connected with the government, including Dongan, Collector Matthew Plowman, and Captain Jervais Baxter of the garrison, made plans speedily to leave the colony.[9] Their departure failed to stop rumors of a French invasion aided by internal subversion, or of an Indian rising led by Andros, or of an attack by a French and Indian force led by Andros, or of a conjunction of Dongan and Andros sweeping down to rally the crypto-Catholics and seize New York for King James.[10] Nicholson, the council, the mayor and aldermen, and the militia officers denounced "seditious" people for spreading these rumors, but with little effect.[11] Tension continued to mount until the council issued an order commanding Dongan to return to the city where he could be kept under observation, thus placating the anti-Catholics. New York was slowly slipping from control.

The first direct action taken against the government originated in Long Island. The easternmost towns of Suffolk County received word from Boston about events there urging them to follow Boston's example. The "freeholders" of the county then formulated a declaration protesting against the "heavy burdens" placed on them by an "arbitrary power."[12] In order to secure English liberties from popery and French invasion they decided to seize control of the forts in New York City ("our headquarters") and Albany, and to secure the money lately extorted from them by the "enemies of peace and prosperity." Queens and Westchester counties, following the lead of Suffolk, tossed out their old magistrates, elected new ones, and prepared to march on the city.[13] The militia advanced as far as Jamaica while Nicholson and the council frantically met with their leaders in order to work out a compromise, meanwhile denouncing the militia as "rabble" intent on stirring up sedition. The militia marching on the city gradually dispersed with little harm done to anyone but Nicholson and the council, who were badly frightened at the course of events.[14] Their control over the city also diminished. One sure sign was the refusal of the merchants to pay customs, a levy they now regarded as illegal. The people were increasingly restless despite the attempts of government officials to quiet them.[15]

The beginning of the end for the government came on 31 May. Nicholson took six or seven soldiers of the Boston garrison, who were fleeing from the troubles there, into the fort. This action created a wave of fear in the city because the soldiers were thought to be Catholic reinforcements. Nicholson brought things to a climax by physically threatening Ensign Hendrick Cuyler of the militia when he brought a translator to the fort to clarify Nicholson's orders. During this meeting an anxious Nicholson lost control and reportedly said "there were so many rogues he was not sure of his life."[16] Another report had him scorning the Dutch as a "conquered people" who could not claim the rights of Englishmen.[17] Nicholson's vituperative remarks to Cuyler caused the militia and townspeople to march into the fort (the symbolic seat of the government), disarm the soldiers, and demand the keys of the fort. After consulting the council Nicholson delivered the keys, thereby giving up control of the fort. To all intents and purposes the government had surrendered its authority.[18]

While the council was paralyzed a "Declaration of the Inhabitants and Soldiers" was distributed. This document stated that the people had suffered the oppression of Dongan and his "pensioners" while waiting for orders from the "Prince of Orange." However, when Nicholson brought "papist" soldiers into the fort, harassed Cuyler, and threatened to put New York to the torch, the militia had to take action.[19] Until someone of the Protestant religion was sent over from England with orders for the colony, they would hold the fort. A few days later, on 3 June, the militia issued a similar declaration. In response, Nicholas Bayard, colonel of the militia, attempted to get the militia companies to obey him, but they refused, preferring to join the dissidents in the fort who were now under the command of another militia officer, Jacob Leisler.[20]

The council met on 6 June to discuss these events. They were so demoralized that they could only agree to send Nicholson to England where he could give an account of the events and perhaps save himself from the wrath of the people. By 10 June Nicholson was out of the city, leaving the remaining members of the government in an even more precarious situation.[21]

The city was still seething when on 22 June two commissioners arrived from Connecticut, bringing with them an official order from England to proclaim William and Mary.[22] Jacob Leisler, in charge of the militia in the fort, did so immediately. He also demanded that Van Cortlandt, in his capacity as mayor, do so before the city hall. Van Cortlandt demurred until he met with the aldermen. His refusal brought on his head a torrent of abuse, but Van Cortlandt held his ground until the meeting took place. After the aldermen had sanctioned the proclamation Van Cortlandt still hesitated, suggesting to Leisler that he should do it, which only brought him a second serving of vituperation. Physically threatened and called a papist and a traitor, Van Cortlandt retired with the officials of the city and province and other "loyal gentlemen," to celebrate privately the accession of William and Mary.[23]

Shaken by these events, the ever-narrowing leadership received good news on 24 June when a proclamation arrived confirming all officials in their offices until William and Mary could issue new orders.[24] Using this as a validation of their authority, Van Cortlandt and the others attempted to collect customs. The men commissioned to do so met with violence. It was simply intolerable to the insurgents that those who hesitated to proclaim William and Mary now used their authority to collect customs. The customshouse was filled with angry men, drawn swords, flashing daggers, and great outrage. Bayard, who barely escaped with his life, went into hiding before leaving the city for Albany, while Van Cortlandt kept out of sight. Some of their fellow partisans went to jail for their actions. Philipse played an ambiguous role in these events and remained untouched. Van Cortlandt made one last stand by trying to hold a mayor's court meeting. He and the aldermen were warned not to meet and the session was canceled. With its officers dispersed and its institutions unable to function, the government ceased to exist.[25]

The Rebels in Power

After declaring their loyalty to the new monarchs and harassing the old government out of office, the insurgents moved to create their own government. The captains of the militia remained prominent leaders, but for the future a civil government, separate from the captains, was needed. Copying the actions of the New England colonies, a committee of safety was formed. Spurning any relationship with the old government and its Jacobite commissions, the committee believed it derived its undefined powers from the people. Its members had two immediate concerns—insuring the defense of the city and explaining their actions to Connecticut and Massachusetts. For the former they appointed Jacob Leisler captain of the fort with orders to carry out its reconstruction and the recruiting of a new garrison.[26] In approaching the New England colonies the committee sought to assure them of their good intentions and to request New England's help against the French. They also sent letters with the same intent to King William and the bishop of Salisbury.[27] In these missives they concentrated upon justifying their actions and proclaiming loyalty to the new monarchs. To insure that they received a fair reception, the committee also sent Ensign Joost Stoll to England to present their case. Friendly merchants in England were also called upon to testify to the good character of the members of the committee.[28]

Creating a government proved more complicated than providing a defense. The reconstruction of the fort and improvement of the city defenses required money. To meet this need, the committee appointed Peter Delanoy customs collector, so that the most lucrative source of funds came into its hands. Connecticut and the counties received requests for funds or militiamen. The French immigrants, whom Leisler had helped settle at New Rochelle, immediately notified the committee of their willingness to contribute, a politic move when anti-French feeling was running high.[29] The committee's efforts were insufficient and on 23 July, when news of the outbreak of war with France arrived, it seized the provincial treasury of £773. The discovery of such a large sum of money confirmed the suspicions of many about the fiscal practices of the government and proved discomforting to Stephanus Van Cortlandt, who was called upon to account for its source. When his evidence appeared suspect, each county was asked to forward its receipts in order to verify them with the records.[30] In the meantime, the treasury plus the promised financial aid seemed adequate to the tasks at hand. Thus, real financial hardship was delayed, leaving the need to tax a problem for the future.

The committee faced a more difficult task in providing a system of justice. A major problem, and a major grievance, was the lack of records. The secretary's office was broken into for the remaining archives, and pleas were sent to Boston and England requesting the return of the material taken away by Andros.[31] Other difficulties accompanied the opening of the courts; since the justices of the peace for New York City refused to act for the committee, one of its adherents, Gerardus Beekman, a justice in Kings County, acted as a justice for the city.[32] Opening the mayor's court presented greater problems. The court remained in the hands of those opposed to the committee, and they could not be turned out until the fall elections. When the elections were held, they were characterized by irregularities. The insurgents wanted to be sure that the right people were elected. Fearing the invidious "papist" opposition, they acted to keep its members from influencing the election and, more importantly, from gaining office. They achieved this goal by electing only insurgents. Their actions only confirmed the worst suspicions of their opponents. After the election the new mayor, Peter Delanoy, tried to hold a court of sessions, but the opposition objected because the new government did not hold the city charter. Not to be denied, Delanoy demanded it from the ex-mayor, Stephanus Van Cortlandt. When he refused, a group of men went to his house and forcibly seized it. Armed with the charter, the new magistrates began their regime.[33]

In providing a government the committee of safety had limited goals. The preservation of the colony was the supreme goal and one that was accomplished. A secondary goal of providing a government was slowly realized, and then only in the city. Apart from asking aid in defending New York City, the committee did not try to govern the other regions, which had gained control over their own governments. This situation continued until December when a new central government emerged.

This process was initiated in mid-August when the committee of safety surrendered its primacy. Because it could not always meet conveniently and was uncertain as to when orders would arrive from England, the committee made Leisler commander-in-chief.[34] In its absence he was given the power to do whatever was necessary for the preservation of the province. As its final act the committee collected evidence on the former government and sent it to England. Thus, their records came to an end with the by now familiar charges of an "Arbitrary" power "especially of Late" exercised against them "being alwayes esteemed, as a conquest people." The government had used its power to extract taxes without the consent of the people and without an accounting of how the taxes were spent.[35] With this denunciation the committee put New York in Leisler's hands.

Leisler did not perceive his role as merely that of a caretaker. He saw to the defenses of the city, spied upon the disgruntled members of the old regime, and jailed anyone he deemed seditious.[36] He also managed the elections for a new city government in October 1689, and thus must bear responsibility for the irregularities the insurgents used to gain control over the city government.[37]

Leisler also turned his attention to Albany. Up to this point Albany had hewed its own path as the vitality of the central government waned. On 1 July 1689 the *commissaries* had proclaimed William and Mary in Dutch and English. A month later the civil and military authorities of Albany City and County joined together in a convention awaiting orders from the new monarchs while ignoring the new government in the city because they believed there was no settled government for the province.[38] The convention was especially fearful of French intentions and took steps to strengthen its defenses by asking "Capt." Leisler for one hundred men and supplies. Leisler did not reply to the convention but to Johannes Wendel and J. J. Bleeker, captains in the militia. Without offering aid, he told them to consult the "Common People" about sending representatives to New York City.[39] Denied aid by Leisler, the convention collected a special tax of £367 and sent letters to Boston and Hartford requesting help.[40] October still found Albany acting alone and hoping for the best.

Some of the disputes poisoning New York City found their way up the Hudson: the convention found it necessary to allay suspicions by swearing loyalty to William and Mary and making the soldiers in the garrison take a loyalty oath. Other rumors circulated to the effect that Leisler believed that the officers of the Albany garrison were papists and that men from New York would have to seize Albany and arrest the leading men of the town. As a consequence of these rumors the convention publicly asserted Albany's independence and put Mayor Peter Schuyler in command of the fort.[41] This action was taken on 8 November, the day before Jacob Milborne arrived and began eroding Albany's unity.

After the dispute with Van Rensselaer, Milborne had abandoned New York. He returned in December 1678 and immediately regretted doing so because in November 1677 he had written slightingly of Andros. Andros never forgot such things and with his old adversary back in his hand, he brought Milbourne before the council as a "mutinous" person and turned him over to the sheriff for punishment. Milborne extricated himself from Andros's clutches once again and later exacted his own revenge by dragging Andros into court after his recall to England. Not until 1683, when Andros was safely removed from the scene, did Milborne return to New York and regain his freeman's status in New York City.[42] Obedience to authority was not one of Milborne's strongest characteristics and the events of 1689 gave him ample opportunity to exercise his antiauthoritarianism.

Milborne arrived in Albany on 9 November with fifty men and orders from Leisler to reinforce the garrison. Marching into a crowded city hall Milborne immediately launched into a rousing speech. The clerk of the convention reported his "Discourse to ye Common People" carried the message that:

now it was in there power to free Themselfs from yt Yoke of arbitrary Power and Government under which they had byen so long in ye Reign of yt Illegal king James, who was a Papist, Declaring all Illegall whatever was done and past in his time, yea the Charter of the Citty was null and void Since it was granted by a Papist kings governour and that now ye Power was in the People to choose new Civill and Military officers as they Pleased, challenging all them that had bore office in king James Time to be Illegall, and therefore they must have a free Election.[43]

Here is an argument not previously articulated by the insurgents. Since James II was a "papist," his government was illegal and all acts of that government were void; as a result power returned to the people. It would seem that the radical religious world that Milborne inhabited continued to carry the tradition of political radicalism. The members of the convention refused to accept Milborne's arguments, and he had to settle for turning over his commission.[44]

The next day brought further bad news to the convention. The settlements at Kinderhook and Schenectady, which Albany had always dominated in order to guard the fur monopoly, had been aroused by promises made by Milborne of equal privileges in the fur trade and in wheat bolting.[45] Milborne had rapidly spread the message of political equality and an end to the system of monopolies. Called before a shaken and furious convention, Milborne was unrepentant. The convention denounced his commission from the council of war in New York City as a document signed by "private" men, therefore without force, and refused to obey anyone without orders from William and Mary. Milborne treated them to another speech, which the convention denounced as seditious and positively destructive of their goal of keeping peace in the community. However, by the next day, 11 November, it was apparent that communal solidarity had been broken. Members of the convention could not enter city hall because of a crowd demanding that Milborne's soldiers, who were billeted outside the town, be accepted into the community under the leadership of a local man, Jochim Staats. One hundred people, described by the convention as youths and not freeholders, signed a petition to this effect. Under pressure, the convention had more or less decided to accept the reinforcements if they were placed under its control. The sticking point was a demand by Milborne that the fort be in the hands of a military officer and not Mayor Schuyler. Perhaps suspecting that once Milborne got his men into the fort under the command of one of his own men its problems would rise commensurately, the convention refused to concede this point.[46]

Milborne's actions badly divided Albany. Substantial citizens such as Peter Bogardus, Johannes Wendel, Gabriel Thompson, and even Richard Pretty, the ex-sheriff, were giving aid and comfort to Milborne. Growing confident of his success, Milborne marched his soldiers into town and billeted them with members of his "faction." Treading softly, the convention held a meeting on 14 November with an invited delegation of twelve men picked by the "people." Mayor Schuyler presented evidence to the meeting that the insurgents in New York planned to take charge of the fort and change the government. This evidence was followed by revelations about the convention's negotiations with Milborne, stressing Milborne's unwillingness to accept a civilian leader in the fort. The representatives of the people were convinced that Milborne had been duplicitous, and they finally turned on him, requesting that he accept the convention's terms. He refused and walked out. The next day Milborne attempted a coup by seizing the fort. Thwarted, with his foot literally in the gate, he deployed his men and had them load their weapons. A group of Mohawks observed his actions from a nearby hill. The convention had warned constantly that divisions in the community would cause doubt among the Indians and occasion their going over to the French. Now Milborne had displayed their divisions and imperiled the community. The Mohawks turned out to be allies of the convention; they threatened to attack Milborne's men as soon as they left town. Caught between hostile Indians and apprehensive townspeople, Milborne gave up. He turned over command of his men to five sympathizers from the community and left Albany on 16 November. A strong desire for communal security allowed the convention to thwart Milborne and remain aloof from the new leadership in New York City.[47]

Milborne's undignified retreat reveals the strengths and the weaknesses of the insurgents at this point. His rhetoric in Albany was a heady new wine for many people, particularly in the communities that had been subordinated to Albany, yet he could not rally sufficient support to overcome the convention. Fear of the Indians and of New York's intentions kept Albany to a course of its own. The convention had proclaimed William and Mary but was unwilling to surrender to "private" men from the city. Regionalism still flourished whenever the center was weak. Each area of the colony went its own way, disregarding an illegitimate government in the city, a government becoming ever more radical, if Milborne's rhetoric is any gauge.

December brought the long-awaited news from England. King William had written to Francis Nicholson on 30 July appointing him (temporarily) lieutenant governor. The letter contained a crucial phrase. Without certain knowledge of events in the colonies King William's letter to Nicholson contained a standard phrase. It was addressed to Nicholson or "in his absence to such as for the time being take care for the Preserving the Peace and administring the Lawes in our said Province."[48] This letter was delivered by Captain John Riggs to Van Cortlandt and Philipse, the remaining members of the council. Leisler immediately demanded the letter package and when Van Cortlandt refused, he sent soldiers to seize it. On reading the letter and an accompanying order in council to proclaim William and Mary, Leisler decided he was the one in charge and accepted the temporary commission of lieutenant governor.[49] The choice was simple. The members of what had now become the "Roman Catholic Party" were completely ineligible to administer the colony. Only good Protestants could control the government; therefore Leisler was legitimated, and he moved immediately to create a government.

Leisler formed a council of four representatives from the city and one each from Queens, Kings, Orange, and Westchester counties. Albany and eastern Long Island, still averse to his leadership, were unrepresented. Milborne became the provincial secretary and Leisler's clerk. On 17 December, Leisler appointed men to administer oaths to justices in the counties, and in the days that followed a stream of commissions for civil and military officials flowed to every part of the colony.[50] These actions were the functions of an executive, a position that Leisler quickly adopted. When it came to legislative functions there were problems. The king's brief message did not provide Nicholson, or whoever was in his place, with a commission outlining his powers. Leisler and the new council may have wondered if they had the power to call an assembly. However, since they had been preaching the advisability of holding new elections to establish popular authority, it may be assumed they believed an assembly could be called. The real question was—could they insure the election of a favorable majority? The answer to that was negative. With Albany and Suffolk counties outside their control and the Roman Catholic faction still active, they wanted to avoid an election. Besides, an election during the winter month of December was not feasible. But the problems of raising money and establishing the courts needed resolution and only an assembly could do these things. In the end they grasped the solution of using the acts passed by the assembly in 1683.[51] The acts of a popularly elected assembly were just what they needed.

After resurrecting the legislation of 1683, Leisler first moved on 16 December to put the revenue act in force and three days later opened all of the courts.[52] No sooner was the taxing power proclaimed than the need for courts became evident. Unknown "English freemen" nailed a proclamation over the new government's announcement.[53] The proclamation argued that James, as the duke of York or as king, never approved the acts of the assembly, and since a law must be a grant of the people with royal assent, the acts of the assembly never had the force of law. To exhume the old legislation in 1689 was unreasonable, arbitrary, and against the fundamental rights of English subjects. Leisler's proclamation simply had claimed that the laws of 1683 were still in force. The "English freemen's" argument was on sounder legal grounds although it verged on the polemical by stating that the use of the old acts would cause "brutish slavery." Leisler and the council retaliated by denouncing anyone who could put a "false" construction on laws passed by the freemen represented in an assembly.[54] Their rebuttal went on to quote almost directly from the Charter of Libertyes that legislative authority resided in a governor, council, and an assembly. Using the rhetoric of the charter and its undoubted popular appeal, the new government derided those who made legalistic quibbles. In the end Leisler had the power to do as he wanted. By this time he had adopted the symbols of power, even to the point of taking the governor's pew in the church and having a new seal made recognizing the changes in government.[55] On 30 December he ordered the surrender of all commissions issued by Dongan and Andros. This gave him additional leverage on the opposition, which now had to obey the order or face the new courts.

Leisler entered the new year with his administration established and his enemies on the defensive. To assert his authority Leisler demanded an oath of loyalty from the people.[56] It was reported that he forced subscription to the oath by arguing that evidence of popular support would induce the new government in England to give more privileges to the colony. Some of the more radical insurgents argued that if the home government did not give them what they wanted, they now knew how to lay the government aside.[57] This was another sign of radicalism that may have been beyond Leisler's control.

An Analysis of the Rebel Movement

The movement that destroyed the government received its immediate impetus from the hysteria that grew so swiftly during May 1689. The sources of discontent that had accumulated under Dongan were brought to the boiling point by the rumors from England of war at home and abroad. Controlling this rising tide of fear and uncertainty proved beyond the capacity of the rump government of the dominion. It finally exploded in what Van Cortlandt referred to as the "people's Revolucions."[58] Later a devil theory came into vogue, placing the blame for the events of May and June on the ambitions of Jacob Leisler, the chief leader of the insurgency. However, these events appear to be explosions of frustration rather than the plotting of one individual. Nicholson's foolish actions and words brought hundreds of men into the street and the fort. This "mob" merely forced out Nicholson and the soldiers without spilling blood. Once its purposes were achieved, the group issued a statement of loyalty to the new rulers in England and denounced the actions of the former government.[59] Following protestations of loyalty from the militia, the people entered into an "association" binding themselves to protect one another, fight "evil" persons, and obey officers put over them. They made it clear that they did so because they could no longer obey a government commissioned by King James. As a result all acts of Dongan and Andros were declared null and void. The people also stressed their willingness to defend William and Mary, the Protestant cause, and the lawful rights and liberties of subjects. The articles of association stressed obedience to authority, putting both those who formulated the articles and those who signed them in a rather conservative light. They were merely removing an illegal government and awaiting orders from the new sovereigns. Minimal demands were made and little violence was committed against the members of the government.[60]

In form, the association is an old English means of swearing loyalty to the sovereign while dismantling a despised local government. The people behind it, however, were primarily the Dutch inhabitants of the city. The pent-up frustrations of years of English administration were readily released with the accession of William and Mary. The prince of Orange, leader of their *Patria*, was a figure to arouse the affection of his fellow countrymen in New York. He was also a symbol of the Protestant cause in Europe, now threatened by the Catholic menace of France. The Dutch were facing a French invasion from Canada while governed by a "papist"-controlled government; the accession of William provided them with an outlet for their frustrations, particularly when the government appeared to be ignoring the accession of in order to carry on a "Jacobite" government. According to Councilor Nicholas Bayard the men who joined the association were "almost none but of the Dutch Nation." He added that the "tenth man not knowing what he had signed," but they did so because they were promised that the situation would be restored as it was in 1660.[61] One can imagine the nostalgic impulses that drove the Dutch to believe that the clock would be turned back and that they would govern

New Netherland under a Dutch prince. Such a prospect was a catalyst for action.

Nostalgia alone did not impel the members of the movement. The depression, hatred for Dongan's administration, fear of French intentions, anxieties about the future under the Stuarts, and anti-Catholic hysteria brought many into the streets. Even English inhabitants, who had no old affection for William, joined in the activities of 1689. The participation of the English citizens of the city in the movement was overlooked, in part, because they were still a minority in the community and the movement was largely Dutch. The opponents of the insurgents had other reasons for overlooking the English participants. The members of the old regime who opposed the movement consisted of Englishmen and Dutchmen associated with the English. By characterizing the insurgents as wholly Dutch and a "rabble" they stigmatized their opponents, making them appear illegitimate contenders for power in an English colony. This double aspersion would be used time and again in England against the insurgents.

The men who were looked to for leadership as the rebellion began were the militia captains—Jacob Leisler, Charles Lodwick, Abraham De Peyster, Johannes De Bruyn, Gabriel Minvielle, and Nicholas Stuyvesant. These were the men who marched their men into the fort, defied Bayard, and led in signing the association. Jacob Leisler emerged as their leader.[62] In the weeks prior to the outbreak he had played an ambiguous role, participating in meetings of magistrates and other officials called by Nicholson but he refused to pay customs. During the events of 31 May through 26 June his leadership became vital to the movement. He joined the men whom Hendrick Cuyler had taken into the fort, issued a personal proclamation of loyalty to William and Mary, and called together a committee of safety.[63] This was the first time he had emerged into public life since the Van Rensselaer affair and its aftermath. In the years after this unhappy interlude he had continued to build his fortune but was still kept out of office except that of a militia captain.

The anti-Catholicism that swept New York touched a vital nerve in Leisler, for religion remained a central concern of his life. The controversy with Van Rensselaer revealed his tenacity as a religious polemicist. A deacon of the Dutch church, he withdrew from participation by 1686, probably because of his distrust of the church's leadership.[64] Certainly, after the rebellion got under way his rhetoric was that of a rigid Calvinist. His letters to New England after the failure of his projected invasion of Canada in 1690 are particularly revealing. He wrote,

> Good God, to what excusse do men run themselves into, neither regarding morality or the legible proceedings of the Creator, when his judgements are abroad and carry such remarkable stamps of punishing These Territories.
> For my part I must owne mine and the inequities of the Province, and that we have highly as well as justly minted whatever may befall us. . . .
> Nevertheless, it cannot but one day sadly reflect that a peoples professing Christianity so eminently beyond others, should so basely degenerate beneath the very heathens. . . .
> but when you are searched with candles, it will be known who are guilty of this accursed thing, and your nakedness will be uncovered.[65]

These are the words of an embittered man excoriating his coreligionists. It is easy to see how he was swept along by the anti-Catholic tides. Once he emerged as the leader of the insurgency he denounced his enemies as papists and collected evidence proving the Catholicism of the members of the old government.[66] The events of 1689 were for him an opportunity to restore the true religion and rid the colony of Catholic influences.

Less susceptible of analysis are his other reasons for joining the movement. He probably looked to King William not as the leader of the *Patria* but as the defender of Protestantism. An equally strong motive may have been revenge—revenge on a system and the members of the "court" faction. For all that he was wealthy and related by marriage to the Bayards and Van Cortlandts, Leisler was never brought into the elite group. He probably believed that he had suffered financially at their hands because he had to wage a bitter struggle in court against his relatives over his wife's estate. The ransom he paid the "Turks" and the lost profits of the voyage during which he and his sons were captured remained associated in his mind with the Van Rensselaer affair. He suffered another setback in 1683 when Philipse won a case in the mayor's court that denied him plate worth £500 recovered from a shipwreck. The jury that found against him consisted of ten Englishmen and two Dutchmen—a Van Cortlandt and a Schuyler.[67] Status jealousies are difficult to measure, but there is little reason to doubt that Leisler disliked an elite group that denied him its rewards and attacked his religion. He referred to them as "grandees," a term carrying connotations of Catholicism and of being a Spanish or alien nobleman.[68]

Once Leisler had established himself and staffed the government, it becomes easier to analyze his followers. By then some of the earlier participants in the movement refused to continue and a few others would soon drop out. These included such established figures as Johannes De Peyster, Gabriel Minvielle, Abraham De Peyster, William Beekman, Francis Rombouts, and Nicholas De Meyer. Some new men, such as Charles Lodwick and Stephen De Lancey, thought better of their support too and went over to the opposition.

No lists of any kind survive to illuminate the nature of Leisler's mass support at this time. That he had widespread support is beyond doubt. Even at the very end, when he finally gave up, it was reported that three hundred men surrendered with him.[69] An analysis of voters in later electoral battles in New York City reveals that the Leislerian faction was extremely strong among the Dutch inhabitants and particularly so among Dutchmen who were born about the time of the English conquest and who were taking up family and political responsibilities around 1689.[70] Widespread Dutch support was frequently noted at the time of the insurgent movement, yet the leadership of the movement was far from wholly Dutch, with men such as Samuel Edsall, William Lawrence, and Jacob Milborne in high office. The insurgents were not just Dutchmen alienated by the increasing Anglicization of life in New York. Leisler, in fact, carefully avoided making the movement wholly Dutch. When he requested that the new French immigrants appoint a justice, he insisted the man must speak English.[71]

The motives pulling the insurgents together were varied. Family ties bound together the elite establishment and the family was also an important tie among the insurgents. Samuel Edsall had four sons-in-law—William Lawrence, Benjamin Blagg, Jacob Milborne, and Peter Delanoy—all of whom were prominent Leislerians. Edsall's brother-in-law during his second marriage was Daniel Ternieur of New Haarlem, an insurgent. Milborne's second wife was one of Leisler's daughters, and another of Leisler's daughters was married to Robert Walters, one of the new aldermen in New York City. Another constellation of associations formed around Hendrick Cuyler. His wife was Elsje Ten Brock, daughter of Dirk; his daughter Sara married Peter Van Brugh, while his son Abraham married the daughter of J. J. Bleeker.[72] Members of all these families played prominent roles in Leisler's government. Such interconnections illuminate the importance of the family as a political unit in colonial society.

For the purposes of examining the insurgent movement, fifty-six men have been chosen. They served on the council or were associated with New York City as civil or military officers (including assembly representatives) during Leisler's administration.[73] Accurate information on their economic status is difficult to obtain. Sixteen of them were assessed in 1676 for the new dock. Only one of them, Leisler, had great wealth. No one else came close to his £3,000 assessment. Their modest assessments placed them in the middle class. Two young men involved in the rebellion who had not yet established fortunes of their own in 1676 had fathers with substantial assessments, and two others inherited more modest fortunes. The only other assessment of wealth is derived from the special house tax of 1677. Two individuals were charged the maximum £1; two others were in the middle rank.[74] There is always the problem of underassessment in these tax lists. For instance, Samuel Edsall and William Lawrence owned considerable estates in New Jersey and Long Island that were not recorded in New York City.[75] In most cases, however, one is left with the strong impression that the supporters of Leisler were in the middle class.

In terms of officeholding, thirty-two of the fifty-six never held a civil or military commission. Twelve of the remaining twenty-four had been members of the city government. The other twelve held such offices as *schepen* in the Dutch government, or justice of the peace, and in one case (Gabriel Minvielle) member of the council. The overall picture is one of men outside the group of families that had previously dominated the political and economic life of the city and province.

There was a further bond linking some of these men together. One element that reveals the Dutch aspect of the movement was that two of the insurgents were among the eight who refused to take the loyalty oath in 1674. Two others were the sons of men who had refused. Of the remaining four protesters, two were dead by 1689 and two (Bayard and Kip) had become members of the establishment.[76]

Examining the personnel appointed by Leisler or those elected in the outlying regions reveals different patterns of experience. On Long Island after 1689 truly unpopular officials were simply put out of office by the townsmen. However, the leadership changed very little. When Leisler extended the central government he allowed the townsmen to choose their own leaders, and as a result the men who accepted appointments were townsmen with long careers in local government or government officials such as justices, who retained popular support.[77] Continuity rather than discontinuity of leadership characterized Long Island government. Thus, when dissent appeared on Long Island, Leisler lacked influence over the local leadership and had to send the militia in to quell the disturbances, something never done previously.

As has already been shown, Albany expressed its particularism by denying Leisler's legitimacy. In part, this was a move to gain independence from the city's monopolies. The visits of Nicholas Bayard, Stephanus Van Cortlandt, and other exiles from the city also helped alienate the town's leaders from Leisler. Mayor Peter Schuyler and Robert Livingston, the secretary and treasurer, were related to the Van Cortlandts and the Van Rensselaers, who exerted great influence in the town. Only when Milborne came to Albany and spoke out against monopolies in the outlying towns and in favor of new elections did cracks appear in Albany's unity. Towns such as Schenectady, Kinderhook, and Claverack resented the dominance of Albany and sought a means of escape. Some individuals inside Albany found Milborne's rhetoric tantalizing and many undoubtedly wanted to join their Dutch compatriots in the city. When Albany finally accepted Leisler the men who moved into office were similar to those in New York City.

The new officials were generally men of the middle ranks. Of the thirty-nine individuals involved sixteen were taxed in

1679 for the stockade. Only two (Hans Hendrickson and Robert Sanders) had assessments near the top, while the remainder were spread in the middle ranks. Of the eighteen not taxed, six were from outlying villages and therefore not taxable in Albany. Repeating the pattern of New York City, few men had previously held office. Of the ten who had, only two were prominent. Richard Pretty served as a *commissary* and was for many years sheriff of Albany.[78] Johannes Provoost had been a constable, acting sheriff, assessor, *commissary*, secretary, and delegate to the court of assize, where he argued Albany's case against monopolies.[79] Both men were rivals of Robert Livingston; their jealousy of him may have influenced their actions. Livingston took away Pretty's position as excise collector, and, through his position as secretary and marriage into the Van Rensselaer family, Livingston had diminished Provoost's opportunities for public office. Pretty attacked Livingston in his letters to Milborne and when Leisler obtained a firm grip on Albany in 1690, Pretty drove his rival into exile.[80] One other tie bound together some of the men. In 1681 seven of them had joined together to protest against conditions in the fur trade that reduced their profits.[81] Their protest was ignored, but they evidently remembered it quite well. Thus, the group favoring Leisler in Albany was remarkably similar to that in the city— men of middle standing who had various economic and political grievances. Their popular support came from those who were attracted to a Dutch movement that promised elections and broader trade opportunities.

Leisler remained in power for a little over one year, struggling to legitimatize the insurgents' actions and his own administration. He sent letters to King William and his advisors, reporting favorably on the condition of the province and excoriating the "papist" faction.[82] Royal favor was denied him. Joost Stoll, his emissary, returned in May 1690 with the news that he had failed to gain royal recognition for the insurgents and that a new governor had been appointed. Another envoy, Benjamin Blagg, hurried off in June to plead the insurgents' cause.[83] By this time Leisler was engaged in his greatest enterprise, a combined intercolonial assault on Canada. Even this major initiative did not bring him success or royal favor and, as the year went on, unfavorable responses from England strength-ened the opposition. At home, Leisler's need for money and food for war against the French forced him to collect unpopular taxes. Thus, in New York and abroad he found frustration and resentment.

The Growth of the Opposition

Leisler's government was not unopposed. Indeed, spar-ring with its enemies took a great deal of energy. From the beginning the insurgents were harassed. In turn, they took steps to thwart their real or imagined antagonists, which had the effect of creating a real opposition party. What impelled the insurgents to lash out was fear of Catholic plots and invasion. Rumors and plots to seize New York blossomed constantly in the hot summer weather of 1689: a fire was set in a tower of the fort to blow up the ammunition supply and thus destroy the fort and the city, fleets were sighted bearing down on the harbor, and the insurgents' enemies spread false tales in order to wear down their vigilance.[84] They lived in a world filled with catastrophe, evil, and, in the end, hatred. As protection against plots, anyone coming into the city was seized and taken to the fort for examination. The insurgents scrutinized the letters and actions of the opposition for treasonous activities.[85] "Papists" were disarmed and their "idols" smashed. Gradually more vigorous action was needed. As the committee of safety gained control over the situation it started jailing those accused of sedition. These men were regarded as prisoners of "warre" and were put in jail without trial.[86] Concurrently, a campaign was carried on to collect evidence on the Catholic tendencies and malfeasance of former officials. One man testified that Nicholson had attended mass. The Reverend Mr. Innis, the Anglican minister, was suspected of not following Protestant practices; his Dutch and French peers quickly testified to his soundness in theology and liturgy, but he remained suspect.[87] Stephanus Van Cortlandt was accused of responding to a state-ment about the tax burden by saying "let them be sold for it." In this atmosphere of suspicion and hatred mobs broke into homes and threatened individuals with guns and swords. These activities forced the opposition to leave the city and start a campaign to regain control of the colony.[88]

The resources of the old regime were limited. The small numbers involved in the government were a slim base to build upon, but the actions of the insurgents helped swell their ranks. The mobs put fear in the hearts of many—especially the English. The overwhelmingly Dutch composition of the movement gave rise to rumors about an "ill design" against the English, so much so that the committee of safety and the militia captains issued a declaration stating that the seizure of the fort was "solely" for the service of the Crown and that all should obey the laws and live in peace with their neighbors.[89] The English may have been unconvinced when rumor had Leisler saying "he would do all the English Rogues business for them so that two of them should not be seen to walk together."[90] Another report stated that "there will be very few Englishmen of any reputation left in ye place" unless orders were speedily sent from England.[91] As England was still the place that bestowed legitimacy, it was there that the anti-insurgents sought relief.

As they turned to England, the anti-insurgents began building their case. The one constant theme that emerges in their correspondence is the unworthiness of the insurgents to hold power. Their rhetoric rarely indulged in ethnic slurs but concentrated on class differences. The insurgents were frequently described as a "rabble," or Leisler's "gang," or the "rebels." Slighting references were made to "our Noble Committee of safety," Leisler's "Billingsgate Rhetorick," and how one of the insurgents liked to "show his fine cloaths." They heaped derision on the "rebels'" qualifications for office. Leisler was a man having neither the birth nor the education to govern and was simply discontent with his "station." The social status of various individuals was questioned: Jacob Milborne was vulgar in conversation and suffering from a decayed fortune; Cornelius Pluvier, one of the new aldermen, was described as a poor man who sold beer and rum retail; Joost Stoll, their envoy to the Crown, was constantly referred to as a "dram man"— almost a barkeeper; and Leisler was the "Grand Robber."[92]

The actions of the insurgents were equally reprehensible to the old "court" party. For instance, they disbanded the elite troop of horse in the city militia because it created dissatisfaction among the people. They even went so far as to seize four young gentlemen of "quality" from the "University of Boston." Not only were such low types incapable of ruling, but their loyalty to the new government in England was questionable. How far could one trust "great Ollerverians" or a "Masanello"— the former, a term calling up a great world of sedition in England, the latter recalling a famous rebel.[93] Spilling outrage and venom from their pens, the anti-insurgents described a government that had used the "rabble" to come into power and now consisted of unworthy and seditious people. In doing so they created the personal divisions that would last so long in New York—Leislerians and anti-Leislerians. But in the summer and fall of 1689 the anti-Leislerians could only wait upon orders from England.

The Decline and Fall of Leisler's Regime

In the early morning hours of 9 February 1690 disaster struck in Schenectady. Count Frontenac, the able defender of New France, sent three expeditions of Indians and soldiers crashing into New England and New York. When the raiders withdrew from Schenectady, sixty-two villagers were dead and twenty-seven prisoners stumbled north with their captors. The few remaining survivors struggled across the frozen ground to alert Albany. A rescue party was organized; it struggled after the raiding party all the way to the gates of Montreal—so near, but yet so far.[94] For years fear of such an attack had determined the policy of the governors and the *handlaers* of Albany; now they confronted the terrible reality when the colony was in turmoil. In response the convention decided to go on the offensive. It planned to appeal to Massachusetts, Connecticut, Virginia, and New York City for an invasion of Quebec in the spring.[95] This plan, only roughly thought out, was to become the basis of the first intercolonial action against the French.

Albany had first to resolve its problems with Leisler. Jochim Staats had been sent to Albany in December to take charge of the fort, collect taxes, and hold a "free" election that Leisler hoped would elect "willing" candidates. When Staats presented his credentials, the convention challenged him to show some document from William and Mary conferring authority on Leisler. Staats bluffed and demanded that the people be called together so that he could show them his powers. Refusing to allow a recurrence of what had happened with Milborne, the convention kept Staats from his audience. Having spurned Leisler's initiative once again, it arranged a pageant to build communal solidarity. The magistrates, accompanied by soldiers, marched through the town proclaiming its independence.[96] It was a brave show, but after the attack on Schenectady communal pride fell before French fury, and Leisler could not be resisted. The convention sent delegates to Leisler who in turn sent a three-man commission led by Milborne to bring the town into the fold. The convention, which Leisler blamed for encouraging the French through its refractory practices, was dissolved.[97]

Leisler threw his considerable energies behind a major assault upon New France. The most remarkable feature of his plan was an intercolonial conference called on 2 April to meet on 1 May. Leisler engaged in a wide correspondence with colonial governors as far away as Barbados to elicit attendance at the conference or, alternatively, support for an attack on Canada. When the conference opened, the attendance did not match his expectations. Only the governors of Massachusetts, Plymouth, and Connecticut attended. New Jersey was under the influence of New York exiles and refused to aid their enemy. Virginia's new governor, Francis Nicholson, was hardly a friend of Leisler. Pennsylvania had no governor and did not even reply. Maryland promised 100 men and Rhode Island promised money for any joint enterprise. The results of the conference were mixed. Massachusetts was preoccupied with the eastern frontier; Salmon Falls, New Hampshire, had suffered the same fate as Schenectady and further disasters at Casco and Fort Loyal were to make the east a greater concern. The Bay colony had put its energies into an expedition led by Sir William Phipps against Port Royal in Acadia. Massachusetts, therefore, promised only 160 men; Plymouth agreed to send 60, Connecticut 135, and New York 600 for the expedition against Montreal.[98] The delegates returned home with some hope that they could strike at their old enemies.

The New York conference was significant for it had been called into session and had met without direction from England. This action indicates the growing maturity of the colonies, for in a time of rebellion and war they were able to plan a vigorous counterattack against their enemies. It was a considerable achievement for Leisler. The conference also set in motion the classic strategy that was to dominate future planning of Canadian campaigns. A thrust up the Lake Champlain corridor at Montreal was joined with an attack on the St. Lawrence approaches to Quebec. Before Wolfe could bring off a final victory during the Seven Years' War, many men would thrust their fingers over maps outlining the basic strategy conceived in 1690.[99]

Leisler may have harbored an ambition to lead the expedition, but the necessity of watching his enemies made this impractical. Instead he nominated his chief adviser, Milborne. Leisler did not get his way, for the New England colonies had what amounted to a veto because he needed their aid. They were also suspicious of Leisler. Robert Livingston, now in exile, urged the New England colonies to join the expedition but not to accept Leisler or Milborne as its leader. The result was a letter to Leisler from Secretary Allyn of Connecticut announcing that Milborne was "short of parentage" for such a position.[100] To take his place Allyn suggested the eminently well-born "Major-General" Fitz Winthrop. Winthrop, it was suggested, was a man of reputation, capable of eliciting discipline from the troops. The desire to assault the French finally overcame Leisler's ambitions for his son-in-law and he withdrew his nomination.[101]

Men and supplies for the expedition moved into Albany as the summer began. Only Connecticut met its obligations in men; Massachusetts was too intent on the Phipps expedition against Quebec to help, and the others never met their quotas. Leisler, however, continued to urge action upon all concerned and even launched a three-ship navy against the French.[102] Meanwhile, smallpox broke out among the soldiers and the Iroquois, demoralizing the army. In midsummer Winthrop arrived in Albany to accept his commission and review his command. He left Albany on 30 July only to return on 20 August with nothing to show for his efforts. Winthrop complained of short supplies and dispirited troops, but this was not enough to satisfy an enraged Leisler, who arrived in Albany on 27 August to confront Winthrop. Not only had Leisler lost his chance to smite the "papists," but his means of gaining approval in England vanished with the expedition's failure. His dreams of victory and of receiving the plaudits of the colonists and the appreciation of his monarch were now just that—dreams. In a tantrum he threw Winthrop in jail. The Connecticut government chastised Leisler for his action. Secretary Allyn wrote, "prison is not a catholicon for all State Maladyes though so much used by you." He finished with a warning to Leisler that he had "disobliged al New England" and could no longer rely on their aid. Leisler replied with intemperate letters that revealed his desperation.[103]

Restlessness with Leisler's regime increased during the summer of 1690, creating a severe challenge for Leisler. Secretary Allyn of Connecticut touched upon a sensitive nerve in writing that jails were "so much used by you."[104] Leisler viewed all opposition as papist and therefore treasonable. From the beginning he used the jails to punish his political adversaries. After he launched the expedition against Canada, his opposition had a new issue to seize upon. The soldiers needed supplies and supplies cost money. To get funds Leisler called an assembly to raise a special tax.[105] While mouthing the rhetoric of free elections, the insurgents did not want to give their enemies a chance. As Roelef Swartwout put it in a letter to Milborne: "I admit it ought to be a free election for all classes, but I would be loath to allow those to vote or to be voted for who have refused to this day to take their oath, lest so much leaven might again taint that which is sweet."[106] Because there are no records to indicate how much leaven got into the assembly, it is difficult to judge how representative the assembly was. Suffolk County certainly was unrepresented, for the eastern towns continued their independent ways and refused to send delegates. The assembly passed a tax of three pennies on the pound of assessed valuation—a heavy tax that was ameliorated only by a bill ending all trade monopolies. When the members began to question the number and treatment of prisoners jailed by Leisler, he sent them home.[107] To Leisler's enemies the whole thing was a sham and a fraud. Worse was yet to come, for when supplies were needed for the expedition Leisler began a systematic search for foodstuffs. Leisler's men ferreted them out of hiding places and sent them up the Hudson. Receipts were given in many cases, but were the receipts of an illegal government valid? To Leisler's opponents the answer was no. So, instead of silencing his opposition Leisler supplied it with fuel.[108]

Not that his opposition needed more fuel. Since Leisler's rise to prominence many of his opponents had graced New York's jailhouse. Trials and other legal niceties had been ignored, as most of the prisoners were committed for sedition or treason. After a while, simply to be considered an enemy of the regime was sufficient to insure a stay in the jail. The arrest of major personalities began in January 1690, when Leisler seized a packet of letters going to Boston for transshipment to England.[109] He interpreted the letters to contain seditious and treasonable materials, leading to warrants for the arrest of Bayard, Van Cortlandt, William Nichols (son of Mathias), and Brockholls. Van Cortlandt escaped, as did Brockholls, but Bayard and Nicolls were confined to jail for over a year.[110] The next wave of arrests came after news of Schenectady. A general warrant was issued for all "reputed" papists and those who held commissions from Dongan and Andros. Men such as Van Cortlandt, Robert Livingston, John Tuder, Nicholas Bayard, and William Nicolls became fugitives or prisoners. A warrant was even issued for Dongan, forcing him to leave Long Island and flee to New Jersey, where he joined a growing colony of refugees. Even the captains, crews, and passengers of arriving ships were arrested for sedition. While Leisler's actions may have brought him a measure of security from internal opponents, they kept New York in a turmoil and furthered the cause of the opposition. Harsh treatment and disregard of legal proceedings inflamed a desire for vengeance.[111]

Leisler's long arm reached out to encompass even the ministers of the Dutch Reformed church. Since the new ministers had coexisted with and gained patronage from the old government, they were vulnerable to attack. Domine Henricus Selyns of New York City made the mistake of attesting to the good Protestant character of Bayard and Van Cortlandt. For his opinion he was openly abused in church by Leisler.[112] Domines Rudolphus Varick of Long Island and Godfridus Dellius of Albany were similarly attacked. Dellius felt so threatened that he fled to New England. Varick was not as wise. He went to New Castle but made the mistake of returning. He spent five months in jail accused of treason.[113] Besides dispersing the ministerial group Leisler confiscated church property in New York City and Albany. With Leisler's tacit consent laymen began preaching and carrying on ministerial duties. William Bertoff was particularly active in urging on the "revolting party." This wave of enthusiasm continued after the rebellion, causing a number of communities to live without the services of the regular clergy, even when they returned. In the domines' eyes Leisler had cruelly damaged the Dutch Reformed church and imperiled its existence.[114] Leisler had allowed his own enthusiastic, perhaps by this time messianic, religious views to endanger the most important Dutch institution in New York.

Regional differences also plagued Leisler. Albany smoldered over its loss of independence, and at one time Milborne was forced to leave Albany and to retire to Esopus.[115] Suffolk County retained a cool demeanor. Easthampton, for instance, congratulated Leisler on his accession to power but refused to attend the assembly because to comply meant accepting an administration similar to the "old bondage" they had suffered. Instead, they appealed to the king to return them to Connecticut. The other towns were not as determined and, after an indecisive meeting and a visit from Samuel Edsall, they recognized Leisler, but too late to send representatives to the assembly meeting.[116]

Leisler's enemies in the city remained quiescent until early May 1690. Urged on by the news from England that a governor had been appointed, and perhaps fearing that Leisler's Canadian expedition might bring him into favor in England, the opposition revived. On 19 May an "Address of your Majesties most Dutiful and Loyall Subjects the merchants Traders and others the Principal Inhabitants" was sent to England complaining of rule by an "Isolent Alien (he being none of your Matyes natural borne subject)."[117] Assisted by a rabble, the petition continued, Leisler had illegally imprisoned his opponents, plundered their homes, ruined trade, and abused the domines.

Thirty-six men, most of them members of the old "court" faction, some of whom were Leisler's former allies (Abraham De Peyster, Stephen De Lancey, Gabriel Minvielle, and Charles Lodwick), appended their signatures. Even the leaders of the French church joined in this protest.[118]

A more dangerous exploit followed on the heels of the petition. There may have been a plan for a rising, but the only action that occurred was an attack upon Leisler as he walked about town. Leisler dodged the blows of his assailants until his supporters came to his rescue. The alarm went up and people came in arms to the city to defend the government. The result was jail for the assailants and their friends and a good time for the "country" people, who quartered themselves in their homes.[119] This incident only further deepened the animosity between the parties. Citing the possibility of an invasion by King James's army in Ireland, Leisler forced everyone to take an oath to defend the fort. His embittered opponents could only promise to crush the "Dutch Plott" when the government came into their hands.[120]

The next overt threat came from Long Island. Dissatisfied with heavy taxes and Leisler's "oppressions," 150 men led by Major Thomas Willett started a march on New York City. They were quickly denounced as seditious, and Milborne, the perpetual troubleshooter, took the city militia to quell the rising while Samuel Edsall sailed up Long Island Sound to guard the coast. When the two opponents met, Milborne stood his ground and then fired into the townsmen. Willett escaped to New England after leaving the field with his wounded. The city militia satisfied themselves by looting the homes of Willett and the other leaders before returning to the city. Now even more antagonistic, the English inhabitants of Queens County sent a petition to the secretary of state denouncing the "usurpers" and "oppressors" who, they claimed, had stripped their wives and daughters and seized their estates. The townsmen demanded relief from the "monsters of men."[121]

The opposition's main campaign was not fought in New York, but in England. Both sides knew that, ultimately, decisions made in the mother country would decide their fate, and throughout the colony men waited for a "settlement" from

England. Knowing this, Leisler had sent representatives to England to plead the insurgents' cause, obtain royal approval for their actions, and get a new commission. They failed to gain approval from the Crown. Meanwhile, his enemies conducted their own vigorous campaign.[122] In a political system in which patronage and influence at court were paramount, the anti-Leislerians had an edge over their opponents. William and Mary did not sweep the boards clean when they came to power. Instead, they took over a functioning system that responded to former officeholders. William Blathwayt, for instance, still had considerable influence over colonial policy, and his protégés prospered. When Francis Nicholson returned to England he remained in favor and was quickly sent back to North America as lieutenant governor of Virginia. Andros, Randolph, and the others eventually returned to England and to other offices.[123] Their misfortune was not a permanent affliction; their influence and, more important, that of their patrons, kept them in favor. They, in turn, influenced policymakers about events in New York.

The letters sent from New York to Old and New England were filled with the already familiar vituperations. They described Leisler's followers as a "gang" or a "rabble," Leisler as "madman," a "drunkard," and an "oppressor of protestants." His arrests were described in detail, as were his threats, such as how the "best people" would be pressed for service on privateers. Rumors circulated that Leisler would leave New York as soon as he collected the taxes, reported to be as much as £4,000. The abuse sank to extremely low levels. The Schenectady massacre was Leisler's fault because he "perverted [that] poor people by his seditious letters now founde all bloody upon Shinechtady streets, with ye notions of a free trade, boalting and thus they are destroyed." He was also blamed for the deaths of the soldiers who died in Albany of a "bloody flux" from the "fishy" pork sent to them after it was "stolen" from the merchants. Leisler's more extravagant actions, such as throwing Winthrop in jail, were widely recounted.[124] These constant attacks on his regime bore fruit in England.

Without as persistent and knowledgeable an agent as Increase Mather, or one of the stature of Sir William Phipps, Leisler was unlikely to succeed in gaining official recognition for his movement or himself. Stoll and Blagg could not influence the inexorable movement of the imperial bureaucracy. New York affairs came before the Lords of Trade on 26 April 1689. By 2 May they recommended "speedy" action because of the French threat. The government gave little or no consideration to maintaining the Dominion of New England because it was too preoccupied with domestic affairs and the French war. It moved instead to appoint a governor and recruit a new garrison as its first order of business. By 25 September 1689 Colonel Henry Sloughter was designated the new governor and orders were issued to recruit new soldiers for the garrison. Sloughter revealed his opinions about New York in a set of proposals presented to the Lords of Trade.[125] He characterized New York as a province governed by a "rabble" and threatened by invasion. The proposals for defending New York against attack suggest strongly that Nicholson and merchants such as William Antelby, Gerrard Van Heythusen, Jacob Harwood, Ralph Lodwick, and Richard Merriweather were supplying intelligence about New York to Sloughter.[126] His other suggestions reflect the ambitions of the New York establishment. He asked for the annexation of the Jerseys, Connecticut, and Pennsylvania and that New York City be the only port for export trade. His characterization of the insurgents as "rabble" did not bode well for them—nor did the composition of his council. Philipse, Van Cortlandt, Bayard, Thomas Willett, and other enemies of Leisler were returned to power. When the Lords of Trade later turned over to Sloughter for comment the materials presented to them for investigation by Blagg and other friends of the insurgents, one has to wonder if his mind was not already closed.[127]

By the beginning of 1690 Sloughter had been commissioned and had made most of his arrangements for New York. Tragically, he took an incredibly long time to get to his post. He finally sailed on the *Archangel* on 29 November 1690. When the captain of the *Archangel* made a tack on 2 January 1691, only one ship in the convoy followed him. This navigational fiasco brought further tragedy to New York, for after sighting Bermuda on 9 January 1691, the *Archangel* ran aground on it the next day. The new garrison sailed on without its commander.[128]

Major Richard Ingoldsby arrived on 30 January 1691, and

the next day he demanded that Leisler surrender the fort. Leisler refused until he saw a royal commission, and both sides began to call up reinforcements. Ingoldsby then demanded the release of the prisoners, which Leisler refused to do as he feared that the "papists" would join together and disturb the peace.[129] A standoff ensued. Ingoldsby did not have the royal commission; that was in Bermuda with Sloughter. Leisler refused to acknowledge anything less.

The members of the old government and their adherents rallied to Ingoldsby, as did the English from Long Island, declaring that Leisler held New York as one would a foreign province. Leisler recruited between two and three hundred "desperadoes" while Ingoldsby mustered his two companies and four to five hundred men in the city. With tension at a high pitch Secretary Allyn of Connecticut and Gerardus Beekman, one of his strongest adherents, urged Leisler to be cautious.[130] Leisler, however, was beyond caution. On 17 March he demanded the disbanding of Ingoldsby's forces. Ingoldsby refused, stating that he and the newly appointed councilors were the king's officers and that only a "public enemy" would attack them. Shortly thereafter Leisler fired upon the royal troops, and during the resulting exchange men were killed and wounded. Leisler and his followers, now confined to the fort, kept up a desultory gunfire that lasted for two days until, on 19 March, the *Archangel* sailed into the harbor. In the eyes of his enemies Leisler now compounded his original mistake by refusing to admit Sloughter to the fort immediately. The men in the fort, unlike Leisler, were unwilling to argue over legal technicalities and began going over the walls.[131]

Protesting his rectitude, Leisler surrendered the fort on 20 March. Bayard and Nicolls, freed from jail to take their place on the council, joined the others who had suffered under Leisler and bent their efforts to gain revenge. Sloughter had orders to investigate Leisler's activities and make recommendations to the king. These were quickly forgotten as the men who surrounded him demanded far more than an investigation. Instead Leisler and his leading officers were brought to trial for treason and murder. During the trial Leisler and Milborne refused to plead and maintained a dignified pose before their enemies. Their trial, marked by many irregularities, produced a predictable result and unfortunately Sloughter acquiesced to the sham. He went through the motion of requesting guidance from the newly created assembly, which avoided this package of political dynamite by claiming a lack of jurisdiction.[132] The precedent set in Dyre's trial, of referring the issues to England, was forgotten or rejected in the headlong rush to revenge.

In the shadow of the scaffold Leisler made an eloquent speech stating his case.[133] His actions had not been motivated by personal gain, but by a desire to serve the Crown and the cause of Protestantism. To many who heard his protestations, he was, and would remain, a hero. To many others he was an archfiend. His death was an end and a beginning. Stephanus Van Cortlandt, reflecting on the demise of his enemy, wrote,"I am afraid wee shall lead but a troublesome life here."[134] He was correct in fearing the ghost, not the body. For the next generation New York was embroiled in bitter feuding between Leislerians and anti-Leislerians for political supremacy. The Glorious Revolution left an inglorious legacy of hatred and vituperation.

❦ Part IV
Conclusion

10 ❧ A Time of Troubles

In assessing Leisler's Rebellion and its aftermath, one first turns to the failure of the government in both the short and long term. The immediate cause of Leisler's Rebellion was the loss of authority by the central government. A young, inexperienced caretaker with a few members of the ruling elite proved incapable of controlling events. As in 1680, a power vacuum invited disorder. Complaints and petitions were soon overrun by overt deeds until the collapse at the center was obvious to all. The colony then split into its constituent parts.

The long-term failure of the government was due to the estrangement of the people and the government. The authoritarian system of government, and the governors and their elite clique who administered it, are best characterized as power without principle. With the possible exception of Nicolls, the governors sought only their own and the duke's profit. None of this changed after 1685; in fact, Dongan created the worst regime of all. As a result, the people could only live in hope of further changes imposed from the outside or collapse at home. In the meantime the English petitioned for a return to Connecticut while the Dutch prayed for a fleet from home. When the government became too overbearing each group was willing to speak out against a particular imposition or to resist passively. The government viewed any form of resistance as sedition and the records are cluttered with the burning of petitions, threats to individuals, and occasional physical punishment. These actions tended further to erode the relationship between the people and the government. What then was the bond that kept the colony together?

The colonists were unwilling to overthrow a properly constituted government. It did after all validate their local courts and land grants. A respect for legitimate authority also kept in check major grievances until authority faltered. Throughout the colonies a search for legitimacy was a constant factor in political development.[1] The belief that legitimacy ultimately resided in England frequently led to a form of political paralysis. This was obvious in such situations as when Governor Lovelace hesitated to act, stating, "ye whole frame of ye Government standing at this tyme . . . all business wayting upon that breath that must animate this little body Politique of ours," or when the people of New England accepted the Dominion of New England after a long struggle against the home government.[2] Only when legitimate authority faltered, or was shown to be illegitimate, did the colonists act. Leisler's staying power, once he gained control of the government, can be partly attributed to his appearing to be legitimated by William and Mary. Challenging him was a serious matter until he was rejected in England.

Nevertheless, the desire for legitimacy was balanced by the colonists' concern for their rights as Englishmen or a concern among the Dutch for their residual rights. The English planters of Long Island, and later the English merchants, continually articulated the rights of Englishmen. Time after time the townsmen of the island requested an assembly where they could control taxation and guarantee themselves the undefined "rights of an Englishman." Ultimately they got an assembly and produced the Charter of Libertyes articulating their concept of the relationship between the governed and the government. Unfortunately, this achievement was snuffed out when James came to the throne and instituted the dominion. The people could only contemplate further years of prerogative government by a narrowly based elite during a period of economic depression, threats from New France, and a continuance of the Catholic Stuarts in England.

Given this background, one is struck by the insurgents' lack of purpose once they seized control. The insurgents swore loyalty to the new monarchs and promised to await their orders. But no demands were lodged at Whitehall for structural changes in the government. Compared to the vigorous campaign of Increase Mather to preserve independence for Massachusetts Bay, or the agitation of the Marylanders for an end of the proprietary, New York was inert.[3] Leisler's assembly was not much of a force for change either. It was brought into being to pass laws within a limited context. Those communities, candidates, and voters thought to bear animosity toward the insurgents were excluded. When the members still insisted on raising unpopular issues, Leisler quickly sent them home. Before going home the assembly did end New York City's monopoly of bolting, baking, and transporting wheat. Nothing was done about the fur trade or New York City's control over exporting and importing. The old economic system was not dismantled, perhaps because of the lack of time, but more likely because of Leisler's need for the revenue generated by customs. Thus, 1689 did not fulfill the old ambitions of many New Yorkers for an end to privilege.

There was one positive trend during this period—the independence of the regions. During the rebellion and the changes of government prior to 1689, the local governments kept functioning.[4] The most vigorous level of government to emerge from this period was that of the locality. Town courts met, roads were repaired, fences were mended, and all the other functions that created the pattern of life at the local level were maintained. It was from this solid base that popular politics emerged and future leaders trained. Men moved up the political ladder in full view of their neighbors. Failure was rewarded with a return to the body politic—success, with long years in office. This system of advancement created a core of local leaders vital to the functioning of the town or county. When a man went to the assembly he went as a delegate for his neighbors, to meet with similar men. The assemblies were aggregations of local representatives first, and only later the destroyers of executive authority.[5] Loyalty in colonial times began with the town, extended later to the province, and only at the very end approached all of English North America. In the seventeenth century the boundaries of the town or county were as far as a man's loyalty extended.

In the aftermath of the rebellion the government settled upon New York conformed to the pattern of the royal colonies. There was a powerful governor appointed by the Crown who, along with his council, administered the colony. And, at last, there was an established assembly that quickly became the tool used by Albany and Long Island to strip the city of its monopolies. The old resentments built up during the years of privilege were vented and each region then retreated to protect its own narrow interests.[6] Geography could not be overcome, however.

The city was situated on a superb harbor and lay at the center of many natural trading routes. The government remained there and the influence of the mercantile elite continued unabated. Not until the Revolution would the regions complete the process and settle the government in Albany. Although they could strip New York City of government, they could not diminish its allure. They could only nourish a grumpy jealousy of what was an American phenomenon.

The rebellion set the fate of the Dutch. In past changes of government they had attempted to preserve the rights guaranteed in the articles of surrender. In 1689, with the prince of Orange on the throne of England, many of the Dutch felt they could not only secure their rights but also diminish the pressures of Anglicization. This prospect, of course, proved ephemeral. The Dutch could not escape their fate of being the first Europeans to confront the pressures of English culture and society in North America. Unique in the seventeenth century, their poignant struggle was just the first of many such encounters. The Glorious Revolution and anti-Catholic hysteria gave them the opportunity to fulfill their atavistic impulses. Unfortunately, the prominence of the Dutch in the rebellion only made it easier for the old "court" party to rally support in England. In Whitehall English control mattered more than the fulfillment of Dutch patriotism. Nor would the Dutch be in a position, as they had been in the past, of bargaining with the new government to keep their rights. This time it was a completely English settlement. Only in isolated communities, particularly on the upper Hudson River, would Dutch cultural patterns remain strong well into the eighteenth century.

The rebellion impressed upon New York a new pattern of party or interest. Prior to the rebellion, New York was divided into the "city" versus the "country," or perhaps a better definition would be "insiders" versus everyone else. There were two causes for this configuration: first, the extensive distances between the centers of population; second, the structure of government created by the duke of York. Centered upon an executive who was a needy, and occasionally greedy, soldier who relied upon the merchants to finance the government, the system proved eminently corruptible. Those admitted to the council or New York City government became part of a clique that had as its goal greater wealth for itself. The growth of a group that aggrandized more and more the community's wealth as the result of favoritism created tremendous strains in a still-fluid social system. When this group also frequently assessed taxes that never provided for a proper defense or met the costs of the government, the "outs" were justified in becoming jealous.

The "outsiders" or "country" group got their chance in 1680 to express their contempt for the system. They ignored the central government and expressed their feelings about the system in the Charter of Libertyes. In 1689 the situation was more complex because of the ethnic factor; once again, however, the "court" group was attacked. New men moved into the positions they vacated and gained control of the government. This time it was not simply a matter of ignoring the central government, but of replacing it. The men who came to power had been denied in the past; they were not to be stopped in 1689.

The dynamics of Leisler's regime created new but equally deep and bitter divisions that lasted until the 1720s. Leisler believed he had to protect the Protestant cause from all "papists." To do so, he disregarded the law and common decency toward those whom he considered to be his enemies. His desire to gain legitimacy through the success of the Canadian expedition gave full rein to his worst instincts when he jailed any and all critics. His victims were unforgiving and gained a full measure of vengeance in 1691. As a result, the Leislerian/anti-Leislerian contest was on. The new royal government with its assembly and strong executive provided the context for the new struggles. The political infighting was the continuation, on a greater scale and with more heat, of the conflict between the old "court" and "country" groups. Vehement denunciations and slanderous personal attacks characterized the struggle for power in the new system. Frequently the quarrels were passed on to England for solution, making New York a playground for imperial politicians. If there is a silver lining to this cloud it comes from the fact that as the elite groups battled for power they brought more men into the political process, creating a larger active base in the colony's political life.

The members of the elite group survived the rebellion and

reestablished their economic and social position. The Livingston, Van Cortlandt, Schuyler, Philipse, Van Rensselaer, and other families would dominate life in New York in the eighteenth century. They proved the chief beneficiaries of the period of central authority. It had allowed them to aggrandize economic opportunity and political power in a way analogous to the development of the Virginia elite under Governor Berkeley. Preferred families throughout the colonies established their position and closed the doors of opportunity behind them.

The late seventeenth century was a decisive, formative period. A chaotic mélange of individuals, groups, and regions struggled for economic, political, and social dominance. The potential for the future was mixed, and in New York the contests created by these disruptive forces continued for a very long time. Diverse in peoples, religions, and economic interests, it was unlike the more stable, less diverse colonies such as Virginia. Pluralism, so often considered a modern American characteristic, was present in the seventeenth century. By the eighteenth century the other middle colonies shared this diversity. Recently it has been argued that the diversity of the middle colonies created the conditions that made possible democratic politics. Competing elites created "factions" and "interests" that fought for votes and influence. This pattern of political activity, rather than the homogeneity of Virginia, was the precursor of modern American politics.[7] These developments lay shrouded by time for those New Yorkers who lived during the time of troubles.

Abbreviations
Notes
Bibliography
Index

❧ Abbreviations

Albany Minutes of the Court	A. J. F. Van Laer, ed. *Minutes of the Court of Albany, Rennselaerswyck and Schenectady, 1668–1680*. 3 vols. Albany, N.Y., 1926.
BM Addl. MSS	Additional MSS, British Museum, London, England.
CCM	New York (Colony Council). *Calendar of Council Minutes, 1668–1783*. Edited by Berthold Fernow and A. J. F. Van Laer. New York State Library Bulletin No. 58, History 6. Albany, N.Y., 1902.
CO	Colonial Office MSS. Public Record Office, London, England.
CSPC	Great Britain, Public Record Office. *Calendar of State Papers, Colonial Series, America and West Indies, 1574–1736*. 42 vols. Edited by W. Noel Sainsbury, et al. London, 1860–1953.
CSPD	Great Britain, Public Record Office. *Calendar of State Papers, Domestic, of the Reign of Charles II*. 28 vols. Edited by Mary A. E. Green, et al. London, 1860–1938.
Cal. Hist. MSS	New York (colony). *Calendar of Historical Manuscripts in the Office of the Secretary of State, Albany, New York*. Vol. 1. *Dutch Manuscripts 1630–1664*. Albany, N.Y., 1865. Vol. 2. *English Manuscripts, 1664–1776*. Albany, N.Y., 1866.
DAB	Allen Johnson, ed. *Dictionary of American Biography*. 20 vols. New York, 1928–37.
DNB	Leslie Stephen and Sidney Lee, eds. *Dictionary of National Biography*. 63 vols. London, 1885–1900.
Doc. Hist.	E. B. O'Callaghan, ed. *The Documentary History of the State of New York*. 4 vols. Albany, N.Y., 1850–51.
Executive Council	New York (Colony Council). *Minutes of the Executive Council: Administration of Francis Lovelace, 1668–1673*. 2 vols. Edited by Victor H. Paltsits. Albany, N.Y., 1910.
General Entries	New York (colony). *Colonial Records. General En-*

	tries, 1664–1665. New York State Library Bulletin, History, No. 2. Albany, N.Y., 1899.
MCC	New York (city). *Minutes of the Common Council of the City of New York, 1675–1776*. 8 vols. Edited by Frederick Osgood, et al. New York, 1905.
MCM	Mayor's Court Minutes MS, microfilm copy, Queens College Library, Queens, N.Y.
Mass. Hist. Soc. *Collections*	Massachusetts Historical Society, *Collections*. Boston, 1792–.
N.Y. Col. Docs.	E. B. O'Callaghan and Berthold Fernow, eds. *Documents Relative to the Colonial History of the State of New York*. 15 vols. Albany, N.Y., 1856–87.
N.Y. Col. Laws	New York (colony). *Colonial Laws of New York from the Year 1664 to the Revolution*. 5 vols. Albany, N.Y., 1894–96.
N.Y. Col. MSS	New York Colonial MSS. New York State Library, Albany, N.Y.
N.Y. Eccl. Rec.	Edward T. Corwin, ed. *Ecclesiastical Records of the State of New York*. 7 vols. Albany, N.Y., 1901–16.
NYHS, *Collections*	New York Historical Society, *Collections*. New York, 1811–.
New Jersey Archives	W. A. Whitehead, et al. *Archives of the State of New Jersey, 1631–1800*. 30 vols. Newark, N.J., 1880–1906.
Not. Arch.	Amsterdam Notarial Archives MSS, microfilm, English Summaries and translations, Queens College Library, Queens, N.Y.
PCC	Prerogative Court of Canterbury, Public Record Office, London, England.
PRO	Public Record Office, London, England.
Pennsylvania Archives	Samuel Hazard, et al., eds. *Pennsylvania Archives*. 9 series, 138 vols. Philadelphia and Harrisburg, 1852–1949.
RNA	New York (city). *The Records of New Amsterdam from 1653–1674*. 7 vols. Edited by Berthold Fernow. New York, 1897.
WOL	Warrants, Orders, Passes, Letters, Hue and Cry, 1674–1679, MS, New York State Library, Albany, N.Y.

 Notes

CHAPTER 1

1. Stuyvesant to the West India Company, 24 September 1661 (N.S.), E. B. O'Callaghan and Berthold Fernow, eds., *Documents Relative to the Colonial History of the State of New York*, 14:506, hereafter cited as *N.Y. Col. Docs.* Thomas Willett came to Plymouth Plantation from Leyden in 1629. Because of his knowledge of Dutch he soon began trading with New Netherland.

2. Report of the Commissioners on Long Island, 15 January 1664 (N.S.), *N.Y. Col. Docs.*, 2:400–401. Ensign Nyssen to Stuyvesant, 21 April 1664 (N.S.), ibid., 13:368.

3. Charles Wilson, *Profit and Power*, pp. 1–77 and Keith Feiling, *British Foreign Policy*, pp. 28–138; D. W. Davies, *A Primer of Dutch Seventeenth Century Overseas Trade*, passim.

4. Samuel Pepys, *The Diary of Samuel Pepys*, p. 31. A discussion of the state of English opinion can be found in Gerald B. Hertz, *English Public Opinion After the Restoration*, pp. 14–49. Feiling, *British Foreign Policy*, pp. 97–101.

5. Wilson, *Profit and Power*, pp. 112–15. Another account can be found in the article on Holmes in Leslie Stephen and Sidney Lee, eds., *Dictionary of National Biography*, 9:1088–91, hereafter cited as *DNB*.

6. Richard S. Dunn, *Puritans and Yankees*, p. 152. See also Robert C. Black, *The Younger John Winthrop*, pp. 219–31, 279–82.

7. For a favorably biased work on John Scott, see Lilian T. Mowrer, *The Indomitable John Scott*, passim. A record of his petition for a proprietary of his own can be found in Thomas Hutchinson, ed., *Collection of Original Papers Relative to the History of the Colony of Massachusetts Bay*, 2:104–5. This petition was referred to the Council for Foreign Plantations but there is no record that it was ever considered. See also Black, *The Younger Winthrop*, pp. 236–43.

8. See the essay on Maverick in Allen Johnson, ed., *Dictionary of American Biography*, 6:432–33, hereafter cited as *DAB*, and also Bernard Bailyn, *The New England Merchants in the Seventeenth Century*, pp. 114–16.

9. Great Britain, Public Record Office, *Calendar of State Papers, Colonial Series, America and West Indies, 1547–1736*, 5, no. 3; hereafter cited as *CSPC*.

10. *N.Y. Col. Docs.*, 3:39–41. Other documents with similar opinions can be found in the New York Historical Society, *Collections* (1869), pp. 22–28, hereafter cited as NYHS, *Collections*, and Egerton MS, 2395, fols. 397–411, British Museum.

11. NYHS, *Collections* (1869), pp. 1–14, 19–22. Charles M. Andrews, *The Colonial Period of American History*, 3:54 asserts that Maverick wrote all of his letters to Clarendon in this period while living in New Amsterdam. The evidence in the letters leaves no doubt, however, that Maverick was in London, as he frequently refers to visits with Clarendon and also to his willingness to call on him at any time.

12. The committee consisted of Edmund Waller, a Mr. Denham, and two of the most important men on the Council for Foreign Plantations, Thomas Povey and Martin Noell. The actions of the committee can be traced in *CSPC*, 5, nos. 54, 56, 64. The letter to the colonies can be found in ibid., 5, no. 66. The report on the council is in ibid., no. 88.

13. NYHS, *Collections* (1869), pp. 35–37. Lord Windsor arrived in Barbados July 1662, *CSPC*, 5, no. 365.

14. *CSPC*, 5, no. 370.

15. This special committee was formed to consider the king's title to New Nether-

land, how the Dutch had intruded, their strength, trade, government, and the means to force their surrender. Its major meeting is reported in Colonial Office Papers 1/17/no. 113, hereafter cited as CO, Public Record Office, London, hereafter referred to as PRO.

16. Henry L. Schoolcraft, "The Capture of New Amsterdam," pp. 674–93, argues that financial ruin of the Royal African Company became apparent in early 1664, precipitating the invasion. The report in n. 15 can be dated through a reference to Dutch trade figures "last year" in 1662. This argues against Schoolcraft's conclusion.

17. *CSPC*, 5, no. 432.

18. Scott tried to rouse the English settlers against the Dutch. *N.Y. Col. Docs.*, 2:507; CO 1/18/no. 15, PRO. See also *CSPC*, 5, no. 647.

19. Wilson, *Profit and Power*, pp. 92–94, 108, 122–23. *Pepys Diary*, 4:95, 98. Andrews, *Colonial Period*, 3:52–53. Stephen S. Webb, "Brave Men and Servants to His Royal Highness," pp. 55–80.

20. This coalition can be traced in Violet Barbour, *Henry Bennet, Earl of Arlington*; Louise F. Brown, *The First Earl of Shaftesbury*; Wilson, *Profit and Power*, pp. 92–94. For Downing, see Wilson, *Profit and Power*, pp. 94–96, and John Beresford, *The Godfather of Downing Street*, passim.

21. *Pepys Diary*, 4:93, and Feiling, *British Foreign Policy*, pp. 130–31.

22. *CSPC*, 4, no. 618. The meetings of the company were held in the duke's quarters, Wilson, *Profit and Power*, pp. 112–13. N. Japikse, *De Verwikkelingen Tuschen de Republick en Engeland van 1660–1665*, pp. 346–53.

23. Feiling, *British Foreign Policy*, p. 132.

24. Additional MSS, 15896, fols. 54–55, British Museum, hereafter cited as BM Addl. MSS.

25. J. S. Clarke, ed., *The Life of James the Second*, 2:399. For information on Ford's activities, see John R. Woodhead, *The Rulers of London, 1660–1689*; *Pepys Diary*, 1:249, 277, 375; Great Britain, Public Record Office, *Calendar of Treasury Books*, 5, pt. 1:443, 548; Dennis T. Witcombe, *Charles II and the Cavalier House of Commons, 1663–1674*, p. 201. Ford's enmity toward the Dutch was deepened in 1661 when he and his partners lost a ship worth £8,585 due to the Dutch East India Company, Japikse, *De Verwikkelingen*, Appendix, 35; Great Britain, Public Record Office, *Calendar of State Papers, Domestic, of the Reign of Charles II*, 3:525, 527, hereafter cited as *CSPD*.

26. See the *DNB*, 4:1287–89. Also V. Vale, "Clarendon, Coventry and the Sale of Naval Offices, 1660–1668," pp. 107–25.

27. *DNB*, 2:361–63, for Berkeley and ibid., 3:1117–19, for Carteret, *CSPC*, 5, nos. 427, 408. Also Leo F. Stock, ed., *Proceedings and Debates of the British Parliaments Respecting North America*, 1:280, 295.

28. Additional MSS, 7091, fol. 88, Cambridge University Library, and *CSPC*, 5, no. 3.

29. Francis C. Turner, *James II*, pp. 69–70, and Robert C. Ritchie, "The Duke of York's Commission of Revenue," pp. 177–78.

30. *N.Y. Col. Docs.*, 3:47–50. John Scott estimated the revenues from Long Island alone at £3,000, *N.Y. Col. Docs.*, 2:400–401.

31. The original patent can be found in Chancery 66/3058, PRO. Printed copies can be seen in *N.Y. Col. Docs.*, 2:295–98, and Aaron Leaming and Jacob Spicer, *The Grants, Concessions, and Original Constitutions of the Province of New Jersey*, pp. 3–8. The rapid movement of the patent through the seals can be seen in *CSPC*, 5, nos. 676, 677, 678, 683, 685; or more succinctly in Andrews, *Colonial Period*, 3:57.

32. Downing to Clarendon, 6 May 1664, T. H. Lister, *Life and Administration of Edward, Earl of Clarendon*, pp. 315–21. England's claim to this area was based upon the voyage of John Cabot along the east coast of North America. *CSPC*, 5, no. 624. York had to extinguish a prior English claim to his new proprietary. James Alexander, the earl of Stirling, was granted most of York's land by Charles I. Clarendon, acting on behalf of his son-in-law, engaged to pay £3,500 to Stirling's heirs to obtain their deed. The deed was turned over, but the money was never paid. Isabel M. Calder, "The Earl of Stirling and the Colonization of Long Island," pp. 74–95.

33. See *DAB*, 13:515–16, and *Notes and Queries*, 2nd ser., 8:214–16. At the time of

his appointment Nicolls was a captain of York's company stationed at Portsmouth. *CSPD*, 3:285.

34. *CSPC*, 5, no. 623.

35. These instructions were the result of many hearings. Egerton MSS 2395, fol. 396, British Museum, and CO 1/18/no. 46, PRO. The public instructions can be found in *N.Y. Col. Docs.*, 3:51–55, and the secret ones, ibid., pp. 57–61.

36. New York (colony), *Colonial Records, General Entries, 1664–1665*, pp. 74–77, hereafter cited as *General Entries*. Nicolls and Cartwright to Lord Arlington, n.d., ibid., pp. 74–77.

37. Stuyvesant wrote a long justification for his actions which reports on the armaments in New Amsterdam. *N.Y. Col. Docs.*, 2:367. The way in which the New England Commission fooled everyone is explained, *N.Y. Col. Docs.*, 2:366.

38. *General Entries*, pp. 80–81. The letter is dated 19 August 1664.

39. Stuyvesant to the *Commissaries* at Esopus, 19 August 1664, *N.Y. Col. Docs.*, 13:392–93; Stuyvesant to the Dutch towns on Long Island, 18 August 1664, ibid., 2:376.

40. Nicolls to Captain John Youngs, ibid., 14:555. The Dutch attitude is recorded in: New York (city), *The Records of New Amsterdam from 1653–1674*, 5:110, hereafter cited as *RNA*. John Underhill wrote later to John Winthrop, Jr., about the difficulties he experienced in restraining the militia from plundering the Dutch. Thus it appears the Dutch fears were well founded. Massachusetts Historical Society, *Collections*, 4th ser., 7:190–91, hereafter Mass. Hist. Soc., *Collections*.

41. Langdon G. Wright, "Local Government and Central Authority in New Netherland," pp. 7–29. Thomas J. Condon, *New York Beginnings*, pp. 144–72.

42. Nicolls demanded Stuyvesant's surrender on 20 August 1664, *General Entries*, pp. 81–82. His letter claimed that the surrender was necessary because the king could not allow foreigners, "how near soever they be allyed," to continue to occupy his dominion. The events from the Dutch side can be traced in the account of Domine Samuel Drisius, *N.Y. Col. Docs.*, 3:393–94.

43. Nicolls to Winthrop, 22 August 1664, *General Entries*, p. 84. Winthrop forwarded this information the same day to Stuyvesant, Mass. Hist. Soc., *Collections*, 4th ser., 4:527–29.

44. An account of the interviews can be found in *N.Y. Col. Docs.*, 2:444–45; 13:393–94.

45. Testimony of two Dutch soldiers, ibid., pp. 508–9. See also Edmund B. O'Callaghan, *History of New Netherlands*, 2:531.

46. "Remonstrance," *N.Y. Col. Docs.*, 2:248–50.

47. "Articles of Capitulation," ibid., pp. 250–53.

48. Testimony of two soldiers, ibid., pp. 508–9. Those soldiers who wanted to remain were granted fifty acres of land in article 19 of the surrender terms. The *Gideon* was given permission to leave on 9 September, *General Entries*, pp. 184–85.

49. Cartwright's commission, 10 September 1664, *General Entries*, p. 105. De Decker's punishment, ibid., p. 109. He was given ten days to leave. The agreement regarding Albany, *General Entries*, pp. 112–14. In exchange for the fur monopoly the town agreed to furnish houses to be used as barracks for a garrison and also to supply a certain amount of food and money.

50. Treaty, *N.Y. Col. Docs.*, 3:67–68.

51. Carr's commission, *General Entries*, p. 104; and instructions, ibid., pp. 125–27.

52. Carr to Nicolls, 13 October 1664, *N.Y. Col. Docs.*, 3:73–74. Articles of Surrender, 1 October, ibid., p. 71. See John R. Brodhead, *The History of the State of New York*, 2:202–52, and C. A. Weslager, *The English on the Delaware*, pp. 176–202. Report on the Surrender of New Netherland, *N.Y. Col. Docs.*, 2:369. See also Brodhead, *New York*, 2:51–52 and O'Callaghan, *New Netherlands*, 2:537–38. The only extant report on Carr's actions states that the soldiers were supposedly sold into slavery. This is a Dutch report designed to have an impact in the Netherlands. So the term "slavery" is probably an exaggeration. If they were sold into slavery it would be the only incidence of white slavery in North America. See Winthrop D. Jordan, *White Over Black*, p. 134.

53. Nicolls to Arlington, October 1664, *N.Y. Col. Docs.*, 3:68–70. Maverick to Winth-

rop, 9 November 1664, Mass. Hist. Soc., *Collections*, 4th ser., 7:309–11.

54. Commissioners to Carr, 24 October 1664, *General Entries*, p. 121. Commissioners to Nicolls, giving him permission to go, 24 October 1664, ibid., pp. 121–22.

CHAPTER 2

1. Edmund B. O'Callaghan, *The History of New Netherlands*, 1:540.

2. The most convenient way to trace the growth of New York City is in the monumental six-volume work of I. M. Stokes, *The Iconography of Manhattan Island*.

3. Ibid., 6:73–79, 100, 123–24.

4. *RNA*, 6:286–88.

5. As will be explained in chapter eight the multiplier of six has been used in calculating the city's population. The magistrates also estimated the population at 1,500 in 1664. Ibid., pp. 110–15.

6. New York had this reputation as early as 1647. Isaac Jogues's description of Manhattan reprinted in J. Franklin Jameson, ed., *Narratives of New Netherland, 1609–1664*, p. 259.

7. The *Gideon* of Amsterdam arrived in New Netherland just before the invasion fleet in August 1664 with 290 slaves. Microfilm copy of the Amsterdam Notarial Archives, 3189, N. 8, 23 March 1666, Queens College Library, Queens, N.Y., hereafter cited as Not. Arch.

8. Nicolls to York, November 1665, *N.Y. Col. Docs.*, 3:106.

9. James Riker, *Revised History of New Harlem*, pp. 228–29.

10. John E. Pomfret, *The Province of East New Jersey*, pp. 1–26.

11. C. A. Weslager, *Dutch Explorers, Traders and Settlers in the Delaware Valley*, pp. 129–58, 185–214.

12. The best source at the present time for Long Island is Benjamin F. Thompson, *History of Long Island*.

13. The rise of the whale hunts can be traced in the *Records of the Town of East-Hampton*, pp. 188, 199, 270–72, 321, 378–79, 380–82.

14. Ed. by Gabriel Furman (London, 1701), pp. 6–7.

15. Lovelace to Benedict Arnold, governor of Rhode Island, 5 July 1669, *N.Y. Col. Docs.*, 14:624.

16. Daniel Denton, *A Brief Description of New York*, p. 19.

17. Jasper Danckaerts, *Journal of Jasper Danckaerts*, p. 196. A. J. F. Van Laer, ed., *Minutes of the Court of Albany, Rensselaerswyck and Schenectady, 1668–1680*, 1:96–97, hereafter cited as *Albany Minutes of the Court*.

18. The *commissaries* forced out the Lutheran minister, the Rev. Jacobus Fabricius, *Albany Minutes of the Court*, pp. 62–66; they refused to consider a Lutheran petition complaining about harassment, ibid., pp. 144–45; or to allow bell ringing prior to Lutheran services, ibid., p. 208.

19. Nicolls to Clarendon, 30 July 1665, NYHS, Collections (1869), pp. 74–77.

20. Thomas J. Condon, *New York Beginnings*, pp. 87–143. Van cleaf Bachman, *Peltries or Plantations*, pasim.

21. Condon, *New York Beginnings*, pp. 116–72.

22. Langdon G. Wright, "Local Government and Central Authority," pp. 7–29.

23. York's distrust of elected bodies is made clear in his letters to Governor Edmund Andros, 6 April 1675, *N.Y. Col. Docs.*, 3:230–31, and 28 January 1676, ibid., p. 235.

24. For a discussion of Connecticut's charter, see Charles M. Andrews, *The Colonial Period of American History*, 2:132–42. For a list of the Long Island representatives to the General Court, see James T. Adams, *The History of the Town of Southampton*, pp. 71–72. Robert C. Black, *The Younger John Winthrop*, pp. 279–80. Boundary agreement, *General Entries*, pp. 135–36. John Winthrop, Jr., owned Fisher's Island, which Nicolls turned over to him and gave the privileges of a manor. Black, *Younger Winthrop*, p. 282. See also Thompson, *History of Long Island*, 1:389. New York Colonial Manuscripts, 23, fol. 5, New York State Library, Albany, N.Y., hereafter cited as N.Y. Col. MSS. Nicolls to Howell and Young, 1 December 1664, *General Entries*, pp. 132–33.

25. Nicolls to the inhabitants of Long Island, February 1665, *N.Y. Col. Docs.*, 14:564. A shorter version of this letter, without a preamble discussing the loss of "Civil Libertyes" under the Dutch, was sent to the Dutch towns. See ibid., p. 565.

26. Nicolls defined freemen as "all persons rated accordingly to their Estates, whether English or Dutch." Ibid. The towns that had been sending delegates to the Connecticut General Court probably continued to follow their past procedures. See *Records of East-Hampton*, 1:140, 194, and Adams, *Southampton*, p. 71.

27. Nicolls to Jamaica, 2 January 1665, *N.Y. Col. Docs.*, 3:562–63. For examples of the numerous land cases, see Flushing v. Jamaica, *General Entries*, p. 143, and others, ibid., pp. 144–45. A commission was appointed at the meeting to investigate disputes, *N.Y. Col. Docs.*, 14:565–66.

28. A list of the deputies can be found in *N.Y. Col. Docs.*, 11:565.

29. J. W. Case, ed., *Southold Town Records*, 1:358–59.

30. For an account of the various surviving copies of the laws, see Morten Pennypacker, *The Duke's Laws*, passim. The laws are in New York (colony), *The Colonial Laws of New York from the Year 1664 to the Revolution*, 1:6–71, hereafter cited as the *N.Y. Col. Laws*. An interesting commentary on the laws can be found in Wesley Frank Craven, *The Colonies in Transition*, pp. 74–78.

31. For Nicolls's legal career, see Paul M. Hamlin and Charles E. Baker, eds., *Supreme Court of Judicature of the Province of New York*, 1:19. Hamlin and Baker's three-volume study is an indispensable guide to the early history of New York's legal system.

32. Pennypacker, *Duke's Laws*, pp. 22–26. George L. Haskins and Samuel Ewing, "The Spread of Massachusetts Law in the 17th Century," pp. 413–18. Thomas Ludwell, secretary of Virginia, to Nicolls, 7 December 1664, Blathwayt Papers, Box 1, BL 8, Henry E. Huntington Library, San Marino, Cal. Ludwell wrote that he was sorry to hear the first set of laws he sent went astray. Some of the sections in the Duke's Laws closely parallel parts of the Virginia code. For example, see the regulations on churchwardens, William H. Hening, *The Statutes at Large . . . A Collection of all the Laws of Virginia*, 2:51–52. For Nicolls's comment on Maryland, see Pennypacker, *Duke's Laws*, pp. 22–26.

33. Nicolls to Clarendon, 30 July 1665, NYHS, *Collections* (1869), p. 77.

34. The following discussion is derived from *N.Y. Col. Laws*, 1:6–71.

35. A. E. McKinley, "The Transition from Dutch to English Rule in New York," pp. 706–7. This article is a very useful guide to the various political institutions that were melded together in New York.

36. Pennypacker, *Duke's Laws*, pp. 22–26.

37. Ibid.

38. Declaration of the Deputies of Long Island, 1 March 1665, *N.Y. Col. Docs.*, 3:91.

39. Pennypacker, *Duke's Laws*, pp. 22–26.

40. Thompson, *Long Island*, 3:631–34. Nicolls to Clarendon, 30 July 1665, NYHS, *Collections* (1869), pp. 74–77.

41. *N.Y. Col. Laws*, 1:24–26. For York's feelings, see *N.Y. Col. Docs.*, 3:218.

42. Black, *Younger Winthrop*, p. 282, and *General Entries*, pp. 157–58, for the order for Fisher's Island. For Giles Sylvester's testimony, see *CSPC*, 5, no. 75. He petitioned the king in 1661 for freedom from the harassment he was getting from New Haven, ibid., no. 52. The grant from Nicolls, 31 May 1666, Mass. Hist. Soc., *Proceedings*, 2nd ser., 4:290–91. The Sylvesters were Quakers with family branches in London, Shelter Island, and Barbados. Shelter Island acted as a refuge for Quakers persecuted in New England. *CSPC*, 5, no. 89. For a note on the family, see Mass. Hist. Soc., *Proceedings*, 2nd ser., 4:270.

43. The manors of Pelham and Fordham are discussed in Howard Pell, *The Pell Manor*, and Harry C. W. Melick, *The Manor of Fordham and Its Founder*. Fox Hall was patented on 16 October 1672, *N.Y. Col. Docs.*, 13:459–60. Petition of the people of Westchester, 22 August 1664, ibid., pp. 391–92.

44. Julius Goebel, *Some Legal and Political Aspects of the Manors in New York*. Goebel argues that the grants were also made to allow the manors to organize their own defenses under the militia sections of the Duke's Laws. This seems unlikely since Fisher's Island is just a few miles from New London, Connecticut, and could receive help easily

from there, and the Shelter Island patent has a clause exempting the island from the militia system. This was probably in deference to the Sylvester family's Quaker beliefs. See also Herbert A. Johnson, "The Advent of Common Law in Colonial New York," in George A. Billias, ed., *Law and Authority*, pp. 83–84.

45. Resolutions and Directions for Settlement of Government in Delaware, 21 April 1668, *N.Y. Col. Docs.*, 12:462. Carr's Proposals, June 1671, ibid., pp. 558–61. He asked for a stronger fort at New Castle, a ban on upriver trade beyond New Castle by nonresidents, completion of a road to Maryland, and a constable to enforce these regulations. New York (Colony Council), *Minutes of the Executive Council*, 2:597–98, 606–8, 688–89, hereafter cited as *Executive Council*. Commission for Wharton, 9 April 1672, *N.Y. Col. Docs.*, 12:495. Cantwell was acting as sheriff in August 1672, ibid., pp. 674–76. The council authorized the bailiwick on 17 May 1672, ibid., 1:121–26.

46. Lovelace to Governor Philip Carteret, 18 September and 13 October 1672, *N.Y. Col. Docs.*, 13:466–67. Indenture for sale, 13 April 1670, *Executive Council*, 1:338–42, warrant for possession, 3 May 1670, ibid., p. 344.

47. The patents, *Executive Council*, pp. 345–54; Commission for Mayhew, 8 July 1671, ibid., pp. 368–69. Mayhew was given two votes in the affairs of the government. Council minutes, 29 June 1671, ibid., p. 94; proposals for settling a government on Nantucket, June 1671, ibid., pp. 358–59. Secretary Nicolls to Nantucket, 24 April 1673, ibid., pp. 376–77. Nicolls issued a receipt for the quitrent and acknowledged their gift of feathers to the governor. Andros's instructions to Anthony Brockholls, Caesar Knapton, and Mathias Nicolls, 13 June 1677, *N.Y. Col. Docs.*, 3:248–49.

48. Order regulating the civil and military affairs at Esopus, 25 October 1671, *N.Y. Col. Docs.*, 13:459–60.

49. *RNA*, 5:183–85, 248–50. See also *General Entries*, pp. 171–74. This change had been considered by Nicolls for some time. On his way to Boston in the winter of 1665, Sir George Cartwright had stopped in Plymouth Plantation and spoken to Thomas Willett about becoming the first mayor. Cartwright to Nicolls, 4 February 1665, *N.Y. Col. Docs.*, 3:87–88.

50. *RNA*, 5:251.

51. For the appointments, see ibid., pp. 248–50, 255. The aldermen were Thomas Delaval, Oloff Van Cortlandt, Johannes Van Brugh, Cornelius Van Ruyven, and John Laurence.

52. The seal and robes were presented on 5 October 1669, ibid., 6:196–200. The first government by double nomination was chosen on 8 October 1669, ibid., pp. 200–201. On 10 October 1670 Lovelace appointed Mathias Nicolls and John Laurence aldermen even though they were not nominated. Ibid., pp. 260–63.

53. Ibid., 5:252–55, 267.

54. Orders for the Government of Albany, 2 August 1671, *Executive Council*, 2:548–49.

55. The garrison commander sat with the *commissaries* regularly, especially over Indian affairs. See Instructions to Captain Baker, August 1668, ibid., 1:387–90. For the extension of Salisbury's powers, see the extraordinary session of the town council with Lovelace's representative Delaval, 1 November 1670, *Albany Minutes of the Court*, 1:196–97. On 2 October 1672 Salisbury was appointed a justice of the peace also, *Executive Council*, 2:441–42. This shows Lovelace's disregard of any boundaries between civilian and military authority.

56. S. G. Nissenson, *The Patroon's Domain*, passim. Van RensSelaer grant, 18 October 1664, *General Entries*, p. 119. The agreement is outlined in Jeremias Van Rensselaer's letters to his brother, Jan Baptist, in October 1664. A. J. F. Van Laer, ed., *Correspondence of Jeremias Van Rensselaer*, pp. 361–67. The first payment was made to Nicolls, 15 November 1664. It consisted of 100 *schepels* (bushels) of wheat and 308 boards, ibid., p. 369.

57. These figures are compiled from the annual elections held in the city in October. See *RNA*, pp. 5, 6, passim. For the councilors, see S. C. Hutchins, *Civil List and Forms of Government of the Colony and State of New York*, pp. 17–18.

58. Topping's career is outlined in Adams, *Southampton*, pp. 74–75. He acted as a

representative to the General Court in Connecticut.

59. The most complete account of Willett's life is Elizur Y. Smith, "Captain Thomas Willett," pp. 404–17.

60. Lovelace traced his career in a petition to York, Rawlinson MSS, A, 173, fol. 186, Bodleian Library, Oxford University.

61. For Van Ruyven, see *Executive Council*, 1:39–40. He was the chief financial officer of the West India Company but stayed on in New York and was an alderman five times.

62. For Laurence, see Stokes, *Iconography*, 6:461–62; W. E. Laurence, "The Laurence Pedigree," pp. 121–31.

63. Order, 16 June 1672, *N.Y. Col. Docs.*, 13:464.

64. Nicolls had a long and influential career. As secretary of the province and one of the very few barristers in New York, he played a role in every major court proceeding at the assize and sessions for over twenty years. In 1683 during the first session of the assembly he was elected speaker. He carved out a substantial estate in Islip, Long Island. *DAB*, 13:514–15.

65. Delaval identified himself as a surveyor general of the customs in a petition of 24 June 1675, Rawlinson MSS, A, 173, fol. 186, Bodleian Library, Oxford University. In the *CSPD*, 1:213, August 1660 he is identified as a customs collector at Dunkirk. The customs commissioners claimed him as one of their officers, 15 October 1664, High Court of Admiralty, 15/8, fol. 1, PRO. The soldiers of the garrison complained about Delaval's high prices. "Petition of all the Soldiers in the Garrison of Fort James, 21 November 1664," New Netherlands Collection MS, New York Historical Society, New York City.

66. For Steenwyck, see David T. Valentine, *Manual of the Corporation of the City of New York*, 1864, pp. 648–64; *DAB*, 13:558–59; *Executive Council*, 1:63–64. For his trading activities, see *RNA*, 7:87–91; Van Laer, *Jeremias Van Rensselaer*, pp. 454, 466; W. H. Brown et al., eds., *Archives of Maryland*, 49:37. For his wealth, see New York (city), *Minutes of the Common Council of the City of New York*, 1:30, hereafter cited as *MCC*.

67. For an interesting analysis of local communities and their relationship with other institutions, see Darrett B. Rutman, "The Social Web: A Prospectus for the Study of the Early American Community," pp. 57–88.

CHAPTER 3

1. The history of the garrison is traced in Stanley M. Pargellis, "The Four Independent Companies of New York," pp. 96–123.

2. "An establishment of pay for ye officers and soldiers of my colony of New York," 1 July 1674, *N.Y. Col. Docs.*, 3:220. "Estimate of the militia by Colonel Nicolls," 1668, N.Y. Col. MSS, 22, fol. 50.

3. "A brief state of the King's Private Revenue," B.M. Addl. MSS, 15, 896, fol. 54. "Ordinance sent to New York from 1664 to 1674," CO/324/4, fol. 45, PRO. Some English garrisons were as much as three years in arrears of salary at this time. John Shy, *Toward Lexington*, pp. 20–28.

4. Delaval is identified as the *commissary* by the soldiers in a petition protesting his lack of supplies for the garrison. "Petition of all the soldiers in the Garrison of Fort James," 21 November 1664, New Netherland Collection MS, New York Historical Society.

5. Nicolls placed a special tax on New York City to support the garrison. *RNA*, 5:221–25. Governor Lovelace diverted 4,297.4 guilders from the liquor excise to the use of the garrison. N.Y. Col. MSS, 24, fol. 133–34. He also charged a special levy for repairs to the fort. *New York's Colonial Archives: Transcriptions of the Records between the Years 1673–1675*. New York State Historian's *Annual Report*, pp. 166–71, hereafter cited as *Annual Report* (1896).

6. "Estimate of the militia by Colonel Nicolls," N.Y. Col. MSS, 22, fol. 50. Nicolls to Arlington, 9 April and October 1666, *N.Y. Col. Docs.*, 3:113–15, 68–70. Nicolls to Clarendon, 7 April 1666, NYHS, *Collections* (1869), pp. 113–17.

7. Nicolls to Arlington, 9 April 1666, *N.Y. Col. Docs.*, 3:113–15.

8. Additional MSS, 7091, fols. 140–41, Cambridge University Library.

9. Will written on 1 May 1672 on board the *Royal Prince*. He was killed during the battle of Sole Bay. Coventry MSS, 106, fol. 136, Longleat House, Wiltshire, England.

10. For the problems of Lovelace's estate, see *N.Y. Col. Docs.*, 3:587–88, and N.Y. Col. MSS, 24, fols. 102, 115, 127.

11. Nicolls to Clarendon, 30 July 1665, NYHS, *Collections* (1869), pp. 74–77.

12. Lease from York to Berkeley and Carteret, 23 June 1664. W. A. Whitehead et al., eds., *Archives of the State of New Jersey, 1631–1800*, 1st ser., 1:8–10, hereafter cited as *New Jersey Archives*. Release, 24 June 1664, ibid., pp. 10–14. For an analysis of this transaction, see Charles M. Andrews, *The Colonial Period of American History*, 3:138, n. 1.

13. Nicolls to York, n.d., *N.Y. Col. Docs.*, 3:105.

14. *N.Y. Col. Docs.*, 14:573. The manner of assessing estates was outlined in the Duke's Laws. *N.Y. Col. Laws*, 1:59–62.

15. Nicolls to Oyster Bay, 31 March 1666, *N.Y. Col. Docs.*, 14:574. Warrants, Orders, Passes, Letters, Hue and Cry MSS, II, fol. 68, New York State Library, Albany, N.Y., hereafter cited as WOL.

16. Nicolls to Justice Hicks of Hempstead, 20 April 1666, *N.Y. Col. Docs.*, 14:578. Nicolls to Jonas Wood, 21 May 1666, ibid., p. 582. Nicolls characterized the Brookhaven rioters as "men ill affected to the Government, some of whom have also spoken words tending to ye deregacon of his Majties Authority, settled in these parts."

17. Nicolls to Sheriff Topping, 19 April 1666, ibid., p. 577.

18. Benjamin F. Thompson, *History of Long Island*, 3:631–34.

19. *N.Y. Col. Laws*, 1:92. To make their point the members of the assize made an example of the chief troublemakers. John R. Brodhead, *The History of the State of New York*, 2:108.

20. Nicolls to Underhill, 7 May 1666, *N.Y. Col. Docs.*, 14:580–81.

21. Court of Assize Minutes MSS (1666–69), fol. 77, New York State Library, Albany, N.Y.

22. Nicolls to Underhill, 7 May 1666, *N.Y. Col. Docs.*, 14:580–81.

23. Nicolls to Clarendon, 7 April 1666, NYHS, *Collections* (1869), pp. 113–17.

24. Nicolls to (unknown), 7 May 1666, WOL, II, fols. 61–62.

25. Nicolls to Hempstead, Oyster Bay, Jamaica, Flushing, and Newton, 27 August 1666, *N.Y. Col. Docs.*, 14:585–86. Nicolls to Sheriff Wells, 10 November 1666, ibid., p. 590. *N.Y. Col. Laws*, 1:73–82. This session of the assize also edited and refined the language and content of the Duke's Laws.

26. *Records of the Town of East-Hampton*, 1:241–42.

27. *N.Y. Col. Laws*, 1:90.

28. Van Ruyven to Peter Stuyvesant, 7 August 1666, *N.Y. Col. Docs.*, 2:472–73.

29. *N.Y. Col. Laws*, 1:44, 80, 93.

30. Ibid., p. 93.

31. John Pell to John Winthrop, 2 May 1666, Mass. Hist. Soc., *Collections*, 5th ser., 1:410–12. Nicolls to Albany [January 1667], *N.Y. Col. Docs.*, 3:143. A record book of New York City patents was compiled at a later date with the first patents registered in 1667, CO/5/1134, PRO.

32. As quoted in James Riker, *Revised History of New Harlem*, p. 245.

33. For the patents, see Thompson, *Long Island*, Flushing, 2:181; Brookhaven, 1:410–11; Easthampton, 1:311–12; Newtown, 2:139–40; Huntington, 1:467; Smithtown, 1:454; Gravesend, 2:177; Flatlands, 2:183–84; Flatbush, 2:201; Brooklyn, 2:220; Bushwyck, 2:157–58; New Harlem, Riker, *Harlem*, pp. 226–27; Hempstead, Frederick Van Wyck, ed., *Long Island Colonial Patents*, pp. 150–53.

34. Townspeople of Oyster Bay to Nicolls, 10 January 1668, John Cox, ed., *Oyster Bay Town Records*, 1:33–34. Nicolls wrote to the town, 16 December 1667, threatening them with having to leave the colony unless "those scales of darkness will faull from your eyes." Ibid., p. 35.

35. The Lloyd family avoided payment until 1689. Lloyd Family Papers, NYHS, *Collections* (1926), pp. 42–44, 70–77.

36. *N.Y. Col. Laws*, 1:80.

37. J. Thomas Scharf, ed., *History of Westchester County*, 1:84.

38. Thompson, *Long Island*, 1:366–67.

39. Jeremias Van Rensselaer to his brother Richard, 25 August 1671, A. J. F. Van Laer, *Jeremias Van Rensselaer*, pp. 439–42.

40. Nicolls to Arlington, October 1664, *N.Y. Col. Docs.*, 3:68–70. See also Maverick to Winthrop, 9 November 1664, Mass. Hist. Soc., *Collections*, 4th ser., 1:309–11. Maverick reports that some planters in Maryland wanted to fill the commission's supply ship, the *William and Nicholas*. Part, if not all, of the *William*'s cargo came from Virginia; John Darcy to Cartwright, 3 February 1665, CO/1/19, fol. 27, PRO. Darcy reports he was consigning 400 hogsheads of tobacco to Nicolls.

41. Only one ship, the *William and Mary*, is recorded in the Port Books as leaving for New York; Exchequer, Class 190, Pieces 50/5 and 52/1, PRO. The nature of the port books and the loss of so many other customs records mean that we cannot conclude that other ships did not sail to New York.

42. For an example of the certificates of denization, see *General Entries*, pp. 183–85.

43. Order, 26 October 1664, ibid., pp. 122–23. In this order Nicolls admits his action is contrary to the Navigation Acts but insists that it was necessary to encourage the people.

44. Permits to Steenwyck and his partners, 13 December 1664, ibid., p. 137. Permit to Steenwyck to load the *Hopewell* for Holland, ibid., pp. 148–49.

45. Order on the payment of duties, 26 November 1664, *General Entries*, pp. 133–34. The property of the company was seized on 24 December 1664, ibid., pp. 140–41. On 29 December all magistrates were ordered to turn in a true account of the company's property. Ibid., pp. 142–43.

46. *RNA*, 5:160–61.

47. Nicolls to Arlington, 9 April 1666, *N.Y. Col. Docs.*, 3:113–15.

48. Stuyvesant to York, n.d., ibid., pp. 163–64. Stuyvesant to King Charles, 23 October 1667, ibid., pp. 164–65. Stuyvesant noted that Dutch agricultural tools were different from English ones and must be imported from the Netherlands.

49. Referral order, 17 October 1667, *CSPC*, 5, no. 1613, and *N.Y. Col. Docs.*, 3:165–66.

50. Council for Trade to the King, n.d., *N.Y. Col. Docs.*, 3:175–76, and the order in council, 18 November 1668, ibid., pp. 177–78.

51. Contracts selling the permit, 27 February 1668, Not. Arch., 2784, N. 492, N. 494. Petition, 11 December 1668, *N.Y. Col. Docs.*, 3:178–79. Order in council granting their request, 11 December 1668, ibid., p. 179. York tried to establish a free trade between Scotland and New York; however, this was defeated by the Farmers of the Customs, ibid., pp. 180–82.

52. As quoted in Stanley N. Katz, *Newcastle's New York*, p. 28.

53. Testimony of Thomas Lovelace [1674], Rawlinson MSS, A, 173, fol. 186, Bodleian Library, Oxford University, Oxford, England. For some of their land transactions, see ibid., fol. 185, and *RNA*, 6:286–88. Samuel Hazard et al., eds., *Pennsylvania Archives*, 2nd ser., 5:651–52, hereafter cited as *Pennsylvania Archives*. Samuel Maverick reported to Richard Nicolls that the *Good Fame* was costly to build, 15 October 1669, *N.Y. Col. Docs.*, 3:185. His other ship transactions are recorded in Lovelace to Richard Nicolls, 19 May 1672, Coventry MSS, 76, fol. 257, Not. Arch., 3502, N. 320, and Mass. Hist. Soc., *Collections*, 3rd ser., pp. 10, 79–80. For Lovelace's accounts, see N.Y. Col. MSS, 22, fols. 115, 116; 24, fols. 115, 127, 169, 102. Not. Arch., 3504, pt. 1, N. 339; 3496, pt. 2, N. 295; 3206, N. 21, N. 22; 3207, N. 25. The relationship between Lovelace and Bedloo can be traced in *N.Y. Col. Docs.*, 2:651. N.Y. Col. MSS, 22, fols. 115, 116. WOL, 2, fols. 233–34.

54. 7 July 1668, *RNA*, 6:138–41.

55. *Executive Council*, 2:522–23 and 9 March 1671, ibid.

56. 22 October 1670, ibid., 1:56–58. This overland trade was very important to the New England fur traders. Bernard Bailyn, *The New England Merchants in the Seventeenth Century*, p. 60.

57. Jeremias Van Rensselaer to Richard Van Rensselaer, 25 August 1671. Van Laer,

Jeremias Van Rensselaer, pp. 439–42. Reports of hard times circulated as far as the Carolinas, "Extracts of Carolina affairs," November 1671, *CSPC*, 7, no. 664, and January 1672, ibid., no. 746.

58. *RNA*, 6:286–88; *Executive Council*, 1:80, 519–20.

59. *Executive Council*, 1:88–91.

60. Order to the justices, 23 May 1671, ibid., pp. 520–21. Court of assize meeting 4–7 October 1671, *Annual Report* (1896), pp. 171–75.

61. *N.Y. Col. Docs.*, 14:661.

62. For the export permits, see *Executive Council*, 1:139–44; 2:521–22; Assize meeting, 2–7 October 1672, *Annual Report* (1896), pp. 175–80.

63. As early as 1659 the magistrates watched the quality and size of bread loaves closely. Arthur E. Peterson and George W. Edwards, *New York as an Eighteenth Century Municipality*, pp. 42–45. For later regulations, see *RNA*, 6:111, 113, 266, and *Executive Council*, 1:175–77.

64. *Executive Council*, 1:184–87.

65. Order to Thomas Chatfield, customs officer at Easthampton, 15 October 1665, *N.Y. Col. Docs.*, 14:608, 612–13.

66. Charles R. Street, *Huntington Town Records*, 1:113–14. Hicks, *Records of the Towns of North and South Hempstead*, p. 260. Stephanus Van Cortlandt to Maria Van Rensselaer, April 1669, A. J. F. Van Laer, ed., *Correspondence of Maria Van Rensselaer*, pp. 9–10; Jeremias Van Rensselaer to Jan Baptist Van Rensselaer, 1669, Van Laer, *Jeremias Van Rensselaer*, pp. 412–13.

67. Lovelace to Hempstead, Flushing, Jamaica, Newtown, and Oyster Bay, 10 February 1669, *N.Y. Col. Docs.*, 14:615.

68. Warrant to Sheriff Robert Coe, 12 October 1669, ibid., p. 626.

69. Petition to court of assize, 2 November 1669, ibid., pp. 731–32.

70. Answer to the petition, n.d., ibid., pp. 632–33.

71. Court of assize meeting 3–6 November 1669, *Annual Report* (1896), pp. 162–66.

72. For the membership of the assize, see *Executive Council*, 2:423. The session is recorded in *Annual Report* (1896), pp. 166–71.

73. *Annual Report* (1896), pp. 166–71.

74. Town meeting, Jamaica, 10 December 1670, Josephine C. Frost, *Records of the Town of Jamaica*, pp. 47–48. The town of Huntington issued a similar petition on 21 February 1671. At the next court of sessions this petition was burned as seditious. Street, *Huntington Records*, 1:163–65.

75. "Declaration of ye severall justices . . . ," 21–22 December 1670, *Executive Council*, 2:485.

76. "Order for the libels . . . ," 29 December 1670, ibid., pp. 485–86. See also the council minutes for the same day, ibid., 1:66.

77. James T. Adams, *The History of the Town of Southampton*, p. 89. The letter, dated 15 February 1671, was signed by fifty townsmen. Council minutes, *Executive Council*, 1:80.

78. The letter was dated 9 March 1671, *Executive Council*, 2:525–26. The commission to Delaval and the others, 9 March 1671, ibid., pp. 524–25.

79. Records of East-hampton, 1:337. J. W. Case, *Southold Town Records*, 1:339. *CSPC*, 7, no. 875.

80. Order in Council, 3 July 1672, *N.Y. Col. Docs.*, 3:197–98.

81. Isaac N. Stokes, *Iconography of Manhattan Island*, 2:222, 278, 309.

82. Nicolls and Maverick to Governor Benedict Arnold and William Burton, deputy governor of Rhode Island, 23 September 1664, *General Entries*, pp. 107–8.

83. Riker, *Harlem*, p. 245.

84. Instructions to Captain Baker, August 1668, *Executive Council*, 2:387–90.

85. Instructions to Brodhead, 23 October 1665 in Marius Schoonmaker, *The History of Kingston*, p. 51.

86. Samuel Maverick reported, "There is a good correspondence kept between the English and Dutch and to keep it the closer, sixteen (ten Dutch and six English) have

had a constant meeting at each other's houses in turn." Maverick to Nicolls, 5 July 1669, *N.Y. Col. Docs.*, 3:182–84.

87. The discussions can be found in *RNA*, 5:142–44. The oath does not ask them to fight against the Netherlands. *N.Y. Col. Docs.*, 3:74–77.

88. Nicolls to Magistrates of New York City, 18 October 1664, *General Entries*, pp. 118–19.

89. The climactic interview can be found in *RNA*, 5:144–45, and the list of names, *N.Y. Col. Docs.*, 3:74–77. Only twenty-nine people, eight of whom were soldiers, obtained permission to leave on the *Unity*. Few substantial people decided to leave; even Peter Stuyvesant took the oath. *General Entries*, pp. 139–40.

90. The chief complaints against the soldiers were of assault and theft. See *RNA*, 5:211–13, 260–62. On one occasion twenty soldiers raided a household, ibid., pp. 138–40. There was a rise in other activities obnoxious to the city fathers as they had to exile women for prostitution. Ibid., pp. 269–72; 6:10. One soldier who assaulted a civilian was made to run the gauntlet and then banished, punishment intended to reduce these incidents. David T. Valentine, ed., *Manual of the Corporation of the City of New York* (1847), p. 353.

91. Governor William Berkeley to Nicolls, 7 December 1664, Blathwayt Papers, Box 1, fol. 69, Henry E. Huntington Library, San Marino, Cal. This letter contains the only comment on the mutiny, as Nicolls never mentioned it in his correspondence to England. "Petition of all the soldiers," 21 November 1664, New Netherland Collection MSS, New York Historical Society, New York City.

92. Nicolls's retention of jursidiction over the soldiers was commented on, *RNA*, 5:317–19.

93. The soldiers had asked to be put into homes in their petition to Nicolls. His request to the magistrates and their response, ibid., 5:206–9.

94. This meeting began with complaints from three Dutch inhabitants about assaults committed by soldiers. Ibid., pp. 211–13.

95. Ibid., pp. 221–25. The tax continuation, ibid., 6:1–5, 74–77, 101–3.

96. Esopus Court of Sessions MS, I, fols. 197, 246–50, microfilm in the Queens College Library, Queens, N.Y. Reports of fighting in the river communities reached Sir George Cartwright in Boston. Cartwright to Nicolls, 15 April 1665, *N.Y. Col. Docs.*, 3:93–94.

97. Instructions to Captain Baker, August 1668, *Executive Council*, 2:381–90. Nicolls to *Commissaries* of Albany [January 1677], ibid., p. 143.

98. Instructions to Brodhead, 23 October 1665 in Schoonmaker, *Kingston*, p. 51.

99. N.Y. Col. MSS, 12, fol. 28. For the complaints of the Dutch, ibid., fol. 22, and also *N.Y. Col. Docs.*, 13:407–8.

100. For an account of the riot, see *N.Y. Col. Docs.*, 13:407–8, and "Papers that concern the Esopus Mutiny." Ibid., 13:406–14.

101. Private Instructions to the Commission for Esopus, n.d., Ibid., 3:149–50.

102. Sentence of the Governor, 16 February 1666, Valentine, *Manual* (1847), pp. 357–58. All of the convicted were eventually allowed to return to Esopus.

103. Order to Carr, 2 August 1669, *Executive Council*, 1:304–12.

104. Order to Carr, 2 August 1669, ibid., pp. 310–12; Council Minutes, 14 September 1669, ibid., p. 37; Lovelace to Carr, 15 September 1669, ibid., pp. 310–12. Council minutes, 18 October 1669, ibid., p. 38; *N.Y. Col. Docs.*, 13:469–71, and also E. A. Louhi, *The Delaware Finns*, p. 137; warrant for transportation of Jacobsen on the ship of Jacques Cousseau, 28 January 1670, *Executive Council*, 1:314–17, 322. On the trial, see Mathias Nicolls to Richard Nicolls, 31 December 1669, *N.Y. Col. Docs.*, 3:186.

105. The most succinct account of the reawakening of New France is in William J. Eccles, *Canada Under Louis XIV*, pp. 24–76. And also, Richard C. Harris, *The Seigneurial System in Early Canada*, pp. 17–19.

106. The expansionary impulse of the Iroquois and its motivation are discussed in George T. Hunt, *The Wars of the Iroquois*, passim; Peter Wraxall, *Peter Wraxall's, An Abridgement of the Indian Affairs . . . In the Colony of New York . . . 1678 to . . . 1751*, pp.

xlii–xlv. The most balanced account is in Allen W. Trelease, *Indian Affairs in Colonial New York*, pp. 52–54, 118–24.

107. Arthur H. Buffinton, "The Policy of Albany and English Westward Expansion," pp. 327–66.

108. During a single storm of this terrible winter two ships in New York harbor were sunk and a great deal of tobacco and salt stored in cellars was lost. Then when the spring thaws began Albany lost forty homes and barns swept away in floods. Stokes, *Iconography*, 4:265. Jeremias Van Rensselaer to Oloff Van Cortlandt, 3 April 1666, Van Laer, *Jeremias Van Rensselaer*, pp. 386–87. Van Rensselaer lost his house, barn, and two breweries. "The Relation of the March of the Governor of Canada," *N.Y. Col. Docs.*, 3:118–19. See also Eccles, *Canada*, p. 40.

109. For an account of the expedition see Edmund B. O'Callaghan, ed., *The Documentary History of the State of New York*, 1:60–70, hereafter cited as *Doc. Hist.* The Du Bois ceremony is recounted in *N.Y. Col. Docs.*, 3:135.

110. *N.Y. Col. Docs.*, 3:143. Nicolls was always careful to congratulate all concerned about the peace kept among them. To sheriff Gerard Swart he wrote, "I am very glad to heare that all affaires are carried out with so much discretion, that not one complaint is made; which is wellcome tydinges to me, and shows that every man walkes in his owne station." Ibid., p. 145.

111. Ambassador Van Gogh to States General, 31 October 1664, State Papers 84/172, fols. 305–6, PRO. Van Gogh reported that the news was already around London of Nicolls's success. The duke heard the details from a Captain Grove, York to King Charles, 15 November 1665, Lambeth Palace MSS, 645, fol. 45, Lambeth Palace, London.

112. Keith G. Feiling, *British Foreign Policy*, p. 134; orders from King Charles, *N.Y. Col. Docs.*, 3:85–86.

113. Cartwright to Nicolls, 5 June 1665, *CSPC*, 5, no. 1008; order of confiscation, 15 June 1665, *General Entries*, pp. 174–75.

114. *RNA*, 5:267.

115. Ibid., pp. 268–69. Nicolls to Clarendon, 30 July 1665, NYHS, *Collections* (1869), pp. 74–77.

116. J. P. Blok, *The Life of Admiral De Ruyter*, pp. 183–98.

117. J. C. M. Warnsink, *Abraham Crijnssen*, pp. 66–70, 162–66.

118. Van Rensselaer to Anna Van Rensselaer, 1668, Van Laer, *Jeremias Van Rensselaer*, pp. 401–3.

119. Nicolls to Clarendon, 20 July 1665, NYHS, *Collections* (1869), pp. 74–77.

120. "The Conditions for new-planters in the Territories of his Royal Highness the Duke of York." Clifford K. Shipton, ed., *Early American Imprints, 1639–1800* (microfiche), no. 98.

121. Nicolls to the inhabitants of Jamaica, 4 January 1665, *N.Y. Col. Docs.*, 14:562–63.

122. Proposal to the Council, 9 April 1669, ibid., 3:180.

123. The farmers estimated an annual £7,000 loss if the petition was granted. Ibid., pp. 181–82.

124. Mathias Nicolls to Richard Nicolls, 31 December 1669, ibid., p. 186. For the whole Scots fiasco, see Peter Gouldesbrough, "An Attempted Scottish Voyage to New York in 1669," pp. 56–62.

125. Maverick to Bond, 30 May 1669, Mass. Hist. Soc., *Collections*, 4th ser., 7:316–18. Maverick wrote that cod was in abundance, 20 whales had been taken in the spring, and 10,000 *schepels* of wheat had already been exported to Boston.

126. Lovelace to the governor of Bermuda, 3 June 1669, *N.Y. Col. Docs.*, 13:424–26.

127. "Extracts of Carolina Affairs, November, 1671," *CSPC*, 7, no. 664, and January 1672, ibid., no. 746. A £10 fine was placed on masters taking emigrants without passports, *N.Y. Col. Docs.*, 14:658.

128. *N.Y. Col. Docs.*, 13:416. Nicolls bought the land at Esopus from the Indians on 7 October 1665, N.Y. Col. MSS, 22, fol. 4. He promised each soldier 30 acres of lowland, 2½ acres of upland, and a share in the woodlot. Lovelace's order, 5 September 1668,

Executive Council, 1:242–45. Answer to the Desires of the Inhabitants at Esopus, 26 September 1668, ibid., pp. 248–49. He promised to supply the soldiers and asked that they not be loaned any money.

129. Executive Council, pp. 294–95. Order from Lovelace, 23 August 1670, ibid., p. 305. Some soldiers tried to withdraw right after they received their allotments, ibid., p. 299. One of the Dutch men also tried to withdraw. He was refused until he could find a replacement. Ibid., p. 297.

CHAPTER 4

1. King Charles to Lovelace, Executive Council, 2:737–39. Keith G. Feiling, British Foreign Policy, pp. 228–344.

2. Lovelace to Major-General Leverett of Boston, 23 April 1672, Executive Council, 2:712–13.

3. Lovelace's order 27 January 1672, ibid., pp. 155–56. His plea to the towns was made in a letter to John Young, 30 May 1672, N.Y. Col. Docs., 14:666.

4. Receipts from various areas of the colony are in Executive Council, 1:133–39, 155–66; 2:700–701, and N.Y. Col. Docs., 14:676.

5. Letter 24 July 1762, Coventry MSS, 76, fols. 259–60, Longleat House.

6. Executive Council, 1:127–29. Lovelace to Winthrop, 26 June 1672, ibid., 2:739. During an earlier threat to peace Lovelace wrote to Winthrop that he was "very zealous to promote a tranquility amongst all whereby Trade, and commerce may not receive any interruption." Mass. Hist. Soc., Collections, 3rd ser., 10:79–80.

7. Declaration, Executive Council, 1:144–45. The confiscation order was issued 25 October 1672, ibid., 2:747–48.

8. Council minutes, 24 May 1672, ibid., 1:127–29.

9. Thomas Ludwell to Lord Arlington, 2 August 1673, N.Y. Col. Docs., 3:204.

10. C. De Waard, ed., De Zeewusche Expeditie, pp. 38–40. Later reports indicated that the decision to invade New York was made while the fleet was in Virginia. The logbook kept by Evertsen shows nothing of the sort happened. Affidavit of William Hayes, 2 December 1673, N.Y. Col. Docs., 3:213–14. Account of the capture of New York by Nathaniel Gould, ibid., pp. 200–203.

11. Lovelace had been considering the mail system during the summer of 1673, Executive Council, 2:794–96. On the way to visit Winthrop, Lovelace, along with Mathias Nicolls, spent time visiting friends, apparently in no hurry. John Allyn to Fitz-John Winthrop, 29 July 1673, Mass. Hist. Soc., Collections, 6th ser., 3:434–35.

12. The following account is compiled from slightly different versions: De Waard, De Zeewusche, pp. 40–44; account of John Sharp (Lovelace's attorney) in two differing versions—Mass. Hist. Soc., Collections, 6th ser., 3:436–44, and "An exact account of the proceedings of the military officers of Fort James, July 29 to the surrender of the Fort," CO/1/30, fols. 117–19, PRO.

13. Lovelace to Winthrop, 31 July 1673, N.Y. Col. Docs., 3:198. He told Winthrop he was going to Long Island to raise the militia. Ibid., pp. 201–2.

14. One of the leading complaints of the Dutch to Evertsen and Binkes was the misuse of taxes and nonpayment of debts by the government. Ibid., 2:578–79. Colve had to charge a special tax to repair a decayed fort. Ibid., p. 685.

15. For the activities of the commission see CSPC, 9, nos. 441, 442, 530. See also Newsletters, 3 March and 9 March 1675, Historical Manuscripts Commission, Twelfth Report, S. H. le Fleming of Lydal, Appendix, 7, no. 1595. The English garrison was shipped home and put into the garrison of Portsmouth. Dartmouth MSS, D, 1778V, fol. 2, William Salt Library, Stafford, Staffordshire, England.

16. The submissions of the towns to the Dutch on 12 August 1673 can be found in N.Y. Col. Docs., 2:580–81; for New Jersey, including the English areas, on 24 August, see ibid., p. 582.

17. Commissioned 9 September 1673, ibid., pp. 609–10. Nicholas Bayard stood next to Steenwyck in influence. He was appointed secretary and receiver general. Ibid., pp. 612–13.

18. Proclamation, 10 September 1673, ibid., pp. 611–12.

19. Petition, 28 August 1673, ibid., pp. 598–600.

20. Their petition 14 August 1673, ibid., pp. 583–84.

21. At a council session on 14 August 1673 the government received the envoys. Ibid., pp. 584–85. The General Court ordered 500 dragoons to be raised on 7 August and on the same day James Richards and William Rosewell were ordered to New York. J. Hammond Trumbull and Charles J. Hoadly, eds., *The Public Records of the Colony of Connecticut*, 2:203–6.

22. Council session, 14 August, *N.Y. Col. Docs.*, 2:584–85. Another account of the meeting can be found in De Waard, *De Zeewusche*, p. 46.

23. *N.Y. Col. Docs.*, 2:584–85, and Robert C. Black, *The Younger John Winthrop*, p. 332.

24. Commission to Knyff, 1 October 1673, *N.Y. Col. Docs.*, 2:620. His report to the council, 19 October, ibid., p. 638. The town's refusal notices, ibid., pp. 639–42. The last ship, with the exception of the *Zeehond*, left on 2 December, *RNA*, 7:31.

25. John Ballyn to Colve, 21 October 1673, *N.Y. Col. Docs.*, 2:651–52. The bearer of the letter was jailed, Mass. Hist. Soc., *Collections*, 5th ser., 7:156–57.

26. Colve to Governor Winthrop, 8 November 1673, *N.Y. Col. Docs.*, 2:660–61, and council meeting, 10 October, ibid., p. 642. Commission and instructions to Steenwyck, 20 October 1673, ibid., p. 648. A journal, kept on the *Zeehond*, of the expedition, ibid., pp. 654–58. The townsmen were seeking even more help. John Winthrop, Jr., reported to his son Fitz-John that representatives of the towns had gone to Boston. Mass. Hist. Soc., *Collections*, 5th ser., 7:158–59.

27. Black, *The Younger Winthrop*, pp. 334–36.

28. Four New England ships were seized and confiscated in November, *N.Y. Col. Docs.*, 2:664. For the trade slump, see Jeremias to Jan Baptist Van Rensselaer, 29 June 1674, A. J. F. Van Laer, *Correspondence of Jeremias Van Rensselaer*, pp. 460–64. A stop was placed on the export of provisions from New York City, *RNA*, 7:35, and regulations were put into effect on 1 May strictly limiting the number of ships going to Albany, ibid., pp. 70–71.

29. The taxes and special assessments can be found in *RNA*, 6:40 and 2:8–15, 49–52. The mortgage was made on 2 May 1674, *N.Y. Col. Docs.*, 2:674. On the same day the extreme measure of confiscating the New York property of all Englishmen who resided in England, New England, Virginia, or Maryland was taken, ibid.

30. Proclamation, 10 December 1673, *N.Y. Col. Docs.*, 2:666. Captain Knyff was appointed 16 January 1674, *RNA*, 7:36–39. The burgomaster's protest, ibid., pp. 39–43. John Sharpe's account of the mood of the city is in his letter to John Winthrop, Jr., 12 May 1674, Mass. Hist. Soc., *Collections*, 3rd ser., 10:108–10.

31. For an account of Dyre see Mariana G. Van Rensselaer, *History of the City of New York in the Seventeenth Century*, 2:170–71. A report on his petition stated he was very knowledgeable about the colonies, 16 January 1674, *Executive Council*, 2:126–27. See his petition, 17 December 1673, CO/389/5, fol. 45, PRO.

32. Dyre's proposal, 27 October 1673, *N.Y. Col. Docs.*, 3:207–8; anonymous memorials, 22 October 1673, ibid., p. 207. Sir John Knight to earl of Shaftsbury, 29 October 1673, ibid., pp. 209–10. Lord Culpepper's proposal, 13 November 1673, CO/1/30, fol. 20, PRO. "Memorialls of what strength will be necessary for the retaking of New York," 3 November 1673, CO/1/30, fol. 199, PRO. One proposal was revealed much later. Captain Wynborne, of the Royal Navy, was at Boston when New York was captured. He requested additional aid from the government of Massachusetts Bay in order to attack New York, and was refused. The magistrates told him they would rather see the colony Dutch than have it come under Lovelace again. *CSPC*, 4, no. 721.

33. *N.Y. Col. Docs.*, 3:211–13.

34. States General to King Charles, 9 December 1673, *N.Y. Col. Docs.*, 2:531. King Charles to the States General, 31 March 1674, ibid., p. 554. Resolutions of the States General, 6 April 1674, ibid., pp. 545–46. John R. Brodhead, *The History of the State of New York*, 2:251.

35. Addl. MSS 1091, fols. 106–9, Cambridge University Library, Cambridge. See Robert C. Ritchie, "The Duke of York's Commission of Revenue," pp. 177–79.

36. Ritchie, "York's Commission," pp. 178–79.

37. For Andros's career see *DAB*, 1:300–301. Brodhead, *New York*, 2:262, and Jeanne Bloom, "Sir Edmund Andros," passim. At about the same time Andros succeeded to his father's position as bailiff of Guernsey and hereditary seigneur of Sausmarez.

38. For details of these episodes, see Robert C. Ritchie, "The Duke's Province," pp. 208–10, 214–16.

39. Andros's commission, *N.Y. Col. Docs.*, 3:215; instructions, ibid., pp. 216–19; and his military commission, ibid., p. 219.

40. Warrant, 6 August 1674, ibid., pp. 226–27.

41. Warrant to seize Lovelace's estate, 6 August 1674, ibid., p. 226. The goods sent by York were valued at over £800. *CSPC*, 7, no. 1328. The goods were shipped customs free, as were those of Andros. Great Britain, Public Record Office, *Calendar of Treasury Books*, 4:554, 564.

42. Van Laer, *Jeremias Van Rensselaer*, pp. 460–64.

43. Jeremias to Richard Van Rensselaer, 3 July 1674, ibid., pp. 464–68. Jeremias to Robert Vastrick, 28 August 1674, ibid., p. 471. In the letter Van Rensselaer writes he is sorry to hear Vastrick "fears" the return of the English.

44. This account of the surrender is derived from the following. Andros to Colve, 22 October 1674, *Doc. Hist.*, 3:67–68. Resolution of the States General, 28 June 1674, *N.Y. Col. Docs.*, 2:730–31. Andros to Colve, 23 October 1674, *Doc. Hist.*, 3:68–69. Commission to Steenwyck and Van Brugh, ibid., pp. 70–71. The "Proposals," ibid., pp. 73–75.

45. Andros refused to accept article 9, which reserved the tappers' excise for the debts of the city, and article 10, which would have reserved the customs for payment of the loans used to rebuild the fort. *Doc. Hist.*, 3:73–75.

46. *RNA*, 7:138. *N.Y. Col. Docs.*, 3:227.

47. Council minutes, 27 November 1674, New York (Colony Council), *Calendar of Council Minutes*, p. 19, hereafter cited as *CCM*.

48. Petition, 1 December 1674, N.Y. Col. MSS, 24, fol. 25.

49. Council minutes, *N.Y. Col. Docs.*, 14:681. On 17 November 1674 the Southold town meeting placed the town under Connecticut and appointed men to meet with Easthampton and Southampton to negotiate with Connecticut. J. W. Case, *Southold*, 1:374–75. See also Richard S. Dunn, "John Winthrop, Jr., Connecticut Expansionist," pp. 19–22.

50. *N.Y. Col. Docs.*, 14:682–83. Winthrop to Andros, 16 December 1674, Mass. Hist. Soc., *Collections*, 5th ser., 7:164–66.

51. *N.Y. Col. Docs.*, 14:683–84. And also Andros to Winthrop, 28 December 1674, ibid., pp. 684–85.

52. Order, 2 November 1674, ibid., 12:513. Council minute, 4 November 1674, *CCM*, p. 19. See also the order, 2 November 1674, *N.Y. Col. Docs.*, 12:513. Andros to Hurley and Marbleton, 11 January 1675, ibid., 13:482.

53. For aspects of Darvall's career see *Executive Council*, 2:522; Isaac N. Stokes, *Iconography of Manhattan Island*, 6:373; Benjamin D. Hicks, ed., *Records of the Town of North and South Hempstead*, 2:87–88, 98–101; *N.Y. Col. Docs.*, 13:546–48.

54. The magistrates were appointed, 17 October 1675, *MCC*, 1:1–2.

55. The appointment of the magistrates can be traced in Brodhead, *New York*, 2:273; *MCC*, 1:1–2, 25–26, 63–64, 69, 74. Those appointed in 1680 continued in office until 1683; New York Miscellaneous MSS, Box 2, No. 21, New York Historical Society, New York City; and Mayor's Court Minutes MSS, microfilm copy, Queens College Library, Queens, N.Y., hereafter cited as MCM. In 1674, 1675, 1676, and 1680 there were five aldermen; however, in 1677, 1678, and 1679 there were six. I have no explanation for these fluctuations.

56. *CSPC*, 7, no. 875. Even in 1672 the petition complained that "the Dutch being chief impose what laws they please." Jasper Dankaerts said of the relationship between

Andros and Philipse, "he [Philipse] and the governor are one." Jasper Dankaerts, *Journal of Jasper Dankaerts*, p. 238.

57. *N.Y. Col. Docs.*, 3:216–19.

58. Werden to Andros, 28 January 1676, *N.Y. Col. Docs.*, 3:246–47.

59. Dyre's commission 2 July 1674, *N.Y. Col. Docs.*, 3:221–22 and instructions, ibid., pp. 222–23. These documents say nothing about royal customs and refer only to "my customs." For Smith, see Great Britain, *Calendar of Treasury Books*, 4:552. His commission is dated 13 May 1673. A John Sharpe was commissioned collector of the royal customs in 1677, WOL, 2: fol. 367. He never appears in the records after this. It should be pointed out that other students of the customs regard those collected as royal customs and Dyre as a royal official. See Thomas C. Barrow, *Trade and Empire*, p. 167, and George L. Beer, *The Old Colonial System*, 2:351–52.

60. Captain John Manning became the scapegoat for the fiasco in 1673. His trial is recorded in N.Y. Col. MSS, 25, fols. 36–53; *Doc. Hist.*, 3:80–82.

61. Lovelace's property was seized by Andros on 25 March 1675. N.Y. Col. MSS, 24, fol. 726. Colve formed a commission to untangle the estates of Lovelace and Delaval. *N.Y. Col. Docs.*, 2:587–88. Isaac Bedloo's widow was similarly enmeshed with Lovelace's estate. N.Y. Col. MSS, 24, fols. 102, 115, 127, 126. Thomas Lovelace also lost a great deal. Rawlinson MSS, A, 137, fol. 186, Bodleian Library, Oxford. Thomas Delaval had the largest claim, £6,000, CO/5/1112, fol. 186, PRO.

62. The duke's first letter to Andros was written on 6 April 1675. It indicated that he had received Andros's letters of 6 November and 4 and 7 December, none of which have survived. *N.Y. Col. Docs.*, 3:230.

63. York to Andros, 28 January 1676, ibid., p. 235.

64. The Easthampton town records contain an exceptionally complete accounting of expenditures: *Records of the Town of East-Hampton*, 2:140–44 for 1684, and pp. 151–63 for 1685. For town expenditures to an individual for a variety of services, see Isaac Platt's bill, 15 March 1687, Street, *Huntington Town Records*, 1:484–85. Andros to George Hall, of Esopus, 13 October 1675, *N.Y. Col. Docs.*, 13:489. Hall was ordered to collect all public debts. Order, 4 July 1676, *Albany Minutes of the Court*, 2:124–31. The *commissaries* were not to collect rates without his approval. Order to Edmund Cantwell, at Delaware, 18 November 1678, *N.Y. Col. Docs.*, 12:412. Andros ordered Cantwell to send the records of a rate Andros heard the magistrates had charged. This order reveals the lack of communication with the Delaware settlements.

65. Order, 17 September 1675, after Andros had met with them on 4 September 1675. *Albany Minutes of the Court*, 2:17, 22. Extract of a letter from Andros to Albany, 5 September 1675, ibid., p. 23. Order, 20 September 1676, ibid., pp. 161–62.

66. Excise, 5 September 1676, ibid., pp. 155–60; powder and lead order 28 June 1676, ibid., pp. 123–24; assessment list for stockades, 3 March 1679, ibid., pp. 396–97. Extraordinary court session, 20 April 1677, ibid., p. 225.

67. Commission to Philipse, Delaval, Oloff Van Cortlandt, Steenwyck, and two others, 25 January 1677, *MCC*, 1:39–40. Their report, ibid., pp. 43–46. The list of creditors is interesting. The city owed Andros 6,280 guilders, Philipse 701 guilders, Stephanus Van Cortlandt 1,075 guilders, and Nicholas De Meyer 1,873 guilders.

68. For examples of the fees, see ibid., pp. 27–29, 49, 63. Order, n.d., ibid., pp. 10–11. Regulations on taphouses, 29 January 1676, ibid., pp. 13–14. There were twenty-four taphouses in 1680, ibid., pp. 80–81. Orders, 28 February 1681, ibid., p. 86. Orders, 15 April 1676, ibid., p. 9. Assessment list, 10 November 1676, ibid., pp. 29–37.

69. N.Y. Col. MSS, 25, fol. 56. Even the small villages of Westchester were charged. Mathias Nicolls to Westchester and Eastchester, 19 September 1676, *N.Y. Col. Docs.*, 13:501. "Proportion for each town for new fort building," 1 January 1676. This is a very detailed list of supplies including 100,591 stockades of 12 feet by 4 inches. WOL, 3: fol. 171. Andros's threats began in May, ibid., fol. 195, continued in June, ibid., fol. 201, and climaxed in September, ibid., fol. 210.

70. For the special land tax a street-by-street breakdown of houses and empty lots was created. *MCC*, 1:50–62. Afterward the owners of vacant lots were told to build on them or have them confiscated. N.Y. Col. MSS, 25, fol. 120.

71. These are detailed in Andros's instructions, *N.Y. Col. Docs.*, 3:217. The first renewal of the customs was in 1677, ibid., p. 246.

72. Ibid., pp. 231, 235.

73. A petition of the constables of the east and north ridings requested the opening of the ports. N.Y. Col. MSS, 36, fol. 122. Apparently exemptions were granted in special cases. One captain loaded with whale oil petitioned for and received permission not to come to New York City, *N.Y. Col. Docs.*, 14:735. When the city became the collection center Captain John Collier of the garrison was appointed subcollector on 23 September 1675, ibid., 12:556–57. Council minute, 5 December 1675, ibid., p. 542.

74. Order, 13 August 1677, *N.Y. Col. Docs.*, 14:580.

75. Council minute, 5 August 1675, *CCM*, p. 23. For succeeding rates, see *Doc. Hist.* (1675), 2:253–68; (1676), 2:269–86; (1683), 2:287–314. N.Y. Col. MSS, 29 (1680) fols. 275a–b; (1676) 25, fol. 223; (1677) 26, fol. 163; (1678) 28, fol. 17a; (1675) 24, foll. 147–48.

76. Young's accounts, N.Y. Col. MSS, 29, fol. 275a–b. For the careers of some of the lawyers, see Paul M. Hamlin and Charles E. Baker, *Supreme Court of Judicature of the Province of New York*, 3:306, 393, 397, 408. Mathias Nicolls to the towns, 20 October 1675, *N.Y. Col. Docs.*, 14:704–5. Nicolls asked the towns for payment in produce.

77. Assessment list, *Doc. Hist.*, 2:262–63. Assize meeting October 1676, N.Y. Col. MSS, 25, fol. 197. However, on 4 October 1677 the constables of the east and north ridings again requested a change, *N.Y. Col. Docs.*, 14:730–31. They claimed the rate was double the worth of horses on the market.

78. Complaints of the towns at court of sessions, 10 December 1679, *N.Y. Col. Docs.*, 14:748–49. See the warning to Huntington, 1676, N.Y. Col. MSS, 25, fol. 197.

79. Southold quitrent was one fat lamb, 31 October 1676, J. W. Case, *Southold Town Records*, 2:8–11; same for Oyster Bay, John Cox, ed., *Oyster Bay Town Records*, pp. 307–8, and Southampton, Benjamin F. Thompson, *History of Long Island*, 1:335. Andros put a quitrent into all patents he approved. Ulster County list of patents, "Ulster County Papers," pp. 143–48. For a fuller discussion of quitrents, see Beverly W. Bond, Jr., *The Quit-Rent System in the American Colonies*, pp. 110–13. Bond assumes there were no rents in the Dutch patents. In fact the West India Company charged a tenth of all the produce of the land. See *N.Y. Col. Docs.*, 14:10–13.

80. Order of 26 October 1678 ended the three-year reprieve, *N.Y. Col. Docs.*, 12:609.

81. Order, 6 October 1677, ibid., 13:512–13.

82. One tax list of the three sent by Sheriff Cantwell of Delaware had a total of 81½ bushels of wheat in quitrent payments, ibid., 12:543–45.

83. "List of bids for the excise," 5 December 1675, N.Y. Col. MSS, 25, fols. 51, 53. There were eight bidders, one of whom was Dyre, who came in second. On 10 December 1680 he tried for the weigh-house and lost again, ibid., 29, fol. 264. For the weigh-house, see ibid., 25, fol. 49. John Sharpe, a merchant, had the highest bid.

84. Conditions for farming the weigh-house, 25 November 1675, ibid., 25, fol. 50. Lists of bids 1675–79, ibid., 28, fol. 156. For 1680, see ibid., 29, fol. 264.

85. This amount was collected 23 March 1678; ibid., 27, fol. 48. One other record exists. On 25 March 1679 at least sixteen licenses were granted at £2.8.0 each for a total of £38.8.0; ibid., 25, fol. 67.

86. Werden to Andros, 7 May 1677, *N.Y. Col. Docs.*, 3:246–47.

87. Warrant to Apsley to pay Andros, 18 May 1678, ibid., pp. 267–68.

CHAPTER 5

1. "Answers of Governor Andros to enquiries about New York," 16 April 1678, *N.Y. Col. Docs.*, 3:260–62. Five ships of over 100 tons were owned locally. In contrast Massachusetts had "very many and good ships" of 200 to 300 tons.

2. A petition of July 1677 lists twelve men in Amsterdam who still considered themselves traders to "New Netherland." Ibid., 2:792. Andros did raise questions about a direct legal trade with the Netherlands but was sharply rebuffed. Werden told him the Navigation Acts would not permit such commerce. Ibid., 3:236–38.

3. This typical cargo was registered in Dover. Exchequer Class 190/664/14, PRO, hereafter cited as E 190. The Dover trade in the 1670s can be seen in the following port books: ibid., 663/2, 5, 6; 664/2, 14, 17; 665/4, 11; 666/8, 18, PRO.

4. For examples of the Falmouth trade, ibid., 1043/14, 16; 1044/12, 18, PRO.

5. The *Rebecca* of New York had this typical lading when she left Dover on 3 June 1678. Ibid., 664/17, PRO.

6. This figure is derived from the port books listed in n. 3 and evidence in the Amsterdam Notarial Archives.

7. The total of five merchant vessels sailing directly from England to New York can be taken only as an approximate figure. E 190/50/5; 62/1; 62/5, PRO. *General Entries*, pp. 158–59. The ship *William and Nicholas* that came with Nicolls in 1664 is included.

8. These prices have been collected from a wide variety of sources from all over New York. Surprisingly the geographic price differentials were not great. For the sources, see *RNA*, 7:123–28. *MCC*, 1:18. N.Y. Col. MSS, 28, fol. 164. Benjamin D. Hicks, ed., *Records of the Town of North and South Hempstead*, pp. 95, 137, 152–53, 264–65, 302–3, 400, 421. John Cox, ed., *Oyster Bay Town Records*, 1:55, 83, 90, 129, 159, 161, 191, 229, 274, 310. J. W. Case, *Southold Town Records*, pp. 311, 370, 358. Charles R. Street, ed., *Huntington Town Records*, 1:160–61, 238–39, 330–32, 414, 514–19, 526–28, 264–65. *Records of the Town of East-Hampton*, 1:221, 233, 264–65, 313, 329, 349, 368, 397, 403, 2:124. *Albany Minutes of the Court*, 2:228–34, 3:48–58.

9. Oloff Van Cortlandt to Maria Van Rensselaer, January 1681, A. J. F. Van Laer, ed., *Correspondence of Maria Van Rensselaer*, pp. 45–46. The slump was severe in Albany. *Albany Minutes of the Court*, 3:87, 143–44. Stephanus Van Cortlandt to Maria Van Rensselaer, December 1681, Van Laer, *Maria Van Rensselaer*, pp. 52–54. Maria Van Rensselaer, who was in charge of the patroonship while Stephanus Van Cortlandt, her brother, was director, indicates a scarcity of grain until the spring of 1683. Ibid., pp. 82–83, 105–6. Price declines also affected Massachusetts. William I. Davisson, "Essex County Price Trends," and "Essex County Wealth Trends," pp. 144–85, 291–342.

10. Petition of Benjamin Alford of Boston to ship a "considerable" amount of whale oil direct to London, 20 April 1678, *N.Y. Col. Docs.*, 14:735. Granted by the council. N.Y. Col. MSS, 27, fol. 66. The coopers of Southampton and Easthampton complained in a petition that coopers from Boston traveled to Long Island to compete with them. 13 October 1675, *N.Y. Col. Docs.*, 14:703. They also complained that the Boston coopers did not help train young men, pay rates, and in addition made bad barrels.

11. Forty-two beavers were confiscated in one raid on Schenectady, 4 July 1676. *Albany Minutes of the Court*, 2:124–31. Fines on outsiders for trading illegally were set at 100 guilders for the first offense and 300 for the third, 4 August 1676, ibid., pp. 136–38. Complaints about violations were still being made in 1678. Ibid., pp. 331–36.

12. Orders regulating the fur trade were issued annually, which may be a comment on their effectiveness. For example, ibid., pp. 106–8, 245–46, 393–95. Cases involving the arrest of children, ibid., pp. 340–48, 471–74.

13. New York City merchants bought farms and grain in the Esopus area particularly. Esopus Court of Sessions MS, 2, fol. 547; 3, fol. 29–30, 133, 137, 189, microfilm, Queens College Library, New York City. The volume of this trade is impossible to estimate. Its value to the city merchants caused a warning to be issued to the farmers about their "unclean" wheat, meaning they were mixing grains with foreign substances. Ibid., 2, fol. 509.

14. John E. Pomfret, *The Province of East New Jersey*, pp. 103, 102–29. Robert C. Ritchie, "The Duke's Province," pp. 207–33.

15. The arrival of the new colonists is recorded in *N.Y. Col. Docs.*, 12:579, 584–85. Their vessels were ordered to New York City for clearance, council minute, 25 February 1678, N.Y. Col. MSS, 27, fol. 35.

16. *N.Y. Col. Docs.*, 12:564–65.

17. For the conditions in the cities see Carl Bridenbaugh, *Cities in the Wilderness*, pp. 26–54. For the registration ordinance, 28 February 1677, *MCC*, 1:47. On 20 January 1676 an ordinance set fees at six beavers to become a merchant and two beavers for a tradesman. Ibid., p. 10. On 10 May 1677 it cost Nicolas Blake £8.0.0 to gain the privileges of a freeman, N.Y. Col. MSS, 26, fol. 54. For the various appointments, see *MCC*, 1:20, 22, 25, 38–39, 63, 74, 84.

18. The coopers' agreement specified donations to the poor for those who broke

the agreement. N.Y. Col. MSS, 29, fol. 3. For the council's response, ibid., fol. 2–3c. An illegal agreement between the tanners and shoemakers was similarly treated. NYHS, *Collections* (1893), pp. 430–31.

19. Werden to Andros, 31 January 1676, *N.Y. Col. Docs.*, 3:238. "Edmund Randolph's Report," ibid., pp. 241–42. The position paper has no date but was written after Andros arrived in New York. The author was probably Thomas Delaval, who remained in England attempting to recoup his fortune after 1674. The author of the paper states that Massachusetts would like to have "the place [New York] if they could." The Bostonians were accused of subverting New York by carrying on an illegal trade with Holland that had to be stopped. New York was also recommended as a place from which to mount an attack in order to stop the Bostonians. Coventry MSS, 77, fol. 310, Longleat House

20. Duke to Andros, 6 April 1675, *N.Y. Col. Docs.*, 3:230–31. Werden raised the same objections about setting prices on pieces of eight, 28 January 1676, ibid., pp. 236–38. Werden also refused to send over brass farthings, 15 September 1675, ibid., pp. 232–34.

21. It is an indication of Andros's control that the cases of the coopers and shoemakers were brought before the council and not the city magistrates.

22. Order, 8 August 1678, N.Y. Col. MSS, 27, fol. 175. Prior to this order Andros had issued an order on 12 March 1677 prohibiting "Christians" from going up the river. Indians who caught such men could keep all their goods. *N.Y. Col. Docs.*, 13:502–3. Order directing traffic through New York City, 22 August 1678, ibid., pp. 531–32.

23. Inhabitants of Albany and Rensselaerswyck to Andros, 29 April 1679, *Albany Minutes of the Court*, 2:406.

24. Council minute, 6 May 1679, N.Y. Col. MSS, 28, fols. 86–87. Andros to Albany, 17 May 1679, *Albany Minutes of the Court*, 2:413–14.

25. Cornelius Van Dyck and Johannes Provoost to Andros, 22 May 1679, N.Y. Col. MSS, 28, fol. 99.

26. On 2 July 1678 New Yorkers were stopped from trading in furs, ibid., 27, fol. 144. John Robinson was stopped 14 August 1678. Ibid., fol. 182. Jan Bruyn's case can be followed in ibid., fols. 148, 149, 151, 152, 158, and ibid., 28, fol. 223. For an extended discussion of the Albany monopoly, see Thomas E. Norton, *The Fur Trade in Colonial New York*, pp. 43–59.

27. Timothy Cooper was admitted as a burgher of Albany on 24 August 1675, *Albany Minutes of the Court*, 2:9–12. He acted as Pynchon's attorney in Albany. Ibid., pp. 17–22. On 19 September 1678 he was expelled. N.Y. Col. MSS, 27, fol. 27.

28. *Albany Minutes of the Court*, 2:360–63. Albany's appeal 25 October 1678, N.Y. Col. MSS, 28, fol. 26. Andros's reply, 31 October 1678, *N.Y. Col. Docs.*, 13:533–34.

29. Andros's report, 16 April 1678, *N.Y. Col. Docs.*, 3:260–62.

30. Viewers appointed 25 August 1675, *MCC*, 1:25, and cure masters appointed 16 November 1676, ibid., pp. 38–39.

31. Order, 11 April 1679, *Albany Minutes of the Court*, 2:404.

32. Ibid., pp. 405–8.

33. The excuse used was that there had been several complaints made about the quality of wheat exports. N.Y. Col. MSS, 29, fol. 29. Order of 30 March 1680, *Albany Minutes of the Court*, 2:480–83.

34. The people of Long Island complained bitterly about the monopoly. The constables of the east and north ridings petitioned against it, 4 October 1677, *N.Y. Col. Docs.*, 14:748–49.

35. E 190/62/1, 5; 66/5; 80/1; 89/10; 91/1; 106/1, PRO.

36. The Dutch branch of the family is frequently mentioned in Not. Arch., 3295, N. 97; 3217, N. 39; 3322, N. 103; 3332, N. 289. The heirs of William De Peyster were his trading partners Samuel, Peter, and Abraham. The codicil relating to the latter granted him £1,000 after he had made all of his returns. Prerogative Court of Canterbury, Probate 11/369, p. 36, PRO. Another extensive Anglo-Dutch trading network was that of the Dankeythusen-Vanheythusen-Lodwick. Prerogative Court of Canterbury, Probate 11/414, p. 59. Charles Lodwick, briefly an ally of Jacob Leisler's and later an important

figure in New York, was a member of this family. Hereafter the Prerogative Court of Canterbury is cited as PCC.

37. Delaval returned to England after the Dutch conquest of New York in 1673 to retrieve his fortune after his goods were seized by the Dutch. He petitioned York for compensation. BM Addl. MSS, 18,206, fols. 61 verso–62 verso. Delaval's estate is discussed by James Riker, *Revised History of New Harlem*, p. 809. His will, PCC, Probate 11/ 372, p. 17, PRO.

38. PCC, Probate 11/438, p. 113, PRO. Cullen was associated with Mathew Chitty in a number of deals with Frederick Philipse and De Peyster. Not. Arch., 3403 (no number designated); 3302, N. 97. Jacob Leisler acted as Chitty's attorney in New York City. MCM, 5, fol. 45. Cullen's ventures are frequently recorded in the Dover port books: E 190/667–7; 668–4; 669–16, PRO.

39. John Lewin and Mathew Chitty had the largest account, £1,442. MCM, 5, fols. 211–12.

40. Lawrence H. Leder, *Robert Livingston and the Politics of Colonial New York*, pp. 10–11, 46–49, 52, 83–84. Harwood later acted very badly toward Livingston. Ibid., pp. 111–13. Harwood also traded with alderman John Robinson. MCM, 5, fols. 315–16. Other prominent men who voyaged to New York as factors were William Pinhorne, James Graham, John West, and John White. Charles Wolley, *A Two Years Journal in New York*, p. 101.

41. *MCC*, 1:26.

42. His ship, the *Good Hope*, traveled between England, the West Indies, and New York. He first appeared in New Amsterdam in October 1661, *N.Y. Col. Docs.*, 13:485. He bought an island on the Delaware River, 29 January 1677, ibid., 12:570. In Southampton he paid taxes in 1683, *Doc. Hist.*, 2:304. His house in New York City was near Wall Street, N.Y. Col. MSS, 30, fol. 215. He bought a house in Albany in 1676 and sold it in 1684. Joel Munsell, ed., *Collections on the History of Albany*, 3:135, n. 2, and N.Y. Col. MSS, 32, fol. 49. The incident with Bellingham is related in Wolley, *Two Years Journal*, p. 177. Heathcote left New York for Pennsylvania where he died in 1710. He bequested his estate to his cousin, Caleb, who had a long career in New York politics. Dixon R. Fox, *Caleb Heathcote, Gentleman Colonist*, passim.

43. MCM, 3, fols. 104–5. N.Y. Col. MSS, 25, foll. 234, 237. Heathcote to Andros, 26 October 1676, ibid., fol. 241. Proposals of George Heathcote, 12 December 1676, ibid., fol. 156, and remission of his fine, ibid., fol. 157.

44. Robinson was the only merchant to testify in Heathcote's behalf. Ibid., fols. 221, 234. Delaval, Philipse, and others of Andros's circle testified against Heathcote. Ibid., fols. 221, 234. Dyre demanded the money under orders from Andros. MCM, 4, fol. 96.

45. This action may have been taken because Robinson charged Andros himself with bringing over Dutch goods on the *Unity* of Amsterdam. N.Y. Col. MSS, 26, fols. 30, 39. His trial, MCM, 4, fols. 334–35. Order suspending Robinson's right to trade, 8 August 1678, N.Y. Col. MSS, 27, fol. 176.

46. MCM, 4, fols. 178, 188, 300–301. Andros's activities forced William Darvall to unload part of a cargo on Shelter Island as he feared Andros would seize it—which in fact he did. Not. Arch., 3284, N. 92.

47. Council minute, 10 October 1677, *CCM*, p. 30.

48. "Articles of Complaint against Edmund Andros by Thomas Griffeth, Henry Griffeth, John Harwood and others," 10 May 1678. Massachusetts and New York Miscellaneous MS, 91.1, Massachusetts Historical Society, Boston, Mass.

49. Robson was jailed for sedition. N.Y. Col. MSS, 25, fol. 216.

50. York to Andros, 24 May 1680, *N.Y. Col. Docs.*, 3:283, and Werden to Andros, 24 May 1680, ibid. Werden mentions in a later letter Griffeth's desire to sue Andros. Ibid., p. 286.

51. Ibid., p. 283.

52. This is commented upon negatively, N.Y. Col. MSS, 14, fol. 91.

53. For examples of these complaints against the Quakers, see *N.Y. Col. Docs.*, 14:696–97; N.Y. Col. MSS, 26, fols. 28, 98. Street, *Huntington*, 1:308.

54. Fine for an illegal wedding ceremony, 4 September 1680, *N.Y. Col. Docs.*, 14:752–53. Samuel Scudder was jailed and fined for a "scurrilous" paper and Thomas

Case was fined £40 for disturbing the peace because they protested against these practices. N.Y. Col. MSS, 24, fol. 172.

55. For Billop's career, see *N.Y. Col. Docs.*, 13:485. Werden to Andros, 31 August 1676, ibid., 3:238–40; 12:606–8. Council minute, 24 September 1678, *CCM*, p. 31. Werden to Andros, 10 March 1679, *N.Y. Col. Docs.*, 3:276–77. Commission to Sylvester Salisbury replacing Billop, 1 March 1679, *CSPC*, 10, no. 923.

56. The north and east ridings asked Mathias Nicolls to inform Andros of the abuse they received at the customshouse. *N.Y. Col. Docs.*, 14:748–49.

57. Southampton to Andros, 28 September 1676, ibid., pp. 722–23.

58. The Huntington magistrates were threatened in February 1676, Street, *Huntington*, 1:245, and *N.Y. Col. Docs.*, 14:713–15. They were committed to prison 22 February 1676, and shortly thereafter they were released. *CCM*, pp. 24, 25. The Hemptead affair can be followed in *N.Y. Col. Docs.*, 14:726–27, and N.Y. Col. MSS, 25, fols. 225–30.

59. Andros received complaints about the growing lack of land from Hempstead, Flushing, and Gravesend, N.Y. Col. MSS, 28, fol. 55. *N.Y. Col. Docs.*, 14:732, 750–51.

60. Jasper Dankaerts, *Journal of Jasper Dankaerts*, pp. 244–49.

61. Cargo list, July 19, 1674, *CSPC*, 7, no. 1328. Werden to Andros, 15 September 1675, *N.Y. Col. Docs.*, 3:232–34.

62. Dankaerts, *Journal*, p. 44. Andros wrote to Esopus on 6 January 1676 requesting the wheat he had on Gabriel Minvielle's account, *N.Y. Col. Docs.*, 13:493. On 1 June 1678 orders were issued for the collection of Andros's accounts, N.Y. Col. MSS, 27, fol. 120. The voyages of his sloop are mentioned a number of times. For examples, see *N.Y. Col. Docs.*, 12:571; N.Y. Col. MSS, 29, fol. 69; Dankaerts, *Journal*, p. 166. One paying passenger was left behind May 1679, N.Y. Col. MSS, 28, fol. 89.

63. Werden to Andros, 7 May 1677, *N.Y. Col. Docs.*, 3:244–47. Dankaerts, *Journal*, p. 36. On this voyage they went first to Falmouth where Margareta Philipse bought another ship, which she dispatched to Cape Verde Islands and Barbados. After loading at New York she returned to Falmouth. Ibid., pp. 80–81.

64. MCM, 5, fol. 311. Philipse lost the case.

65. Marie Van Rensselaer to Richard Van Rensselaer, September 1680, Van Laer, *Marie Van Rensselaer*, pp. 37–39.

66. Order to stop distilling, 5 July 1676, *Albany Minutes of the Nourt*, 2:113–36. Dankaerts, *Journal*, pp. 244–49. *N.Y. Col. Docs.*, 3:268. *MCC*, 1:50. N.Y. Col. MSS, 25, fols. 19, 20; 30, 396.

67. Philipse was the garrison *commissary*. After Andros left New York Philipse collected the debts owed him as *commissary*, MCM, 5, 296–97.

68. York to Andros, *N.Y. Col. Docs.*, 3:283.

69. For Lewin's and Woolley's trading activities, see E 190/52/1; 63/8; 62/1, 5; 66/5; 96/1; 53/6, PRO. They were involved in a long court proceeding from 1676 until 1679, when it finally went to England on appeal. N.Y. Col. MSS, 25, fol. 706; 28, fols. 134, 138, 174; 29, fols. 2, 8, 9, 15, 18, 19. Their purchase of a house in the city is recounted by Isaac N. Stokes, *Iconography of Manhattan Island*, 6:133 and *N.Y. Col. Docs.*, 3:286. Werden to Andros, 12 May 1680, *N.Y. Col. Docs.*, 3:286.

70. Lewin's commission, 24 May 1680, *N.Y. Col. Docs.*, 3:279. His instructions, 24 May 1680, ibid., pp. 279–80.

71. Council minute, 29 October 1680, N.Y. Col. MSS, 29, fol. 258.

72. Letter, April 1681, Van Laer, *Maria Van Rensselaer*, p. 48.

73. Maria to Richard Van Rensselaer [January 1682], ibid., p. 57.

74. Minute, 13 September 1681. *MCC*, 1:87. Andros was ordered by Werden to make sure Lewin had this power. Evidently Andros left for England without giving him authority to administer oaths, thereby hampering the investigation, *N.Y. Col. Docs.*, 3:284. The council did help Lewin at times. On 10 October 1681 three men were commissioned to audit the rates of Long Island, N.Y. Col. MSS, 30, fol. 40.

75. "Mr. Lewin's report on the Government of New York," *N.Y. Col. Docs.*, 3:302–8. The report of the hearing, ibid., pp. 314–16. Mr. Robinson may be John Robinson.

76. Ibid., p. 306. Griffeth had sued Andros in chancery; thus his testimony was probably suspect at the hearing. Werden to Andros, 12 May 1681, ibid., p. 286. See also chap. 9, n. 2.

77. Two merchants who were supposedly discriminated against were John Robin-

son and William Pinhorne. Robinson's troubles with Andros have already been outlined previously. Pinhorne was a merchant and a lawyer. He was also the bookkeeper of John Winder. Winder, in turn, traded with Lewin and Wolley, N.Y. Col. MSS, 25, fol. 706.

78. Governor Andros's answer to Mr. Lewin's report, 31 December 1681, *N.Y. Col. Docs.*, 3:308–13.

79. John Gardner to Andros, 21 March 1678, N.Y. Col. MSS, 27, fol. 45. "Declaration of Richard Mann about John Curtis," 9 June 1680, ibid., 29, fol. 113. A warrant was issued for Mann's arrest, 11 June 1680, ibid., fol. 118.

80. Michael Kammen, *Empire and Interest*, pp. 30–39.

81. E 190/106/1, PRO. Robinson was an alderman of the city in 1684. *MCC*, 1:156–57; Lodwick was a captain of the militia. N.Y. Col. MSS, 33, fol. 304. James Graham did not arrive until 1678, but by 1680 he was an alderman. Paul M. Hamlin and Charles E. Baker, *Supreme Court of Judicature of the Province of New York*, 3: 90–98.

CHAPTER 6

1. There were small settlements in Westchester and Ulster counties that have left few records susceptible to analysis.

2. N.Y. Col. MSS, 35, fol. 75.

3. *Doc. Hist.*, 1:690.

4. "List of persons who are to keep in repair the posts set around the town," 5 March 1679. *Albany Minutes of the Court*, 2:396–97. The list as printed has 143 names on it; however, the numbers 30 and 112 are repeated. The total with two added names at the end of the list therefore should be 147. If this is used as a guide to population the figure 147 would be multiplied by 5 to give an approximate population of 735. Throughout the conversion figure of 5 will be used except for New York City. The conversion figure generally used in Europe for the seventeenth century is 4.75. I have rounded it out to 5 to take into account the higher childbirth and survival rates in America at this time. Peter Laslett, "Size and Structure of the Household in England over Three Centuries," pp. 199–223.

5. *Albany Minutes of the Court*, 2:234, 88–89. For home ownership, see *Early Records of the City and County of Albany*, 2:49, in New York State Library, *History Bulletin*, no. 9, and ibid., 3:461–62, in New York State Library, *History Bulletin*, no. 10, and also *Albany Minutes of the Court*, 2:265.

6. N.Y. Col. MSS, 35, fol. 68, and *Doc. Hist.*, 1:279–82.

7. Esopus Court of Sessions MS, microfilm, Queens College Library, Queens, N.Y., fols., 2:481, 484, 499, 547, 133, 137, 226.

8. The most readily available Long Island tax lists are in the *Doc. Hist.*, (1675), 2:253–68; (1676), 269–86; (1683), 287–314. To this point the 1849 edition of the *Doc. Hist.* has been cited; however, in this chapter the larger and easier-to-read 1850 edition is used. For other lists, see N.Y. Col. MSS, 29 (1680), fols. 275a–b; (1676), 25, fol. 223; (1677), 26 fol. 163; (1678), 28, fol. 17a; (1675), 24, fols. 147–48.

9. *N.Y. Col. Laws*, 1:59–62.

10. *Doc. Hist.*, 2:300; *MCC*, 1:36; Benjamin F. Thompson, *History of Long Island*, 3:603; *MCC*, 1:29–37.

11. By the 1660s the average holding in Andover, Mass., was 196.7 acres. Philip J. Greven, Jr., *Four Generations*, p. 59. Kenneth Lockridge estimates that the typical holding in eastern Massachusetts was 150 acres. "Land, Population and the Evolution of New England Society," pp. 64–66.

12. First division of land 25 November 1656 (N.S.), Josephine C. Frost, ed., *Records of the Town of Jamaica*, 1:2. For 1683, see *Doc. Hist.*, 2:301–3.

13. Hempstead forwarded a petition for land from six young men, 17 February 1679, *N.Y. Col. Docs.*, 14:740. Petition from young men of Gravesend, 1 November 1677, ibid., 14:732. Flushing was ordered to grant sixty acres to young men so that they could vote for town officers. N.Y. Col. MSS, 29, fols. 79, 80.

14. *Doc. Hist.*, 2:312–14.

15. Because of the differences in the manner of assessment and computations, comparisons are only approximate. Between 1661 and 1681 the income distribution in

Essex County and Salem, Mass., was as follows: 73.4 percent of the wealth in Essex County was owned by 26.7 percent of the population while 73.3 percent of the population owned 26.6 percent of the wealth. In Salem the figures were as follows: 79.6 percent of the wealth was in the hands of 26.8 percent while 20.4 percent owned 73.2 percent. Donald W. Koch, "Income Distribution and Political Structure in the Seventeenth Century, Salem, Massachusetts," pp. 50–71. In Chester County, Pa., in 1683 wealth was distributed as follows:

Lowest 30%	17.4%
Lower-middle 30%	21.1%
Upper-middle 30%	37.7%
Upper 10%	23.8%

Derived from James T. Lemon and Gary B. Nash, "The Distribution of Wealth in Eighteenth Century America," pp. 1–24.

16. The 1665 list is in *RNA*, 5:221–25; the 1672 list, *Executive Council*, 2:704–9; 1674, *N.Y. Col. Docs.*, 2:699–700; 1676, *MCC*, 2:29–37; 1677, ibid., pp. 50–62.

17. There are 301 assessments, but one for £100 is for two men, "Mr. Rodeney and Joseph Lee." I have counted them as two separate individuals for population purposes but as one for individual assessments. Another change made at this point is to use a conversion figure of six instead of five. The reason for this is that in the first real census of households made in 1703 the relationship between dependents and householders is a multiplier of just over six and not five. *Doc. Hist.*, 1:395–405. In a seaport such as New York there would also be sailors, factors, and others just passing through, all of them tending to enlarge the city's population.

18. *MCC*, 1:64, 73. The position of the carter or cartman is reviewed in Arthur E. Peterson and George W. Edwards, *New York as an Eighteenth Century Municipality*, pp. 63–68.

19. Frederick Philipse was assessed on £13,000 and rated £81.5.0. I believe this is a misprint in the *MCC*, 1:31. The tax on £3,000 was £18.5.0, so it would seem that a one was added before the three, and the eight and one reversed.

20. James A. Henretta, "Economic Development and Social Structure in Colonial Boston," p. 80.

21. Gary B. Nash, *Quakers and Politics*, p. 280.

22. The court of sessions records have many examples of New York City merchants who sued local men over broken contracts. For instance, at the Jamaica sessions 8 December 1675, Assur Levy, Jacob Leisler, and Allard Anthony pressed suits, N.Y. Col. MSS, 25, fol. 55. At the Jamaica sessions in December 1677 Nicholas Bayard collected debts worth 3,906 guilders, ibid., 26, fol. 159. If someone became particularly difficult, the governor issued warrants for an arrest on goods. Delaval received one for a case in Oyster Bay, ibid., fol. 86. The merchants were also in the upriver towns. Esopus Court of Sessions MS, 3, fols. 30, 133, 137, 186, 236, microfilm, Queens College Library, Queens, N.Y.

23. One example was William Darvall, who bought land at Easthampton on 15 March 1679 and can be found trading there for whale oil, whalebone, and iron. See *Records of the Town of East-Hampton*, 2:87, 90–91.

24. A building boom of sorts occurred in the early 1670s. Nicholas De Meyer, Francis Rombouts, and Jacob Leisler were among those who built new houses. Isaac N. Stokes, *Iconography of Manhattan Island*, 2:222, 278, 309.

25. Lawrence H. Leder, *Robert Livingston*, passim.

26. *DAB*, 2:68–69. For his various offices see *RNA*, 5:28–29; 6:15–18, 19, 181–99, 218–23, 229–32, 301–5. Bayard owned the *St. Michael* with Steenwyck. They sent it to Holland in 1676, A. J. F. Van Laer, *Correspondence of Jeremias Van Rennselaer*, p. 454.

27. "Answers of Governor Andros to Enquiries about New York," *N.Y. Col. Docs.*, 3:261.

28. New York (colony), *Calendar of Historical Manuscripts . . .* , 2, English Manuscripts: 8–12, 20–24, hereafter cited as *Cal. Hist. MSS*.

29. Every man was to have 60 acres plus 50 acres for his wife, each child, and servant. *N.Y. Col. Docs.*, 13:485. "Dongans Report . . . " *Doc. Hist.*, 1:161–62.

30. *Doc. Hist.*, 1:659–61. Dongan claimed that the Dutch were still immigrating in

large numbers in his 1687 report. Because he was arguing for more English immigrants to match Dutch numbers his statement must be treated with care. Ibid., pp. 161–62.

31. *Cal. Hist. MSS*, 2, 141–47. See also "Petition of the French Protestants of New York," 9 May 1687, *N.Y. Col. Docs.*, 3:419–20. Order issued 19 July 1687, ibid., pp. 426–27.

32. There was one notorious incident where the nightwatch ganged up on one Englishman. MCM, 4, fol. 172.

33. MCM, 2, 15 March 1675 (no foliation). The Quakers of Oyster Bay were allowed to subscribe to the oath on 9 April 1675, N.Y. Col. MSS, 14, fol. 91.

34. "Petition to the mayor and aldermen," N.Y. Col. MSS, 14, fol. 73.

35. Petition to Andros, 16 March 1675, *N.Y. Col. Docs.*, 2:740–43. Nicholas Bayard hurled this threat, MCM, 2, 17 March 1675 (no foliation). Order for the jailing of the eight, *CCM*, p. 21. On 18 March, 117 took the oath, the next day 76, and on 23 March, 44. This manuscript is damaged but it appears that 310 men took the oath, MCM, 2, 18 March 1675 (no foliation). Report of the commission, 19 March 1675, N.Y. Col. MSS, 24, fol. 76. Bail certificates for all but Steenwyck were recorded, ibid., fols. 77–82. Council minute, 7 April 1675, *CCM*, p. 22.

36. For an account of the trial, see N.Y. Col. MSS, 24, fol. 172. All but De Milt were convicted of trading illegally on 12 October 1675, ibid., fol. 176K. Their sentences, ibid., fol. 186a–k. Bayard was sentenced separately on 13 October 1675, ibid., fol. 163.

37. Petition of the seven, 16 March 1675, *N.Y. Col. Docs.*, 2:740–43.

38. N.Y. Col. MSS, 24, fol. 196. Orders for a new trial, 1 and 2 November 1675, ibid., 25, fols. 5–7.

39. "Petition of the Burghers of New Netherland to the States General," n.d., *N.Y. Col. Docs.*, 2:738–40. States General to Ambassador Van Beuningen, 12 October 1675, ibid., p. 745.

40. 15 September 1675, ibid., 3:232–34.

41. Petitions, 3 November 1675, N.Y. Col. MSS, 25, fols. 9–13. Their sentences, ibid., fols. 14–15.

42. Steenwyck was appointed mayor on 24 November 1683, *MCC*, 1:106–7; Van Brugh became an alderman on 21 November 1679, ibid., p. 74; De Peyster an alderman on 31 October 1676, ibid., pp. 25–26; Bayard an alderman on 24 November 1683, ibid., pp. 106–7, and to the council the following year. S. C. Hutchins, *Civil List*, p. 18; Beekman an alderman, 14 October 1678, *MCC*, 1:69.

43. 20 May 1676, *N.Y. Eccl. Rec.*, 1:684–86.

44. See for instance the court calendars MCM, 4, fols. 80, 177, 670–79.

45. Ibid., fols. 308–51; 5, fols. 8–19. The French jurors represent the growing French community in the proprietary. Their numbers increased rapidly in the 1680s.

46. John M. Murrin, "English Rights as Ethnic Aggression," p. 15.

47. Samuel Megapolensis to a friend, 7 September 1668, *N.Y. Eccl. Rec.*, 1:595–96. Megapolensis to the Classis of Amsterdam, 17 April 1669, ibid., pp. 601–3.

48. Consistory of New York to the Classis, 24 January 1670, ibid., pp. 607–8, 610–11.

49. Lawrence H. Leder, "The Unorthodox Domine," pp. 168–74. *Doc. Hist.*, 3:872–74; Van Laer, *Jeremias Van Rensselaer*, pp. 374–77, 439–42. York to Andros, 23 July 1674, *CSPC*, 7, no. 1330. Van Rensselaer was the family's representative in London and helped obtain a new patent. Werden to Andros, 7 June 1678, *CSPC*, 10, no. 724. The colony received a new patent 4 June 1678 that excluded Albany but allowed the Van Rensselaers to charge rent on every house in town, 4 June 1678, *N.Y. Col. Docs.*, 3:269–70. Andros did not allow them to collect this rent, 31 October 1678, *Albany Minutes of the Court*, 2:362. Petition of Van Rensselaer to Andros, 15 October 1675, to assume the directorship, N.Y. Col. MSS, 24, fol. 158.

50. Council minute, 25 September 1675, *Doc. Hist.*, 3:872–74. John R. Brodhead, *The History of the State of New York*, 2:288.

51. Maria Van Rensselaer to Jan Baptist Van Rennselaer (November 1676), A. J. F. Van Laer, *The Correspondence of Maria Van Rensselaer*, pp. 13–16. She reported that the quarrel set friend against friend.

52. For a summary of his career, see *DAB*, 6:156–57. Stokes, *Iconography*, 6:463. See *MCC*, 1:32, for his assessment of £3,000, the second highest bracket. He maintained a factor in Maryland, *RNA*, 7:74–77. When Maryland sent a delegation to meet the Iroquois the envoys were ordered to get their supplies from Leisler, CO/1/40, no. 56, PRO. For the sort of minor positions he had, see *RNA*, 6:246–52. He owned his own ship, Van Laer, *Maria Van Rensselaer*, pp. 76–77.

53. Milborne related his early life while testifying against John Scott, 6 January 1680. Rawlinson MSS, A, 175, fol. 83, Bodleian Library, Oxford. In an affidavit in a court case he testifies as Delaval's bookkeeper, N.Y. Col. MSS, 26, fol. 179, and Brodhead, *New York*, 2:321.

54. Hearings before the *commissaries*, 23 August 1676 and 2 September 1676, *Albany Minutes of the Court*, 2:146–48, 153–55. The bonds were £1,500 sterling for Van Rensselaer, £1,000 for Leisler, and £500 for Milborne, ibid., pp. 146–48, 150–52.

55. Council minute, 8 September 1676, *Doc. Hist.*, 3:875. Andros to *commissaries*, 16 September 1676, N.Y. Col. MSS, 25, fol. 166. Schaets was sued by ten unnamed members of the congregation, 5 September 1676, *Albany Minutes of the Court*, 2:159, 161–62.

56. Council meeting and warrant, 16 September, *Doc. Hist.*, 3:876. He was taken into custody on 26 September, *Albany Minutes of the Court*, 2:162–64. Warrant, 18 September, *Doc. Hist.*, 3:876–77.

57. *Doc. Hist.*, 3:876–77, 879; meeting, 28 September, *Albany Minutes of the Court*, 2:164–67.

58. He was restored to the pew later, *Albany Minutes of the Court*, 2:291.

59. He was seized along with at least eight other New Yorkers. Report, 17 August 1678, N.Y. Col. MSS, 27, fol. 179. In order to obtain the release of the other passengers a special tax called the "Turks rate" was charged throughout New York. See *N.Y. Col. Docs.*, 13:533, and Charles R. Street, ed., *Huntington Town Records*, 1:254, for instances of "Turks rate" taxation in Albany and Long Island.

60. Their fears for the Reformed church were heightened by the appointment of Anglican ministers to New York. John Gordon was appointed chaplain to the garrison on 19 August 1674, *CSPC*, 7, no. 1345. Charles Wolley served from 1678 to 1680, Charles Wolley, *Two Years Journal in New York*, passim.

61. This account is derived from Van Zuuren's correspondence with the Classis of Amsterdam, 25 June 1681 and 30 October 1681, *N.Y. Eccl. Rec.*, 2:771–80, 790–95.

62. Esopus to the Classis, 22 November 1680, ibid., pp. 748–50.

63. Selyns to the Classis, 22 October 1682, ibid., pp. 827–34; 31 October 1683, ibid., pp. 865–69. Vaarick to the Classis, ibid., pp. 936–56.

64. Selyns to the Classis, 20 September 1685, ibid., pp. 906–9. Van Zuuren to the Classis, 30 October 1681, ibid., pp. 790–95.

65. Special meetings were held with the Indians, 16–30 September 1675, N.Y. Col. MSS, 24, fols. 138, 139, 141. An order was issued 7 October, prohibiting the sale of guns or powder to Indians. *N.Y. Col. Docs.*, 14:700.

66. Connecticut to Andros, 13 January 1675, J. Hammond Trumbull and Charles J. Hoadly, eds., *The Public Records of the Colony of Connecticut*, 2:397–98. There was great fear in Albany at King Philip's approach. Maria Van Rensselaer to Richard Van Rensselaer, December 1675, Van Laer, *Maria Van Rennselaer*, pp. 16–17. At Esopus there was a panic, *N.Y. Col. Docs.*, 13:491–92, and the outlying farms were ordered to be abandoned, 10 April 1676, ibid., p. 495.

67. Andros to Connecticut, 20 January 1675, Trumbull and Hoadly, *Connecticut Records*, 2:404–5.

68. Connecticut to Andros, 31 January, ibid., pp. 404–5. In the letter the council wrote, "Theire [the Dutch] exact obedience to his Majesties Lawes may be somewhat questioned . . . the enemie do boast of great supply from those parts about Albany."

69. Council minute, 17 January 1676, *N.Y. Col. Docs.*, 14:711. The charges were printed in Boston, 7 December 1675. *Narrative of the Progress of the War* in Clifford K. Shipton, ed., *Early American Imprints*, no. 206.

70. Order, 11 March 1676, N.Y. Col. MSS, 25, fol. 90. His trial and sentence, ibid., fol. 184. He finally recanted and asked for a remission of his fine. Ibid., fol. 220. Two

other Englishmen got into similar trouble. They charged the Indians were able to get powder at Albany. The court had them brought in by the sheriff and after they were questioned they thought better of their charges. *CCM*, p. 24, and *Albany Minutes of the Court*, 2:86, 64. When his son was harshly treated in a trial a few years later, Loveridge complained that he was denied the rights of an Englishman by the Albany magistrates. Loveridge to the council, 23 April 1678, N.Y. Col. MSS, 27, fol. 77.

71. Petition to the King, 9 April 1678, *N.Y. Col. Docs.*, 3:258–59. Order in council, 9 April 1678, ibid., p. 259.

72. *DAB*, 10:164–65; Paul M. Hamlin and Charles E. Baker, *Supreme Court of Judicature of the Province of New York*, 3:192–95.

73. There is no good account of Philipse. For information on his activities, see *RNA*, 6:143, 144–45; 8:114–17; Robert Bolton, *History of the County of Westchester*, 2:417–19; *Albany Minutes of the Court*, 2:430; Mariana G. Van Rensselaer, *History of the City of New York*, 2:172–73; Joel Munsell, ed., *Collections on the History of Albany*, 3:124–25; *N.Y. Col. Docs.*, 2:699; NYHS, *Collections* (1892), p. 88.

74. Oloff Van Cortlandt to Maria Van Rensselaer, 16 January 1678, and Stephanus Van Cortlandt to Maria, 1 November 1682, Van Laer, *Maria Van Rensselaer*, pp. 19–20, 42.

75. Oloff Van Cortlandt to Maria, 10 August 1682, ibid., pp. 72–74, and Stephanus to Maria, 10 August 1682, ibid., pp. 72–74, 75. Killiean was apprenticed to silversmith Jeremiah Drummer, and his sureties were Richard Pattischal and John Usher. John Darvall to Maria, 24 October 1682, ibid., pp. 80–81.

76. For one of their deals see *Albany Minutes of the Court*, 2:409–11.

77. Philipse genealogy, Edward H. Hall, *Philipse Manor Hall*, pp. 38–42.

78. Schuyler genealogy, D. R. Gerlach, *Philip Schuyler*, p. 314. Verplank "Verplank Geneology," *New York Geneaological and Biographical Record*, 24 (1903). Teller, ibid., 2 (1871): 139–40. Cuyler, ibid., 3 (1872): 81–82. Loockermans, ibid., 8 (1887): 11–16. Van Brugh, ibid., 56 (1925): 212–13. Van Cortlandt, Bolton, *Westchester*, 1:50.

79. Bolton, *Westchester*, 1:417, and *RNA*, 7:114–17. For cases when Livinston was the attorney for these men see *Albany Minutes of the Court*, 2:65–69, 81–88, 91–99, 331–36.

80. Lawrence H. Leder, *Robert Livingston*, pp. 129–60.

81. Leisler's later dislike for the English may have stemmed from the fact that he had done everything expected for success but was never admitted to power. Leisler Genealogy, *New York Genealogical and Biographical Record*, pp. 145–50. One of his daughters, Susannah, married Michael Vaughton, a protégé of Governor Dongan.

CHAPTER 7

1. A sign that Andros expected to return was the presence of his wife in New York until November 1681. Stephanus Van Cortlandt to Maria Van Rensselaer, December 1681, A. J. F. Van Laer, ed., *Correspondence of Maria Van Rensselaer*, pp. 52–54. Wait Winthrop reported to his brother, 19 December 1681, that Andros was bedeviled in the courts, Mass. Hist. Soc., *Collections*, 5th ser., 8:423–24. Andros petitioned the duke for relief from arrests and law suits and York ordered his solicitors to take charge, 15 December 1683, BM Addl. MSS, 24,928, fol. 14. One of these cases was a suit by Jacob Milborne, son-in-law of Jacob Leisler, for false arrest in New York. Milborne v. Andros, *N.Y. Col. Docs.*, 3:300–301. It is reported Milborne won £45, John R. Brodhead, *The History of the State of New York*, 2:356.

2. York ordered Brockholls to replace Andros, York to Andros, 24 May 1680, *N.Y. Col. Docs.*, 3:283. Maria to Richard Van Rensselaer, January 1682, Van Laer, *Maria Van Rensselaer*, pp. 56–58.

3. S. C. Hutchins, *Civil List*, p. 18. Wait Winthrop wrote to his brother Fitz-John, 19 December 1681, reporting that Nicolls was in Scotland visiting the duke, Mass. Hist. Soc., *Collections*, 5th ser., 7:423–24. Brodhead, *New York*, 2:355.

4. Brockholls to Andros, 17 September 1681, *N.Y. Col. Docs.*, 3:289.

5. York to Andros, 7 May 1677, ibid., p. 246.

6. "Randolph's Welcome Back Again," January 1680, Robert N. Tappan and A. T. S. Goodrich, eds., *Edward Randolph*, 3.61.

7. Brockholls married Susanna Schrick, 2 May 1681, *Albany Minutes of the Court*, 3:113. Dyre's illness was reported in a letter of Brockholls to Werden, 14 May 1681, *N.Y. Col. Docs.*, 13:549.

8. *N.Y. Col. Docs.*, 13:549. York to Brockholls, 8 August 1681, ibid., 3:292.

9. Dyre missed his first trial before the mayor's court and had to post £300 bond for his appearance. When the council refused to consider the case they referred it back to the mayor's court. They, in turn, refused to consider the case because they did not have the power to try capital crimes. MCM, 5, fols. 270–73.

10. The proceedings can be traced in the records of the special court of assize, 29 June 2 July 1681, NYHS, *Collections* (1912), pp. 8 15.

11. The letter referring the case gave as a reason "the Present Confusion and Disorder in the Government here." Ibid., pp. 11–12. Dyre's petition for relief, *N.Y. Col. Docs.*, 3:318–21. Dyre ultimately became surveyor general of colonial revenues, 27 December 1683, *CSPC*, 11, no. 1486.

12. For a biography of Tuder see Paul M. Hamlin and Charles E. Baker, *Supreme Court of Judicature of the Province of New York*, 3:182–91.

13. NYHS, *Collections* (1912), pp. 13, 22.

14. Ibid., pp. 14, 15. "Petition of the Special Court of Assize," 29 June 1681, as an appendix in Brodhead, *New York*, 2:658.

15. *Albany Minutes of the Court*, 3:134–43. The trade slump had a severe effect in Albany. A petition by twenty-seven merchants asked the *commissaries* to find a method of relieving the situation, ibid., pp. 143–44.

16. The case was considered in an extraordinary session of the court, 29 August 1681, ibid., pp. 153 57. The jury in making its decision said, "The jury bring in an unanimous verdict that in the laws which prevail here they cannot find any provision that such excise as is demanded must be paid, but if the order of the governors must be considered as being law, then the defendant is guilty."

17. Ibid.

18. Ibid., pp. 182–87, 203, 245. Stephanus Van Cortlandt to Maria Van Rensselaer (December 1681), Van Laer, *Maria Van Rensselaer*, pp. 52–54; N.Y. Col. MSS, 30, fol. 86. Officials were left with the fees of their offices as a source of income, *Albany Minutes of the Court*, 3:263–64. On 14 August 1682 the court decided that the rates had to raise 1,000 to 1,100 guilders for the coming year, ibid., pp. 279–81.

19. Brockholls to Delaval, 10 November 1681, *N.Y. Col. Docs.*, 13:552. Brockholls to Delaval, 12 January and 9 March 1682, ibid., pp. 552, 554. Brockholls to Thomas Chambers, 15 January and 6 April 1683, ibid., pp. 566, 569.

20. There is no record of what the petition to the duke contained. Case, *Southold*, 1:217, and Benjamin D. Hicks, ed., *Records of the Town of North and South Hempstead*, p. 101.

21. Charles R. Street, ed., *Huntington Town Records*, 1:315. Captain Josiah Hobart was stirring up Long Island with "seditious" speeches. Brockholls finally arrested him. Brockholls to John Young, 1 November 1681, *N.Y. Col. Docs.*, 14: 762–63. A warrant for his arrest, 10 November 1681, N.Y. Col. MSS, 30, fol. 49.

22. Hempstead did so, 17 September 1681, *Records of Hempstead*, p. 385. Easthampton, 24 September, *Records of the Town of East-Hampton*, pp. 103–4. Huntington, 24 September, Street, *Huntington*, 1:315. Southold, 26 September, Case, *Southold*, p. 166. Oyster Bay, 24 September, John Cox, ed., *Oyster Bay Town Records*, p. 245. Order, 27 September 1681, *N.Y. Col. Docs.*, 14:762.

23. NYHS, *Collections* (1912), p. 25.

24. Ibid., pp. 24–25.

25. Brockholls to Andros, 17 September 1681, *N.Y. Col. Docs.*, 3:281. The full quote is "I have done what possible to gett the Excise kept up, my Endeavors therein have proved ineffectuall—the merchants taking advantage of Courts who Being Scared Refuse to Justifie and maintaine my Ord'rs . . . Here it was never worse. A Govenm't wholly overthrown and in the Greatest Confusion and Disord'r Possible."

26. Ibid., p. 292.

27. MCM, 5, fols. 312, 351. Brockholls apologized, claiming it was all a misunderstanding. It does appear, however, that he gave information to Lewin perhaps to gain favor with York. Ibid., 5, fols. 352–53. For examples of the suits, ibid., 4, fols. 300–301, 304; 5, fol. 18. Albany, in particular, ignored the regulations. Ibid., 5, fol. 44.

28. York to Brockholls, 8 August 1681, N.Y. Col. Docs., 3:292.

29. Joseph E. Illick, *William Penn the Politician*, pp. 21–28 explores the alternative explanations for Penn's grant. For the relationship between York and Penn, Vincent Buranelli, *The King and the Quaker*, pp. 49–66. Werden wrote to William Blathwayt, secretary to the Lords of Trade, requesting the New Castle area. CO/1/46, fol. 118, PRO.

30. Werden wrote to Andros, "I must confess I should be glad were [it] confirmed in the Duke's possession by a better title than this, wch indeed to an ordinary person would not be very secure." 7 May 1677, N.Y. Col. Docs., 3:246–47.

31. Ibid., pp. 291–92.

32. Accounts of the trial, N.Y. Col. MSS, 29, fol. 140 and Jasper Dankaerts, *Journal of Jasper Dankaerts*, pp. 238–44. Dankaerts relates that Andros had a dias constructed in order to sit above the court. For Carteret's view of the trial, see W. A. Whitehead et al., eds., *Archives of the State of New Jersey, 1631–1800*, 1:316–18.

33. Pomfret, *East New Jersey*, pp. 102–129.

34. "Opinion of Sir William Jones," 28 July 1680, N.Y. Col. Docs., 3:285. Whitehead, *New Jersey Archives*, 1:337–45, 366–76.

35. The following account is derived from Agnes M. Whitson, *The Constitutional Development of Jamaica*, pp. 82–107. Jones's decision was widely recognized in the colonies and used to assert local powers. For example, see Peter Force, ed., *Tracts and Other Papers*, 4:45–46.

36. Michael G. Hall, *Edward Randolph*, pp. 204–5.

37. Werden to Brockholls, 11 February 1682, N.Y. Col. Docs., 3:317.

38. York to Brockholls, 28 March 1682, ibid., pp. 317–18.

39. Dongan's career is recounted in *DAB*, 5:364–65; John H. Kennedy, *Thomas Dongan*, passim; and Thomas P. Phelan, *Thomas Dongan*, passim. In contrast to the other governors of New York, Dongan has attracted biographers because of his Catholicism, which, unfortunately, leads his biographers into filiopietism.

40. For the influence of Tangier on other careers, see Stephen S. Webb, "The Strange Career of Francis Nicholson," pp. 513–48. Dongan, however, was unsure of the effects on his career and had to be reassured. William Coventry to Dongan, 27 September 1679, BM Addl. MSS, 25,120, fol. 149.

41. Instructions, 27 January 1683, N.Y. Col. Docs., 3:331–35.

42. Council minute, 13 September 1683, N.Y. Col. Docs., 14:770–71, and CCM, p. 33. In New York City a warrant was issued to take a census of all "freemen householders" prior to the election, MCC, 1:98.

43. West to William Penn, 16 October 1683, Samuel Hazard, ed., *Pennsylvania Archives*, 1st ser., 1:79–80.

44. The address was agreed on at a town meeting, 24 September 1683, *Records of the Town of East-Hampton*, 2:134–35.

45. MCC, 1:205.

46. *Albany Minutes of the Court*, 3:399–401. Marius Schoonover, *The History of Kingston*, p. 75. N.Y. Eccl Rec., 2:863.

47. John Murrin has cast doubt on West's characterization. West wrote his letter to William Penn on Tuesday, 16 October 1683, Hazard, *Pennsylvania Archives*, 1st ser., 1:79–80. However the assembly did not organize until the following week. Perhaps the English representatives from Long Island did not want to travel over the Sabbath. John M. Murrin, "English Rights as Ethnic Aggression," p. 26.

48. A speculative re-creation of the assembly's membership is provided by Murrin, "English Rights," Appendix A, pp. 31–32.

49. York to the Assembly, 2 March 1683, N.Y. Col. MSS, 31, fol. 13. The use of both "Libertyes and Priviledges" is of interest. A liberty, according to the *Oxford English Dictionary*, is a privilege or exceptional right granted to a subject by a sovereign power. A

privilege is a grant to an individual, corporation, or community of special rights and immunities, sometimes to the prejudice of the general right; a franchise, monopoly, or patent. So the title of the charter reveals a desire to gain general and particular rights from York.

50. Whitson, *Jamaica*, p. 82.

51. Gary B. Nash, "The Framing of Government in Pennsylvania," pp. 206–9. John E. Pomfret, *The Province of East New Jersey*, pp. 152–81.

52. The charter can be found in *N.Y. Col. Laws*, 1:111–16. The best account of the charter is David S. Lovejoy, "Equality and Empire," pp. 493–515. Lovejoy stresses the tax revolt as the precipitant for the duke's change of mind. While I agree with him on this, I think he neglects the legal decisions about which Werden queried the commissioners.

53. Parliament still did not have effective recognition of triennial sessions, Lovejoy, "Equality and Empire," p. 505.

54. The charter was sent to Dongan and the council for their assent and read three times between 26 and 30 October, Brodhead, *New York*, 2:661.

55. Lovejoy, "Equality and Empire," pp. 504–5. The extensive personal rights granted by Dongan in the charter remained unchallenged in the colonial period. Hamlin and Baker, *Supreme Court*, 1:146–47.

56. On 14 September 1685, Jews were specifically excluded from exercising their religion by Dongan. He cited the assembly's action guaranteeing freedom of religion only to Christians, *MCC*, 1:168–69. On 12 September 1685 Dongan ruled that Jews could trade only wholesale, not retail. Ibid., pp. 168–69.

57. Pomfret, *East New Jersey*, pp. 56–81. Charles M. Andrews, *The Colonial Period of American History*, 2:100–143. Nash, *Quakers and Politics*, pp. 67–113. The same is true of South Carolina. See M. Eugene Sirmans, *Colonial South Carolina*, pp. 19–54.

58. *N.Y. Col. Laws*, 1:124.

59. Ibid., pp. 116–21.

60. Ibid., pp. 121–23.

61. *N.Y. Col. Docs.*, 3:333.

62. *N.Y. Col. Laws*, 1:125–28.

63. For a discussion of two new courts, of oyer and terminer and of chancery, see Hamlin and Baker, *Supreme Court*, 1:14–23. Dongan credited the assembly for originating the court of oyer and terminer.

64. *N.Y. Col. Laws*, 1:137–41, 165.

65. BM Addl. MSS, 24,927, fol. 35.

66. On 10 March 1684, ibid., fols. 36–37.

67. Ibid., fol. 41. See also a List of Bills delivered to Mr. Graham to get Ingrossed, 7 November 1684, CO/1/56, fol. 15, PRO. Request to York was made on 4 October 1684, BM Addl. MSS, 24,927, fol. 42. There is a memo of October 1684 that states that the duke signed and sealed the charter, *CSPC*, 9, no. 1885.

68. David Ogg, *England in the Reign of Charles II*, 2:606–56.

69. Phillip S. Haffenden, "The Crown and the Colonial Charters," pp. 297–311.

70. The commissioners were immediately ordered to turn over their records to the Lords of Trade, CO/381/5, fol. 90, PRO. "Observations upon the Charter of the Province of New York," *N.Y. Col. Docs.*, 3:357–59.

71. The king's veto message was issued 3 March 1685, *N.Y. Col. Docs.*, 3:357. The only piece of legislation that was approved was the act pertaining to revenue. Draft Instructions to Dongan, 20 May 1686, CO/391/5, fol. 271, PRO.

72. Haffenden, "Crown and Colonial Charters," pp. 452–53.

73. Andros to Blathwayt, 16 September 1678, *N.Y. Col. Docs.*, 3:271–72.

74. Much the same sort of opinions was expressed in two other letters of the same period. Andros to Blathwayt, 27 March 1679 and 12 October 1678, ibid., pp. 277–78, 272–73. For the development of Blathwayt's career see Stephen S. Webb, "William Blathwayt, Imperial Fixer," pp. 3–21.

75. Dongan's designs on the Jerseys are revealed in a letter from the Earl of Perth and other proprietors to Dongan, 22 August 1684, *N.Y. Col. Docs.*, 3:348. The duke's

commissioners treated this idea seriously and called Andros in to discuss it. He agreed with Dongan. BM Addl. MSS, 24,925, fols. 35–36. For Dongan's other plans see his letter to Sunderland, 6 November 1686, CO/1/61, no. 11, PRO; and Dongan to Sunderland, 21 May 1687, CO/1/62, fol. 206, PRO. See also Allen W. Trelease, *Indian Affairs in Colonial New York*, pp. 260–69.

CHAPTER 8

1. The second session of the first assembly met 22 October 1684 and the first session of the second assembly 20 October 1685. There are no records for the election of the second assembly. *N.Y. Col. Laws*, 1:143–277. Thirty-eight laws were passed. Of these, fourteen dealt with legal affairs, three with morals, and three with economic affairs.

2. Dongan's commission, 30 September 1683, and instructions, 27 January 1684. *N.Y. Col. Docs.*, 3:328–29, 331–35.

3. Council membership, S. C. Hutchins, *Civil List*, p. 18. Lewis Morris followed his brother Richard from the Barbados to New York in 1674 when the latter died, leaving an infant son. He was a Quaker of prominence and a shrewd merchant. He established himself in New York City where he was assessed on £1,000 of property in 1676. The iron deposits of New Jersey attracted him and he was one of the first entrepreneurs to develop colonial iron. His ironworks at Tintern reportedly employed sixty to seventy slaves. His prominence led to political office in New York and New Jersey, John E. Pomfret, *The Province of East New Jersey*, p. 147. See also Patricia V. Bonomi, *A Factious People*, pp. 69–70. For Palmer's career as a merchant, lawyer, and officeholder, see Paul M. Hamlin and Charles E. Baker, eds., *Supreme Court of Judicature of the Province of New York*, 1:20; Brodhead, *New York*, 2:289, and *CCM*, p. 25. Dongan not only complained of Young's age, he also reported he "has no estate of his own." CO/1/61, fol. 249, PRO. Santen was involved in a long and acrimonious dispute with Dongan over customs collections. *N.Y. Col. Docs.*, 3:493–501.

4. N.Y. Col. MSS, 24, fol. 115; ibid., 35, fol. 10; *CCM*, p. 139.

5. For example, see N.Y. Col. MSS, 35, fols. 42, 67.

6. Ibid., 34, fols. 12–13; 30, fols. 77, 79; *Cal. Hist. MSS*, 2:154.

7. For Dongan's many appointments, see *Cal. Hist. MSS*, 2:128–33.

8. Marius Schoonmaker, *The History of Kingston*, pp. 77–79, and also *Cal. Hist. MSS*, 2:108. Court of oyer and terminer, 4–6 June 1684. Ulster County MS, U.C. 50 (microfilm), Queens College Library, Queens, N.Y. Their fines were remitted after they admitted they were "ill advised," *Cal. Hist. MSS*, 2:108.

9. *Cal. Hist. MSS*, 102–5. See also *N.Y. Col. Docs.*, 3:337–38. The magistrates wanted control over the merchants and artisans admitted to freemanship, the trade up the Hudson, and all aspects of the flour trade.

10. The mayorality of New York was not an elective position until 1834. During the first election under the new system in 1684 seven names, only one of which was that of an alderman, were presented to Dongan, *MCC*, 1:158–59.

11. Election, 24 November 1683, *MCC*, 1:106–7. For an assessment of Steenwyck's role, see Bayard Still, "New York's Mayorality," pp. 239–56. When Steenwyck died in 1683 his estate was assessed at £15,841, David T. Valentine, ed., *Manual of the Corporation of the City of New York* (1864), 664. The officers appointed with Steenwyck were Nicholas Bayard, John Inians, William Pinhorne, Guleyn Verplanck, John Robinson, and William Cox, aldermen; John Tuder, sheriff; John West, clerk; James Graham, recorder. It was a government in the hands of the English and their sympathizers, *MCC*, 1:106–7, 113, 120.

12. *MCC*, 1:107–14 and *N.Y. Col. Docs.*, 3:334.

13. The aldermen met and decided who was going to represent what ward, *MCC*, 1:112–13. The assessors and constables were elected in December 1683, ibid., pp. 114–15. For an unknown reason the common councilors were not elected until the following February. Ibid., pp. 120–21. The new government met for the first time on 14 February 1684. Ibid., pp. 120–21.

14. The officeholders for 1683, 1684, and 1685 can be found in ibid., pp. 115, 145,

156–57, 170. For De Peyster's career see Hamlin and Baker, *Supreme Court*, 3:56–63.

15. Nicholas Bayard was chairman of two of the committees, *MCC*, 1.120–21.

16. Report of the committee on city revenue, 22 February 1684, ibid., pp. 123–25. Report of the committee on public works, 23 February 1684, ibid., pp. 125–26. Resolves of the Governor and Council, 1 March 1684, ibid., p. 132. Order for taxes, 15 August 1684, ibid., pp. 153–54. William Graverad refused to collect the new taxes and was relieved of office. Special meetings were held in the wards to convince the people of the need for the tax. Ibid., pp. 155–56.

17. The new and revised set of city ordinances was published 15 March 1683. Ibid., pp. 132–40. The cartmen objected to having to clear the streets of refuse every Saturday without compensation. Regulations on cartmen, ibid., p. 136. They were suspended 19 March 1684. Ibid., pp. 146–47. By 6 April some of them had begun submitting to the magistrates. Ibid., p. 148.

18. The magistrates asked for a warrant to conduct the elections on 6 March 1684. The election returns were announced 13 October. On 14 October the magistrates presented a list of seven names to Dongan for him to use in selecting a mayor. Philipse, Van Cortlandt, Pinhorne, Bayard, Graham, Minvielle, and Captain Andrew Boune were the nominees. Only Boune, Minvielle, and Bayard had been elected aldermen. Dongan finally chose Minvielle as the new mayor. Steenwyck was left off the list as he was dying. Ibid., pp. 156–58.

19. The request was made 10 April 1684, *Albany Minutes of the Court*, 3:437–38, 450–51.

20. The new patents generally recite the patent granted by Nicolls, name the new trustees, grant them control of the land and the government, and specify the times of future elections. Some of the patents state the quitrent is for the rights of government, others just for the land. Those that have it as right of government usually have a rent of one lamb. For examples, see *Records of the Town of East-Hampton*, 2:193–204, and Charles R. Street, *Huntington Town Records*, 1:532–43. For Flushing, see N.Y. Col. MSS, 35, fols. 34–36, 57.

21. This process was proceeding in the New England colonies during this period. Ray H. Akagi, *The Town Proprietors of the New England Colonies*, pp. 55–84, and Richard S. Bushman, *From Puritan to Yankee*, pp. 41–103.

22. Lawrence H. Leder, *Robert Livingston and the Politics of Colonial New York*, pp. 23–35.

23. Dongan to King James, 30 September 1685, CO/1/58, fol. 188, PRO.

24. John R. Brodhead, *The History of the State of New York*, 2:453–65, 491.

25. "Dongan's Report," *N.Y. Col. Docs.*, 3:406.

26. On 21 May 1684, the new officers and fees were complained of and on 6 June the council took steps to make sure the new fees were obeyed, *CCM*, p. 39. See also *N.Y. Col. Docs.*, 3:400. Michael Vaughton, Dongan's nephew, was given command of the ship 27 December 1684, *Cal. Hist. MSS*, 2:134. The sloop was ordered out again on June 1686, ibid., p. 144. See Council minutes, 20 September 1686, CO/5/1135, fols. 7–8, PRO; *N.Y. Col. Docs.*, 3:402; N.Y. Col. MSS, 34, fol. 43, for the investigating committee. The two-port restriction is mentioned in a petition of Jacob Leisler, ibid., 35, fol. 54. Dongan refused Andros's request 6 June 1687, ibid., fol. 66. The city was declared the only port, *Cal. Hist. MSS*, 2:136.

27. The court of exchequer was authorized 14 December 1685, *N.Y. Col. Docs.*, 3:390. For a discussion of its powers and operations see Hamlin and Baker, *Supreme Court*, 1:30–36.

28. Many warrants were issued beginning in 1684. N.Y. Col. MSS, 34, fols. 11, 16, 32, 57; 35, fol. 39; *Cal. Hist. MSS*, 2:121, 132, 137, 138.

29. Wesley Frank Craven, *The Southern Colonies in the Seventeenth Century*, pp. 127–28.

30. For an example of the letter, see John Cox, *Oyster Bay Town Records*, p. 271. For the orders, see *CCM*, pp. 37, 38.

31. For the commissioner's discussions, see BM Addl. MSS, 24,937, fol. 426. See also Werden to Dongan, 24 August and 1 November 1684, *N.Y. Col. Docs.*, 3:349–50, 351–52.

32. *Cal. Hist. MSS*, 2:134. Warrant to John Harlow and Henry Filkin of the city of New York, 15 April 1685, ibid., p. 143. Warrant to the sheriffs, 16 March 1685, ibid., pp. 135, 137.

33. "Dongan's Report," *N.Y. Col. Docs.*, 3:397.

34. Dongan wrote to the town demanding repatenting and quitrents, or a trial in the court of exchequer, Street, *Huntington*, 1:436. On 12 April 1686 a town meeting opposed giving up their patent. Ibid., p. 440. For similar cases, see CO/1/60, fols. 304–5, PRO.

35. Cox, *Oyster Bay*, p. 285. J. W. Case, *Southold Town Records*, 1:421.

36. The Easthampton controversy began with a letter from Dongan to Sheriff Joseph Fordham, 23 March 1685, *Records of East-Hampton*, 2:155–56. Josiah Hobart to Dongan, 13 July 1685, ibid., p. 168. Their grievances for the assembly were formulated 21 September. Ibid., pp. 168–69. Order, 19 November 1685, *Cal. Hist. MSS*, 2:126. Information of the attorney general, 19 November 1685, *Doc. Hist.*, 3:351–59. Special levy, 24 January 1687, *Records of East-Hampton*, 2:204.

37. On 16 October 1686 Huntington paid Dongan £10, Street, *Huntington*, 1:468–69. On 10 November 1686 the town decided to go to New York City and recant. On 24 November they voted for the additional gift of £20 to Dongan and made Palmer a patentee. Ibid., pp. 470–71. James Graham also got into the act and his services cost the town £177. Benjamin F. Thompson, *History of Long Island*, 2:15–16. For Hempstead and Flushing, see Benjamin D. Hicks, ed., *Records of the Town of North and South Hempstead*, pp. 485–86; *Cal. Hist. MSS*, 2:108, 114; for Brookhaven, Thompson, *Long Island*, 1:410–11. New York City paid Dongan £300 and secretary Spragg £25 in April 1686, Brodhead, *New York*, 2:437–39. Albany paid on 21 July 1686, Dongan MS, New York Historical Society, New York City.

38. The recipients were men like John West, John Tuder, and John Lawrence, *Cal. Hist. MSS*, 2:35, 36, 39.

39. Like his predecessors, Dongan acquired land and engaged in trade. Besides the land he obtained on Long Island he had a 5,100-acre manor (Castletown) on Staten Island. He mortgaged it for £2,172 to Robert Livingston; Leder, *Robert Livingston*, pp. 52–53. For his trade activity, N.Y. Col. MSS, 35, fol. 40. The quote is from "Dongan's Report," *N.Y. Col. Docs.*, 3:406. William Blathwayt suspected Dongan and asked Van Cortlandt to investigate Dongan's accounts. Van Cortlandt refused as he did not have such powers in his commission. Van Cortlandt to Blathwayt, 23 October 1688, Blathwayt MSS, 9, New York (microfilm from Colonial Williamsburg), Henry E. Huntington Library, San Marino, Cal.

40. "Accounts of Stephanus Van Cortlandt and James Graham . . . ," N.Y. Col. MSS, 34, Pt. II, fol. 12.

41. Herbert L. Osgood, *The American Colonies in the Seventeenth Century*, 2:359–60.

42. *Doc. Hist.*, 1:274–75. The total bill is broken down into counties; Suffolk was to pay £434, Ulster £408, and Albany £240.

43. J. Hammond Trumbull and Charles J. Hoadly, eds., *The Public Records of the Colony of Connecticut*, 3:126, 129, 493.

44. J. R. Bartlett, ed., *Records of Rhode Island*, 3:236.

45. Pomfret, *East New Jersey*, pp. 86–87, 257, 298–99, and Aaron Leaming and Jacob Spicer, eds., *Grants, Concessions, and Original Constitutions of the Province of New Jersey*, p. 274.

46. Allen W. Trelease, *Indian Affairs in Colonial New York*, pp. 278–82. Edmund Randolph to the Lords of Trade, 8 October 1688, *N.Y. Col. Docs.*, 3:567–69. Livingston's account, *CSPC*, 12, no. 1727.

47. The 1687 tax, N.Y. Col. MSS, 35, fol. 67. New York City sold lands worth £293 to meet its costs, *MCC*, 1:190, and CO/5/1031, no. 86, PRO. The second tax, *N.Y. Col. Docs.*, 3:475–77. The 1688 tax, *Doc. Hist.*, 1:274–75, and *CSPC*, 12, no. 1873. The city's share of Andros's tax was £434, *MCC*, 1:201.

48. CO/1/63, nos. 50, 56, PRO. See also Van Cortlandt to Blathwayt, n.d., Blathwayt MSS, 9, New York (microfilm), Huntington Library.

49. Dongan to the Lord President, n.d., *N.Y. Col. Docs.*, 3:428–30. Same to same, 12 September 1687, ibid., pp. 477–78.

50. Dongan to Lord President, 22 February 1687, ibid., pp.420–21. "Dongan's Report," ibid., p. 392. Spragg to Sunderland, 25 November 1686, *CSPC*, 12, no. 1014. Santen to Blathwayt, 14 September 1686, Blathwayt MSS, 10, New York (microfilm), Huntington Library.

51. Dongan to Blathwayt, 11 August 1685, *N.Y. Col. Docs.*, 3:363–64.

52. Carl Bridenbaugh, *Cities in the Wilderness*, p. 143.

53. Fletcher to the Board of Trade, *N.Y. Col. Docs.*, 4:159.

54. In his report of 1687, Dongan complained of the loss of the Delaware tobacco and trade. Ibid., 3:393–99.

55. See Gary B. Nash, "The Quest for the Susquehanna Valley," pp. 113–27, and Robert C. Ritchie, "The Duke's Province," pp. 221–27.

56. Curtis P. Nettels, "Economic Relations of Boston, Philadelphia and New York," p. 208; Gary B. Nash, *Quakers and Politics*, pp. 56–66. Instructions to John Palmer, 8 September 1687, *N.Y. Col. Docs.*, 3:475–77. Gabriel Minvielle to Werden, n.d., ibid., p. 361. Dongan to Sunderland, 25 October 1687, CO/1/63, fols. 251–53, PRO. Address of the mayor and common council to the king, n.d., *N.Y. Col. Docs.*, 3:424–25. Van Cortlandt stated that rum imports declined from 12,080 gallons to 4,161 gallons in one year and peltries from 30,000 to 12,000. Van Cortlandt to Blathwayt, n.d., Blathwayt MSS, 9, New York (microfilm), Huntington Library.

57. Bernard Mason, "Aspects of the New York Revolt of 1689," pp. 172–73.

58. Santen to Blathwayt, 14 September 1686, Blathwayt MSS, 10, New York (microfilm), Huntington Library.

59. See n. 63. Maria Van Rensselaer wrote to her brother-in-law Richard, " land is getting to be much in demand and brings big money, owing to the increase in population and the rapid falling off of trade, and that there is no land, no matter how far from the place, but is being bought." A. J. F. Van Laer, *Correspondence of Maria van Rensselaer*, pp. 145–51. The land boom may also have been encouraged by Dongan, who was very interested in his fees from the grants.

60. There were at least two voyages to Africa, N.Y. Col. MSS, 34, Pt. II, fols. 39, 46, 77.

61. MCM, 5, fols. 44–46. When caught trading, the Albany merchants pled ignorance and apologized to the city. See also *CCM*, pp. 132, 136, 141–42.

62. "Reasons presented to the governor by the mayor and aldermen to prohibit bolting in any other place but this city," 6 April 1684, *MCC*, 1:149–50.

63. Complaints were voiced in an extraordinary session of the *commissaries*, 3 May 1683. *Albany Minutes of the Court*, 3:348. The Esopus communities also complained. "Petition of the inhabitants of Ulster County," 1687, Paltsits Collection and Miscellaneous MSS, New York Historical Society, New York City.

64. Extraordinary session of the magistrates, 28 June 1683, *Albany Minutes of the Court*, 3:366.

65. Extraordinary session of the magistrates, 16 June 1683, ibid., pp. 364–65.

66. Van Dyck's orders, 10 April 1684, ibid., pp. 437–38.

67. The only economic legislation of consequence was the bill for the encouragement of trade and navigation passed 22 October 1684, *N.Y. Col. Laws*, 1:143–73.

68. Gary B. Nash, "The Free Society of Traders," pp. 147–73.

69. The letter was received 21 May 1684, *CCM*, p. 39. This was a very timely interference from Barbados. It would be interesting to know if such ex-Barbadians as Lewis Morris or John Palmer, who were very close to Dongan, had elicited such a complaint.

70. *MCC*, 1:152–53. York to Dongan, 26 August 1684, *N.Y. Col. Docs.*, 3:349–59. In a letter to Dongan, Werden ordered him always to act to prosper New York City, 1 November 1684, ibid., pp. 351–52.

71. Petition of Jacob Leisler, 7 April 1687. N.Y. Col. MSS, 35, fol. 54. "Bill to Prevent Fraud . . . ," 14 March 1687, ibid., fol. 43. The magistrates let the excise for only £5, ibid., fol. 62.

72. "Petition of Richard Blackledge on behalf of the soap boilers . . . ," 6 March 1688, ibid., fol. 132.

73. Mason, "Aspects of the Revolt," pp. 172–73. Mason uses the assessment total of £100,937 for the year 1676 to show the decline. This was a special tax, not a regular provincial rate.

74. Charles W. Long and William T. Davis, *Staten Island*, p. 128.

75. *Doc. Hist.*, 1:279, 659.

76. The council refused their petition to escape militia duty, N.Y. Col. MSS, 35, fols. 35–36.

77. By 9 May 1689 it was reported the men in Queens County had taken up their arms over their pay arrears. NYHS, *Collections* (1868), pp. 254–55.

78. Jacob Leisler asked for the return of the records from Boston, 4 March 1690. *Doc. Hist.*, 2:184–85. Complaints from New York elicited an order in council to Massachusetts to return the records. 30 April 1690, *N.Y. Col. Docs.*, 3:711–12.

CHAPTER 9

1. Andros to the Lords of Trade, 4 October 1688, in Michael G. Hall, Lawrence H. Leder, and Michael Kamman, eds., *The Glorious Revolution in America*, p. 98.

2. For their careers in the dominion, see Viola F. Barnes, *The Dominion of New England*, passim.

3. NYHS, *Collections* (1868), pp. 241–45.

4. Ibid., pp. 244–45.

5. Ibid., pp. 245, 272–74. Council to Andros, 1 May 1689, ibid., pp. 250–51.

6. His career is recounted in Stephen S. Webb, "The Strange Career of Francis Nicholson," pp. 513–48. See also Bruce T. McCully, "From North Riding to Morocco," pp. 534–57.

7. Council meeting, 22 May 1689, NYHS, *Collections* (1868), pp. 265–66.

8. For an arid discussion as to whether or not the status of the government made the rebellion a rebellion, see Jerome R. Reich, *Leisler's Rebellion*, pp. 14–75.

9. For the influence of a generalized belief as a focusing agent in times of stress, see Neil J. Smelser, *Theory of Collective Behavior*, pp. 79–130. "Deposition of Nicholas Brown," 13 September 1689, *Doc. Hist.*, 2:27; *CSPC*, 13:902; *N.Y. Eccl. Rec.*, 2:1041–45. Baxter withdrew in May, NYHS, *Collections* (1868), p. 267. Dongan had retired from office to enjoy his estate on Long Island, John R. Brodhead, *The History of the State of New York*, 2:521.

10. NYHS, *Collections* (1868), pp. 259–62, 272–73; CO/5/1081, no. 61, PRO; and *Doc. Hist.*, 2:5–6.

11. CO/5/1081, no. 5, PRO.

12. "Declaration of the Freeholders of Suffolk County, Long Island," *N.Y. Col. Docs.*, 3:577.

13. Nicholson to Lords of Trade, 15 May 1689, ibid., p. 575.

14. Council to Captain Howell, 4 May 1689, NYHS, *Collections* (1868), pp. 252–53. One of the chief complaints of the Queens County men was that they had not been paid for their previous services in Albany. The council agreed to pay them but only after ordering the county to settle the arrearages from its taxes. Ibid., pp. 254–55.

15. Nicholson to Lords of Trade, 15 May 1689, *N.Y. Col. Docs.*, 3:575. Council meetings, 20, 22 May 1689, NYHS, *Collections* (1868), pp. 282–84.

16. NYHS, *Collections* (1868), pp. 286–87. "Deposition of Hendrick Cuyler," 10 June 1689, ibid., pp. 292–93.

17. "Deposition of Charles Lodwick," 25 July 1689, ibid., p. 295.

18. Ibid., pp. 268–88. The officers of the militia refused to intervene. Ibid., pp. 288–90.

19. *Doc. Hist.*, 2:10. A slightly different text exists in CO/5/1081, no. 6, PRO.

20. The "Declaration of the Militia," 3 June 1689, was approved by the six captains and about four hundred men. CO/5/1081, no. 10. Jacob Leisler issued his own declaration on 3 June with the intent of letting the world know the insurgents had not acted rashly. *Doc. Hist.*, 2:4. Captains Lodwick, Minvielle, De Peyster, and De Bruyn

and their men marched from the parade ground to join Leisler and the others in the fort. NYHS, *Collections* (1869), pp. 269–70.

21. NYHS, *Collections* (1869), pp. 270–72.

22. John Tuder to Nicholson, August 1689, *N.Y. Col. Docs.*, 3:616–18. Van Cortlandt to Andros, 9 July 1689, ibid., p. 595.

23. Van Cortlandt to Andros, 9 July 1689, ibid., pp. 590–98. "Abstract of Colonel Bayard's Journal," ibid., p. 600.

24. Ibid., p. 596.

25. "Abstract of Bayard's Journal," ibid., pp. 602–3, 596.

26. "Journal of the Council of Safety," CO/5/1081, fols. 111–37, PRO; and *Doc. Hist.*, 2:11.

27. Leisler to William and Mary, 20 August 1689, *N.Y. Col. Docs.*, 3:614–16. Leisler to Bishop of Salisbury (the famous Whig historian Gilbert Burnet), ibid., pp. 654–57.

28. Leisler called upon Gerrard Vanheythusen and Nicholas Cullen, among others, to help them. *Doc. Hist.*, 2:13–14. Stoll's mission and his proceedings are in *N.Y. Col. Docs.*, 3:602–3, 629–32.

29. Robert Bolton, *History of the County of Westchester*, 1:381.

30. Delanoy had been a financial officer in the city previously. *MCC*, 1:171, 193. "Journal of the Council," CO/5/1081, fols. 111, 112, 127, PRO. Van Cortlandt to Nicholson, 5 August 1689, *N.Y. Col. Docs.*, 3:609–10.

31. An inventory of the records was completed 24 July 1689, N.Y. Col. MSS, 36, fol. 13. Leisler to Salisbury, 7 January 1690, *N.Y. Col. Docs.*, 3:654–59. Leisler to Boston, 4 March 1690, *Doc. Hist.*, 2:184–85. Van Cortlandt was blamed for sending the records to Boston, inflaming the people against him. Van Cortlandt to Randolph, 13 December 1689, CO/5/1081, no. 78, PRO. Removal of the records was described as a "mean business." NYHS, *Collections* (1868), pp. 296–97.

32. "Journal of the Council," CO/5/1081, fol. 135, PRO.

33. The elections were confirmed 14 October 1689. *Doc. Hist.*, 2:35. Van Cortlandt to Andros, 18 December 1689, Blathwayt MSS, 9, New York (microfilm), Huntington Library.

34. Leisler's commission, 16 August 1689, *Doc. Hist.*, 2:23–24.

35. "Journal of the Council," CO/5/1081, fols. 136–37, PRO.

36. Leisler to William and Mary, 20 August 1689, *N.Y. Col. Docs.*, 3:614–16. Leisler to "Governor of Boston," 28 August 1689, *Doc. Hist.*, 2:25–27.

37. Those elected, including Leisler's son-in-law, Robert Walters, were all members of the insurgent group. *Doc. Hist.*, 2:35.

38. Ibid., pp. 7, 80.

39. The convention refused permission to anyone who wanted to leave Albany because of the French threat. Ibid., pp. 84, 88–89. Leisler's answer was dismissed by the convention on 14 September. Ibid., pp. 92–93. The convention snubbed Leisler by addressing him as "Capt." He had already adopted the title of commander-in-chief. Ibid., p. 80.

40. Connecticut sent Captain Jonathan Bull with eighty-seven men. He arrived 25 November 1689 and left in March 1690. Ibid., pp. 132, 210.

41. Twenty-six soldiers took the oath and one refused. Ibid., pp. 99–101, 105–8, 112–13.

42. Brodhead, *New York*, 2:321. Jacob Milborne v. Edmund Andros, *N.Y. Col. Docs.*, 3:300–301 and MCM, 5, fol. 45. When he returned to New York, Milborne was a merchant and agent for Sir Thomas Griffeth and Edward Griffeth. All three sued Andros in chancery and one of the debtors' courts (the poultry counter) for debt, assault, and damages. The case dragged on for years in chancery. See court actions Chancery, 7/3/62; 33/257, fol. 394; 7/576/37; 33/259, fol. 90. His brother, William, was an Anabaptist preacher in Boston who helped oust Andros in 1689. "Extract of Bayard's Letter," 23 September 1689. *N.Y. Col. Docs.*, 3:620–21.

43. *Doc. Hist.*, 2:113–14.

44. Ibid., p. 115.

45. Ibid., pp. 116–17.

46. Ibid., pp. 120–27.

47. Ibid., pp. 129–32.

48. *N.Y. Col. Docs.*, 3:606.

49. Certificate of Van Cortlandt and Philipse, 13 December 1689, ibid., p. 649. Van Cortlandt to Randolph, 13 December 1689, CO/5/1081, no. 78, PRO. Van Cortlandt had returned to the city only to have the letters taken from him.

50. The council was formed on 11 December from individuals who were active on the committee of safety or friends of the committee. *Doc. Hist.*, 2:15, 45. The members were Peter Delanoy, Samuel Staats, Hendrick Jansen Van Veurden, and Johannes Vermilje for the city. Samuel Edsall for Queens County, Gerardus Beekman for Kings, Thomas Williams for Westchester, and William Laurence for Orange. For the other offices, see *Doc. Hist.*, 2:48, 49, and *Cal. Hist. MSS*, 2:185–92.

51. N.Y. Col. MSS, 36, fol. 142, no. 72.

52. Ibid., fol. 142, no. 65. Leisler frequently used the courts of oyer and terminer and of exchequer against his enemies because he controlled appointments of the justices.

53. "Proclamation by the English Freemen of New York," 19 December 1689, CO/5/1081, no. 84, PRO.

54. *Doc. Hist.*, 2:50–51.

55. Van Cortlandt to Andros, 18 December 1689, Blathwayt MSS, 9, New York, (microfilm), Huntington Library. Brodhead, *New York*, 2:599.

56. *Doc. Hist.*, 2:53.

57. "Bayard's Narrative," 13 December 1689, *N.Y. Col. Docs.*, 3:648.

58. Van Cortlandt to Andros, 9 July 1689, *N.Y. Col. Docs.*, 3:590.

59. "Address of Militia of New York to William and Mary," June 1689, *N.Y. Col. Docs.*, 3:583–84.

60. "Form of Association proposed to the inhabitants," CO/5/1081, no. 26, PRO. For other "associations" see Stuart E. Prall, ed., *The Puritan Revolution*, pp. 211–38. For English patterns of rebellion, see Anthony Fletcher, *Tudor Rebellions*, passim. Leisler's rebellion is similar to the "Church and King" riot described by George Rudé, *The Crowd in History*, pp. 135–47.

61. "Bayard's Narrative," *N.Y. Col. Docs.*, 3:639.

62. The opposed positions on Leisler's role and motives are found in Reich, *Leisler's Rebellion*, passim, which is very favorable, and Brodhead, *New York*, 2:536–49, who despised Leisler.

63. NYHS, *Collections* (1868), pp. 272–73. New Netherland MSS, fol. 33, New York Historical Society, New York City. "Leisler's Declaration . . . ," 3 June 1689, *Doc. Hist.*, 2:4. "Journal of the Council of Safety . . . ," 6 June 1689, CO/5/1081, fol. 111, PRO.

64. His name does not appear on Domine Henricus Selyn's list of members of his church, even though Leisler's wife was still a communicant. NYHS, *Collections*, 1 (1841): 392–99. He may well have objected to Selyn, who like Nicholas Van Rensselaer, was very close to Andros and later Dongan. Leisler did not limit his criticism to the establishment. He was equally harsh on the Quakers. *N.Y. Col. Docs.*, 3:654–59.

65. Leisler to Governor Treat, 1 January 1691, *Doc. Hist.*, 2:316–19. Leisler to [Boston], 30 September 1690, ibid., pp. 300–303.

66. CO/5/1081, no. 16, 1–14, PRO, and *CSPC*, 13, no. 902.

67. Leder, "Unorthodox Domine," pp. 166–76. Leisler v. Philipse, 16 January 1683, MCM, 5, fol. 103.

68. Leisler to "Governor of Boston," 9 August 1689, *Doc. Hist.*, 2:21–22. The term "Grandee" was frequently used to describe members of elite groups in the late seventeenth century. "Nathaniel Bacon, esq. his manifesto . . . ," *Virginia Magazine of History and Biography* 1 (1893): 55–58. "Complaint from Heaven . . . ," W. H. Browne, ed., *Archives of Maryland*, 4:146.

69. Governor Henry Sloughter to Nottingham, 27 March 1691, *N.Y. Col. Docs.*, 3:756–57.

70. Thomas J. Archdeacon, "The Age of Leisler—New York City, 1689–1710," pp. 63–82.

71. D. Bourepos, pastor of the French Colony, to Leisler, 20 October, 1690, *Doc. Hist.*, 2:304–5.

72. Edsall's career and family are recounted in *New York Genealogical and Biographical Record*, 13 (1882): 191–93. For Cuyler, ibid., 3 (1872): 81–82.

73. For the appointment or election of these individuals see *Doc. Hist.*, 2:15, 35, 45, 48–49, 291, 303–4, 307, and *MCC*, 1:204.

74. Tax lists are in *MCC*, 1:29–37, 50–62.

75. For Edsall see *New York Genealogical and Biographical Record*, 13 (1882): 191–93. Lawrence, ibid., 3 (1872): 409.

76. Steenwyck and Luyck were dead. The men who had signed the petition to Andros and joined with Leisler were William Beekman, Johannes De Peyster. The sons were Peter De Milt (Anthony De Milt), Peter Van Brugh (Johannes Van Brugh). *N.Y. Col. Docs.*, 2:740–43.

77. *Cal. Hist. MSS*, 2:185–89.

78. For Pretty, see *Albany Minutes of the Court*, 2:99, 143; 3:88, 372, 506.

79. Provoost's career can be followed in ibid., 1:24; 2:160, 224, 360, 439; 3:40, 163.

80. Lawrence II. Leder, *Robert Livingston and the Politics of Colonial New York*, pp. 3–53, 64–67. Pretty to Milborne, 15 January 1690, *Doc. Hist.*, 2:59–60.

81. *Albany Minutes of the Court*, 3:144.

82. Leisler to the King, 7 January 1690, *N.Y. Col. Docs.*, 3:653–54. Leisler to the Bishop of Salisbury, 7 January 1690, ibid., pp. 654–57.

83. Stoll's unsuccessful embassy can be traced in, "Representations of Joost Stoll . . . ," 16 November 1689, ibid., pp. 629–32, and "Account of Joost Stoll's Proceedings," 16 November 1689, ibid., pp. 602–3; CO/391/6, fol. 299, PRO. Blagg made his case to the Lords of Trade in October 1690, ibid., fol. 352, after presenting a petition to them on 23 June. *N.Y. Col. Docs.*, 3:735–36.

84. Affidavits concerning Andros, *N.Y. Col. Docs.*, 3:659. Leisler to Governor Treat, 9 August 1689, *Doc. Hist.*, 2:21–22. For other examples see, *N.Y. Col. Docs.*, 3:589–90, 654–59, 614–16, and *Doc. Hist.*, 2:406.

85. Captain McKenzie to Nicholson, 15 August 1689, *N.Y. Col. Docs.*, 3:612–14. Depositions of John Dischington and Philip French, ibid., pp. 586–87; *Doc. Hist.*, 2:7–9; "Bayard's Narrative," ibid., p. 682.

86. Leisler to Governor to Treat, 7 August 1689, *Col. Doc.*, 2:20–21. "Journal of the Council," CO/5/1081, fol. 119, PRO.

87. Affidavits, CO/5/1081, no. 16, 1–14, PRO; *Doc. Hist.*, 2:27. McKenzie to Nicholson, 15 August 1689, *N.Y. Col. Docs.*, 3:612–14. "Journal of the Council," CO/5/1081, fols. 120–121.

88. For Van Cortlandt's statement, see "Journal of the Council," ibid., fol. 134. See also "Bayard's Narrative," *N.Y. Col. Docs.*, 3:683–84.

89. The by-laws for Captain Lodwick's militia company ordered the men to make no national distinctions. NYHS, *Collections* (1868), pp. 293–94. "Journal of the Council," CO/5/1081, fol. 116, PRO.

90. "Bayard's Narrative," *N.Y. Col. Docs.*, 3:672.

91. McKenzie to Nicholson, 19 August 1689, CO/5/1081, no. 49, PRO.

92. See the letters of Van Cortlandt, John Tuder, and Bayard for this campaign. *N.Y. Col. Docs.*, 3:598–99, 609–10, 611–12, 616–18, 633–34. Van Cortlandt to Andros, 18 December 1689, Blathwayt MSS, 9, New York (microfilm), Huntington Library. Van Cortlandt to Blathwayt, 18 December, ibid.; "Bayard's Narrative," *N.Y. Col. Docs.*, 3:669, 674, 676.

93. "Journal of the Council," CO/5/1081, fol. 128, PRO. McKenzie to Nicholson, 19 August 1689, ibid., no. 49. Bayard first uses the term "Mansanello" in his "Narrative," *N.Y. Col. Docs.*, 3:668. Tuder to Nicholson, August 1689, ibid., pp. 616–18.

94. Allen W. Trelease, *Indian Affairs in Colonial New York*, p. 301.

95. *Doc. Hist.*, 2:159, 168.

96. Ibid., pp. 51–52, 144–54.

97. Commission, 4 March 1690, *N.Y. Col. Docs.*, 3:702–3.

98. *Doc. Hist.*, 2:211, 237–40, 242, 254–56.

99. Charles M. Andrews, *The Colonial Period of American History*, 3:130–31.

100. Milborne's commission, 25 May 1690, *Doc. Hist.*, 2:240–41. Livingston to Connecticut, 11 April 1690, *N.Y. Col. Docs.*, 3:703–7. Same to same, 9 May 1690, ibid., pp. 728–29, 730–31. Secretary John Allyn of Connecticut to Leisler, 27 May 1690, N.Y. Col. MSS, 36, fol. 86. Leisler to Governor Treat, 20 June 1690, *Doc. Hist.*, 2:265.

101. Leisler to Connecticut, 11 April 1690, *N.Y. Col. Docs.*, 3:703–7.

102. Ships commissions, May 1690, *Doc. Hist.*, 2:250–51.

103. Trelease, *Indian Affairs*, pp. 303–4. Leisler to Connecticut, 30 September 1689, *Doc. Hist.*, 2:300–3. Leisler to Governor Treat, 1 January 1691, ibid., pp. 316–19. Richard S. Dunn, *Puritans and Yankees*, pp. 287–94.

104. Allyn to Leisler, 1 September 1690, *Doc. Hist.*, 2:288–90.

105. Writ for assembly elections, 20 February 1690, N.Y. Col. MSS, 35, fol. 29.

106. *Doc. Hist.*, 2:230–31.

107. Van Cortlandt to Andros, 19 May 1689, *N.Y. Col. Docs.*, 3:717.

108. N.Y. Col. MSS, 36, fols. 36, 39, 125, and *Doc. Hist.*, 2:68, 432.

109. "A Modest and Impartial Narrative . . . ," *N.Y. Col. Docs.*, 3:661.

110. Warrant, 17 January 1689, *Doc. Hist.*, 2:60.

111. General warrant, 15 February 1689, ibid., p. 71. The warrant for Dongan was accompanied with warrants for prominent leaders of Queens County such as Thomas Willet and Thomas Hicks. Ibid., p. 71; *N.Y. Col. Docs.*, 3:701. A captain, his crew, and passengers were arrested 7 June 1690, ibid., p. 264. Other notables for whom warrants were issued included Edward Antill, Peter Marius, Thomas Wenham, Jacobus De Key, Brant Schuyler, and Phillip French. *Doc. Hist.*, 2: 70, 71, 262, 278, 279.

112. "Certificate of the clergy of New York in favor of Messrs. Cortlandt and Bayard," 11 June 1690, *N.Y. Col. Docs.*, 3:588, and *Doc. Hist.*, 2:431.

113. Leisler to Shrewsbury, 20 October 1690, *N.Y. Col. Docs.*, 3:751–54. Selyns, Varick, Dellius to Classis of Amsterdam, 12 October 1692, *N.Y. Eccl. Rec.*, 2:1041–45. Varick to Classis, 9 April 1693, ibid., pp. 1048–53.

114. "Defense of Dellius against charges of Lord Bellomont," 13 October 1699, *N.Y. Eccl. Rec.*, 2:1394–97. Varick to the Classis, 9 April 1693, ibid., pp. 1048–53. Selyns, Varick, and Dellius to the Classis, 12 October 1692, ibid., pp. 1041–45.

115. Leisler to Milborne, 19 May 1690, *Doc. Hist.*, 2:247–48.

116. *N.Y. Col. Docs.*, 3:187–88. Charles R. Street, ed., *Huntington Town Records*, 1:71–73.

117. *N.Y. Col. Docs.*, 3:748–49.

118. Bolton, *Westchester*, 1:381.

119. *Doc. Hist.*, 2:262–63. Leisler believed that the attack was caused by success of the Jacobites in Ireland. Leisler to John Coode, 27 June 1690, ibid., pp. 266–69. Lawrence H. Leder, ". . . Like Madmen Through the Streets," pp. 405–15.

120. Order, 7 June 1690, *Doc. Hist.*, 2:264. "A Memorial of What has Occurred in New York . . ." ibid., p. 55.

121. Deposition of Henry Cravenraedt, 16 December 1690, CO/5/1036, no. 3, PRO. Orders to Milborne and Edsall, 28, 30 October 1690, *Doc. Hist.*, 2:309–10. All of the courts on the island were suspended until the whole island was "reduced" to peace. *N.Y. Col. Docs.*, 3:307. An extraordinary court martial was ordered to punish the rebels. *Doc. Hist.*, 2:310. John Clapp to the Secretary of State, 7 November 1690, *N.Y. Col. Docs.*, 3:754–56.

122. Benjamin Blagg appeared before the lords and was just as ineffective as Stoll. Lords of Trade meeting, 3 October 1680, CO/391/6, no. 352, PRO.

123. Stephen S. Webb, "William Blathwayt, Imperial Fixer: Muddling Through to Empire, 1689–1717," pp. 373–415.

124. Van Cortlandt to Nicholson, 18 December 1689, Blathwayt MSS, 9, New York (microfilm), Huntington Library. Livingston to Andros, 14 April 1690, *N.Y. Col. Docs.*, 3:708–10. Leisler to Milborne, 18 May 1690, *Doc. Hist.*, 2:247–48. Van Cortlandt to Andros, 19 May 1690, *N.Y. Col. Docs.*, 3:715–19. Livingston to Nicholson, 7 June 1690, ibid., pp. 727–28. Van Cortlandt to Blathwayt, 5 June 1690, Blathwayt MSS, 9, New York (microfilm), Huntington Library. Livingston to Andros, 14 April 1690, *N.Y. Col.*

Docs., 3:708–10. Livingston to Nicholson, 7 June 1690, ibid., pp. 727–28. Joseph Dudley to Blathwayt, 5 February 1691, CO/5/856, no. 140, PRO. Nicholson to Lords of Trade, 4 November 1690, CO/5/1305, no. 50, PRO. Isaac Melyn to Leisler, 11 December 1690, Doc. Hist., 2:316.

125. N.Y. Col. Docs., 3:622.

126. "Petition of the merchants trading to New York," 19 December 1689, ibid., pp. 651–53.

127. Instructions to Sloughter, 31 January 1690, ibid., pp. 685–91. A memo recounting the strengths and weaknesses of potential councilors was prepared for the lords, CO/5/1081, no. 94, PRO. Mathias Nicolls was superannuated, Nicholas De Meyer—old and ill, and most of the others were simply "rich and good man." Lords of Trade to Sloughter, 17 October 1690, N.Y. Col. Docs., 3:750.

128. Log of the Archangel, Admiralty 51/55 pt. 1, PRO. See also Andrews, Colonial Period, 3:128n.

129. Ingoldsby to Leisler, NYHS, Collections (1868), p. 300. Warrant to Samuel Moore, 30 January 1691, ibid., pp. 300–301. Leisler to Ingoldsby, 14 February 1691, ibid., pp. 302–3.

130. "Declaration of the Freeholders and Inhabitants of Long Island . . . ," n.d., ibid., pp. 304–5. Joseph Dudley to Leisler, 11 March 1691, CO/37/25, no. 25, PRO. Sloughter to Nottingham, 27 March 1691, N.Y. Col. Docs., 3:756–57. Chidley Brooke to Sloughter, 12 March 1691, CO/37/25, no. 37, PRO. See also Brodhead, New York, 2:635.

131. Van Cortlandt to Blathwayt, 6 April 1691, Blathwayt MSS, 4, New York (microfilm), Huntington Library. Sloughter to Nottingham, 27 March 1691, N.Y. Col. Docs., 3:756–57. Log of the Archangel, Admiralty, 51/55, pt. 1, PRO.

132. Lawrence H. Leder, "Records of the Trials of Jacob Leisler," pp. 431–57. "Memorial of the Court Proceedings," NYHS, Collections (1868), p. 313. Julius Goebel, Jr., and T. Raymond Naughton, Law Enforcement in Colonial New York, p. 83. Reich, Leisler's Rebellion, pp. 115–26. Six other men, Mindert Coerton, Thomas Williams, Johannes Vermilye, Abraham Brasier, Abraham Gouverneur, and Gerardus Beekman, escaped their death sentences. Samuel Edsall and Peter Delanoy were acquitted for unexplained reasons. For an account of the execution and its aftermath, see Mariana G. Van Rensselaer, History of the City of New York in the Seventeenth Century, 2:523–68. Van Cortlandt to Nicholson, 23 May 1691, Blathwayt MSS, 9, New York (microfilm), Huntington Library.

133. Doc. Hist., 2:213–15.

134. Van Cortlandt to Nicholson, 23 May 1691, Blathwayt MSS, 9, New York (microfilm), Huntington Library. Van Cortlandt shared a common belief that if Leisler was not put to death there would be another rising.

CHAPTER 10

1. Michael Kammen, People of Paradox, pp. 31–56, and David S. Lovejoy, The Glorious Revolution in America, pp. 271–93.

2. Executive Council, 1:310–12.

3. Kenneth B. Murdock, Increase Mather, pp. 211–61. For Maryland, see Lois G. Carr and David W. Jordan, Maryland's Revolution in Government, pp. 146–79.

4. For the vigor of local government at this time and in the future, see Carr and Jordan, Maryland's Revolution, pp. 228–29. Warren W. Billings, "The Causes of Bacon's Rebellion," pp. 408–35. Patricia U. Bonomi, "Local Government in Colonial New York: A Base for Republicanism," pp. 29–50.

5. Michael Kammen, Deputyes and Libertyes, pp. 52–68.

6. Patricia U. Bonomi, in her A Factious People, fully explores the divisive tendencies in New York after 1691.

7. Patricia U. Bonomi, "The Middle Colonies," pp. 63–92. Milton M. Klein, The Politics of Diversity, 11–45, 183–200.

~ Bibliography

Primary Sources

Manuscripts
Berkshire County Record Office, *Reading, England*
    Downshire Manuscripts
Bodleian Library, Oxford University, *Oxford, England*
    Clarendon Manuscripts
    Rawlinson Manuscripts
British Museum, *London*
    Additional Manuscripts
    Egerton Manuscripts
Cambridge University Library, *Cambridge, England*
    Additional Manuscripts
Friends Library, *London*
    Penn Manuscripts
Henry E. Huntington Library, *San Marino, Cal.*
    Blathwayt Papers, *microfilm copy from Colonial Williamsburg*
Lambeth Palace, *London*
    Lambeth Palace Manuscripts
Longleat House, *Wiltshire, England*
    Coventry Papers
Massachusetts Historical Society, *Boston*
    Massachusetts and New York Miscellaneous Manuscripts
New York Historical Society, *New York City*
    Dongan Manuscripts
    New Netherland Collection Manuscripts
    New York Miscellaneous Manuscripts
    Paltsits Collection and Miscellaneous Manuscripts
New York State Library, *Albany, N.Y.*
    Court of Assize Minutes Manuscripts
    New York Colonial Manuscripts
    Warrants, Orders, Passes, Letters, Hue and Cry Manuscripts
Public Record Office, *London*
    Admiralty
    Chancery 7, 33, 66
    Colonial Office, 1, 5, 389, 391
    Exchequer 190
    High Court of Admiralty
    Prerogative Court of Canterbury

State Papers, Foreign
Queens College Library, *New York City*
    Amsterdam Notarial Archives, *microfilm*
    Esopus Court of Sessions Manuscripts, *microfilm*
    New York City Mayors Court Minutes Manuscripts, *microfilm*
Franklin D. Roosevelt Library, *Hyde Park, N.Y.*
    Livingston-Redmond Manuscripts
William Salt Library, *Stafford, Staffordshire, England*
    Dartmouth Manuscripts

Published

Bartlett, John R. *Records of the Colony of Rhode Island and Providence Plantations in New England*. 10 vols. Providence: A. C. Greene, 1856–65.

Browne, W. H., et al., eds. *Archives of Maryland*. 65 vols. Baltimore, Md.: Maryland Historical Society, 1883–1952.

Case, J. W., ed. *Southold [L.I.] Town Records*. 2 vols. Southold, N.Y.: Printed by order of the towns of Southold and Riverhead, 1882–84.

The Clarendon Papers. New York Historical Society, *Collections*, for the year 1869. New York: New York Historical Society, 1870.

Corwin, E. T., ed. *Ecclesiastical Records of the State of New York*. Albany, N.Y.: J. B. Lyon, state printer, 1901–16.

Cox, John, ed. *Oyster Bay Town Records, 1653–1763*. 6 vols. New York: T. A. Wright, 1916–31.

Dankaerts, Jasper. *Journal of Jasper Dankaerts, 1678–1680*. Edited by Burleigh J. Bartlett and J. Franklin Jameson. Original Narratives of Early American History. New York: Charles Scribner's Sons, 1913.

Denton, Daniel. *A Brief Description of New York*. Edited by Gabriel Furman. New York: W. Gowans, 1845.

De Waard, C., ed. *De Zeewusche Expeditie naar De West Onder Cornelius Evertsen Den Jonge, 1672–1674*. S' Gravenhage: Martinius Nijhoff, 1928.

Force, Peter, ed. *Tracts and Other Papers Relating Principally to the Colonies in North America*. 4 vols. Washington, D.C.: Printed by Peter Force, 1836–46.

Frost, Josephine C., ed. *Records of the Town of Jamaica, Long Island, New York, 1656–1751*. 3 vols. New York: The Long Island Historical Society, 1914.

Great Britain. Public Record Office. *Calendar of State Papers, Colonial Series, America and West Indies, 1574–1736*. 42 vols. Edited by Noel Sainsbury, et al. London: Her Majesty's Stationery Office, 1860–1953.

————. *Calendar of State Papers, Domestic, Charles II*. 28 vols. Edited by Mary A. E. Green, et al. London: Her Majesty's Stationery Office, 1860–1938.

————. *Calendar of Treasury Books Preserved in the Public Record Office, 1660–1718*. 32 vols. Edited by William Shaw. London: Her Majesty's Stationery Office, 1904–57.

_____. _Calendar of Treasury Papers_. 6 vols. Edited by Joseph Redington and William A. Shaw. London: Her Majesty's Stationery Office, 1868–97.

_____. _Historical Manuscripts Commission, Twelfth Report, Papers of S. H. le Fleming of Rydal_. London: Her Majesty's Stationery Office, 1890.

Greene, Evarts, and Virginia D. Harrington, comps. _American Population Before the Federal Census of 1790_. New York: Columbia University Press, 1932.

Hamlin, Paul M., and Charles E. Baker, eds. _Supreme Court of Judicature of the Province of New York, 1691, 1704_. 3 vols. New York: New York Historical Society, 1952–59.

Hazard, Samuel, et al., eds. _Pennsylvania Archives_. 9 series, 138 vols. Philadelphia and Harrisburg: J. Stevens & Co. and others, 1852–1949.

Hening, William W., ed. _The Statutes at Large Being a Collection of all the Laws of Virginia, 1619–1792_. 13 vols. Richmond Va.: Samuel Pleasants, junior, printer to the Commonwealth, 1809–23.

Hicks, Benjamin D., ed. _Records of the Town of North and South Hempstead, Long Island, New York_. 8 vols. Jamaica N.Y.: Long Island farmer print., 1896–1904.

Hough, F. B., ed. _Papers Relating to the Island of Nantucket, Martha's Vineyard and Other Islands Adjacent Known as Duke's Country While Under the Colony of New York_. Albany, N.Y.: J. Munsell, 1856.

_____. _Papers Relating to Pemaquid and Parts Adjacent in the Present State of Maine, Known as Cornwall County when Under the Colony of New York_. Albany, N.Y.: Weed, Parsons & Co., 1856.

Hutchins, S. C., comp. _Civil List and Forms of Government of the Colony and State of New York_. Albany, N.Y.: Weed, Parsons & Co., 1869.

Hutchinson, Thomas, ed. _Collection of Original Papers Relative to the History of the Colony of Massachusetts Bay_. Boston, 1769. Reprinted for the Prince Society, Albany, N.Y.: J. Munsell, 1865.

Jameson, J. Franklin, ed. _Narratives of New Netherland_. New York: Charles Scribner's Sons, 1909.

Leaming, Aaron, and Jacob Spicer, eds. _The Grants, Concessions, and Original Constitutions of the Province of New Jersey_. Philadelphia: W. Bradford, 1752. Reprinted, Somerville, N.J.: Honeyman & Company, 1881.

Massachusetts Historical Society. _Collections_, 1792–. Boston: Massachusetts Historical Society, 1792–.

_____. _Proceedings_, 1859–. Boston: Massachusetts Historical Society, 1859–.

Papers of the Lloyd Family of the Manor of Queen's Village, Lloyd's Neck, Long Island, New York. New York Historical Society, _Collections_ for the years 1926–27. 2 vols. New York: New York Historical Society, 1927.

Munsell, Joel, ed. _The Annals of Albany_. 10 vols. Albany, N.Y.: J. Munsell, 1850–59.

————. *Collections on the History of Albany From its Discovery to the Present Time*. 4 vols. Albany, N.Y.: J. Munsell, 1865.

New York (city). *Minutes of the Common Council of the City of New York, 1675–1776*. 8 vols. Edited by Herbert L. Osgood, et al. New York: Dodd, Mead and Company, 1905.

————. *The Records of New Amsterdam from 1653 to 1674*. 7 vols. Edited by Berthold Fernow. New York: Knickerbocker Press, 1897.

New York (colony). *Calendar of Historical Manuscripts in the Office of the Secretary of State, Albany, New York*. Vol. 1. *Dutch Manuscripts, 1630–1664*. Vol. 2. *English Manuscripts, 1664–1776*. Edited by Edmund B. O'Callaghan. Albany, N.Y.: Weed, Parsons & Co., 1866.

————. *Colonial Laws of New York from the Year 1664 to Revolution*. 5 vols. Albany, N.Y.: J. B. Lyon, state printer, 1894–96.

————. *Colonial Records. General Entries, 1664–1665*. New York State Library Bulletin, History, No. 2. Albany, N.Y.: The University of the State of New York, 1899.

————. *Colonial Records of the State, 1664–1673*. Appendix G in the New York State Historian's *Annual Report*, 1896, pp. 133–369. Albany and New York: Wynkoop, Hallenbeck Crawford Co., 1896.

————. *Early Records of the City and County of Albany and Colony of Rensselaerswyck*. 4 vols. Edited by J. Pearson. New York State Library, History Bulletins. Albany: Weed, Parson & Co., 1916.

————. *Laws and Ordinances of New Netherland, 1638–1674*. Edited by Edmund B. O'Callaghan. Albany, N.Y.: Weed, Parsons & Co., 1868.

————. New York Historical Society. *Collections*, 1811–. New York: New York Historical Society, 1811–.

————. *New York's Colonial Archives: Transcriptions of the Records between the Years 1673–1675*. Appendix L in the New York State Historian's *Annual Report*, 1897, pp. 157–436. Albany and New York: Wynkoop, Hallenbeck Crawford Co., 1898.

New York (Colony Council). *Calendar of Council Minutes, 1668–1783*. Edited by Berthold Fernow and A. J. F. Van Laer. New York State Library Bulletin No. 58, History 6. Albany, N.Y.: University of the State of New York, 1902.

————. *Minutes of the Executive Council: Administration of Francis Lovelace, 1668–1673*. 2 vols. Edited by Victor H. Paltsits. Albany, N.Y.: J. B. Lyon Co., 1910.

O'Callaghan, Edmund B., ed. *The Documentary History of the State of New York*. 4 vols. Albany, N.Y.: Weed, Parsons & Co., 1850–51.

————, and Berthold Fernow, eds., and John R. Brodhead, comp. *Documents Relative to the Colonial History of the State of New York*. 15 vols. Albany, N.Y.: Weed, Parsons & Co., 1856–87.

Pearson, Jonathan, and A. J. F. Van Laer, trans. and eds. *Early Records of the City and County of Albany, and Colony of Rensselaerswyck, 1656–1675*. Albany, N.Y.: The University of the State of New York, 1869–1919.

Pepys, Samuel. *The Diary of Samuel Pepys*. Edited by Henry B. Wheatley. 10 vols. London: G. Bell, 1928.

Records of the Town of East-Hampton, Long Island. 5 vols. Sag Harbor, N.Y.: J. H. Hunt, publisher, 1887–1905.

Shipton, Clifford K., ed. *Early American Imprints, 1639–1800*. Worcester, Mass. Microcard edition of Charles Evans, ed. *American Bibliography: A Chronological Dictionary of all Books, Pamphlets, and Periodical Publications Printed in the United States of America . . . , 1639–1820*. 12 vols. Chicago: Blakeley Press, 1903–34. Reprinted 16 vols. New York: Peter Smith, 1941–59.

Stock, Leo F., ed. *Proceedings and Debates of the British Parliaments Respecting North America*. 5 vols. Washington, D.C.: The Carnegie Institute of Washington, 1924–41.

Street, Charles R., ed. *Huntington Town Records*. Huntington, N.Y.: The "Long Island" Print., 1887–89.

Sylvester Papers. Massachusetts Historical Society *Proceedings*. Boston: The Massachusetts Historical Society, 1869.

Tappan, Robert T., and A. T. S. Goodrich, eds. *Edward Randolph: Including His Letters and Official Papers from New England, Middle and Southern Colonies in America*. Boston: Prince Society, 1898–1909.

Trumbull, J. Hammond, and Charles J. Hoadly, eds. *The Public Records of the Colony of Connecticut*. 10 vols. Hartford, Conn.: The Case, Lockwood & Brainard Company, 1850–90.

"Ulster County Papers." *New York Genealogical and Biographical Record*, 2 (1871): 143–48.

Valentine, David T., ed. *Manual of the Corporation of the City of New York*. New York: J. W. Bell & Others, 1841–70.

Van Laer, A. J. F., ed. and trans. *Correspondence of Jeremias Van Rensselaer, 1651–1674*. New York: The University of the State of New York, 1932.

———, ed. and trans. *Correspondence of Maria Van Rensselaer, 1664–1689*. Albany, N.Y.: The University of the State of New York, 1935.

———, ed. and trans. *Minutes of the Court of Albany, Rensselaerwyck and Schenectady, 1668–1680*, 3 vols. Albany, N.Y.: The University of the State of New York, 1926.

Van Wyck, Frederick, ed. *Long Island Colonial Patents*. Boston: A. A. Beauchamp, 1935.

———, ed. *Select Patents of New York Towns*. Boston: A. A. Beauchamp, 1938.

———, ed. *Select Patents of Towns and Manors*. Boston: A. A. Beauchamp, 1938.

Wharton, Walter. *Walter Wharton's Land Survey Register, 1675–1679*. Edited by Albert C. Myers. Wilmington, Del.: Historical Society of Delaware, 1955.

Whitehead, W. A., et al., eds. *Archives of the State of New Jersey, 1631–1800*. 30 vols. Newark, etc.: Daily Journal and Others, 1880–1906.

The Winthrop Papers. Massachusetts Historical Society *Collections*. Boston: Massachusetts Historical Society, 1863–1902.

Wolley, Charles. *A Two Years Journal in New York and Part of Its Territories*. London, 1701.

Wraxall, Peter. *Peter Wraxall's An Abridgement of the Indian Affairs . . . In the Colony of New York . . . , 1678–1751*. Edited by Charles H. McIlwain. Cambridge, Mass.: Harvard University Press, 1915.

Secondary Works

Books

Adams, James T. *The History of the Town of Southampton*. New York: Hampton Press, 1918.

Akagi, Ray H. *The Town Proprietors of the New England Colonies: A Study of Their Development, Organization, Activities, and Controversies, 1620–1770*. Reprint, Gloucester, Mass.: Peter Smith, 1963.

Andrews, Charles M. *The Colonial Period of American History*. 4 vols. New Haven, Conn.: Oxford University Press, 1934–38.

Bachman, Van Cleaf. *Peltries and Plantations: The Economic Policies of the Dutch West India Company in New Netherland, 1623–1639*. Baltimore, Md.: Johns Hopkins University Press, 1969.

Bailey, Rosalie F. *The Nicoll Family and Islip Grange. . . .* New York: John B. Watkins Company, 1940.

Bailyn, Bernard. *Education in the Forming of American Society: Needs and Opportunities to Study*. Chapel Hill, N.C.: University of North Carolina Press, 1960.

————. *The New England Merchants in the Seventeenth Century*. Cambridge, Mass.: Harvard University Press, 1955.

Barbour, Violet. *Henry Bennet, Earl of Arlington*. Washington, D.C.: American Historical Association, 1914.

Barnes, Viola F. *The Dominion of New England: A Study in British Colonial Policy*. New Haven, Conn.: Yale University Press, 1923.

Barrow, Thomas C. *Trade and Empire: The British Customs Service in Colonial America, 1660–1765*. Cambridge, Mass.: Harvard University Press, 1967.

Beer, George L. *The Old Colonial System*. 2 vols. New York: The Macmillan Company, 1912.

————. *The Origins of the British Colonial System, 1578–1660*. New York: The Macmillan Company, 1922.

Beresford, John. *The Godfather of Downing Street: Sir George Downing, 1623–84*. London: R. Cobden-Sanderson, 1925.

Black, Robert C. *The Younger John Winthrop*. New York: Columbia University Press, 1966.

Blok, J. P. *The Life of Admiral De Ruyter*. London: E. Benn, Limited, 1933.

Bolton, Robert. *History of the County of Westchester from its First Settlement*. 2 vols. New York: C. F. Roper, 1848.

Bond, Beverly W., Jr. *The Quit-Rent System in the American Colonies*. New Haven, Conn.: Yale University Press, 1919.

Bonomi, Patricia U. *A Factious People: Politics and Society in Colonial New York*. New York: Columbia University Press, 1971.

Bridenbaugh, Carl. *Cities in the Wilderness: The First Century of Urban Life in America, 1625–1742*. New York: Alfred A. Knopf, 1964.

Brodhead, John R. *The History of the State of New York, 1609–1691*. 2 vols. New York: Harper & Brothers, 1853.

Brown, Louise F. *The First Earl of Shaftsbury*. New York: Appleton-Century, 1933.

Buranelli, Vincent. *The King and the Quaker*. Philadelphia: University of Pennsylvania Press, 1962.

Bushman, Richard S. *From Puritan to Yankee: Character and the Social Order in Connecticut, 1690–1765*. Cambridge, Mass.: Harvard University Press, 1967.

Calder, Isabel M. *The New Haven Colony*. New Haven, Conn.: Yale University Press, 1934.

Carr, Lois G., and David W. Jordan. *Maryland's Revolution in Government, 1689–1692*. Ithaca, N.Y.: Cornell University Press, 1974.

Clark, George. *The Later Stuarts*. Oxford: The Clarendon Press, 1934.

Clarke, James S., ed. *Life of James II*. London: Longman, 1816.

Condon, Thomas J. *New York Beginnings: The Commercial Origins of New Netherland*. New York: New York University Press, 1968.

Craven, Wesley Frank. *The Colonies in Transition, 1660–1713*. New York: Harper & Row, 1968.

———. *New Jersey and the English Colonization of North America*. Princeton, N.J.: Van Nostrand Co., 1964.

———. *The Southern Colonies in the Seventeenth Century, 1607–1689*. Baton Rouge, La.: Louisiana State University Press, 1949.

Davies, D. W. *A Primer of Dutch Seventeenth Century Overseas Trade*. The Hague: Martinius Nijhoff, 1961.

Demos, John. *A Little Commonwealth: Family Life in Plymouth Colony*. New York: Oxford University Press, 1970.

Dunn, Richard S. *Puritans and Yankees: The Winthrop Dynasty of New England, 1630–1717*. Princeton, N.J.: Princeton University Press, 1962.

Eccles, William J. *Canada Under Louis XIV, 1663–1701*. New York: Oxford University Press, 1964.

Elting, Irving. *Dutch Village Communities on the Hudson River*. Baltimore, Md.: The Johns Hopkins University Press, 1886.

Feiling, Keith G. *British Foreign Policy, 1660–1672*. London: Macmillan and Co., 1930.

Fletcher, Anthony. *Tudor Rebellions*. London: Longmans, 1968.

Fox, Dixon R. *Caleb Heathcote, Gentleman Colonist: The Story of a Career in the Province of New York, 1692–1721*. New York: Charles Scribner's Sons, 1926.

Gerlach, D. R. *Phillip Schuyler and the American Revolution in New York, 1733–1777*. Lincoln, Neb.: University of Nebraska Press, 1964.

Goebel, Julius. *Some Legal and Political Aspects of the Manors in New*

York. Baltimore, Md.: Order of the Colonial Lords of Manors in America, 1928.

———, and T. Raymond Naughton. *Law Enforcement in Colonial New York: A Study of Criminal Procedure*. New York: The Commonwealth Fund, 1944.

Greven, Philip J., Jr. *Four Generations: Population, Land, and Family in Colonial Andover, Massachusetts*. Ithaca, N.Y.: Cornell University Press, 1970.

Hall, Edward H. *Philipse Manor Hall at Yonkers, New York*. New York: The American Science and Historic Preservation Society, 1912.

Hall, Michael G. *Edward Randolph and the American Colonies, 1676–1703*. Chapel Hill, N.C.: University of North Carolina Press, 1960.

———, Lawrence H. Leder, and Michael Kammen, eds. *The Glorious Revolution in America*. Reprint, New York: W. W. Norton & Co., 1972.

Harris, Richard C. *The Seigneurial System in Early Canada: A Geographical Study*. Madison, Wis.: University of Wisconsin Press, 1966.

Hertz, Gerald B. *English Public Opinion After the Restoration*. London: T. F. Unwin, 1902.

Hollingsworth, T. H. *Historical Demography*. Ithaca, N.Y.: Cornell University Press, 1969.

Hunt, George T. *The Wars of the Iroquois: A Study in Intertribal Relations*. Madison, Wis.: University of Wisconsin Press, 1940.

Illick, Joseph E. *William Penn the Politician*. Ithaca, N.Y.: Cornell University Press, 1965.

Insh, George P. *Scottish Colonial Schemes, 1620–86*. Glasgow: Maclehose, Jackson & Co., 1922.

Japiske, N. *De Verwikkelingen en Tuschen de Republik en England van 1660–1665*. Leiden: S. C. van Doesburgh, 1900.

Johnson, Allen, and Dumas Malone, eds. *Dictionary of American Biography*. 22 vols. New York: Charles Scribner's Sons, 1928–44.

Jordan, Winthrop D. *White Over Black: American Attitudes Toward the Negro, 1515–1812*. Chapel Hill, N.C.: University of North Carolina Press, 1968.

Kammen, Michael. *Deputyes and Libertyes: The Origins of Representative Government in Colonial America*. New York: Alfred A. Knopf, 1969.

———. *Empire and Interest: The American Colonies and the Politics of Mercantilism*. Philadelphia: J. B. Lippincott Co., 1970.

———. *People of Paradox: An Inquiry Concerning the Origins of American Civilization*. New York: Alfred A. Knopf, 1972.

Katz, Stanley N. *Newcastle's New York: Anglo-American Politics, 1732–1753*. Cambridge, Mass.: Harvard University Press, 1968.

Kennedy, John H. *Thomas Dongan Governor of New York, 1628–1688*. Washington, D.C.: Catholic University of America, 1930.

Kessler, Henry H., and Eugene Rachlis. *Peter Stuyvesant and His New York*. New York: Random House, 1959.

Klein, Milton M. *The Politics of Diversity: Essays in the History of Colonial New York*. Port Washington, N.Y.: Kennikat Press, 1974.

Leach, Douglas. *Flintlock and Tomahawk: New England in King Philip's War*. New York: W. W. Norton, 1966.

Leder, Lawrence H. *Robert Livingston and the Politics of Colonial New York, 1654–1728*. Chapel Hill, N.C.: University of North Carolina Press, 1961.

Leng, Charles W., and William T. Davis. *Staten Island, Its History and People*. New York: Lewis Historical Publishing Company, 1930.

Lister, T. H. *Life and Administration of Edward, Earl of Clarendon*. 3 vols. London: Longman, Orne, Brown, Green, and Longmans, 1838.

Lockridge, Kenneth. *A New England Town: The First Hundred Years*. New York: W. W. Norton, 1970.

Louhi, E. A. *The Delaware Finns*. New York: Humanities Press, 1925.

Lovejoy, David S. *The Glorious Revolution in America*. New York: Harper & Row, 1972.

McKee, Samuel. *Labor in Colonial New York, 1664–1776*. New York: Columbia University Press, 1935.

Melick, Harry C. *The Manor of Fordham and Its Founder*. New York: Fordham University Press, 1950.

Morgan, Edmund S. *The Puritan Family: Religion and Domestic Relations in Seventeenth Century New England*. Boston: Trustees of the Public Library, 1944.

Mowrer, Lilian T. *The Indomitable John Scott: Citizen of Long Island, 1632–1704*. New York: Farrar, Straus and Cudahy, 1960.

Murdock, Kenneth B. *Increase Mather: The Foremost American Puritan*. Cambridge, Mass.: Harvard University Press, 1925.

Nash, Gary B. *Quakers and Politics: Pennsylvania, 1681–1726*. Princeton, N.J.: Princeton University Press, 1968.

Nettels, Curtis P. *The Money Supply of the American Colonies Before 1720*. Madison, Wis.: University of Wisconsin Press, 1934.

Nissenson, S. G. *The Patroon's Domain*. New York: Columbia University Press, 1937.

Norton, Thomas E. *The Fur Trade in Colonial New York, 1686–1776*. Madison, Wis.: University of Wisconsin Press, 1974.

O'Callaghan, Edmund B. *The History of New Netherlands*. 2 vols. 2nd ed. New York: D. Appleton and Company, 1855.

––––––. *Origin of Legislative Assemblies in the State of New York*. Albany, N.Y.: Weed, Parsons & Co., 1861.

Ogg, David. *England in the Reign of Charles II*. 2 vols. Oxford: Clarendon Press, 1934.

Osgood, Herbert L. *The American Colonies in the Seventeenth Century*. 3 vols. New York: Macmillan Company, 1904. Reprinted, 1930.

Pell, Howland. *The Pell Manor*. Baltimore, Md.: Order of Colonial Lords of Manors in America, 1917.

Pennypacker, Morten. *The Duke's Laws: Their Antecedents, Implications and Importance*. Anglo-American Legal History Series, ser. 1, no. 9. New York: New York University School of Law, 1944.

Peterson, Arthur E., and George W. Edwards. *New York as an Eigh-*

teenth Century Municipality. New York: Columbia University Press, 1917.

Phelan, Thomas P. *Thomas Dongan Colonial Governor of New York, 1683–1688*. New York: P. J. Kenedy & Sons, 1933.

Pomfret, John E. *The Province of East New Jersey, 1609–1702: The Rebellious Proprietary*. Princeton, N.J.: Princeton University Press, 1962.

————. *The Province of West New Jersey, 1609–1702: A History of the Organization of an American Colony*. Princeton, N.J.: Princeton University Press, 1956.

Powell, Sumner C. *Puritan Village: The Formation of a New England Town*. New York: Wesleyan University Press, 1963.

Prall, Stuart E., ed. *The Puritan Revolution: A Documentary History*. New York: Anchor Books, 1968.

Reich, Jerome R. *Leisler's Rebellion: A Study of Democracy in New York, 1664–1720*. Chicago: University of Chicago Press, 1953.

Riker, James. *Revised History of New Harlem*. New York: New Harlem Publishing Co., 1904.

Rudé, George. *The Crowd in History, 1730–1848*. New York: John Wiley & Sons, 1964.

Scharf, J. Thomas, ed. *History of Westchester County, New York*. 2 vols. Philadelphia: L. E. Preston & Co., 1886.

Schoonmaker, Marius. *The History of Kingston, New York*. New York: Burr Printing House, 1888.

Schuyler, George W. *Colonial New York: Phillip Schuyler and His Family*. 2 vols. New York: Charles Scribner's Sons, 1885.

Schuyler, Montgomery. *Richard Nicolls First Governor of New York, 1664–1668*. Baltimore, Md.: Order of Colonial Lords of Manors in America, 1928.

Shy, John. *Toward Lexington: The Role of the British Army in the Coming of the American Revolution*. Princeton, N.J.: Princeton University Press, 1965.

Sirmans, M. Eugene. *Colonial South Carolina: A Political History, 1663–1763*. Chapel Hill, N.C.: University of North Carolina Press, 1966.

Slafter, Edmund F. *Sir William Alexander and American Colonization*. Boston, Mass.: Prince Society, 1873.

Smelser, Neil J. *The Theory of Collective Behavior*. New York: Free Press of Glencoe, 1963.

Smith, William. *The History of the Province of New York*. 2 vols. New York Historical Society, *Collections*, vols. 4–5. New York: New York Historical Society, 1829–30.

Stephen, Leslie, and Sidney Lee, eds. *Dictionary of National Biography*. 22 vols. London: Oxford University Press, 1917–.

Stokes, Isaac N. *Iconography of Manhattan Island 1498–1909*. 6 vols. New York: R. H. Dodd, 1916–28.

Tanner, Edwin P. *The Province of New Jersey, 1664–1738*. New York: Columbia University, Longmans, Green & Co., Agents, 1908.

Thompson, Benjamin F. *History of Long Island from its Discovery and*

Settlement to the Present Time. 3 vols. 3rd ed. New York: R. H. Dodd, 1918.

Trelease, Allen W. *Indian Affairs in Colonial New York: The Seventeenth Century*. Ithaca, N.Y.: Cornell University Press, 1960.

Turner, Francis C. *James II*. New York: Eyre & Spottiswoode, 1948.

Valentine, David T. *History of the City of New York*. New York: G. P. Putnam & Company, 1853.

Van Rensselaer, Mariana G. *History of the City of New York in the Seventeenth Century*. 2 vols. New York: Macmillan Company, 1909.

Vaughan, Alden T. *The New England Frontier: Puritans and Indians, 1620–1635*. Boston, Mass.: Little, Brown & Co., 1965.

Warnsink, J. C. M. *Abraham Crijnssen de Vesovering van Suriname en Zijn Aanslag op Virginie in 1667*. Amsterdam: N. v. Noord-hollandsche Vitgeversmaatschappij, 1936.

Weslager, C. A. *Dutch Explorers, Traders and Settlers in the Delaware Valley, 1609–1664*. Philadelphia: University of Pennsylvania Press, 1961.

──────. *The English on the Delaware, 1610–1682*. New Brunswick, N.J.: Rutgers University Press, 1967.

White, Philip L. *The Beekmans of New York in Politics and Commerce, 1647–1877*. New York: New York Historical Society, 1956.

Whitson, Agnes M. *The Constitutional Development of Jamaica, 1660–1729*. Manchester, England: Manchester University Press, 1929.

Wilson, Charles. *Profit and Power: A Study of England and the Dutch Wars*. London: Longmans, Green & Co., 1958.

Wilson, James G., ed. *Memorial History of the City of New York*. 4 vols. New York: New York Historical Company, 1892.

Witcombe, Dennis T. *Charles II and the Cavalier House of Commons, 1663–1674*. Manchester, England: Manchester University Press, 1966.

Woodhead, John R. *The Rulers of London, 1660–1689*. London: London & Middlesex Archaeological Society, 1965.

Zuckerman, Michael. *Peaceable Kingdoms: New England Towns in the Eighteenth Century*. New York: Alfred A. Knopf, 1970.

Zwierlein, Frederick. *Religion in New Netherland*. Rochester, N.Y.: J. P. Smith, 1910.

Articles

Archdeacon, Thomas J. "The Age of Leisler—New York City, 1689–1710: A Social and Demographic Interpretation." In *Aspects of Early New York Society and Politics*. Edited by Jacob Judd and Irwin H. Polishook. Tarrytown, N.Y.: Sleepy Hollow Restorations, 1974.

Bailyn, Bernard. "Politics and Social Structure in Virginia." In James M. Smith, ed., *Seventeenth Century America: Essays in Colonial History*. Chapel Hill, N.C.: University of North Carolina Press, 1959.

Baker, Charles E., and Kenneth Scott. "Renewal of Governor Nicolls Treaty of 1665 with the Esopus Indians." *New York Historical Society Quarterly* 36 (July 1953): 251–72.

Barbour, Viola. "Dutch and English Merchant Shipping in the Seventeenth Century." *Economic History Review* 2 (1930): 261–90.

Billings, Warren W. "The Causes of Bacon's Rebellion, Some Suggestions." *Virginia Magazine of History and Biography* 78 (1970): 408–35.

Bonomi, Patricia U. "Local Government in Colonial New York: A Base for Republicanism." In *Aspects of Early New York Society and Politics*. Edited by Jacob Judd and Irwin H. Polishook. Tarrytown, N.Y.: Sleepy Hollow Restorations, 1974.

————. "The Middle Colonies: An Embryo of the New Political Order." In *Perspectives on Early American History: Essays in Honor of Richard B. Morris*. Edited by Alden Vaughan. New York: Harper & Row, 1973.

Buffington, Arthur H. "The Policy of Albany and English Westward Expansion." *Mississippi Valley Historical Review* 8 (1922): 327–66.

Calder, Isabel M. "The Earl of Stirling and the Colonization of Long Island." *Essays in Colonial History Presented to Charles McLean Andrews by his Students*. New Haven, Conn.: Yale University Press, 1931.

Davisson, William I. "Essex County Price Trends: Money and Markets in Seventeenth Century Massachusetts." *Essex Institute Historical Collections* 103 (1967): 144–85.

————. "Essex County Wealth Trends: Wealth and Economic Growth in Seventeenth Century Massachusetts." *Essex Institute Historical Collections* 103 (1967): 291–342.

De Valinger, Leon, Jr. "The Burning of the Whorekill, 1673." *Pennsylvania Magazine of History and Biography* 74 (October 1950): 473–87.

Dunn, Richard S. "John Winthrop, Jr., Connecticut Expansionist." *New England Quarterly* 29 (1956): 3–26.

Gouldesborough, Peter. "An Attempted Scottish Voyage to New York in 1669." *Scottish Historical Review* 40 (April 1961): 56–62.

Haffenden, Philip S. "The Crown and the Colonial Charters, 1675–1688." *William and Mary Quarterly*, 3rd ser., 15 (July and October 1958): 297–311, 452–66.

Haskins, George L., and Samuel Ewing. "The Spread of Massachusetts Law in the Seventeenth Century." *University of Pennsylvania Law Review* 106 (1958): 413–18.

Henretta, James A. "Economic Development and Social Structure in Colonial Boston." *William and Mary Quarterly*, 3rd ser., 22 (January 1965): 75–92.

Johnson, Herbert A. "The Advent of Common Law in Colonial New York." In *Law and Authority in Colonial America*. Edited by George A. Billias. Barre, Mass.: Barre Publishers, 1965.

Koch, Donald W. "Income Distribution and Political Structure in the Seventeenth Century, Salem, Massachusetts." *Essex Institute Historical Collections* 105 (1969): 50–71.

Kupp, Jan. "Aspects of the New York–Dutch Trade Under the English, 1670–1674." *New York Historical Society Quarterly* 78 (1974): 139–47.

Laslett, Peter. "Size and Structure of the Household in England over Three Centuries." *Population Studies* 23 (1969): 199–223.

Laurence, W. E. "The Laurence Pedigree." *New York Genealogical and Biographical Record* 3 (1872): 121–31.

Leder, Lawrence H. ". . . Like Madmen Through the Streets: The New York City Riot of June 1690." *New York Historical Society Quarterly* 34 (1955): 405–15.

————. "Records of the Trials of Jacob Leisler and His Associates." *New York Historical Society Quarterly* 36 (1952): 431–57.

————. "The Unorthodox Domine: Nicholas Van Rennselaer." *New York History* 35 (April 1954): 166–76.

Lemon, James T., and Gary B. Nash. "The Distribution of Wealth in Eighteenth Century America: A Century of Change in Chester County, Pennsylvania, 1693–1802." *Journal of Social History* 2 (1968): 1–24.

Lockridge, Kenneth. "Land, Population and the Evolution of New England Society, 1630–1790." *Past and Present* (April 1968), pp. 62–80.

Lovejoy, David S. "Equality and Empire: The New York Charter of Liberties, 1683." *William and Mary Quarterly*, 3rd ser., 21 (October 1964): 493–565.

McCully, Bruce T. "From North Riding to Morocco: The Early Years of Governor Francis Nicholson, 1655–1686." *William and Mary Quarterly*, 3rd ser., 19 (October 1962): 534–57.

McKinley, A. E. "The Transition from Dutch to English Rule in New York: A Study in Political Imitation." *American Historical Review* 4 (July 1901): 693–724.

Mason, Bernard. "Aspects of the New York Revolt of 1689." *New York History* 30 (April 1949): 165–80.

Nash, Gary B. "The Framing of Government in Pennsylvania: Ideas in Contact with Reality." *William and Mary Quarterly*, 3rd ser., 23 (April 1966): 183–209.

————. "The Free Society of Traders and the Early Politics of Pennsylvania." *Pennsylvania Magazine of History and Biography* 89 (April 1965): 147–73.

————. "The Quest for the Susquehanna Valley: New York, Pennsylvania and the Seventeenth Century Fur Trade." *New York History* 48 (January 1967): 3–27.

Nettles, Curtis P. "Economic Relations of Boston, Philadelphia and New York, 1680–1715." *Journal of Economic and Business History* 3 (February 1931): 185–215.

————. "England's Trade with New England and New York." *Publications of the Colonial Society of Massachusetts* 28 (1930–35): 322–49.

Pargellis, Stanley M. "The Four Independent Companies of New York." *Essays in Colonial History Presented to Charles McLean Andrews by His Students*. New Haven, Conn.: Yale University Press, 1931.

Ritchie, Robert C. "The Duke of York's Commission of Revenue." *New York Historical Society Quarterly* 58 (1974): 177–87.

———. "London Merchants, the New York Market, and the Recall of Sir Edmund Andros." *New York History* 57 (January 1976): 5–30.

Rutman, Darret. "The Social Web: A Prospectus for the Study of Early American Community." In *Insights and Parallels: Problems and Issues of American Social History*. Edited by William L. O'Neill. Minneapolis, Minn.: Burgess Publishing Co., 1973.

Schoolcraft, Henry L. "The Capture of New Amsterdam." *English Historical Review* 22 (October 1907): 674–93.

Smith, Elizur Y. "Captain Thomas Willett, First Mayor of New York." *New York History* 21 (October 1940): 404–17.

Stern, Steve J. "Knickerbockers Who Asserted and Insisted: The Dutch Interest in New York Politics, 1664–1691." *New York Historical Society Quarterly* 78 (1974): 113–38.

Still, Bayard. "New York's Mayorality: The Formative Years." *New York Historical Society Quarterly* 47 (July 1963): 239–56.

Sutherland, Stella. "Colonial Statistics." *Explorations in Entrepreneurial History* 5 (1967): 58–107.

Vale, V. "Clarendon, Coventry and the Sale of Naval Offices, 1660–1668." *Cambridge Historical Journal* 12 (1956): 107–25.

Webb, Stephen S. "Brave Men and Servants to His Royal Highness: The Household of James Stuart in the Evolution of English Imperialism." *Perspectives in American History* 7 (1974): 55–82.

———. "William Blathwayt, Imperial Fixer: From Popish Plot to Glorious Revolution." *William and Mary Quarterly*, 3rd ser., 25 (January 1968): 3–21.

———. "William Blathwayt, Imperial Fixer: Muddling Through to Empire, 1689–1717." *William and Mary Quarterly*, 3rd ser., 26 (October 1969): 373–415.

———. "The Strange Career of Francis Nicholson." *William and Mary Quarterly*, 3rd ser., 23 (October 1966): 513–48.

Wright, Langdon G. "Local Government and Central Authority in New Netherland." *New York Historical Society Quarterly* 57 (1973): 7–29.

Unpublished Materials

Bloom, Jeanne. "Sir Edmund Andros: A Study in Seventeenth Century Colonial Administration." Ph.D. dissertation, Yale University, 1962.

Luidens, John Pershing. "The Americanization of the Dutch Reformed Church." Ph.D. dissertation, University of Oklahoma, 1969.

McAnear, Beverly. "Politics in Provincial New York, 1689–1761." Ph.D. dissertation, Stanford University, 1935.

Murrin, John M. "English Rights as Ethnic Aggression: The English Conquest, the Charter of Liberties of 1683 and Leisler's Rebellion in New York." Paper read at the American Historical Association Meeting, San Francisco, 1973.

Ritchie, Robert C. "The Duke's Province: A Study of Proprietary New York, 1664–1685." Ph.D. dissertation, University of California, Los Angeles, 1972.

Wright, Langdon G. "Local Government in Colonial New York, 1640–1710." Ph.D. dissertation, Cornell University, 1974.

Index

DATE

NOV 23

HIGHSMITH 45-102

PRINTED IN U.S.A.